Justiciability of Political Questions in South Africa: A Comparative Analysis

Justiciability of Political Questions in South Africa: A Comparative Analysis

Mtendeweka Owen Mhango

eleven international publishing

Published, sold and distributed by Eleven International Publishing
P.O. Box 85576
2508 CG The Hague
The Netherlands
Tel.: +31 70 33 070 33
Fax: +31 70 33 070 30
email: sales@elevenpub.nl
www.elevenpub.com

Sold and distributed in USA and Canada
Independent Publishers Group
814 N. Franklin Street
Chicago, IL 60610, USA
Order Placement: +1 800 888 4741
Fax: +1 312 337 5985
orders@ipgbook.com
www.ipgbook.com

Eleven International Publishing is an imprint of Boom uitgevers Den Haag.

ISBN 978-94-6236-918-4
ISBN 978-94-6274-076-1 (e-book)

PREFACE

Professor Mhango's thesis on the political question doctrine is more or less an investigation into one of the branch-plants of the century-old principle of justiciability enunciated by the US Supreme Court in *Marbury v. Madison* by way of constitutional interpretation and which has made its way into the South African democratic constitutional adjudication with the coming of a truly democratic Constitution with all its accoutrements – the rule of law, supremacy of the Constitution; separation of powers; entrenchment of human rights and fundamental freedoms; social justice and deep-rooted and extensive system of judicial review. The Constitution of South Africa does not, in any place, mention either the term 'justiciability' or 'political question' in its provisions. But, its recognition of the principle of justiciability is embedded in its guarantee of the right of access to the courts "to have any dispute that can be resolved by the application of law".

A perusal of the Mhango thesis clearly conveys to the reader the fact that the foregoing quotation from Section 34 of the Constitution means that the courts can only hear and determine "any dispute that is justiciable" or "any justiciable dispute". In light of the US common law precedents since the *Marbury v. Madison* judgement, there has been some understanding of what that meant in common law jurisprudence; hence the South African courts did not have to interpret that expression in vacuum. In other words, as much as the Constitution did not go further and explain what is "resolved by the application of law", the courts had to develop the common law to accommodate that expression in contemporary constitutional adjudication. In the final analysis, it is the courts that have worked out and must continue to develop the boundaries of what it can adjudicate upon, thus, culminating in imposing limitations of the proper subject matter of its adjudicative province.

The political question doctrine is therefore one of the self-imposed principles where the courts fear to tread. So, quite apart from the courts being guided by the principle of justiciability, they are also guided by the constitutional principle of separation of powers, which clearly mandates them to exercise judicial authority leaving political, policy, executive and administrative decision-making processes to the executive arm of government, while law making is quintessentially that of the legislature. Because these powers have accordingly been distributed by the Constitution, and since the Constitution is the supreme law, its prescripts must be observed by all organs of State or there will be a violation of the Constitution. Again, compliance with the law laid down by the Constitution is the essential fabric of the rule of law, hence non-compliance thereof is a breach of the Constitution. In the final analysis, a court that descends into the political arena of conflict and takes it upon itself to adjudicate a purely political question that belongs to the political class, goes against all these constitutional principles and cannot therefore be said to be performing a judicial function. Similarly, such a court cannot take over the law-making process except to the extent that Sections 39(1) and (2) or any other provision in the Constitution of South Africa permits otherwise.

There can be no doubt that one is here dealing with one of the most difficult areas of contemporary constitutional jurisprudence – an area where only a few constitutional law scholars venture into. It is for this reason and other intellectual contributions made in Professor Mhango's thesis that it is now being presented to you, the reader, in the form of a book: *Justiciability of Political Questions in South Africa: A Comparative Analysis*, which must be seen as having taken the subject into a new era of constitutional jurisprudence not only in South Africa but also the whole of Africa and the common law world.

This book has come at a time when political jargons predominate public discourse; at a time when expressions like "judicial overreach" is bandied around while the listener could surmise, without any fear of contradiction, a total absence of any understanding of the phrase by the very person uttering the words, especially when the political operatives play to the gallery with that term. The political question doctrine is an aspect of judicial self-restraint such that when it is invoked, it stands on the way of any likelihood of a judgement degenerating into judicial overreach. It is, as much as justiciability, tied to the question of a court's jurisdiction for if the subject matter of the dispute is a political question destined to be answered by the political branch, then, it is non-justiciable, and therefore, the court to which the issue was taken for resolution will lack the jurisdiction to hear and determine that particular dispute.

In this book, Professor Mhango deals comprehensively with the conceptual overview of the political question theory. He traces its origins to American jurisprudence and brings up to date through case law and academic writings to its modern application in the US constitutional jurisprudence. He also traces, in three separate chapters, how the political question doctrine as a concept of constitutional adjudication entered the modern juridical space of three African jurisdictions, as to how the courts in these jurisdictions have received and applied the doctrine and how it has evolved in these three African jurisdictions: Ghana, Nigeria and Uganda. He also investigates the development and application of a comprehensive political question doctrine in South Africa where the courts have been slow in embracing, articulating and developing a comprehensive political question doctrine. To that extent, the author has made recommendations for improvement. In other words, this book covers the origins, applications and developments of the political question doctrine in five common law jurisdictions: United States; Ghana; Uganda; Nigeria; and South Africa.

This book is the first of its kind in contemporary constitutional jurisprudence and must serve as an encouragement to emerging African legal scholars to enter the field. It is, therefore, a compulsory read and, I so recommend it to legal academics, judges, legal practitioners and students of constitutional law and adjudication in South Africa, Southern Africa, Africa and the common law world as a whole.

Chuks Mathew Okpaluba
Adjunct Professor, University of Fort Hare,
Research Fellow, University of South Africa,
Research Fellow, Centre for Human Rights, University of the Free State.

POLOKWANE
12 December 2018

Table of Contents

Acknowledgements

In 2011, I struck a conversation with a senior government official when he delivered a paper at a conference where we both attended. We shared mutual concerns about how courts in South Africa readily entertain disputes involving purely political questions and how this impacted on separation of powers. The conversation sparked my interest to examine separation of powers and the possibility for South African courts to apply some version of the political question doctrine. I decided to examine this question.

I started my writing during 2012 following the announcement by the government of South Africa that it would commission an investigation to assess the impact of decisions of the Constitutional Court and Supreme Court of Appeal on the transformation of society. One of the aspects of this investigation, which caught my attention for purposes of this project, was its spotlight on separation of powers issues.

Like with most intellectual projects, I am grateful to the many people who made this project possible. My gratitude goes first to Professors Ntombizozuko Dyani-Mhango and Chuks Okpaluba who patiently commented on my draft thesis, the three members of the examining committee, and the two blind reviewers and editors at Eleven International Publishing.

I would also like to acknowledge that this work is based on the research supported by the National Research Foundation of South Africa and the National University of Lesotho.

Finally, and most importantly, I want to thank my family: my parents Cuthbert Kambutu Ganje Mhango and Jean Kalinga-Mhango, who have always stood by me, and especially *mwanakazi wane* Professor (Dr) Ntombizozuko Dyani-Mhango, and my children, Nia, Tapokelera and Takondwa 'TK'. Their love, support and encouragement mean more than words can ever express.

List of Abbreviations

GFIP	Gauteng Freeway Improvement Project
GLR	Ghana Law Reports
GLRD	Ghana Law Reports Digest
Constitution 1996	Constitution of the Republic of South Africa, 1996
NWLR	NigerianWeekly Law Reports
NYU J Int'l L & Pol	New York University Journal of International Law and Policy
SC	Nigeria Supreme Court Law Reports
SCA	Supreme Court of Appeal of South Africa
SCGLR	Supreme Court of Ghana Law Reports
TSAR	The Journal of South African Law
US Supreme Court	United States Supreme Court

Introduction

Section 34 of the Constitution of the Republic of South Africa, 1996 outlines the scope of judicial authority as encompassing the resolution of any dispute that can be resolved by the application of law. The courts have developed several justiciability canons that restrain the adjudication of disputes, such as standing, mootness, ripeness and the prevention of advisory opinions. These justiciability canons determine who can bring a lawsuit in court, when can such lawsuit be brought as well as what substance may be adjudicated by the courts.

This book focuses on another justiciability canon – the political question doctrine – a distinct species of justiciability because of its distinct results when applied to a case. Generally, a court must abstain from reaching the merits of a case in the absence of a live controversy, ripeness or standing. Likewise, a court must abstain from determining the merits of a case in the presence of mootness, a hypothetical or political question.

The political question doctrine arises from the principle of separation of powers and, in the main, provides that certain questions of constitutional law are allocated to the discretion of the elected branches of government for resolution. As a result, such questions are non-justiciable and require the judiciary to abstain from deciding them because not doing so intrudes unduly into the functions of the elected branches of government. The underlying theme throughout the book is that such questions must find resolution in the democratic process.

Through a comparative analysis, this book examines the origins and current application of the political question doctrine in selected countries with a view to obtain lessons for South Africa. The book places particular emphasis on the early pronouncements of the doctrine by the US Supreme Court. It then reviews modern pronouncements of the doctrine in the constitutional jurisprudence of several countries, including Ghana, Uganda and Nigeria. It argues that while elements of the doctrine and its theory exist in the South African jurisprudence, it is important for the Constitutional Court to articulate and develop it into a coherent doctrine taking into account lessons from those countries. I offer some suggestions in this regard.

The book argues that the political question doctrine is an appropriate legal mechanism through which the judiciary can address the recent problematic proliferation of cases brought to the courts that raise non-justiciable political questions and threaten the legitimate role of the courts in South African democracy.

Chapter 1 introduces the background to the political question doctrine as well as the theories that underpin it. Chapter 2 examines the origins of the political question doctrine and places particular emphasis on the early constitutional commentaries and application of the doctrine (referred to as the traditional or classic political question doctrine) by the US Supreme Court. According to one of the early authorities, *Marbury v. Madison*, the political question doctrine requires that a case be dismissed when the text and structure of the Constitution demands it. However, in the early 1900s, the US Supreme Court gradually began to apply prudential considerations to dismiss cases for both textual and prudential considerations. These prudential considerations became more pronounced when *Baker v. Carr* was decided. The chapter also examines the modern application of the doctrine in American constitutional jurisprudence.

Chapter 3 examines the application of the political question doctrine in Ghana. It seeks to determine the status of the political question doctrine and whether the doctrine is firmly part of Ghanaian constitutional law. The chapter examines the theoretical underpins of the courts embracing the political question in Ghana, including the validity of the jurisprudential justifications offered by the courts, with a view to deriving lessons for South Africa.

In Uganda, courts have considered and applied the political question doctrine since the 1960s as a function of the principle of separation of powers. Chapter 4 examines the history, development and trends in the application of the political question doctrine in Ugandan jurisprudence. The chapter draws lessons for South Africa.

Chapter 5 examines the application of the political question doctrine in Nigeria. Since it is evident from the cases and academic commentaries that Nigerian courts adopted the political question doctrine as pronounced by the US Supreme Court in *Baker v. Carr* and formulated a refined doctrine for Nigeria, the chapter reviews recent case law in Nigeria and the United States to determine the current status of the political question doctrine in Nigeria. The chapter discusses the theoretical underpins of the courts embracing the political question in Nigeria, including the validity of the justifications offered by the courts, and draws lessons from Nigeria's experience for possible application in South Africa.

Chapter 6 explores the development and current status of the political question doctrine in South Africa. The chapter departs from the premise that there exists a body of law that justifies judicial abstention from deciding some types of constitutional questions. This chapter argues that while the doctrine or elements of it exist in South African jurisprudence, the Constitutional Court should articulate and develop it into a clear doctrine. The study offers some suggestions in this regard and in the process criticizes opponents of the political question doctrine in South Africa.

Finally, in a brief conclusion, I advocate for the development of a classical strand of the political question doctrine. I stress the importance of developing a coherent doctrine by considering the consequences of failure to implement a doctrine. Whether my submissions will be implemented will depend largely on the open-mindedness of judges, lawyers and politicians in South Africa.

1 Conceptual Overview

1.1 Introduction

Section 34 of the Constitution of the Republic of South Africa, 1996 (hereinafter as the Constitution or the Constitution 1996), outlines the scope of judicial authority as encompassing the resolution of any dispute that can be resolved by the application of law. The courts in South Africa have developed several justiciability canons that dictate the circumstances where courts may adjudicate disputes, such as standing,[1] mootness,[2] ripeness[3] and the prevention of advisory opinions.[4] These justiciability canons emanate from the consti-

1 *See, Ferreira v. Levin* 1996 1 BCLR 1 (CC), at paras. 162-169, 223-238; *Albutt v. Centre for the Study of Violence and Reconciliation* 2010 3 SA 293 (CC), at paras. 32-35; *Port Elizabeth Municipality v. Prut NO* 1996 4 SA 318 (E); *New Party of South Africa v. Government of the Republic of South Africa* 1999 3 SA 191 (CC), at para. 106; *Kruger v. President of the Republic of South Africa* 2009 1 SA 417 (CC), at paras. 20-27; *Bio Energy Afrika Free State v. Freedom Front Plus* 2012 2 SA 88 (FB), at paras. 13-18 and I. Currie & J. de Waal, *The Bill of Rights,* 6th edn, Juta, Cape Town, 2013, pp. 72-84. *See also,* Z. Motala & C. Ramaphosa, *Constitutional Law: Analysis and Cases,* Oxford University Press, Cape Town, 2002, p. 103 (arguing that the Constitution adopts different standards on standing depending on whether the plaintiff's case is based on a mere claim of wrongdoing on the part of the defendant versus a claim of wrongdoing that affects rights protected in the Bill of Rights, and noting that in the former instance the standards are more rigid whereas in the latter instance the standard for standing are more flexible).

2 *See, National Coalition of Gay and Lesbian Equality v. Minister of Home Affairs* 2000 2 SA 1 (CC), at para. 21; *S v. Dlamini* 1999 4 SA 623 (CC), at para. 27; *Janse van Rensburg NO v. Minister of Trade and Industry* 2001 1 SA 29 (CC), at paras. 9-10; *President of the Ordinary Court Martial v. Freedom of Expression Institute* 1999 4 SA 682 (CC), at paras. 7-8. *See also,* Motala & Ramaphosa, 2002, pp. 115-116 (noted that mootness is not fully developed in South Africa and is unlikely to mirror the American approach because even if an issue becomes moot, South African courts might still need to consider some aspects of the merits. Further noting that despite the fact that the Constitutional Court in *JT Publishing v. Minister of Safety and Security* considered mootness as a barrier to adjudication, it is unlikely that the barrier will be absolute) and *Wiese v. Government Employees Pension Fund* 2012 6 BCLR 599 (CC), at paras. 21-24 (holding that the issues between the parties were moot due to recent legislative interventions).

3 *See, National Coalition of Gay and Lesbian Equality v. Minister of Home Affairs,* at para. 21; *Chairman, State Tender Board v. Digital Voice Processing (Pty) Ltd* 2012 2 SA 16 (SCA), at paras. 16-21; *Ritcher v. Minister of Home Affairs* 2009 3 SA 615 (CC), at para. 40; *S v. Friedland* 1996 8 BCLR 1049 (W); *Transvaal Agricultural Union v. Minister of Land Affairs* 1997 2 SA 621 (CC); *Minister of Education v. Harris* 2001 4 SA 1297 (CC), at para. 19; *Legal Aid South Africa v. Magidiwana* 2014 4 All SA 570 (SCA), paras. 17-18. Motala & Ramaphosa, 2002, p. 113 (noting that Justice Kriegler in *Ferreira v. Levin,* at para. 199, described ripeness as serving the useful purpose of highlighting that the business of a court is generally retrospective, and it deals with situations or problems that have already ripened or crystalized and not with prospective hypothetical problems).

4 *National Coalition of Gay and Lesbian Equality v. Minister of Home Affairs,* at para. 21; *S v. Friedland* 1996 8 BCLR 1049 (W); *Radio Pretoria v. Chairman, Independent Communications Authority of South Africa* 2005 1 SA 47 (SCA), at para. 15; *Rand Water Board v. Rotek Industries (Pty) Ltd* 2003 4 SA 58 (SCA), at para. 26 and*Corruption Watch NPC and Others v. President of the Republic of South Africa and Others* [2018] ZACC 23.

tutional imperative to respect separation of powers and the recognition of the inherent limitations of judicial review in a constitutional democracy.[5]

What has yet to be fully developed in South Africa, as part of the family of justiciability canons, is a coherent political question doctrine. As Margit Cohn has correctly observed, in some jurisdictions like the United Kingdom, Israel and other common law systems, justiciability is narrowly understood to only relate to the political question doctrine – "abstention from review due to political sensitivity".[6]

To illustrate the significance and sensitivity of these issues, in 2010, President Jacob Zuma made an important speech in Parliament at the farewell ceremony of the former Chief Justice Sandile Ngcobo, where he discussed, among other things, his views about limits of judicial review, the principle of separation of powers and its effects on the resolution of political questions or disputes. Zuma said that:

> We reiterate our view that there is a need to distinguish the areas of responsibility between the judiciary and the elected branches of the state, especially with regards to policy formulation. The executive, as elected officials, has the sole discretion to decide policies for government. The principle of separation of powers means that the encroachment of one arm of the state on the terrain of another should be discouraged, and there should be no bias in this regard. We respect the powers and role conferred by our Constitution on the legislature and the judiciary. At the same time, we expect the same from these very important institutions of our democratic dispensation. The executive should be allowed to conduct its administration and policy making work as freely as it possibly could. The powers conferred on the courts could not be regarded as superior to the powers resulting from a mandate given by the people in a popular vote. To provide support to the judiciary and free the courts to do their work, it would help if political disputes were resolved politically.[7]

---

5 *See generally, National Treasury v. Opposition to Urban Tolling Alliance* 2012 6 SA 223 (CC) and *Magidiwana v. President of the Republic of South Africa* 2013 11 BCLR 1251 (CC). *See also*, C. Okpaluba & M. Mhango, 'Between Separation of Powers and Justiciability: Rationalising the Constitutional Court's Judgement in the Gauteng E-tolling Litigation in South Africa', *Law Democracy Development*, Vol. 21, 2017, pp. 1-24.

6 M. Cohn, 'Form, Formula and Constitutional Ethos: The Political Question/Justiciability Doctrine in Three Common Law Systems', *American Journal of Comparative Law*, Vol. 59, 2011, p. 677.

7 The Presidency, 'Judiciary Must Respect Separation of Powers – Jacob Zuma', available from www.politicsweb.co.za/documents/judiciary-must-respect-separation-of-powers-jacob (last accessed 1 November 2011). *See also*, Editorial, 'SA Is Courting Abuse', *Business Day*, 22 November 2016 (noting that behind this bewildering number of cases lies a deep constitutional issue, the notion of a separation of powers between the operational, legislative and judicial arms of government. Increasingly, the courts are being called upon to settle disputes that, arguably, should be dealt with by other constitutional or political institutions, and that the courts should not be the port of call in a political dispute).

The above statement is perhaps the most recent reference to the theme of the political question doctrine by a politician in South Africa.[8] The first reference to the notion of the political question theory in South Africa is found in *Brown v. Leyds No.*[9] In that case, the Supreme Court of the Transvaal had to consider whether the court had the power to test the validity of acts of the legislature. The court relied heavily on American authorities and found that it had the power of judicial review or testing rights, but recognized that such power was not absolute.[10] In other words, while accepting the power of judicial review, the court rejected the proposition that the judiciary was capable of deciding every question brought before it and noted that "if any proposition may be considered as a political axiom, this we think, may be so considered".[11]

As a member of the justiciability family, the political question doctrine arises from the functionality of the principle of separation of powers and, in the main, provides that certain constitutional questions are constitutionally allocated to the discretion of elected branches of government for resolution.[12] As a result, such questions are non-justiciable and require

8 For a discussion about former South African President Paul Kruger's views on judicial review and the notion of the political question theory *see*, J. Dugard, *Human Rights and the South African Legal Order*, Princeton University Press, Princeton, 1978, pp. 14-36 (commenting on the decision in *Brown v. Leyds NO* 4 Off Rep 17 (1897), which applied the concept of judicial review, Kruger said the Court is free as a fish is free to swim in a net. Kruger is known for his controversial and critical views concerning the power of judicial review and is said to have characterized the principle of judicial review as a principle of the devil and warned judges not to follow the devil. Given his critical views of the power of judicial review, it is more than likely that Kruger would have supported the political question doctrine for South Africa since it represents the judicial effort to ensure that courts do not hamper the functioning of the political branches). *See also*, A. Endicott, 'The Judicial Answer? Treatment of the Political Question Doctrine in Alien Tort Claims', *Berkeley Journal of International Law*, Vol. 28, 2010, p. 538 (arguing that the political question doctrine represents a judicial effort to ensure that the courts do not hamper the functioning of the political branches); and K. O'Regan, 'A Forum for Reason: Reflections on the Role and Work of the Constitutional Court', *South African Journal on Human Rights*, Vol. 28, 2012, p. 132 (arguing that courts in South Africa must exercise restraint and not impede the functioning of government because the legislature and, indirectly, the executive are democratically elected arms of government, whose office is determined by popular vote. In support for the proposition that courts should exercise restraint in the area of policy formulation, she argues that courts are institutionally ill-placed to make the complex decisions that policy requires because they have no experience in the field of policy formulation).

9 *Brown v. Leyds NO* 4 Off Rep 17 (1897).

10 *Brown v. Leyds NO* 29-31. For further discussion of the *Brown v. Leyds NO* and its effects including how American authorities influenced that judgment, *see*, G.N. Barrie, 'Impeachment on the Highveld: The Dismissal of Chief Justice Kotze by President Kruger on 16 February 1898', *TSAR*, 2014, p. 817.

11 *Brown v. Leyds NO* 29-30.

12 *See, United Democratic Movement v. Speaker of the National Assembly and Others* 2017 (8) BCLR 1061 (CC), at para. 64 (holding that the Constitution allocated to the National Assembly the discretion to determine the voting procedure in a motion of no confidence in the President); *Economic Freedom Fighters v. Speaker of the National Assembly and Others* 2016 (3) SA 580 (CC), at para. 93 (holding that the Constitution allocates exclusively to the National Assembly the discretion to decide how to hold the executive to account); M. Redish, 'Judicial Review and the Political Question', *Northwestern Law Review*, Vol. 79, No. 5, 1984, p. 1031; K. Breedon, 'Remedial Problems at the Intersection of the Political Question Doctrine, the Standing Doctrine and the Doctrine of Equitable Discretion', *Ohio Northern University Law Review*, Vol. 34, 2008, p. 523 (explaining that the purpose of the political question doctrine is two-fold. The first, rooted

the judiciary to abstain from deciding them because failure to do so unduly intrudes into the functions reserved for the politically accountable branches of government.[13] The underlying theme is that such questions must find resolution in the political process.[14]

In the above statement, Zuma called for the development of a political question doctrine (without mentioning it by name) for South Africa. There is authority and general support for the doctrine in South Africa generally and abroad.[15] One notable authority and support

in the Constitution's separation of powers, is to ensure proper judicial restraint against exercising jurisdiction when doing so would require courts to assume responsibilities that are assigned to the political branches. The second is to ensure the legitimacy of the judiciary by protecting against issuing orders that courts cannot enforce); H. Wechsler, *Principles, Politics, and Fundamental Law,* Harvard University Press, Cambridge, Massachusetts, 1961, pp. 11-14; K. Yoshino, 'Restrained Ambition in Constitutional Interpretation', *Willamette Law Review,* Vol. 45, No. 2, 2009, pp. 557-559 (arguing that the political question doctrine is a doctrine of justiciability, noting that other such doctrines include standing, ripeness, mootness and the bar on advisory opinions; that the justiciability doctrines underscore the idea that there can be rights without judicially enforceable remedies); G. LaTourette, 'Global Climate: A Political Question?', *Rutgers Law Journal,* Vol. 40, 2008, pp. 261, 281 (arguing that the political question doctrine is a function of the separation of powers); *Martin v. Mott* 12 Wheat 29, 25 US 19 (1872) (endorsing the proposition that certain questions of constitution law are exclusively allocated to the political branches of government).

13 Redish, 1984, p. 1031; Breedon, 2008, p. 523; Wechsler, 1961, p. 11; Yoshino, 2009, pp. 559-560; LaTourette, 2008, p. 225. *See also, Economic Freedom Fighters v. Speaker of the National Assembly and Others* 2016 (3) SA 580 (CC) (where the Court abstained from deciding the question of whether the National Assembly failed to hold the executive to account in relation to a Public Protector's report finding that it was not open to the judiciary to prescribe to Parliament how it should hold the executive to account).

14 Redish, 1984, p. 1031; Wechsler, 1961, p. 11.

15 For South African authorities on the subject, *see,* S. Ngcobo, 'Why Does the Constitution Matter?' Gallagher Estate, Johannesburg 2016, pp. 21-22, available from www.hsrc.ac.za/en/events/events/public-lecture-chief-justice-sandile-ngcobo-june-2016 (generally supportive of the political question doctrine and arguing that the political question doctrine is a useful starting point in considering limits on the power of judicial review in South Africa); *Mazibuko, Leader of the Opposition in the National Assembly v. Speaker of the National Assembly (Mazibuko)* 2013 4 SA 243 (WCC) (where, like Zuma, the high court problematizes the use of courts to resolve political disputes short of calling for a political question doctrine. The high court, based on separation of powers concerns, abstained from determining whether parliament should have allowed opposition parties to move a motion of no confidence against the president suggesting that that was a political question); *United Democratic Movement v. President of the Republic of South Africa* 2002 11 BCLR 1179 (CC) (explaining that political questions are of no concern to the Court); *In re: Certification of the Constitution of the Republic of South Africa* 1996 10 BCLR 1253 (CC) (pronouncing that the court has no mandate to express any view on the political choices made by the framers of the Constitution); *Mazibuko, Leader of the Opposition in the National Assembly v. Sisulu MP Speaker of the National Assembly* 2013 (6) SA 249 (CC) (2013), at para. 83 (Jafta J minority opinion) (where the dissenting opinion agreed with the high court in *Mazibuko* and without mentioning the political question doctrine suggest that political disputes should not be resolved in courts but rather find resolution in the process); C. Okpaluba, 'Justiciability, Constitutional Adjudication and the Political Question in a Nascent Democracy: South Africa', *South African Public Law,* Vol. 18, No. 2, 2003 & 2004, p. 331 (part 1) and p. 131 (part 2) (advocating for the political question doctrine in South Africa). For foreign authorities, *see, Marbury v. Madison*; *Luther v. Borden* 48 US 1 (1849); *Balarabe Musa v. Auta Hamza* (1983) 3 NCLR 229 (applying the political question doctrine in Nigeria); *Onuoha v. Okafor* (1983) NSCC 494 (applying the political question doctrine in Nigeria); E. Nwauche, Is the End Near for the Political Question Doctrine in Nigeria?, *in* C. Fombad & C. Murray (Eds.), *Fostering Constitutionalism in Africa,* Pretoria University Law Press, Pretoria, 2010, pp. 31-60 (discussing the political question doctrine in Nigeria); *Ghana Bar Association v Attorney General (Ghana Bar Association)* [2003-2004] SCGLR 250 (holding that the appointment of a Chief Justice was a political

(although not directly addressing Zuma) for the political question doctrine is obtained from the US Supreme Court case in *Marbury v. Madison,* where Chief Justice Marshall held that:

> the province of the court is not to inquire how the executive ... perform duties in which they have discretion. Questions, in their nature political ... can never be made in this court.[16]

Marshall reasoned that since some conduct by the political branches is judiciary examinable and others not, the judiciary must develop a rule of law to guide courts in the exercise of its jurisdiction in those appropriate cases.[17] He emphasized the need for such a rule by recognizing that the executive is endowed with certain important political powers, which it has to apply using its own discretion, and is only politically accountable.[18] As Marshall noted, to aid the executive in the performance of its duties, the head of the executive is expressly permitted to appoint certain office bearers, who serve at his pleasure.[19]

Furthermore, the Chief Justice made an important observation that when office bearers are appointed by the President as head of the executive to aid him fulfil his constitutional tasks

---

question); *Attorney General v. Major General David Tinyefuza* Constitutional Appeal No. 1 of 1997 (SC) (unreported) (holding that the political question doctrine prevents courts from deciding questions involving military policy); *Centre of Health Human Rights v. Attorney-General,* Constitutional Petition No. 16 of 2011; A. Bickel, *The Least Dangerous Branch,* Yale University Press, New Haven, 1962 (advocating for the prudential political question doctrine); I. Imam *et al.*, 'Judicial Activism and Intervention in the Doctrine of Political Questions in Nigeria: An Analytical Exposition', *African Journal of Law and Criminology,* Vol. 1, No. 2, 2011, p. 50 (advocating for the political question doctrine in Nigeria); P. Mulhern, 'In Defense of the Political Question Doctrine', *University of Pennsylvania Law Review*, Vol. 137, 1988, p. 97 (defending the political question doctrine); F. Scharpf, 'Judicial Review and the Political Question: A Functional Analysis', *Yale Law Journal*, Vol. 75, No. 5, 1966, p. 517; M. Tushnet, 'Law and Prudence in the Law of Justiciability: The Transformation and Disappearance of the Political Question Doctrine', *North Carolina Law Review*, Vol. 80, 2002, p. 1203.

16 *Marbury v. Madison,* 1803, p. 170.

17 *Marbury v. Madison,* 1803, p. 165. *See also,* J. Cole, 'The Political Question Doctrine: Justiciability and the Separation of Powers', Congressional Research Service, 2014, www.fas.org/sgp/crs/misc/R43834.pdf; J. Story, *Commentaries on the Constitution of the United States With a Preliminary Review of the Constitutional History of the Colonies and States, Before the Adoption of the Constitution*, Hilliard Gray & Co, Cambridge, 1833, pp. 346-347 (arguing that questions that are confided exclusively to the political branches are not judiciary examinable); T.M. Cooley, *A Treatise on the Constitutional Limitations Which Rest Upon the Legislative Power of the States of the American Union*, Little, Brown & Co, Boston, 1868, p. 41 (arguing that where the a constitutional question is constitutionally addressed to the discretion of one department of government, a rule must prevail that a decision made by that department is final and not examinable by any other department or tribunal).

18 *Marbury v. Madison,* 1803, p. 165 and Cole, 2014, pp. 2-3.

19 *Marbury v. Madison,* 1803, p. 165 and Cole, 2014, pp. 2-3.

> whatever opinion may be entertained of the manner in which executive discretion may be used, still there exists, and can exist, no power to control that discretion ... [because] [t]he subjects are political ..., and, being entrusted to the executive, the decision of the executive is conclusive ... [and] can never be examinable by the courts.[20]

I will argue that Marshal's pronouncements are applicable in South Africa.

Since *Marbury v. Madison* was decided, Professor Joseph Story argued, with great emphasis in support of the classical political question proposition, that:

> ... in measures exclusively of a political, legislative or executive character, it is plain, that as the supreme authority, as to these questions, belongs to the legislative and executive departments, they cannot be re-examined elsewhere. Thus, congress having the power to declare war, to levy taxes, to appropriate money, to regulate intercourse and commerce with foreign nations, their mode of executing these powers can never become the subject of re-examination in any other tribunal ... yet cases may readily be imagined, in which a tax may be laid, or a treaty made, upon motives and grounds wholly beside the intention of the constitution. The remedy, however, in such cases is solely by an appeal to the people at the elections ... but where the question is of a different nature, and capable of judicial inquiry and decision, there it admits of a very different consideration.[21]

And to add to this, Cooley has, with equal force and brevity, remarked that:

> ... every department of the government and every official of every department may at any time, when a duty is to be performed, be required to pass upon a question of constitutional construction. Sometimes the case will be such that the decision when made must, from the nature of things, be conclusive and subject to no appeal or review, however erroneous it may be in the opinion of other departments or other officers; but in other cases the same question may be required to be passed upon again before the duty is completely performed. The first of these classes is where, by the constitution, a particular question is plainly addressed to the discretion or judgment of some one department or officer, so that the interference of any other department or officer, with view to the substitution of its own discretion or judgment in the place of that to

20 *Marbury v. Madison*, 1803, p. 166.
21 Story, 1833, pp. 346-347.

> which the constitution has confided the decision, would be impertinent and intrusive. Under every constitution cases of this description are to be met with; and though it will sometimes be found difficult to classify them, there can be no doubt, when the case is properly determined to be one of this character, that the rule must prevail which makes the decision final.[22]

Since these remarks were made, US Federal and State courts have consistently adhered to the rule that the judiciary is barred from reviewing cases that revolve around discretionary policy choices and value determinations constitutionally delegated, for resolution, to the elected branches of government.[23]

There is also support for the political question doctrine in the case law from Uganda, Nigeria and Ghana. These cases provide the basis for the view that the final resolution of political questions, which are constitutionally allocated to the discretion of the elected branches of government, rests with those branches.[24] Further, the doctrine finds support in a number of leading constitutional scholars.[25]

Proponents of the doctrine have dismissed their opponents, whose opposition, according to Mulhern, is largely premised on two connected assumptions: (1) that the judiciary is the only institution with authority and capacity to interpret the Constitution and (2) that to limit such judicial monopoly threatens the rule of law in ways that undermine the supremacy of the Constitution.[26] Instead, these proponents defend the political question doctrine on the basis that the judiciary shares responsibility for interpreting the Constitution with the elected branches of government and deem the doctrine as one of the devices the judiciary employs to define this division of or shared responsibility.[27]

---

22 Cooley, 1868, p. 41.

23 *See, Corrie v. Caterpillar* 503 F 3d 974 (9th Cir 2007), at p. 980 (holding that courts have no charter to review and revise legislative and executive action); *Vieth v. Jubelirer* 541 US 267 (2004) (holding that the judicial department has no business entertaining the claim because the question is entrusted to one of the political branches or involves no judicially enforceable rights.); *Japan Whaling Assoc v. American Cetacean Society* 478 US 221 (1986).

24 R. Barkow 'More Supreme Than Court? The Fall of the Political Question Doctrine and the Rise of Judicial Supremacy', Columbia Law Review, Vol. 102, No. 2, 2002, p. 237.

25 Bickel, 1962; Scharpf, 1966 and Wechsler, 1961. *See also*, J. Jaffe, 'The Political Question Doctrine: An Update in Response to Recent Case Law', Ecology Law Quarterly, Vol. 38, 2011, p. 1037.

26 See, Mulhern, 1988, pp. 99-100; I.M. Rautenbach, 'Policy and Judicial Review – Political Questions, Margins of Appreciation and the South African Constitution', *TSAR*, 2012, p. 28.

27 Mulhern, 1988, p. 101; I. Currie & J. de Waal, The Bill of Rights Handbook, Juta, Cape Town, 2005, p. 394, no. 184 (arguing that courts are not solely responsible for interpreting the Constitution) and L. Fisher & N. Devins, Political Dynamics of Constitutional Law, West Publishing, St Paul, Minnesota, 1992, p. 10 (arguing that the elected branches have both the authority and the competence to engage in constitutional interpretation); *Attorney General v. Tinyefuza*, 2001 (holding that the judiciary is not the only constitutional organ with interpretive power); *United States v. Butler* 297 US 1 (1936) 87 (Stone J., dissenting) (arguing that courts are not the only agency of government that must be assumed to have the capacity to govern) and Story, 1833, pp. 345-347.

It is important to mention that prior to 1994, South Africa was governed under the system of parliamentary supremacy in which the judiciary enjoyed limited review powers. In reviewing legislative acts, judicial powers were limited to determining whether Parliament had complied with its legislative procedures and never about the substance of its acts. The judiciary could not invalidate the conduct of government on the basis that it violated basic human rights because there was no bill of rights. This is because under the system of parliamentary supremacy, courts are required to abide by the wishes of the political majority in Parliament.[28] Hence, the major constitutional change that occurred in South Africa during 1994 is that parliamentary supremacy was replaced with the system of constitutional supremacy, whereby the judiciary is vested with express and wide judicial review powers and mandated to enforce the Constitution by declaring invalid any law, conduct or decision of the political majority that contravenes the Constitution.[29]

1.2 Theoretical Framework

1.2.1 The Classical Political Question Theory[30]

The classical political question doctrine is one of two main versions of the doctrine that has emerged since *Marbury v. Madison* was decided. It is predicated on the theory that the existence of the doctrine hangs solely on the text or structure of the constitution. It requires courts to focus on the language of a constitution and determine whether it assigns some interpretive discretion or complete deference to any of the political branches.[31] In other words, under the classical political question doctrine, one has to demonstrate an explicit constitutional provision on the basis on which the doctrine may be invoked by a court to abstain from adjudicating a matter in absolute deference to the relevant political branch's interpretive power or decision.[32]

Because of its constitutional source, the classical political question doctrine is not discretionary but a constitutional command.[33] If the text of a constitution does not provide a basis, the political question doctrine can never be invoked. No scholar has comprehen-

28 I. Currie & J. de Waal, The New Constitutional and Administrative Law, Juta, Cape Town, 2001, p. 64.

29 *Id.*, p. 64.

30 Also referred to as the textualist view or the traditionalist view of the political question doctrine.

31 Barkow, 2002, pp. 333-334; Z. Shemtob, 'The Political Question Doctrines: *Zivotofsky v. Clinton* and Getting Beyond the Textual–Prudential Paradigm', *The Georgetown Law Journal,* Vol. 104, 2016, pp. 1017-1019; Wechsler, 1961, pp. 7-15; Story, 1833, pp. 345-347 and Cooley, 1868, p. 41 (emphasizing a textual basis for the political question doctrine).

32 Barkow, 2002, pp. 333-334.

33 Scharpf, 1966, pp. 518, 550; Wechsler, 1961, p. 8; *Warth v. Seldin* 422 US 490 (1975), at pp. 499-500; *Corrie v. Caterpillar* 403 F Supp 2d 1019 (2005); *Corrie v. Caterpillar* (2007), p. 979.

sively investigated the merits of the classical political question theory than Professor Wechsler. In articulating the essence of the classical political question theory and what it entails, Wechsler has strongly remarked that all

> what the political question doctrine can defensibly imply is that the courts are called upon to judge whether the Constitution has committed to another agency of government the autonomous determination of the issue raised.[34]

If a textual commitment is found to exist, then the courts are bound not to hear the case.[35] This is the essence of the classical strand of the political question doctrine.

1.2.2 *The Prudential Political Question Theory*

The prudential political question doctrine theory generally encompasses self-imposed restraints that arise at the judiciary's discretion rather than by the command or the text of a constitution.[36] The theory is predicated upon the outcome of an examination of the likely consequences of a court asserting its jurisdiction and prevents the judiciary from interfering in matters in which it lacks institutional competence to protect its legitimacy and avoid conflicts with the political branches.[37] Unlike the classical theory, the prudential theory is not based solely on an interpretation of a constitutional provision.[38]

Despite the fact that prudential considerations in the application of the political question doctrine have been applied since the judgement in *Luther v. Borden*, these considerations became prominent following the decisions in *Colegrove v. Green* and *Baker v. Carr.*[39] Justice

---

34 Wechsler, 1961, pp. 7-8. In support of Wechsler's proposition, *see*, Story, 1833, pp. 345-347 and Cooley, 1868, p. 41.

35 Shemtob, 2016, p. 1017, fn. 127 (stating that Wechsler found comfort in the following dicta from *Cohens v. Virginia* 19 US (6 Wheat.) 264, 404 (1821) "it is most true that this court will not take jurisdiction if it should not; but it is equally true, that it must take jurisdiction if it should."). For examples of cases applying Wechsler's understanding of the political question doctrine, *see*, *Massachusetts v. Laird* 400 US 886 (1970) (Douglas J., dissenting) and *Roudebush v. Hartke* 405 US 15 (1972), p. 30 (Douglas J., dissenting).

36 *See*, *Warth v. Seldin*, pp. 499-500; *Corrie v. Caterpillar*, 2007.

37 Barkow, 2002, pp. 253, 333-334; Shemtob, 2016, pp. 1013-1017.

38 Barkow, 2002, p. 253.

39 Bickel, 1962, p. 111 (justifying the prudential version of the political question doctrine); *Nixon v. United States* 506 US 224 (1993) (where Chief Justice Rehnquist ignored the prudential considerations and merged the first two factors in *Baker v. Carr*, at p. 228 noting that "the concept of a textual commitment to a coordinate political department is not completely separate from the concept of a lack of judicially discoverable and manageable standards for resolving it"). *See also*, *Oregon v. Mitchel* 400 US 112 (1970) (where on the question of whether Congress had exceeded its powers by enfranchising eighteen-year-olds and establishing residency requirements for presidential elections, Justice Harlan dissented claiming such questions were inappropriate for judicial resolution because they lay beyond the institutional competence of the judiciary and were thus best left for congressional determination); *see*, *Reynolds v. Sims* 377 US 533 (1964), pp. 589-592 (where in his dissenting opinion Justice Harlan emphasized prudential considerations).

Powell was one of the few strong advocates of the prudential strand of the doctrine. His view was that "the political-question doctrine rests in part on prudential concerns calling for mutual respect among the three branches of government".[40] The courts have highlighted Powell's view to point out that the first three factors established under *Baker v. Carr* (discussed below) focus on the classical version of the doctrine, whereas the final three factors are prudential considerations that counsel against judicial intervention.[41]

1.2.3 *Separation of Powers*

The political question doctrine is often and correctly deliberated upon as part of the larger debate about the legitimacy of the institution of judicial review and separation of powers.[42] Hence, the debate around the objectives, legitimacy, justifications and scope of the power of judicial review and the separation of powers are premised on the general understanding that in the absence of an express authorization for judicial review, there is a rich body of jurisprudence that justifies judicial review and restraint on courts from deciding certain category of questions.[43] What is also clear in this debate is that the body of case law that favours the political question doctrine points to the fact that the doctrine is simply a separation of powers' issue concerning the scope of the powers of the political branches vis-à-vis the judiciary.

As one former Chief Justice of South Africa has correctly observed, the role of the judiciary under the Constitution 1996 must be understood in the context of the principle of separation of powers.[44] The latter principle is often traced to the theories of John Locke and Baron de Montesquieu.[45] In his *Second Treatise of Civil Government*, Locke justified the separation of powers by arguing that

---

40 *Goldwater v. Carter* 444 US 996 (1979), p. 1000 (Powell J., concurring). *See also*, *Nixon v. United States*, 506 US 224 (1992) (Souter J., concurring) (noting that applying the political question doctrine requires case-by-case attention to prudential concerns); *Wang v. Masaitis* 416 F 3d 992 (9th Cir 2005) (discussing Justice Powell's approach).

41 *Goldwater v. Carter*, pp. 998-111; *Wang v. Masaitis*, at pp. 996-1006; *Corrie v. Caterpillar* (2007).

42 Ngcobo, 2016, p. 23; M. Thomas & C. Johnson, 'Note, a Dialogue on the Political Question Doctrine', *Utah Law Review*, 1978, p. 523; L. Hand, The Bill of Rights, Harvard University Press, Massachusetts, 1958, pp. 715-716; Bickel, 1962, pp. 183-198.

43 *Premier of the Eastern Cape v. Ntamo* 2015 6 SA 400 (ECB) and '*Certification of the KwaZulu-Natal Constitution*' 1996 11 *BCLR* 1419.

44 Ngcobo, 2016, p. 23.

45 U. Mubig 'At the Roots of European Legal Culture: Crossborder Influences of Locke and Montesquieu', Fundamina: A Journal of Legal History, Vol. 15, No. 2, pp. 119-120 (arguing that "from Montesquieu's citing of Locke, one should not infer an intention to adopt Locke's separation of legislative and executive powers. The reference to Chapter 12 of Locke's The Second Treatise of Government should also not induce an overestimation of the reception of Locke in Montesquieu's main work. Montesquieu's ideal of a distribution of powers and Locke's call for a separation of powers are distinct").

> it may be too great temptation to human frailty, apt to grasp at power, for the same person who has the power to make laws, to have also on their hands the power to execute them.[46]

Decades later, Montesquieu proposed the principle of the *trias politica* or separation of powers among the executive, legislative and judicial branches of government as a way to manage the over-concentration of power. The motivation for his proposal was that:

> When the legislative and executive powers are united in the same person, there can be no liberty, because apprehensions may arise lest the same monarch or senate should enact tyrannical laws to execute them in a tyrannical manner. Were the power of judging joined with the legislative, the life and liberty of the subject would be exposed to arbitrary control, for the judge would then be the legislator. Were it joined to the executive power, the judge might behave with all the violence of an oppressor.[47]

Montesquieu's work has had a profound influence in the constitutional development of many countries in the world such as the United States and South Africa before and after 1994.[48] In the United States, Montesquieu's thesis greatly influenced the framers of the US Constitution during the drafting of that constitution.

In his contributions to the *Federalist Papers*, which defended the proposed US Constitution, Madison, one of the framers of that constitution, heavily cited and discussed Montesquieu's theories with approval and asserted that:

> The accumulation of all powers, legislative, executive and judiciary, in the same hands, whether of one, a few, or many, and whether hereditary, self-appointed or elective, may justly be pronounced the very definition of tyranny.[49]

---

46 J. Locke, Second Treatise of Government, in M. Cohen & N. Fermon (Eds.), Princeton Readings in Political Thought: *Essential Texts Since Plato*, Princeton University Press, Princeton, 1996, p. 243.

47 B. Montesquieu, The Spirit of the Laws, 1748, p. 163 (translated by Anne Cohler, New York, Cambridge University Press, 1989). *See also*, J. Madison, A. Hamilton & J. Jay, The Federalist Papers, Signet Classic, New York, 1961, p. 300.

48 See, *Brown v. Leyds NO*; P.M. Mojapelo, 'The Doctrine of Separation of Powers (a South African Perspective)', *Advocate*, 2013, p. 38; D. Moseneke, 'Oliver Schreiner Memorial Lecture: Separation of Powers, Democratic Ethos and Judicial Function: Current Developments,' *South African Journal on Human Rights*, Vol. 24, No. 2, 2008, p. 341; D. Moseneke, 'Striking a Balance Between the Will of the People and the Supremacy of the Constitution: Notes', *South African Law Journal*, Vol. 129, No. 1, 2012, p. 9 and S. Seedorf & S. Sibanda, Separation of Powers, in S. Woolman, *et al.* (Eds.), *Constitutional Law of South Africa*, Juta, Cape Town, 2008, p. 12-1; and *Certification Judgment*, at para. 6.

49 Madison, Hamilton & Jay, 1961, p. 298.

While Madison was persuaded by Montesquieu's proposition of separation of powers, he understood and reasoned that it did not entail that "the legislature, judiciary and executive should be wholly unconnected with each other".[50] In this respect, Madison stated that:

> The conclusion I am warranted in drawing from these observations is that a mere demarcation of parchment of the constitutional limits of the several departments is not a sufficient guard against those encroachments which lead to a tyrannical concentration of all the powers of government in the same hands.[51]

Madison's conclusion above was a clear revelation in his understanding that while separation of functions was an accepted notion, more was needed to guard liberty. His thinking led to a deficit in Montesquieu's theory and a refinement of the principle of separation by incorporating the notion of checks and balances as a fundamental feature of separation of powers.[52]

There is another fundamental feature that was born out of Madison's understanding of Montesquieu's theory and that is the institution of judicial review, which Madison understood as being essential. In articulating his view on the role of the judiciary in a government in which the different branches are separated, Madison powerfully observed that:

> It is far more rational to suppose that the courts were designed to be an intermediate body between the people and the legislature in order, among other things, to keep the latter within the limits assigned to their authority. The interpretation of the law is the proper and peculiar province of the courts.[53]

The above views and theories have had a profound influence on the judiciaries' interpretation of these and related questions, particularly the separation of powers and its related concepts of checks and balances and judicial review, in the countries examined in this book.[54]

---

50 *Id.*, p. 305. *See also*, Story, 1833, pp. 8-13 (noting that the framers of the constitution understood that strict separation cannot be maintained).

51 Madison, Hamilton & Jay, 1961,p. 310.

52 *See, Certification of the Constitution of the Republic of South Africa*, 1996 1996 4 SA 744 (CC), at para. 109.

53 Madison, Hamilton & Jay, 1961, p. 466.

54 *See, Dr. James Rwanyarare and Another v. Attorney General* [2000] UGCC 2; *Centre for Health Human Rights & Development & 3 Ors v. Attorney General* [2012] UGCC 4; *Certification of the Constitution of the Republic of South Africa*, at para. 109.

1.2.4 Judicial Review

The seminal case on judicial review is *Marbury v. Madison.*[55] There, the court held that "it is, emphatically, the province and duty of the judicial department to say what the law is".[56] With these words, *Marbury v. Madison* laid the foundation for the exercise of judicial review in modern democracies across the common law world, including South Africa.[57] Despite *Marbury v. Madison* and the growth of the institution of judicial review, there is sufficient authority recognizing that the power of judicial review is not absolute[58] and for others illegitimate.[59] In her study of judicial review, the American constitutional scholar Barkow observed that the above phrase in *Marbury v. Madison* "could be read in isolation to establish limitless constitutional authority in the US Supreme Court to answer all constitutional questions".[60] To the contrary, Barkow argues that this eloquent excerpt from *Marbury v. Madison* cannot be taken out of context or absolutely and that the duty "to say

55 *See*, M. Corbett, 'Judicial Review and the Problems of Southern Africa', *Loyola University Chicago Law Journal,* Vol. 12, No. 2, 1981 p. 181 (arguing that although judicial review was, in a sense, the product of an evolutionary process of thought, the special contribution of *Marbury v. Madison* and the subsequent decisions of the Supreme Court entrenching and diversifying the system of judicial review in America is that they first established it as a working reality, and rendered possible and effective the protection of rights granted by a written constitution against not only executive and administrative acts, but also against parliamentary legislation. Since then, in many instances inspired no doubt by the American examples, about 60 countries throughout the world have adopted some form of judicial review). *See also*, M. Cappelletti, *Judicial Review in the Contemporary World,* Bobbs-Merril, Indiana, 1971, p. 25 (acknowledging the influence of *Marbury v. Madison* in other common law countries noting that our own time has seen the burgeoning of constitutional justice, which has in a sense combined the forms of legal justice and the substance of natural justice. Desirous of protecting the permanent will, rather than the temporary whims of the people, modern states have re-asserted higher law principles through written constitutions. Thus, there has been a synthesis of three separate concepts: the supremacy of certain higher principles, the need to put even the higher law in written form and the employment of the judiciary as a tool for enforcing the constitution against ordinary legislation. This union of concepts first occurred in the United States, but it has since come to be considered by many as essential to the rule of law anywhere).

56 *Marbury v. Madison*, 1803, p. 177.

57 *Marbury v. Madison* contributed to the development of the concept of judicial review in South Africa during the late 1800s. *See*, *Brown v. Leyds NO* (where relying on *Marbury v. Madison* the Supreme Court of the Transvaal declared that it had the power of judicial review); and Dugard, 1978, pp. 18-25.

58 *See*, *Doctors for Life International v. Speaker of the National Assembly* 2006 6 SA 416 (CC) *(Doctors for Life International); International Trade Administration Commission v. SCAW South Africa (Pty) Ltd* 2012 4 SA 618 (CC); *Ghana Bar Association v. Attorney General,* 1995; *National Treasury v. Opposition to Urban Tolling Alliance* 2012 (6) SA 223 (CC) (National Treasury); *De Lange v. Presiding Bishop of the Methodist Church of Southern Africa for the Time Being and Another* 2016 (2) SA 1 (CC); *Luther v. Borden; Zivotofsky v. Clinton,* 2012, p. 1427; *Balarabe Musa v. Auta Hamza,* 1983; and *Ferreira v. Levin,* 1996, at para. 180.

59 *See*, A. Hutchinson, 'A Hard Core Case Against Judicial Review', *Harvard Law Review,* Vol. 121, 2008, p. 64; L.D. Kramer, *The People Themselves: Popular Constitutionalism and Judicial Review,* Oxford University Press, New York, 2004; M. Tushnet, *Taking the Constitution Away From the Courts,* Princeton University Press, Princeton, 1999; J. Waldron 'The Core Case Against Judicial Review', *Yale Law Journal,* Vol. 115, 2006, p. 1353.

60 Barkow, 2002, p. 239. *See also*, M. Paulsen, 'Judging Judicial Review: Marbury in the Modern Era,' *Michigan Law Review*, Vol. 101, No. 8, 2003, p. 2706.

what the law is" does not necessarily imply a judicial monopoly on constitutional interpretation.[61] For Barkow, this duty leaves room for absolute deference to the constitutional interpretation by the political branches because a constitution may contain provisions that dictate an interpretive role or discretion for the politically accountable branches.[62] In this regard, she contends that *Marbury v. Madison* itself contains the seeds for the view that the authority to answer some constitutional questions rests entirely with the political branches.[63]

Similarly, Post and Siegel in their commentary on the notion of popular constitutionalism,[64] which is the notion that people assume active and ongoing control over the interpretation and enforcement of constitutional law, offer another explanation for the proposition of the shared responsibility on constitutional interpretation among the three branches of government. They view "elections as critical moments for expressing the people's active, ongoing sovereignty .... [which] authorize Congress and the President to speak for the people".[65] In this way, they argue, popular constitutionalism can be understood to entail a stringent form of departmentalism – namely that each of the three branches of government possesses independent and coordinate authority to interpret a constitution.[66]

It is in this context that this book discusses the development and the current status of the political question doctrine and theory in South Africa. It does this through a comparative discussion of the application of the doctrine in the United States, Ghana, Nigeria and Uganda. The purpose of this comparative discussion is two-fold. The first is to gain insight into the origins, theory, trends and classical application of the doctrine. The second is to gain insight into the challenges and best practices around the application of the doctrine in those countries. I chose to examine the experiences in the United States because that country is the first, among the common law countries, to articulate a coherent political question doctrine as a constitutional limitation of the power of judicial review; hence, it was important to examine early and most recent applications of the doctrine in the United States. Moreover, as Okpaluba has correctly pointed out in the context of his study of justiciability in the Commonwealth, the United States of America, a common law country

---

61 Barkow, 2002, p. 239. *See also*, Currie & de Waal, 2005, p. 394 and Fisher & Devins, 1992, p. 10.

62 Barkow, 2002, p. 239 and Fisher & Devins, 1992, p. 10. *See also*, H. Monaghan, 'Marbury and the Administrative State,' *Columbia Law Review*, Vol. 83, No. 1, 1983, pp. 7-9.

63 *Id.*; and *Cooper v. Aaron*, 358 US 1 (1958) (noting that even the US Supreme Court has the last say only for a time because being composed of fallible men, it may err. But revision of its errors may be done by legislation or constitutional amendments) (Frankfurter, concurring).

64 This term coined by Larry Kramer. *See*, Kramer, 2004; and L. Kramer, 'Popular Constitutionalism: Circa 2004,' *California Law Review*, Vol. 92, No. 4, 2004, p. 959.

65 *See*, R. Post & R. Siegel, 'Popular Constitutionalism, Departmentalism and Judicial Supremacy,' *California Law Review*, Vol. 92, No. 45, 2004, p. 1031.

66 *Id.*

with the oldest written constitution, is the conventional starting point for any enquiry into the study of judicial review and its limitations.[67]

Additionally, South African courts in both the pre- and post-democratic dispensation eras have relied on the proposition of the power of judicial review enunciated in *Marbury v. Madison*, which I argue includes the limitation of judicial review articulated in that case. For example, as already pointed out, in *Brown v. Leyds No.*, the court endorsed the fundamental principle in *Marbury v. Madison*, including the inherent limitation of judicial review, and other authorities that a law repugnant to a constitution is void and that courts, as well as other departments, are bound by that instrument; that courts have authority to enforce this principle.[68] Despite expressly providing for the power of judicial review in the Constitution, courts in post-democratic South Africa have continually cited with approval the proposition in *Marbury v. Madison*. In *Certification of the KwaZulu-Natal Constitution*,[69] the Constitutional Court refused to certify a constitution for the province of KwaZulu-Natal. The court approvingly cited *Marbury v. Madison* for the proposition that a court of law has the authority to strike down or invalidate legislation and administrative action even when such power of review is not expressly granted in the Constitution or the Bill of Rights concerned.

Similarly, in *Premier of the Eastern Cape v. Ntamo*,[70] the Eastern Cape High Court justified the power of judicial review by approvingly citing *Marbury v. Madison*. The court reasoned that

> it is the constitutional function of the judicial arm of government to determine and resolve justiciable disputes between parties. That function includes deciding disputes as to whether the executive or legislative arms of government, or other organs of state, have acted within or beyond the powers conferred on them by law.[71]

The court noted that this is a function that has, in the jurisprudential tradition of which our Constitution is part, always been entrusted to the courts since the landmark case of *Marbury v. Madison*, and that to the extent it may be suggested that this jurisdiction offends

---

67 C. Okpaluba, 'Justiciability and Standing to Challenge Legislation in the Commonwealth: A Tale of the Traditionalist and Judicial Activists Approaches', *Comparative and International Law Journal of Southern Africa*, Vol. 36, No. 1, 2003, p. 30.

68 *Brown v. Leyds NO* 29-31.

69 '*Certification of the KwaZulu-Natal Constitution*', 1996 (11) *BCLR* 1419.

70 *Premier of the Eastern Cape v. Ntamo.*

71 *Id.*, at para. 1.

the doctrine of the separation of powers, it is an intrusion into the terrain of the other branches of government that is permitted, expressly, by the Constitution.[72]

The further reasons for focusing on Ghana, Nigeria and Uganda are that:

(a) all these countries have some common heritage as recipients of the English common law. And all have constitutionally adopted, among other things, the institution of judicial review and separation of powers that imitate the American system instead of the British system, and the courts from these countries have relied on American authorities, such as *Marbury v. Madison*, in their adjudication of these constitutional concepts.[73] Given the fact that in *Marbury v. Madison* and other related authorities have recognized the political question doctrine as a necessary limitation to the institution of judicial review, it was significant for this book to adopt a comparative approach in the light of their common features. This leads to a further point that was equally made by Dennison in the context of Uganda that if the legal borrowing of the notion of judicial review from the United States by the judiciary in these countries is considered fitting, the legal borrowing of the political question doctrine as a corollary to separation of powers should equally be fitting.[74]

What is more, the comparative study of African countries that have borrowed doctrines, such as the political question doctrine, should be useful in identifying common trends and

---

72 *Id. See also, Dada v. Unlawful Occupiers of Portion 41* [2008] ZAGPHC 48, at para. 24 (justifying judicial review by relying on *Marbury v. Madison*). Other judiciaries in the Southern African region have cited *Marbury v. Madison* with approval; *see, Lekotholi v. Attorney-General* [1994] LSCA 153 (noting that for guidance in respect of laws that collide with the Constitution reference should be made to cases of *Marbury v. Madison*); *S v. Cloete* [2008] NAHC 116 (citing *Marbury v. Madison* on the power to declare laws invalid); *African Personnel Services v. Government of Namibia* [2008] NAHC 148 (citing *Marbury v. Madison* on power to declare law invalid); and *Cowigan (Pty) Ltd & Others v. Thwala* [2012] SZSC 25 (discussing judicial review as articulated in *Marbury v. Madison*).

73 *See, Certification of the KwaZulu-Natal Constitution*, at para. 19 (where the South African Constitutional Court refused to certify the KwaZulu-Natal's provincial constitution, and in the process approvingly cited *Marbury v. Madison*); *Premier of the Eastern Cape and Others v. Ntamo* [1] (justified the power of judicial review by approvingly citing *Marbury v. Madison*); *Dr. James Rwanyarare v. Attorney General* (Constitutional Petition No. 5 of 1999) [2000] UGCC 2 (holding that under our Constitution, the courts are given jurisdiction to exercise judicial power and nothing else. In a famous US case of *Marbury v. Madison*, the US Supreme Court held that since the original jurisdiction [of the US Supreme Court] is derived from the Constitution, it follows logically that congress can neither restrict it nor enlarge it. In Uganda, the sole source of the jurisdiction is the constitution. It therefore logically follows the jurisdiction can only be restricted, reduced or enlarged through an amendment to the constitution, and not otherwise. Parliament is empowered to create courts, tribunals, panels, etc., but if they are constituted by judicial officers, Parliament has no power to vest in them jurisdiction that goes outside the exercise of judicial power); *Centre for Health Human Rights & Development & 3 Ors v. Attorney General* (Constitutional Petition No. 16 of 2011) [2012] UGCC 4 (noting that the doctrine of political question emanated from the concept of separation of powers. This doctrine was a creation of court in the case of *Marbury v. Madison* as part of the broader concept of justification – whether or not it is appropriate for court to review the business of other branches of government); and *H Mensah v. Attorney-General* [1996-97] SCGLR 320.

74 B. Dennison, 'The Political Question Doctrine in Uganda: A Reassessment in the Wake of *CEHURD*', *Law, Democracy and Development*, Vol. 18, 2014, p. 280.

problems associated with any potential legal borrowing. While embarking on this comparative analysis, I am mindful of what courts in South Africa have said about reliance on foreign authorities in the interpretation of the Constitution. In this respect, let me draw your attention to what Justice Kriegler once remarked in *Bernstien v. Bester* that:[75]

> ...I wish to discourage the frequent – and, I suspect, often facile – resort to foreign authorities. Far too often one sees citation by counsel of, for instance, an American judgment in support of a proposition relating to our Constitution, without any attempt to explain why it is said to be in point. Comparative study is always useful, particularly where courts in exemplary jurisdictions have grappled with universal issues confronting us. Likewise, where a provision in our Constitution is manifestly modelled on a particular provision in another country's constitution, it would be folly not to ascertain how the jurists of that country have interpreted their precedential provision.[76]

Almost a decade later, Kriegler's counterpart Justice Van der Westhuizen in *Mashavha v. President of the Republic of South Africa and Others*[77] would dismiss an argument (premised on foreign authorities) put forward by the provincial government of KwaZulu-Natal, that:

> South Africa is a huge country with a land mass equivalent to much of mainland Europe. The division into nine provinces recognizes that different areas have vastly different needs that can be dealt with differently in the same way as France and Poland or Denmark and Austria deal with certain matters, including social assistance, differently. In India relief of the disabled and unemployable and the payment of state pensions are matters of exclusive legislative competence for the states in terms of items 9 and 42 of List II in Schedule 7 to the Constitution. Under section 94A of the Canadian Constitution the Parliament of Canada can make laws in relation to old age pensions and supplementary benefits, including disability grants, but no such law shall affect the operation of any law present or future of a provincial legislature in relation to any such matter. In other words, there is dual competence subject to a provincial override.[78]

75 *Bernstien v. Bester* 1996 2 SA 751 (CC), at para. 133.
76 *Id.*
77 *Mashavha v. President of the Republic of South Africa* 2005 2 SA 476 (CC).
78 *Id.*, at para. 48.

The above argument was advanced to persuade the Constitutional Court to interpret Section 126(3)[79] of the Interim Constitution of South Africa Act 200 of 1993 to prevent the national government from overriding the power of provinces to regulate social assistance matters. In dismissing the argument, Justice Van der Westhuizen reasoned that:

> The submissions put forward on behalf of the fifth respondent ignore the political, social and economic history of South Africa. There are countless vast differences between this country and the other countries referred to by the fifth respondent. The way social assistance is structured and administered in Denmark and Austria, or even Canada, or India, can hardly be compared to the South African situation. Our history is well known. It is one of colonialization, apartheid, economic exploitation, migrant labour, oppression and balkanization. Gross inequalities were deliberately and legally imposed as far as race and also geographical areas are concerned. Not only were there richer and poorer provinces, but there were homelands, which by no stretch of the imagination could be seen to have been treated on the same footing as 'white' South Africa, as far as resources are concerned. These inequalities also applied to social assistance – an area of governmental responsibility very closely related to human

---

79 Section 126 of the Interim Constitution Act 200 of 1993 provided:
Legislative competence of provinces 126.

1. A provincial legislature shall subject to subsections (3) and (4), have concurrent competence with Parliament to make laws for the province with regards to all matters that fall within the functional areas specified in Schedule 6.
2. The legislative competence referred to in subsection (1) shall include the competence to make laws that are reasonably necessary for or incidental to the effective exercise of such legislative competence.
3. An Act of Parliament that deals with a matter referred to in subsection (1) or (2) shall prevail over a provincial law inconsistent therewith, only to the extent that:
   a. it deals with a matter that cannot be regulated effectively by provincial legislation;
   b. it deals with a matter that, to be performed effectively, requires to be regulated or co-ordinated by uniform norms or standards that apply generally throughout the Republic;
   c. it is necessary to set minimum standards across the nation for the rendering of public services;
   d. it is necessary for the determination of national economic policies, the maintenance of economic unity, the protection of the environment, the promotion of inter-provincial commerce, the protection of the common market in respect of the mobility of goods, services, capital or labour, or the maintenance of national security; or
   e. the provincial law materially prejudices the economic, health or security interests of another province or the country as a whole.
4. An Act of Parliament shall prevail over a provincial law, as provided for in subsection (3), only if it applies uniformly in all parts of the Republic.
5. An Act of Parliament and a provincial law shall be construed as being consistent with each other, unless, and only to the extent that, they are, expressly or by necessary implication, inconsistent with each other.
6. A provincial legislature may recommend to Parliament the passing of any law relating to any matter in respect of which such legislature is not competent to make laws or in respect of which an Act of Parliament prevails over a provincial law in terms of subsection (3).

> dignity. The history of our country and the need for equality cannot be ignored in the interpretation and application of section 126(3).[80]

However, unlike concerns against reliance on foreign case law expressed in the above authorities, the issues and problems ventilated in this book are universal and shared among all modern constitutional democracies, whose constitutions are founded on the separation of powers, and courts in the countries being compared to have grappled with them in the same way as South African courts have attempted.[81]

Moreover, as mentioned, the concepts that form the essence of the discussions in this book – separation of powers and judicial review – were all manifestly modelled on the American system, which renders it suitable for us to ascertain how the jurists in these countries have dealt with these universal issues. The countries that I review have also relied on each other's case law to interpret their respective constitutions.

(b) the African countries being examined have all adopted supreme constitutions since the last fifty years or so. Although these constitutions are generally similar in design to South Africa's Constitution, the courts in those countries have already considered, developed and applied the political question doctrine in determining political controversies on a number of occasions that offer a useful analogy. In this regard, I explore the origins and current application of the political question doctrine in these countries with a view to draw lessons for South Africa.

The book advances the argument that while the political question theory exists in the South African jurisprudence, this has yet to mature into a clear and transparent doctrine. It will call on the judiciary to develop a clear doctrine for South Africa and make suggestions in this regard. The need for such a development could be illustrated by the following hypothetical questions.

---

80 *Mashavha v. President of the Republic of South Africa*, at para. 51. For other cases where the Court warned against transplanting into South African jurisprudence legal doctrines from other countries where the constitutional provisions are different from South Africa's. *See, Prinsloo v. Van der Linde and Another* 1997 (3) SA 1012 (CC), at paras. 18-20; *S v. Lawrence, S v. Negal; S v. Solberg* 1997 (10) BCLR 1348 (CC); 1997 (4) SA 1176 (CC), at paras. 141-142.

81 *See, Mazibuko*, p. 33 (criticizing the use of courts to fight political issues and commenting that "I regret the need to emphasise this point, but it appears to me to be vital to the future integrity of the judicial institution. An overreach of the powers of judges, their intrusion into issues which are beyond their competence or intended jurisdiction or which have been deliberately and carefully constructed legally so as to ensure that the other arms of the state to deal with these matters, can only result in jeopardy for our constitutional democracy."). On appeal, *see, Mazibuko v. Sisulu* 2013 6 SA 249 (CC), at para. 83 (Jafta J., minority opinion) (noting at the outset that "political issues must be resolved at a political level; that our court should not be drawn into political disputes, the resolution of which falls appropriately within the domain of other fora established in terms of the Constitution").

Suppose for a moment that a citizen of South Africa brought an action seeking judicial review of the recent decisions of the President of South Africa to cause South Africa to enter into a treaty establishing the India, Brazil, South Africa (IBSA)[82] and later the Brazil, Russia, India, China and South Africa (BRICS),[83] under the theory that the decisions were irrational and have not produced benefits for South Africans in whose name and welfare the powers of government should be exercised.

In such a challenge would the courts have a judicial or legal standard to determine the dispute? If not, what would be the justification for a decision that the judiciary should not determine the dispute? If the judiciary were to decide to hear the dispute, would it impermissibly interfere with the functioning of the executive and legislature, who are constitutionally entrusted with the powers and discretion to enter into treaties? Would the judiciary be correctly accused of pronouncing on matters of policy or substituting its own notions of what is wise and politic with that of the executive or legislature? Does the power of judicial review, under the Constitution, authorize the judiciary to sit in judgement of the wisdom of what the legislature and executive branches do in their respective constitutional areas of expertise and discretion? Would not the political question doctrine assist the judiciary to avoid the temptation to impermissibly intrude into the terrain of the political branches that the then President Chaskalson warned about in *Ferreira v. Levin*?[84] These are some of the concerns that President Zuma probably had in mind in his statement quoted above. These questions must be understood in the light of, among others things, Section 231 of the Constitution, which delegates, to the political branches, the discretion to negotiate and enter into international agreements. Noticeably, under the Constitution, the decision to enter into international agreements is expressly and exclusively allocated to the discretion of the political branches of government.[85]

82 Formalized by the Brasilia Declaration of 6 June 2003.

83 *See*, the Contingent Reserve Arrangement Treaty of the BRICS countries signed on 15 July 2014.

84 *Ferreira v. Levin*, at para. 183 (warning courts against a broad construction of certain provisions of the Constitution so as to not overshoot the mark and trespass upon the terrain that is not rightly for the courts).

85 *See, President of the Republic of South Africa v. Quagliani, President of the Republic of South Africa v. Van Rooyen and Another; Goodwin v. Director-General, Department of Justice and Constitutional Development* 2009 4 BCLR 345 (CC); and *Glenister v. President of the Republic of South Africa* 2011 3 SA 347 (CC) (Glenister). *But see, Law Society of South Africa and Others v. President of the Republic of South Africa and Others* [2018] ZACC 5, at paras. 76-92 (*SADC Tribunal* case, 2018) (where in invalidating the President's signature on the 2014 Protocol on the Tribunal in the Southern African Development Community to disband the SADC Tribunal established under the Treaty of the Southern African Development Community 1992, the Court held that in its participation of international relations the South African national executive cannot approve anything that undermines our Bill of Rights ... it thus lacked the authority to sign any international agreement that seeks to frustrate the pre-existing right of South Africans to access justice at the SADC Tribunal that was secured for them by Parliament. The executive lacks the authority to negotiate and sign away fundamental and treaty right of access to justice and to potentially prejudice citizens of other SADC countries in that manner. To the extent that the executive purported to do so, the President's conduct in signing the protocol is unconstitutional... It follows that considerations of comity and the quest for sound

Legal authorities from Ghana, Nigeria, Uganda, the United States and other jurisdictions suggest that a court, presented with the above hypothetical questions, would invoke the political question doctrine or some other similar principle and abstain from intervening in the matters. In South Africa, the problem is that the law is uncertain and the cases that have reflected on similar questions do not provide a clear answer. It is not clear whether or when a court in South Africa would hear and pronounce substantively on a matter involving purely political questions, which the Constitution allocated and grants discretion over such matter to the political branches.

Throughout this book, by political questions I refer to those questions that have, through the text or structure of the Constitution, been allocated, for resolution, to the discretion of the elected branches or those questions for which there is no judicial standard to determine them. In short, the question cannot be resolved through the application of the law. A non-justiciable political question has a similar meaning in this book.

The uncertainty over how to resolve these questions in South Africa is exacerbated by the fact that the Constitution 1996 expressly granted the courts the power of judicial review. In my own view, the effect of this is that the courts have been less inclined to organically develop the institution of judicial review, including the determination of its scope and limitations, like courts in other countries have done. Although the Constitutional Court has recognized the limits of the power of judicial review in the context of separation of powers cases such as the landmark case of *Doctors for Life International* and *Economic Freedom Fighters v. Speaker of the National Assembly*,[86] it has not successfully devised a rule of law to be applied in future cases to give effect to this recognition. Notwithstanding this uncertainty, recent cases such as *Economic Freedom Fighters v. Speaker of the National*

---

diplomatic relations cannot assist the President [executive] in his endeavor to insulate his signature from constitutional invalidation).

86 *Economic Freedom Fighters v. Speaker of the National Assembly*, at para. 93; *United Democratic Movement v. Speaker of the National Assembly and Others*, at paras. 59-64. *See also*, *Economic Freedom Fighters v. Speaker of the National Assembly* 2018 (2) SA 571 (CC) (*Impeachment case*) (Mogoeng, dissenting), at paras. 252-253 (explaining that "We said in [*Economic Freedom Fighters v. Speaker of the National Assembly*] that ours is a less intrusive role and that we are not to prescribe to the National Assembly what mechanics to adopt for holding the President accountable... Similarly, in [*United Democratic Movement v. Speaker of the National Assembly and Others*] we chose not to prescribe a secret ballot voting procedure to the Assembly for a motion of no confidence. This, in circumstances where there is already a strong constitutional pointer to a secret ballot, for electing the President and other constitutional office-bearers, as the implicitly appropriate method for voting him or her out of office. Our appropriate self-restraint was again informed by our ever abiding consciousness of the vital strictures of our powers and our super-alertness to impermissible encroachment on Parliament's powers. We could ... have decided that a secret ballot was the only appropriate voting procedure for a motion of no confidence. But sensitivity to the dictates of separation of powers forbade us. For, it is for the National Assembly to make that choice, not the Judiciary. Respect for separation of powers again constrained us from directing the Speaker to schedule a debate on a motion of no confidence on a particular date. We remitted the request to the Speaker to have the motion tabled in terms of whatever procedure she considered appropriate.").

Assembly, United Democratic Movement v. Speaker of the National Assembly and Others[87] and *National Treasury* reflect a new sign of maturity in South Africa's approach to the political question theory.

To illustrate, in *National Treasury*, the Constitutional Court lifted an interdict against a controversial government policy and emphasized that the duty to formulate and implement public policies lies at the heartland of executive function and domain.[88] The Constitutional Court observed that the judiciary is not well suited to make decisions of that nature because such decisions are constitutionally delegated to the coordinate political branches.[89] In his concurring opinion in *National Treasury*, Justice Froneman found that it is a contravention of separation of powers for a court to intrude by granting an interdict against the implementation of government policy to fund infrastructure projects by means of

---

87 *United Democratic Movement v. Speaker of the National Assembly and Others* 2017 (8) BCLR 1061 (CC).

88 *National Treasury* [67]. *See also*, *Electronic Media Network Limited and Others v. e.tv (Pty) Limited and Others* 2017 (9) BCLR 1108 (CC), at paras. 1-2 (held that "ours is a constitutional democracy, not a judiciocracy. And in consonance with the principle of separation of powers, the national legislative authority of the Republic is vested in Parliament whereas the judicial and the executive authority of the Republic repose in the Judiciary and the Executive respectively. Each arm enjoys functional independence in the exercise of its powers. Alive to this arrangement, all three must always caution themselves against intruding into the constitutionally-assigned operational space of the others, save where the encroachment is unavoidable and constitutionally permissible. Turning to the Executive, one of the core features of its authority is national policy development. For this reason, any legislation, principle or practice that regulates a consultative process or relates to the substance of national policy must recognise that policy-determination is the space exclusively occupied by the Executive.").

89 *National Treasury*, at para. 68. *See also*, *Arakaki v. Lingle* 305 F Supp 2d 1161 (2004); *Corriee v. Caterpillar*, p. 980; *State of Idaho v. Freeman* 529 F Supp 1107 (1981); J. Nzelibe, 'The Uniqueness of Foreign Affairs', *Iowa Law Review*, Vol. 89, No. 942, 2004, p. 941; L. Seidman, 'Secret Life of the Political Question Doctrine', *John Marshall Law Review*, Vol. 37, 2003, pp. 442-443; J. Choper, 'The Political Question Doctrine: Suggested Criteria', *Duke Law Journal*, Vol. 54, 2005, p. 1457; *El-Shifa Pharmaceutical Industries Co v. US* 607 F 3d 836 (2010) (holding that the political question doctrine is essentially a function of the separation of powers, and excludes from judicial review those controversies which revolve around policy choices and value determinations constitutionally committed for resolution to the halls of Congress or the confines of the Executive Branch); S. Banner & J. May, 'American Electric Power Company Inc et al, Petitioners v State of Connecticut, et al, Respondents', *Valparaiso University Law Review*, Vol. 46, No. 2, 2012, p. 459 (arguing that the Constitution's text commits certain tasks to branches other than the judiciary); *Native Village of Kivalina v. ExxonMobil Corp* 663 F Supp 2d 863 (2009) (noting that the political question doctrine serves to prevent the federal courts from intruding unduly on certain policy choices and value judgments that are constitutionally committed to Congress or the executive branch); *Oetjen v. Central Leather* Co 246 US 297 (1918) (holding that the conduct of the foreign relations of our government is committed by the Constitution to the executive and legislative departments of the government, and the propriety of what may be done in the exercise of this political power is not subject to judicial inquiry or decision); *United States v. Belmont* 301 US 324 (1937) (emphasizing the exclusive competence of the executive branch in the field of foreign affairs).

tolling the roads on a user-pay principle[90] because that matter resides in the heartland of national executive.[91]

Furthermore, Justice Froneman declared that "the playing field for the contestation of executive government policy is the political process, not the judicial one" because in his view the

> courts of this country do not determine what kind of funding should be used for infrastructural funding of roads and who should bear the brunt for that cost. The remedy in that regard lies in the political process.[92]

It will be maintained that Justice Froneman's opinion is a validation that the text of the Constitution envisages political accountability when it comes to the remedy for certain constitutional or political questions and is another reminder of the need for the judiciary in South Africa to develop a coherent political question theory in order to implement its obligation to ensure that the courts are conscious of their vital limits.

Lastly, the judgement in *Economic Freedom Fighters v. Speaker of the National Assembly* is another important contribution to the theory of the political question doctrine discourse in South Africa. There, the Constitutional Court endorsed the above principle – that the text of the Constitution envisages political accountability when it comes to the remedy for certain constitutional or political questions. This endorsement was made in the context of its determination of whether the National Assembly breached its constitutional obligation

---

90 The Cabinet took a decision in 2007 that approved an extensive upgrade of roads in the economic hub of the Gauteng province as part of the GFIP.

91 *National Treasury*, at para. 84. There are other matters in the Constitution that are committed to the elected branches of government. *See, President of the Republic of South Africa and Another v. Hugo* 1997 6 BCLR 708 (CC) (recognizing that the exercise of pardon powers is committed to the executive branch). In addition, Sections 206(1) and 207(2) of the Constitution commit policing matters to the executive branch such that it is free to structure the South African Police Service without substantive judicial scrutiny. *See, Glenister*, 2011, at paras. 65, 120 and 162 (holding that the elected branches of government are free to decide where to locate a specialized corruption-fighting unit. In this case, the elected branches had decided to locate such unit within and not without the South African Police Service as previously was the case).

92 *National Treasury*, at paras. 93-95. *See also*, Sections 59; 85(2)(d); 118; 195(1)(e); 72 of the Constitution 1996. *See also, Chief Enyi Abaribe v. the Speaker Abia State House of Assembly & Ors*, (2003) 14 NWLR (pt. 788) 466 (explaining that "in cases involving political questions appeal for relief does not belong here. Appeal must be to an informed, civically militant electorate. In a democratic society like ours, relief must come through an aroused popular conscience that sears the conscience of the people's representatives."); *Schneider v. Kissinger* 412 F 3d 190 (2005) (in addressing concern about the effects of leaving political questions to the political process, the court reasoned that the lack of judicial authority to oversee the conduct of the executive branch in political matters did not leave executive power unchecked because political branches effectively exercise checks and balances on each other in the area of political questions); and J. Story, *Commentaries on the Constitution*, William S. Hein & Company, New York, 1905, p. 525 (arguing that in cases involving questions exclusively of political character, the supreme authority as to these questions belongs to the political branches of government and that the remedy in such cases is solely by an appeal to people at the elections).

to hold the President to account in the manner in which it handled the Public Protector's report titled "Secure in Comfort".[93] In addressing this question, the Constitutional Court unanimously observed that the Constitution neither gives details on how the National Assembly is to discharge the duty to hold the executive to account nor are the mechanisms for doing so outlined in the Constitution.[94] It reasoned that the National Assembly must be construed as having "been given the leeway to determine how best to carry out its constitutional mandate".[95]

As a consequence, it unanimously held that:

> It falls outside the parameters of judicial authority to prescribe to the National Assembly how to scrutinize executive action, what mechanisms to establish and which mandate to give them, for the purpose of holding the Executive accountable and fulfilling its oversight role of the executive or organs of State in general. The mechanics of how to go about fulfilling these constitutional obligations is a discretionary matter best left to the National Assembly. Ours is a much broader and less intrusive role. ...these are some of the vital limits on judicial authority and the Constitution's design to leave certain matters to other branches of government.[96]

In the above rulings, the Court seems to identify the basic contours of judicial review.[97] The effect of the above Constitutional Court's judgement is that a rule of law has emerged, which provides that where the Constitution assigns an obligation to a politically accountable branch of government and gives it discretion on how to discharge the obligation in question, it "falls outside the parameters of judicial authority to prescribe" to that branch of govern-

93 *See*, '*Secure In Comfort*', Report No. 25 of 2013/2014, www.publicprotector.org/sites/default/files/Legislation_report/Final%20Report%2019%20March%202014%20.pdf (last accessed 15 September 2016).

94 *Economic Freedom Fighters v. Speaker of the National Assembly*, at para. 43.

95 *Id.*, at para. 87.

96 *Id.*, at para. 93.

97 Ngcobo, 2016, p. 23; M. Mhango, 'Is It Time for a Coherent Political Question Doctrine in South Africa? Lessons from the United States', *African Journal of Legal Studies*, Vol. 7, No. 4, 2014, p. 471. Redish, 1984, pp. 5-10; and *Doctors for Life International*, at para. 26.

ment how to discharge that obligation.[98] This is precisely what the classical strand of the political question theory advocates.[99]

98 Ngcobo, 2016, p. 23; Mhango, 2014, p. 471; Redish, 1984, pp. 5-10 and *Economic Freedom Fighters v. Speaker of the National Assembly*, at para. 93. Recently, in *United Democratic Movement v. Speaker of the National Assembly and Others*, at paras. 59-69, the Constitutional Court reiterated that the absence in the Constitution of a prescribed voting procedure for a motion of no confidence in the President means that National Assembly has the discretion to determine the voting procedure in a particular instance. It found that that discretion has been delegated to the Speaker of the National Assembly. *See also, Economic Freedom Fighters and Others v. Speaker of the National Assembly and Another* 2018 (3) BCLR 259 (CC) (*Impeachment case*), at paras. 252-255 (Mogoeng, dissenting) (emphasizing the need for the court to adhere to the political question theory-based principle in *Economic Freedom Fighters v. Speaker of the National Assembly* and *United Democratic Movement v. Speaker of the National Assembly and Others*, 2017).

99 Story, 1833, pp. 345-347; and *Marbury v. Madison*.

2 The Genesis and Modern Application of the Political Question Doctrine in the United States

2.1 Introduction

This chapter examines the genesis of the political question doctrine. It traces the origins of the doctrine from the opinions of Alexander Hamilton, one of the framers of the US Constitution, and Chief Justice Marshall in *Marbury v. Madison*.[1] The chapter focuses its discussion on US Supreme Court jurisprudence. It divides the discussion into areas where the classical political question is applied, as well as the prudential political question.

Lastly, it separately surveys a number of federal and state court cases where the political question doctrine has been applied over the years. It concludes that the political question doctrine remains good law in the United States and will likely endure as an important part of American constitutional culture where certain category of cases will be excluded from judicial review. This is despite the criticism and the fact that in recent jurisprudence, some questions remain unanswered concerning the future of the doctrine.

2.2 Early Application of the Classical Political Question Doctrine

The political question doctrine is as old as the elemental principle of judicial review.[2] In the well-regarded case of *Marbury v. Madison*,[3] Chief Justice Marshall first expressed the recognition by the judiciary of the existence of a class of cases constituting:

> political act belonging to the executive department alone, for the performance of which entire confidence is placed by our Constitution in the supreme executive; and for any misconduct respecting which the injured individual has no remedy.[4]

1 *Marbury v. Madison* 5 US (1 Cranch) 137 (1803).
2 *Antolok v. United States* 873 F 2d 369 (DC Cir 1989), p. 379.
3 *Marbury v. Madison*, 1803, p. 164.
4 *Id.*

Additionally, Marshall announced what has now come to be known as the political question doctrine and held that:

> the province of the court is ... not to inquire how the executive or executive officers perform duties in which they have discretion. Questions, in their nature political or which are, by the constitution and laws, submitted to the executive, can never be made in this court.[5]

Marshall's reasoning was that because some conduct by the political branches is judiciary examinable and others not, it was important for the judiciary to develop a rule of law to guide courts in the exercise of its jurisdiction in those appropriate cases where they cannot intervene.[6] He emphasized the need for such a rule by conceding to the fact that the executive is constitutionally endowed with certain important political powers, which it has to apply using its own discretion, and is only politically accountable.[7]

Eventually, Chief Justice Marshall established a rule that:

> where the heads of departments are the political or confidential agents of the executive, merely to execute the will of the president, or rather to act in cases in which the Executive possesses a constitutional or legal discretion, nothing can be more perfectly clear than that their acts are only politically examinable. But where a specific duty is assigned by law, and individual rights depend upon the performance of that duty, it seems equally clear that the individual who considers himself injured has a right to resort to the laws of his country for a remedy.[8]

The above reasoning and holding in *Marbury v. Madison* gave birth to what will, in later years, be commonly known as the political question doctrine.[9] With this holding, the *Marbury v. Madison* Court instructed the judiciary to dismiss cases if the constitution's text, structure or theory signifies that an issue should be decided by an elected branch of government.[10] Furthermore, based on this holding, *Marbury v. Madison* recognized a clear

5 *Id.*, p. 170.

6 *Id.*, p. 165. *See also*, Cole, 2014, pp. 2-3.

7 *Id.*

8 *Marbury v. Madison*, 1803, p. 170.

9 Some scholars have argued that the political question doctrine may have originated from the earlier cases in *Ware v. Hylton* 3 US (3 Dall) 199 (1796); *Martin v. Mott* 25 US (12 Wheat) 19 (1872). *See*, L. Peitzman, 'The Supreme Court and the Credentials Challenge Cases: Ask a Political Question, You Get a Political Answer', *California Law Review*, Vol. 62, No. 4, 1974, p. 1350, fn. 31.

10 R. Pushaw, 'Judicial Review and the Political Question Doctrine: Reviving the Federalist Rebuttable Presumption Analysis', *North Carolina Law Review*, Vol. 80, No. 4, 2002, pp. 1192-1193.

difference between legal questions that the judiciary must decide and political questions they must allow the political branches to remedy.[11]

As Fallon has commented, *Marbury v. Madison* not only represents the fountainhead of judicial review having ruled that it is the duty of the judiciary to say what the law is, but also furnishes the canonical statement of the necessary and appropriate role of the judiciary in a constitutional system founded on the principle of separation of powers.[12] It is for this reason that some commentators have defended the political question doctrine on separation of powers grounds arguing that the US Constitution assigns responsibility for interpreting or enforcing certain constitutional provisions to the elected branches of government.[13] The classical political question doctrine emanated from these pronouncements in *Marbury v. Madison* and forms part of any meaningful discussion of that case.[14] Since *Marbury v.*

11 *See*, S. Shrewsbury, '*Marbury v. Madison*: The Origins and Legacy of Judicial Review', *Military Law Review*, Vol. 173, 2002, p. 166; O. Stephens, 'John Marshall and the Confluence of Law and Politics, *Tennessee Law Review*, Vol. 71, 2004, p. 245 and L. Price, 'Banishing the Specter of Judicial Foreign Policymaking: A Competence-Based Approach to the Political Question Doctrine', *New York University Journal of International Law & Politics*, Vol. 38, 2006, p. 331.

12 *See*, R. Fallon, 'Marbury and the Constitutional Mind: A Bicentennial Essay on the Wages of Doctrinal Tension', *California Law Review*, Vol. 91, No. 1, 2003, p. 5.

13 E. Chemerinsky, *Constitutional Law*, Aspen Law & Business, New York, 2001, p. 77; Imam et al., 2011, pp. 55-56; *Koohi v. United States* 976 F 2d 1328 (9th Cir 1992) and *EEOC v. Peabody W Coal Co* 400 F 3d 774 (9th Cir 2005), at p. 785.

14 *See*, Story, 1833, pp. 345-347; Cooley, 1868, p. 41; Szurkowski, 2014, p. 353 (explaining that in the years following *Marbury v. Madison*, the US Supreme Court applied the classical version of the political question doctrine, under which courts have not only the ability, but also the obligation to decide cases or controversies that come before them, unless the Constitution has committed the power to decide the issue to another branch of government. Accordingly, early applications of the political question doctrine focused closely on constitutional text and structure); Scharpf, 1966, p. 518 (noting that the compatibility with the logic of *Marbury v. Madison* requires that the political question doctrine be understood as the command of the Constitution); Barkow, 2002, pp. 248-249 (discussing that the classic political question doctrine has its roots from utterances of Alexander Hamilton and Chief Justice Marshall in *Marbury v. Madison* noting that Hamilton recognized a constitutionally based political question doctrine, which has come to be known as the classic political question doctrine. She notes that Hamilton was not alone in acknowledging that resolution of certain constitutional questions belongs to the political branches. She acknowledges that Marshall also advocated the same view that some questions are committed by the Constitution to the absolute discretion of the Congress or the President and there is no place for judicial oversight. Unlike Hamilton, Madison identified key factors to identify political questions: the subjects are political; they respect the nation, not individual; they involve areas that the Constitution vests the political branches with discretion. And that the two areas where this would apply were foreign affairs and nomination of candidates to the Senate). *See also*, R. Pushaw, 'Justiciability and Separation of Powers: A Neo-Federalist Approach', *Cornell Law Review*, Vol. 81, No. 2, 1996, p. 424 (arguing that Hamilton foreshadowed the political question doctrine); D. Cole, 'Challenging Covert War: The Politics of the Political Question Doctrine', *Harvard International Law Journal*, Vol. 26, 1985, p. 164 (recognizing three aspects of the political question doctrine: the classical or constitutional version, which is "the most important and most persuasive aspect of doctrine"). For Alexander Hamilton's views about the political question doctrine, *see*, A. Hamilton, The Judiciary, *in* C. Rossiter (Ed.), *The Federalist Paper No. 78*, Signet Classic, New York, 1999, p. 466 (arguing that "If it be said that the legislative body are themselves the constitutional judges of their own powers and that the construction they put upon them is conclusive upon the other departments it may be answered that this

Madison, the US Supreme Court has refined and applied the classical political question doctrine in a number of cases.[15] A few of these cases are significant and require some detailed discussion.

No discussion of the classical political question can be all-embracing without the consideration of *Luther v. Borden*. This was a trespass case where the plaintiff challenged the Rhode Island charter government under the republican form of government in terms of the Guaranty Clause of the US Constitution.[16] When the lawsuit was launched, Rhode Island was still being governed under a charter established by King Charles II in 1663.[17] As part of this lawsuit, the plaintiff challenged the charter government as a violation of the Guaranty Clause, which provides that the "United States shall guarantee to every State in this Union a Republican form of government."[18] The question before the US Supreme Court was which government was to be recognized as the republican government. The US Supreme Court, through Chief Justice Taney,[19] declined to adjudicate the case on the basis that the issue was a political question. It held that:

> Under this article of the Constitution, it rests with Congress to decide what government is the established one in a State. For as the United States guarantee to each State a republican government, Congress must necessarily decide what

cannot be the natural presumption where it is not to be collected from any particular provisions in the Constitution.").

15 *See, Luther v. Borden*; *M'Culloch v. Maryland* 17 US (4 Wheat) 316 (1819), p. 325 (where the court held that Congress, rather than the courts, determines the boundaries of the Necessary and Proper Clause to the Constitution); *Pacific States Telephone*, 223 US 118 (1912), at pp. 141-142; *Rhode Island v. Massachusetts* 37 US (12 Pet) 657 (1838) (Taney J., dissenting) (holding that the powers given to the courts of the United States by the constitution are judicial powers; and extend to those subjects, only, which are judicial in their character; and not to those that are political. And whether the suit is between states or between individuals, the matter sued for must be one that is properly the subject of judicial cognizance and control in order to give jurisdiction to the Court to try and decide the rights of the parties to the suit. Contests for rights of sovereignty and jurisdiction between states over any particular territory, are not the subjects of judicial cognizance and control, to be recovered and enforced in an ordinary suit; and are, therefore, not within the grant of judicial power contained in the constitution); *Colegrave v. Green* 328 US 549 (1946); *Gray v. Sanders* 372 US 368 (1963); *Reynolds v. Sims* 377 US 533 (1964) (holding that some questions raised under the Guaranty Clause are non-justiciable); *Wesberry v. Sanders* 376 US 1 (1964); *Avery v. Midland Country* 390 US 474 (1968); *Wells v. Rockefeller* 394 US 542 (1969) and *New York v. United States* 505 US 144 (1992) 185 (holding that not all claims under the Guaranty Clause present non-justiciable political questions).

16 United States Constitution Art. IV, Section 4.

17 *Luther v. Borden*, at pp. 3, 35 and 48.

18 United States Constitution Art. IV, Section 4.

19 Following *Marbury v. Madison*, Chief Justice Taney was the first to explicate the political question doctrine. *See, Rhode Island v. Massachusetts*, at p. 752 (where in a dissenting opinion Chief Justice Taney explicated the political question doctrine. The court first accepted jurisdiction of a suit by one state against another involving a disputed boundary line. Taney dissented on the ground that Rhode Island was attempting to secure a ruling on what was a political rather than a properly judicial question. He felt that the court would have had jurisdiction rights of property, rather than rights of sovereignty, been involved, but they were not).

> government is established in the State before it can determine whether it is republican or not. And when the senators and representatives of a State are admitted into the councils of the Union, the authority of the government under which they are appointed, as well as its republican character, is recognized by the proper constitutional authority. And its decision is binding on every other department of the government, and could not be questioned in a judicial tribunal.[20]

Essentially, despite that the language in the Guaranty Clause textually assigns the guarantee of a republican government to the whole United States instead of a particular branch of government, the court adopted an interpretation that the clause assigns to the Congress the authority to determine the validity of the charter government. The US Supreme Court reasoned that given that the Guaranty Clause had assigned to Congress the determination of which government was the lawful state government, it declined to adjudicate the matter.

One of the significance of *Luther v. Borden* is that it was the first case that applied and began to define the classical political question theory by establishing the principle that matters assigned to the discretion of Congress could also present political questions. This was a significant pronouncement because *Marbury v. Madison*, before that, had only established the principle that discretion constitutionally vested in the executive would present political questions. While *Luther v. Borden* was decided on the basis of classical political question theory, the US Supreme Court observed some prudential considerations that weighed against the court's exercise of judicial review, such as the chaos that would have erupted if the state government was invalidated.[21]

Scholars have repeatedly cited *Luther v. Borden* as another authority for the classical political question, and as a decision that has conventionally provided the classical expression of the distinction between non-justiciable political questions and justiciable ones.[22] As elaborated in the discussion of the cases below, other commentators have observed that since *Luther v. Borden*, the US Supreme Court began to inter-mingle classical and prudential considerations in the application of the political question doctrine.[23]

---

20 *Luther v. Borden*, at p. 42. *See also*, T. Grove, 'The Lost History of the Political Question Doctrine', *New York Law Review*, Vol. 90, 2015, p. 1908 (arguing that *Luther v. Borden* was not a political question case).

21 *Luther v. Borden*, at pp. 39-40. *See also*, Szurkowski, 2014, pp. 353-354 (describing *Luther v. Borden* as the case where the court began to consider prudence and noting that even as prudence began to be considered the court hesitated to base its political question discussion on prudence alone).

22 J. Pettinato, 'Executing the Political Question Doctrine', *Northern Kentucky Law Review*, Vol. 33, 2006, p. 71 and Szurkowski, 2014, p. 353, fn. 58 (emphasizing that *Luther v. Borden* was decided based on classical considerations).

23 Szurkowski, 2014, pp. 353-354 (discussing the court's application of prudential considerations); Shemtob, 2016, p. 1001; M. Finkelstein, 'Judicial Self-Limitation', *Harvard Law Review*, Vol. 37, No. 3, 1924, pp. 344-345 (discussing the courts' application of prudential considerations and advocating for the use of the political question doctrine in those matters of which the court, at a given time, will be of the opinion that

In *Pacific States Telephone*,[24] the US Supreme Court was presented with another challenge arising from the Guaranty Clause. The following context is what gave rise to this case. During the late 19th century, state legislatures were perceived as corrupt and indebted to railroad companies and large corporations.[25] To curb this problem, a number of states adopted measures imposing direct democracy in which laws could be enacted directly by the people.[26] Oregon was one of the states at the forefront of this direct democracy movement. In 1902, the State of Oregon amended its constitution and adopted the initiative and referendum. This amendment, while retaining an existing clause vesting the exclusive legislative power in a General Assembly consisting of a Senate and House of Representatives, added the following provision:

> But the people reserve to themselves power to propose laws and amendments to the constitution and to enact or reject the same at the polls, independent of the legislative assembly, and also reserve power at their own option to approve or reject at the polls any act of the legislative assembly.

As Williams has correctly noted, the effect of this amendment is that it empowered citizens to petition to have statutory or constitutional measures put on the ballot for adoption and approval directly by the people.[27]

Pursuant to this constitutional amendment and legislative measures to give effect to this amendment,[28] the people of the State of Oregon initiated a law that was voted on and promulgated by the Governor in 1906.[29] The new law approved a two-percent tax on the gross receipts of telephone and telegraph companies as a license fee for doing business

it is impolitic or inexpedient to take jurisdiction) and M.F. Weston, 'Political Questions', *Harvard Law Review*, Vol. 38, No. 3, 1925, pp. 298-299, 331 (advocating the use of the political question doctrine in the Lochner era social legislation).

24 *Pacific States Telephone & Telegraph v. Oregon. See also*, N.R. Williams, 'Direct Democracy, the Guaranty Clause, and the Politics of the 'Political Question' Doctrine: Revisiting *Pacific Telephone*', *Oregon Law Review*, Vol. 87, 2008, p. 979 (noting that the same day as it handed down its decision in *Pacific States Telephone & Telegraph v. Oregon*, the Court also issued its decision in *Kiernan v. City of Portland* 223 US 151 (1912) that involved a Guaranty Clause challenge to direct democracy at the local level, the Supreme Court unthinkingly dismissed the Guaranty Clause challenge as non-justiciable on the basis of *Pacific States Telephone & Telegraph v. Oregon*).

25 C. Hoesly, 'Reforming Direct Democracy: Lessons from Oregon', *California Law Review*, Vol. 93, 2005, p. 1191; Williams, 2008, pp. 979-1004.

26 Hoesly, 2005, p. 1191; Williams, 2008, pp. 979-1004. *See also*, D. Schuman, 'The Origin of State Constitutional Direct Democracy: William Simon U'Ren and the Oregon System', *Temple Law Review*, Vol. 67, 1994, p. 948 and H. Linde, 'Who Is Responsible for Republic Government', *University of Colorado Law Review*, Vol. 65, No. 4, 1994, p. 713.

27 Williams, 2008, p. 979. *See also, Kadderly v. City of Portland*, 74, p. 710 (Or. 1903)(where Supreme Court of Oregon held that direct law making by the voters was consistent with a republican form of government).

28 *See*, 24 February 1903, General Laws 1903.

29 25 June 1906, General Laws 1907.

within the State of Oregon.[30] Pacific States Telephone, an Oregon corporation, refused to pay the newly initiated tax, and the State Oregon sued to collect the unpaid taxes. Pacific States Telephone defended the suit on, among other grounds, the basis that the tax was unconstitutional because the process that gave rise to it violated the Guaranty Clause of the US Constitution.[31]

The Oregon Supreme Court summarily rejected Pacific States Telephone's constitutional claim.[32] In *Pacific States Telephone*, the US Supreme Court dismissed the case for lack of jurisdiction, holding that a constitutional challenge to the initiative and referendum power under the Guaranty Clause presented a non-justiciable political question. Justice White, who wrote for the unanimous court, began his analysis with a statement that almost entirely suggested the outcome of the case. He said that:

> We premise by saying that, while the controversy which this record presents is of much importance, it is not novel. It is important, since it calls upon us to decide whether it is the duty of the courts or the province of Congress to determine when a State has ceased to be republican in form and to enforce the guarantee of the Constitution on that subject. It is not novel, as that question has long since been determined by this court conformably to the practise of the Government from the beginning to be political in character, and therefore, not cognizable by the judicial power, but solely committed by the Constitution to the judgment of Congress.[33]

Following this statement of law, Justice White, after citing *Luther v. Borden* as authority, explicated why the issues, as phrased by the Pacific States Telephone, were not justiciable. He noted that Pacific States Telephone did not argue that it could not be required to pay the impugned license tax or that it was denied an opportunity to be heard as to the amount for which it was taxed, or that there was anything inherent in the tax or involved intrinsically in the law that violated any of its constitutional rights.[34] Justice White emphasized that "if such questions had been raised, they would have been justiciable, and therefore would have required the calling into operation of judicial power."[35]

On the other hand, Justice White noted, the challenge on the impugned statute was of a different kind. In White's characterization:

30 *Pacific States Telephone & Telegraph v. Oregon*, at pp. 135-136.
31 *Id.*, at p. 138.
32 *Kadderly v. City of Portland.*
33 *Pacific States Telephone & Telegraph v. Oregon*, at p. 133.
34 *Id.*, at p. 150.
35 *Id.*

> its essentially political nature is at once made manifest by understanding that the assault which the contention here advanced makes it not on the tax as a tax, but on the State as a State. It is addressed to the framework and political character of the government by which the statute levying the tax was passed. It is the government, the political entity, which (reducing the case to its essence) is called to the bar of this court not for the purpose of testing judicially some exercise of power assailed on the ground that its exertion has injuriously affected the rights of an individual because of repugnancy to some constitutional limitation, but to demand of the State that it establish its right to exist as a State, republican in form.[36]

Furthermore, in the course of his reasoning, Justice White noted a few prudential considerations that would have been brought to bear if the case was sustained. He observed that:

> the propositions each and all proceed alone upon the theory that the adoption of the initiative and referendum destroyed all government republican in form in Oregon. This being so, the contention, if held to be sound, would necessarily affect the validity not only of the particular statute which is before us, but of every other statute passed in Oregon since the adoption of the initiative and referendum. And indeed the propositions go further than this, since, in their essence, they assert that there is no governmental function, legislative or judicial, in Oregon, because it cannot be assumed, if the proposition be well founded, that there is at one and the same time one and the same government which is republican in form and not of that character.[37]

Based on the above reasoning, Justice White held that the case presented by the plaintiff was not within the US Supreme Court's jurisdiction and therefore dismissed the writ of error for want of jurisdiction. The interpretation of the Guaranty Clause in both *Luther v. Borden* and *Pacific States Telephone* has been criticized by academics for, among other reasons, imposing an absolute political question bar in all Guaranty Clause cases.[38]

36 *Id.*, at pp. 150-151.

37 *Id.*, at p. 141.

38 *See*, R. Pushaw, 'Bush v. Gore: Looking at Baker v. Carr in a Conservative Mirror', *Constitutional Commentary,* Vol. 18, No. 2, 2001, p. 362 (arguing that the court imposed such an absolute political question bar in *Pacific States Telephone & Telegraph v. Oregon,* which dismissed a corporation's claim that a state law passed by initiative rather than statute rendered its government non-republican); R. Pushaw, 'The Presidential Election Dispute, the Political Question Doctrine, and the Fourteenth Amendment: A Reply to Professors Krent and Shane', *Florida State University Law Review,* Vol. 29, No. 2, 2001, p. 603 (arguing that most guarantee clause cases were dismissed as non-justiciable and noting that although *Luther v. Borden* did not hold that all claims under the Guaranty Clause raised political questions, the Court created such an absolute prohibition in 1912); *Highland Farms Dairy v. Agnew*, 300 US 608, at pp. 609-612 (1937) (involving a state

Another criticism has come from Professor Williams, who has criticized the premise on which *Luther v. Borden,* and subsequently *Pacific States Telephone,* was decided; that the Guaranty Clause commits its enforcement to Congress and the President, not to the courts. Williams has remarked that there is no support for the view that the Constitution entrusts the enforcement of the Guaranty Clause exclusively to the political branches.[39] He correctly points out that the text of the Guaranty Clause, which should be the foundation of any textually demonstrable commitment of the issue, does not expressly (or exclusively) mandate the resolution of Guaranty Clause issues to the political branches.[40] Relying on the language of the text, he further argues that the Guaranty Clause refers to the United States, not Congress or the President, as the guarantor of republican government, and there is nothing in the term United States that necessarily excludes the federal judiciary.[41]

legislative delegation to an agency of the power to set milk prices); Ohio ex rei. *Bryant v. Akron Metro Park Dist* 281 US 74 (1930), at p. 79 (dealing with a rule requiring that state statutes could not be invalidated absent the agreement of all but one state court justice); *Mountain Timber Company v. Washington* 243 US 219 (1916), at pp. 234-235 (concerning a worker's compensation law); *Ohio ex rel Davis v. Hildebrant* 241 US 565 (1916) (rejecting to determine the political question of whether the invalidation of a state reapportionment statute by referendum violated the guarantee clause); *O'Neill v. Leamer* 239 US 244 (1915), at pp. 244-248 (involving a statutory delegation to the courts of the power to establish drainage districts) and *Marshall v. Dye* 231 US 250 (1913), at pp. 256-257 (pertaining to Indiana's constitutional amendment procedure).

39 Williams, 2008, at p. 1003; E. Chemerinsky, 'Cases Under the Guaranty Clause Should Be Justiciable', *University of Colorado Law Review,* Vol. 65, No. 4, 1994, pp. 872-879 (pointing many obvious flaws with the argument that an entire government would need to be declared unconstitutional); A. Savitzky, 'The Law of Democracy and the Two *Luther v. Borden's*: A Counter History', *New York University Law Review,* Vol. 86, 2011, p. 2045 (noting that the court in *Pacific States Telephone & Telegraph v. Oregon* projected *Luther v. Borden's* sovereignty crisis onto a straight question of constitutional interpretation); R. Hasen, Leaving the Empty Vessel of 'Republicanism' Unfilled: An Argument for the Continued Non-Justiciability of Guaranty Clause Cases *in* B. Cain & N. Mourtada-Sabbah (Eds.), *The Political Question Doctrine and the Supreme Court of the United States,* Lexington Books, Lanham, 2007, pp. 75-79 (accepting that the argument in *Pacific States Telephone & Telegraph v. Oregon* was weak) and C. Engberg, 'Note, Taking the Initiative: May Congress Reform State Initiative Lawmaking to Guarantee a Republican Form of Government?', *Stanford Law Review,* Vol. 54, No. 3, 2001, p. 579 (criticizing *Pacific States Telephone & Telegraph v. Oregon* use of the political question doctrine for challenges to actions of state governments). *See also,* A. Bonfield, 'The Guarantee Clause of Article IV, Section 4: A Study in Constitutional Desuetude', *Minnesotta Law Review,* Vol. 64, No. 3, 1962, p. 513 and T. Smith, 'The Rule of Law and the States: A New Interpretation of the Guaranty Clause', *Yale Law Journal,* Vol. 93, No. 3, 1984, p. 561 (arguing that relegating the enforcement of the guarantee clause exclusively to Congress is problematic. He offers a new theory of the guaranty clause. By interpreting the clause to guarantee the rule of law in the states through requiring that states observe their own constitutions and laws, and noting that the guaranty clause is a justiciable source of constitutional standards, and that those standards proceed from the fundamental and statutory law of the states themselves). *But see,* A. Bickel & B. Schmidt, *History of the Supreme Court of the United States: The Judiciary and Responsible Government, 1910-21,* Cambridge University Press, Cambridge, 1984, p. 311 (praising the decision in *Pacific States Telephone & Telegraph v. Oregon* as an exercise of self-restraint by the US Supreme Court).

40 Bickel & Schmidt, 1984, p. 311, citing W. Wiecek, *The Guarantee Clause of the United States Constitution,* Cornell University Press, Ithaca, 1972, p. 264 (arguing further that Congress is in an exceptionally poor position to guarantee republican government in the states).

41 Bickel & Schmidt, 1984, p. 311.

2.3 Early Application of the Prudential Political Question Doctrine

Following the judgement in *Pacific States Telephone*, the US Supreme Court decided two other important Guaranty Clause cases where prudential considerations featured prominently. In *Colegrave v. Green*,[42] three persons who were qualified to vote in congressional districts of the State of Illinois, which had much larger populations than other congressional districts of that State, brought a lawsuit in a federal district court in Illinois to restrain officers of the State from arranging for an election, in which members of Congress were to be appointed. The lawsuit alleged that the congressional districts created by Illinois legislation lacked compactness of territory and approximate equality of population, and sought a declaration of invalidity under the US Constitution and other laws. The district court dismissed the lawsuit. Justice Frankfurter, who wrote the main judgement of the US Supreme Court, reasoned that:

> To sustain this action would cut very deep into the very being of Congress. Courts ought not to enter this political thicket. The remedy for unfairness in districting is to secure State legislatures that will apportion properly, or to invoke the ample powers of Congress. The Constitution has many commands that are not enforceable by courts, because they clearly fall outside the conditions and purposes that circumscribe judicial action ... Violation of the great guaranty of a republican form of government in States cannot be challenged in the courts.[43]

With this reasoning, Justice Frankfurter dismissed the challenge on political question grounds. Justice Rutledge concurred in the main judgement and found the case to be justiciable, but concluded that the district court had equitable discretion to decline to exercise jurisdiction in light of the delicate relationship between Congress and the states in determining congressional districts.[44] As Pushaw has noted, many cases followed *Colegrove v. Green* in repelling constitutional attacks on state electoral laws, usually based on Frankfurter's reasoning.[45] The next important case affected by the Guaranty Clause is *Baker v. Carr*.

---

42 *Colegrave v. Green* 328 US 549 (1946).

43 *Id.*, p. 556.

44 *Id.*, at pp. 564-566.

45 Pushaw, 2001, p. 363. *See, e.g., Kidd v. McCanless* 352 US 920 (1956) (per curiam); *see also Matthews v. Handley* 361 US 127 (1959) (per curiam); *Radford v. Gary* 352 US 991 (1957) (per curiam); *Anderson v. Jordan* 343 US 912 (1952) (per curiam); *Remmey v. Smith* 342 US 916 (1952) (per curiam); *Tedesco v. Board of Supervisors*, 339 US 940 (1950) (per curiam); *Colegrove v. Barrett* 330 US 804 (1947) (per curiam); *Turman v. Duckworth* 329 US 675 (1946) (per curiam) and *MacDougall v. Green* 335 US 281, 284 (1948) (per curiam).

In *Baker v. Carr*, the US Supreme Court was presented with the task to determine whether an equal protection challenge to the State of Tennessee's malapportionment of the state legislature is a non-justiciable political question. In his majority opinion, Justice Brennan, undermined a century-old line of precedent including *Colegrove v. Green* and held that the question of state legislative reapportionment was justiciable, but did so under the Equal Protection Clause even though the case presented issues which fell squarely under the Guaranty Clause.[46] As one commentator has correctly pointed out "not only did *Baker* upend *Colegrove's* conclusions, but it also dramatically revised *Colegrove's* reasoning."[47] The case of *Baker v. Carr*[48] is perhaps the most famous articulation of the criteria for determining what constitutes a non-justiciable political question. Justice Brennan persuaded a majority of the justices to set out what is often described as the modern articulation of the political question doctrine.[49]

In his analysis, Justice Brennan transformed the political question doctrine by basing it entirely on separation of powers grounds and not on federalism grounds as previous cases had done and by urging a case-by-case analysis to determine its application.[50] In explaining the contours of the doctrine, Justice Brennan proclaimed that in the Guaranty Clause cases and in the other political question cases, it is the relationship between the judiciary and the coordinate branches of the federal government and not the federal judiciary's relationship to the States, which gives rise to the political question.[51] In this case, Brennan found that the question was "the consistency of state action with the Federal Constitution. We have no question decided, or to be decided, by a political branch of government coequal with this Court" to warrant the application of the doctrine.[52] Brennan, then announced six criteria for assessing whether a case may be dismissed under the political question doctrine.[53] These criteria are:

1. textually demonstrable constitutional commitment of the issue to a coordinate political department;
2. a lack of judicially discoverable and manageable standard for resolving it;
3. the impossibility of deciding without an initial policy determination of a kind clearly for non-judicial discretion;

46 Smithm, 1984, p. 563; Pushaw, 2001, p. 362; Pushaw, 2001, p. 606.
47 Shemtob, 2016, p. 1007.
48 *Baker v. Carr.*
49 *Id.*, at pp. 197-198. For authorities describing *Baker v. Carr* as the modern articulation of the political question doctrine, *see*, Shemtob, 2016; Jaffe, 2011, p. 1037; Grove, 2015, p. 1913 (arguing that *Baker v. Carr* articulated a new political question doctrine).
50 *Baker v. Carr*, at pp. 210-211.
51 *Id.*, at p. 210.
52 *Id.*, at p. 226.
53 *Id.*, at p. 217.

4. the impossibility of a court's undertaking independent resolution without expressing lack of the respect due to coordinate branches of government;
5. an unusual need for unquestioning adherence to a political decision already made; or
6. the potentiality of embarrassment from multifarious pronouncements by various departments on one question.[54]

According to Justice Brennan, the existence of one criterion is sufficient to invoke the political question doctrine. It has been strongly observed that the most important considerations were "a textually demonstrable constitutional commitment of the issue to a coordinate political department and a lack of judicially discoverable and manageable standards for resolving it".[55]

Nonetheless, Justice Brennan emphasized the limited reach of the political question doctrine arguing that it must be used sparingly in the context of demonstrable political questions devoted to the elected branches and not simply to political cases.[56] He noted that the "mere fact that the suit seeks protection of a political right does not mean it presents a political question."[57]

Importantly, Justice Brennan explained that the benefit and purpose of the political question doctrine is to preserve the separation of powers principle and minimize claims that have the potential to undermine this principle.[58] His counterpart Justice Douglas, who concurred in the judgement, agreed with Brennan's separation of powers concerns. He put it differently by stating "where the constitution assigns a particular function wholly and indivisibly to another department, the federal judiciary does not intervene."[59]

In the aftermath of *Baker v. Carr*, some members of the US federal bench have gone as far as to suggest that the classical political question doctrine serves to prevent the federal courts from intruding unduly on certain policy choices and judgements that are constitutionally committed to the US Congress or the executive branch.[60] According to this view, a non-justiciable political question exists when, to resolve a dispute, a court must make a

54 *Baker v. Carr. See also*, L. Tribe, *American Constitutional Law*, Foundation Press, New York, 1988, p. 96 (discussing the different strands of the political question doctrine announced in *Baker v. Carr*).

55 *Vieth v. Jubelirer* 541 US 267 (2004), p. 278; Pushaw, 2001, p. 364; and Pushaw, 2001, p. 607.

56 *Baker v. Carr*, at p. 217.

57 *Id.*, at p. 209. *See also, Zivotofsky v. Clinton* (noting that courts cannot avoid their responsibility merely because the issue have political implications)(Roberts J), citing *INS v. Chadha* 462 US 919 (1983), at p. 943; and Justice Sotomayor (noting that a court may not refuse to adjudicate a dispute merely because a decision may have significant political overtones) and E. Gil, 'Judicial Answer to Political Question: The Political Question in the United States and Israel', *Boston University Public Interest Law Journal*, Vol. 23, No. 2, 2014, p. 253 (noting that where there is no legal question, there should be no judicial review).

58 *Baker v. Carr*, at p. 209. *See also, Lane v. Halliburton* 529 F 3d 548 (2008).

59 *Baker v. Carr*, at p. 246.

60 *Koohi v. United States* 976 F 2d 1328 (9th Cir 1992).

policy judgement of a legislative or executive nature, rather than resolve the dispute through the application of the law.[61]

A further benefit of the political question doctrine for Brennan is that it minimizes unwarranted judicial intrusion into the operations of the other branches of government and allocates decisions making to the branches of government that have superior expertise in particular areas. Professor Scharpf is an advocate of this view and has argued, for example, that the US Supreme Court has rightly treated many constitutional issues concerning foreign policy as political questions because of the greater information and expertise of the other branches of government.[62]

Nearly four decades ago, Professors Bickel and Scharpf offered one of the most compelling academic defences of the political question doctrine. In their commentaries, Bickel and Scharpf treat the political question doctrine as one of the devices that the judiciary utilize to define their relationship with other branches and acknowledge that courts share responsibility for interpreting constitutional provisions with those branches of government.[63] According to Bickel and Scharpf, entangling the judiciary with the other institutions of the political system in ways that would not benefit the nation is imprudent.[64] For Bickel and Scharpf, the doctrine provides the judiciary with techniques for refraining from deciding cases on the merits when doing so would be unwise.[65] Since *Baker v. Carr* was decided, the US Supreme Court has dismissed a number of cases on the basis of the doctrine. In the discussion that follows, a few of these cases are discussed to demonstrate how the test in *Baker v. Carr* was employed subsequent to being developed.

2.4 Supreme Court Jurisprudence Post Baker v. Carr

2.4.1 *Powell v. McCormack*

One of the first cases that applied the political question doctrine is *Powell v. McCormack*.[66] In this case, Adam Powell was denied by the House of Representatives to take up his seat in the House because he was under investigation for unethical and possibly illegal financial dealings.[67] Powell challenged this refusal on the basis that he had been duly elected by the voters of the 18th Congressional District of New York to the 90th US Congress.[68] It is

61 *EEOC v. Peabody W Coal Co* 400 F 3d 774 (9th Cir 2005).
62 Scharpf, 1966, pp. 567, 583-584.
63 Bickel, 1962, pp. 183-197; Scharpf, 1966, p. 538.
64 *Id.*
65 Tushnet, 2002, pp. 1203-1204.
66 *Powell v. McCormack* 395 US 486 (1969).
67 *Id.*, at pp. 489-490.
68 *Id.*, at pp. 489-495.

important to mention that during the 89th Congress, the House Committee on Education and Labor was investigated for its expenditures during Powell's chairmanship.[69] The report surrounding the investigation concluded that Powell had engaged in improper expenditures, including deceiving House of Representatives authorities about travel expenses and certain illegal salary payments to Powell's wife at his discretion.[70] However, no formal disciplinary action was taken against Powell and he was subsequently elected to the 90th Congress.[71] Powell claimed that the House of Representatives could not deny him the right to seat because he met the constitutional qualifications for public office contained in Article 1, Section 2 of the US Constitution.[72]

During trial, the House of Representatives argued that Powell's claim presented a political question because "there has been a textually demonstrable constitutional commitment to the House of the adjudicatory power to determine Powell's qualifications."[73] On the contrary, Powell advanced the argument that

> the qualifications expressly set forth in the Constitution were not meant to limit the long-recognized legislative power to exclude or expel at will, but merely to establish standing incapacities, which could be altered only by a constitutional amendment.[74]

In his view, the House of Representatives simply decides whether a duly elected member satisfied the qualifications but as to what these qualifications consisted of is not at the discretion of the House of Representatives.[75] In conceding to Powell's proposition, the US Supreme Court held that the issue before it was not a non-justiciable political question.[76] It rejected the arguments of the House of Representatives that the Constitution vested Congress with the exclusive power to judge the qualifications of its own members.[77] The US Supreme Court found that the political question was not applicable in the case, and that although the House of Representatives possessed constitutional authority to determine

69 *Id.*, at pp. 489-490.

70 *Id.*, at pp. 489-490.

71 *Id.*, at pp. 489-490.

72 Art. 1, Section 2 of the United States Constitution provides "no person shall be a representative who shall not have attained to the Age of twenty five Years, and been seven Years a Citizen of the United States, and who shall not, when elected, be an Inhabitant of that State in which he shall be chosen."

73 *Powell v. McCormack*, at p. 519, quoting *Baker v. Carr*, p. 217; United States Constitution Art. I, Sect. 5, Clause 1.

74 *Powell v. McCormack*, at p. 522.

75 *Nixon v. United States* 506 US 224 (1993), p. 237 (distinguishing *Powell v. McCormack* from the issue in *Nixon v. United States*).

76 *Powell v. McCormack*, at p. 550.

77 United States Constitution Art. I, Sect. 5.

whether a member met the minimum qualifications provided in the Constitution, it had no discretion to establish additional qualifications.[78]

2.4.2 *Gilligan v. Morgan*[79]

Gilligan v. Morgan is another important political question doctrine case. It arose from events on the campus of Kent State University, in which the Ohio National Guard was called in by the Governor of the State of Ohio to impose public order. The National Guard fired live bullets into an unarmed crowd, killing four students and injuring others.[80] The plaintiffs filed suit challenging the actions of the Governor by calling in the National Guard. They challenged the use of arms and sought, among other things, the US Supreme Court to develop standards for the training, kind of weapons and scope and kind of orders to control the actions of the National Guard and assume and exercise a continuing judicial surveillance over the National Guard to assure compliance with whatever training and operations procedures approved by the court.[81]

The US Supreme Court rejected the relief sought by the plaintiffs. It ruled that because the issue involved military training and procedures, it was textually committed to the political branches and therefore did not warrant judicial review.[82] Relying on the first two factors in *Baker v. Carr*, the court held that the case involved non-justiciable political questions. It reasoned that:

> It would be difficult to think of a clearer example of the type of governmental action that was intended by the Constitution to be left to the political branches directly responsible – the Judicial Branch is not – to the electoral process. Moreover, it is difficult to conceive of an area of governmental activity in which the courts have less competence. The complex, subtle, and professional decisions regarding the composition, training, equipping, and control of a military force are essentially professional military judgments, always subject to civilian control

78 *Powell v. McCormack*, at p. 550. *See also*, T. Sandalow, 'Comment on Powell v. McCormack', *UCLA Law Review*, Vol. 17, 1969, p. 164 (critically discussing the court decision in *Powell v. McCormack*) and D. Ellis, 'Powell v. McCormack and the Power to Expel: Some Unanswered Questions Regarding the Framers' Intent', *Georgia Law Review*, Vol. 5, No. 2, 1971, p. 203.

79 *Gilligan v. Morgan* 413 US 1 (1973).

80 *Id.*, at p. 3.

81 *Id.*, at p. 6. For an example of judicial supervision over a defendant, *see*, *Black Sash Trust v. Minister of Social Development and Others* [2017] ZACC 8; 2017 (5) BCLR 543 (CC); 2017 (3) SA 335 (CC)(where the Constitutional Court granted a supervisory order to the South African Social Security Agency (SASSA) and Cash Paymaster Services (Pty) Limited involving the administration of a contract between the two parties in which Cash Paymaster Services (Pty) Limited was expected to, among other things, submit to the Court audited statement of the expenses incurred, the income received and the net profit earned under the contract.)

82 *Gilligan v. Morgan*, at p. 10.

> of the Legislative and Executive Branch. The ultimate responsibility for these decisions is appropriately vested in branches of the government that are periodically subject to electoral accountability. It is this power of oversight and control of military force by elected representatives and officials that underlies our entire constitutional system.[83]

Despite this reasoning, the US Supreme Court explicated that its decision did not mean that the

> the conduct of the National Guard is always beyond judicial review or that there may not be accountability in a judicial forum for violations of law or for specific unlawful conduct by military personnel.[84]

Instead, the US Supreme Court held only that no such questions were presented in this case to warrant judicial review.

2.4.3 *Nixon v. United States*[85]

In *Nixon v. United States*, the US Supreme Court found a non-justiciable political question. The case centred around a federal district court judge, Walter Nixon, who was impeached by the US House of Representatives when he failed to resign after being convicted of perjury and therefore continued to collect his salary.[86] The Senate successfully instituted impeachment proceedings against him.[87] The judge was eventually convicted and removed by the full Senate.[88]

After his Senate conviction, Nixon brought a suit arguing that Senate Rule XI violated the constitutional grant of authority to the Senate to try all impeachments pursuant to Article I, Section 3, Clause 6, of the US Constitution. He argued that the impeachment proceedings in place under Senate rules, which had been adopted by the Senate to try impeachments before a committee and to forward the transcript of the proceedings to the whole Senate for a vote, fell short of the constitutional requirement that he be granted a

83 *Id.*
84 *Id.*
85 *Nixon v. United States* 506 US 224 (1993). *See also*, J. Blum, 'How Much Process Is Due: The Senate Impeachment Trial Process After *Nixon v. United States*', *Catholic University Law Review*, Vol. 44, No. 1, 1994-1995, p. 243 (arguing that the trial-by-committee process challenged in *Nixon v. United States* not only satisfies the Constitution's due process requirement, but, in light of severe time constraints on today's Senate, is necessary as the most efficacious process available).
86 *Nixon v. United States*, at p. 226.
87 *Id.*, at p. 228.
88 *Id.*

trial.[89] Essentially, Nixon maintained that the Senate was constitutionally obligated to give him a trial before the full Senate and not just a Senate committee.

The US Supreme Court found that Nixon's claim was a non-justiciable political question. It held that if the judiciary

> may review the actions of the Senate in order to determine whether that body tried an impeached official, it is difficult to see how the Senate would be functioning independently and without … interference.[90]

In applying the test formulated in *Baker v. Carr*, the US Supreme Court reasoned that the constitutional text provided no standards that the judiciary could detect the limits of the word try, and as a result, the proceedings of the Senate were beyond judicial review.[91]

2.5 Criticism of the Six-Factor Test in Baker v. Carr

The political question doctrine as formulated in *Baker v. Carr* has been welcomed by some and criticized by other scholars and jurists.[92] The major criticism is that despite the six factors that form part of the inquiry, the doctrine remains poorly defined.[93] In her commentary, Breedon has critically observed that while *Baker v. Carr* developed a six-factor test for governing the existence of a political question, no lucid framework for employing the test has emerged, nor has the US Supreme Court explicated the terms that comprise the six factors.[94] Breedon has identified the effect of the failure by the judiciary to articulate the doctrine's contours and comprehensive framework arguing that some of the factors in *Baker v. Carr* significantly overlap with other justiciability doctrines like standing, which permit courts to dismiss cases when certain circumstances are met.[95] She urges that in the

---

89 *Id.*, at p. 238.

90 *Id.*, at p. 231.

91 *Id.*, at pp. 233-238. *But see, Impeachment case*, at para. 196 (ordering the National Assembly in South Africa to establish a permanent committee, prescribe its rules including its composition).

92 For some critical comments against *Baker v. Carr, see*, R. Layman, 'Aftermath of *Baker v. Carr*', *William & Mary Law Review*, Vol. 4, No. 2, 1963, p. 93 and P. Neal, 'Baker v. Carr: Politics in Search of Law', *Supreme Court Review*, 1962, p. 252.

93 *See, Zivotofsky v. Clinton* (noting that as this case illustrates, the proper application of *Baker v. Carr* six factors has generated substantial confusion in the lower courts) (Sotomayor, concurring), at p. 1431; *Tel-Oren v. Libyan Arab Republic* 726 F 2d 774, 803 n. 8 (DC Cir1984) (Bork J., concurring); *U.S. ex rel. Joseph v. Cannon* 642 F 2d 1373, 1379 (1981) (noting that the political question doctrine's precise contours are ambiguous); *District of Columbia v. United States Dep't of Commerce* 789 F Supp 1179, 1184 (DD Cir 1992) (demonstrating that the scope and rationale of the doctrine remain unclear) and C. Nelson, 'Originalism and Interpretive Conventions', *University of Chicago Law Review*, Vol. 70, No. 2, 2003, p. 598.

94 *See*, Mulhem, 1988, pp. 106-108.

95 Breedon, 2008, p. 524.

absence of a lucid doctrine from the judiciary delineating the precise limits of the political question doctrine, in relation to other doctrines with overlapping interests, lower courts may be more likely to misapply the doctrine.[96]

In his study of the transformation of the political question doctrine, Professor Tushnet has also highlighted the problematic overlap between the doctrine and other justiciability doctrines like standing.[97] Tushnet goes further to criticize *Baker v. Carr* for its doctrinalization of the doctrine and its impossible attempt to convert into a set of legal rules an approach to adjudication that had been predicated on some judicial flexibility.[98] In his view, this was a mistake because prudence cannot be captured in rules.[99] For Tushnet, the effects of the doctrinalization of the political question doctrine substantially reduced the possibility of the US Supreme Court's deploying the doctrine.[100] It is because of similar concerns by Breedon and Tushnet that Barkow discouraged courts from the use of the prudential strand of the doctrine because in her view, it seeks to solve the same problem as standing and equitable discretion, but gives courts more flexibility.[101]

As alluded to earlier, the political question doctrine, as formulated by American courts, particularly in cases like *Baker v. Carr*, has had a profound influence in the development of constitutional jurisprudence of many countries, especially the ones being examined in the subsequent chapters. Naturally, there is a need to consider the possible implications that may arise from the fact that a number of countries, particularly Ghana, Nigeria, and Uganda, have considered, applied and developed well-established jurisprudence around the political question doctrine. In some cases, this jurisprudence was heavily influenced by Justice Brennan's pronouncements in *Baker v. Carr*.

In the aftermath of *Zivotofsky v. Clinton*, a key question, especially among jurists from these countries, is whether *Zivotofsky v. Clinton*, to the extent that it partly undermined *Baker v. Carr*, causes a diversion in the manner in which the six factors in that case should be applied? The jury is still out on this question. Still, as Dennison has explained in the context of Uganda's adoption of the doctrine, legal borrowing is more about political choices than importing legal innovations.[102]

It is important to briefly explain the concept of legal borrowing in order to contextualize and appreciate Dennison's point. The concept has been described as the process of importing legal doctrines or rationales from other legal sources or domains in order to

96 *Id. See, Zivotofsky v. Clinton* (where Sotomayor confirms the confusion in lower court over the six factors in *Baker v. Carr*), at p. 1431.

97 Tushnet, 2002, p. 1235. *But see*, Shemtob, 2016, p. 1004 (discussing how the political question doctrine is distinct from other justiciability doctrines).

98 Tushnet, 2002, p. 1213.

99 *Id.*

100 *Id.*, p. 1235.

101 Barkow, 2002, p. 333.

102 Dennison, 2014, p. 280.

persuade someone to adopt a certain reading of a constitution.[103] Among the benefits of legal borrowing, as commentators have noted, is that it helps to restore the generality of law and promote rule of law values.[104] Osiatynski once correctly remarked that legal "borrowing is inevitable because there are a limited number of general constitutional ideas and mechanism."[105]

Likewise, Dennison has drawn attention to the notion of legal borrowing in his discussion of the political question doctrine in Uganda. He has explained that Uganda adopted a framework of separation of powers and judicial review that imitates America's constitutional system. He argues that in the context of this larger picture, Uganda's endorsement of the political question doctrine makes sense adding that "at some point within common law systems the legal heritage of the courts becomes the law of the land [and] origins cease to matter."[106] The suggestion by Dennison is that the political question doctrine has become part of the constitutional law of Uganda, and it is no longer significant to pinpoint where the seeds of the doctrine were borrowed. Hence, Dennison would probably opine that the decision in *Zivotofsky v. Clinton,* to the extent that it undermines aspects of *Baker v. Carr,* will have no significant impact on Uganda's continued application of the doctrine because the doctrine has assumed a life of its own under Ugandan law.

In addition, Dennison would probably point out that since 1966, the political question doctrine has become part of the law of Uganda where courts have developed it consistent with particular circumstances of Uganda, and that it would be too simplistic to expect that *Zivotofsky v. Clinton* would impact these well-established traditions that have developed since the doctrine was adopted in the 1960s. Dennison makes a strong argument in the context of Uganda, which I would submit is applicable to the rest of the countries being examined in this book.

In fact, in *Centre of Health Human Rights v. Attorney-General,*[107] which I discuss in detail in Chapter 4, the plaintiff cited *Zivotofsky v. Clinton* for the proposition that the political question doctrine was disfavoured. This was an attempt by the plaintiffs to persuade the Supreme Court of Uganda to overrule the validity of the political question doctrine in Uganda. Despite this, the Supreme Court in *Centre of Health Human Rights v. Attorney-General* re-affirmed the usefulness and application of the doctrine in Uganda. Notwithstanding my support for Denison's views, it is not clear what the judiciary in Ghana and Nigeria would do if faced with a political question case in the post *Zivotofsky v. Clinton* era. Even with these difficulties of determining whether the political question doctrine

---

103 N. Tebe & R. Tsai, 'Constitutional Borrowing', *Michigan Law Review*, Vol. 108, No. 4, 2009, p. 463.

104 *Id.*, p. 490.

105 W. Osiatynski, 'Paradoxes of Constitutional Borrowing', *International Journal of Constitutional Law*, Vol. 1, No. 2, p. 244.

106 Dennison, 2014, p. 280.

107 *Centre of Health Human Rights v. Attorney-General*, Constitutional Appeal 1 of (2013) 18, at para. 10.

should apply, federal cases in the United States reveal frequent application of the doctrine in federal constitutional adjudication.[108] The next section provides a synopsis of the approach taken by federal courts in applying the doctrine.

2.6 A Survey of Federal Courts' Application of the Political Question Doctrine

One of the areas where the political question doctrine has often featured in lower federal court litigation is foreign affairs. In *Gonzales-Vera v. Kissinger*[109] the plaintiff, a victim and survivor of human rights abuses, carried out by the Chilean government of General Pinochet, brought an action against the United States and former Secretary of State and National Security Advisor, Henry Kissinger, seeking damages for actions, including torture allegedly taken in support of the Pinochet regime. The district court found that the plaintiffs' claims were justiciable but dismissed the action on the grounds that the United States had not waived its sovereign immunity, and that the plaintiffs had failed to state a claim upon which relief can be granted against Dr Kissinger.

The US Court of Appeals, cited as controlling its earlier and related decision in *Schneider v. Kissinger,*[110] affirmed that the plaintiffs' claims were non-justiciable under the political question doctrine. In a judgement written by Judge Ginsburg, the court reasoned that to evaluate the legal validity of the drastic measures taken by the United States to implement its policy with respect to Chile, would require it to delve into questions of foreign policy textually committed to a coordinate branch of government.[111] Ginsburg noted that like the plaintiffs in *Schneider v. Kissinger*, the plaintiffs in this case alleged and challenged drastic measures taken by the United States and Kissinger in order to implement US policy with respect to Chile. The US Supreme Court denied a writ of certiorari in this case.[112]

Another important case that gives us a peak into how federal courts apply the political question doctrine is *Arakaki v. Lingle.*[113] In *Arakaki v. Lingle*, the plaintiffs were citizens

108 *See*, Mulhern, 1988, p. 106 (noting that the political question doctrine is more prominent in the opinions of the lower federal courts); *Doe v. Bush* 322 F 3d 109 (1st Cir 2003) and *Luftig v. McNamara* 373 F 2d 664 (DC Cir 1967). For a discussion of the application of the political question doctrine by state courts, *see*, Grove, 2015, p. 1908.

109 *Gonzales-Vera v. Kissinger* 449 F 3d 1260 (2006).

110 *Schneider v. Kissinger* 412 F 3d 190 (2005) (where the children of a Chilean general and his estate brought suit against the United States and Henry Kissinger for their role in the general's death during the coup of 1970. The district court dismissed the suit for lack of jurisdiction over non-justiciable questions raised by the complaint. The court of appeal affirmed the lower court decision holding that the claims were non-justiciable against the United States and Dr Kissinger for measures allegedly taken in the 1970s to implement the US foreign policy with respect to Chile).

111 *Schneider v. Kissinger*, p. 194.

112 *See, Gonzales-Vera v. Kissinger* 127 SCt 1356 (2007).

113 *Arakaki v. Lingle* 305 F Supp 2d 1161 (2004).

of the State of Hawaii who alleged that various state programs preferentially treat persons of Hawaiian ancestry, in violation of the Fifth and Fourteenth Amendments to the US Constitution and the terms of a public land trust. They brought a lawsuit against the Department of Hawaiian Home Lands (DHHL), the Hawaiian Homes Commission (HHC), the Office of Hawaiian Affairs (OHA), various state officers and the United States. They claimed standing to sue as taxpayers and as beneficiaries of the public land trust.

In a series of orders, the district court held that plaintiffs lacked standing to raise certain claims and that the remaining claim raised a non-justiciable political question. The court dismissed the entire lawsuit. It reasoned that the political question doctrine applied to bar the court's review of the constitutional claim. The district court agreed that the doctrine barred it from reviewing controversies that revolve around policy choices and value determinations constitutionally committed for resolution to Congress or the executive branch. Additionally, the court was persuaded not to exercise jurisdiction in the matter because the political status of Hawaiians was being debated in the US Congress at the time the court was considering the matter, and hence it would be improper for the court to intrude into that political process.

The Court of Appeals affirmed parts of the district court judgement, but reversed the district court's dismissal of the case on political question grounds.[114] The court noted that it had recently addressed the political question doctrine in *Kahawaiolaa v. Norton*[115] in the context of a challenge to the executive's failure to recognize Hawaiians as federal Indian tribes. In *Kahawaiolaa*, native Hawaiians alleged that the Department of Interior had violated the equal protection component of the Fifth Amendment in regulations limiting recognition of new tribes to those American Indian groups indigenous to the continental United States, which meant that native Hawaiians were excluded from eligibility to petition for tribal recognition under the regulations.

The Court of Appeals disagreed with the district court's finding that matters of tribal recognition raise non-justiciable political questions. It found that the plaintiffs did not seek tribal recognition, but rather, they wanted the Department of Interior to allow them to apply for recognition under the same regulatory criteria applied to indigenous peoples in other states. The court concluded that the plaintiffs' suit was not barred by the political question doctrine.

In *Arakaki v. Lingle*, the court found that its reasoning in *Kahawaiolaa* was applicable in the case. It reasoned that a suit that sought to direct Congress to federally recognize an Indian tribe would be non-justiciable as a political question. The court found that no party in this case sought to compel Congress or the President to recognize the tribal status of

114 *Arakaki v. Lingle* 423 F 3d 954 (2005), p. 977.

115 *Kahawaiolaa v. Norton 386 F 3d 1271* (9th Cir 2004), p. 1273, cert. denied by the US Supreme Court 545 US 1114 (2005).

Hawaiians or invited the district court to exercise powers reserved to Congress or to the President. It therefore dismissed the district court's finding and ruling on political question grounds.[116]

In *Corriee v. Caterpillar,*[117] the Court of Appeal dealt with an issue affecting foreign affairs. The case arose out of the conflict in the Middle East. Following the Six Day War in 1967, Israel occupied and took control of the West Bank and Gaza Strip. The defendant, Caterpillar, is the world's leading manufacturer of heavy construction and mining equipment. Among its customers is the Israeli Defence Force, which since 1967 has utilized Caterpillar bulldozers to demolish homes in the Palestinian Territories. According to the plaintiffs' complaint, Caterpillar sold the bulldozers to the Israeli Defence Force, despite its actual and constructive notice that the Israeli Defence Force would use them to further its home destruction policy in the Palestinian Territories; a policy plaintiff contended violated international law. Seventeen members of plaintiffs' families – sixteen Palestinians and one American-were killed or injured in the course of the demolitions.

The family members of individuals, who were killed when the Israeli Defence Force used bulldozers to demolish houses in Palestinian Territories, brought an action against Caterpillar alleging seven claims: (1) war crimes; (2) extrajudicial killing under the Torture

116 *Arakaki v. Lingle*, pp. 973-976.

117 For a discussion of *Corrie v. Caterpillar, see, In re South African Apartheid Litigation* 617 F Supp 2d 228 (2009) 258 (noting that the distinction between this case and the Ninth Circuit's decision in *Corrie v. Caterpillar Inc* is illustrative. In *Corrie v. Caterpillar Inc,* the plaintiffs brought suit against Caterpillar for selling bulldozers to the Israeli Defence Forces under a theory of aiding and abetting extrajudicial killing. The Ninth Circuit dismissed the action under the political question doctrine because the US Government paid for the bulldozers and finding Caterpillar liable for the sales would necessarily require the judicial branch of our government to question the political branches' decision to grant extensive military aid to Israel. In contrast, resolution of this case neither requires this Court to pass judgement on the policy of constructive engagement or the US' relationship with apartheid-era South Africa); *Saldana v. Occidental Petroleum Corporation* 774 F 3d 544 (2014), p. 555 (we remain bound by the Supreme Court's holding in *Oetjen* 302, which we reiterated in *Corrie v. Caterpillar* that the conduct of the foreign relations of our government is committed by the Constitution to the executive and legislative branches and the propriety of what may be done in the exercise of this political power is not subject to judicial inquiry or decision. As the political question doctrine bars us from considering the merits of Plaintiffs' claims, the district court's dismissal of their action is affirmed); *Davoyan v. Republic of Turkey* 116 F Supp 3d 1084 (2013) (invoking the political question doctrine while relying on *Corrie v. Caterpillar*). *See also*, J. Van Detta, 'Some Legal Considerations for EU Based MNES Contemplating High-Risk Foreign Direct Investments in the Energy Sector After Kiobel v. Royal Dutch Petroleum and Chevron Corporation v. Naranjo', *South Carolina Journal of International Law & Business,* Vol. 9, No. 2, 2013, pp. 171-172 (commenting on *Corrie v. Caterpillar* noting that while the courts ultimately dismissed the complaint against Caterpillar, they did not find (1) that corporations were inappropriate ATS defendants, (2) that the FDI of Caterpillar in Israel was outside of the ATS or (3) that the ATS is inapplicable to extraterritorial conduct. Instead, solely because the US government actually paid for Caterpillar's sale of equipment to Israel, the federal court concluded that it could not intrude into our government's decision to grant military assistance to Israel, even indirectly by deciding this challenge to a defence contractor's sales. *Corrie,* therefore, offers little comfort to Alstom.) and G. Sant, 'So Banks Are Terrorists Now? The Misuse of the Civil Suit Provision of the Anti-Terrorism Act', *Arizona State Law Journal,* Vol. 45, No. 2, 2013, p. 592 (discussing *Corrie v. Caterpillar*).

Victim Protection Act 1991; (3) cruel, inhuman or degrading treatment or punishment; (4) violations of the Racketeer Influenced and Corrupt Organizations Act 1961; (5) wrongful death; (6) public nuisance and (7) negligent entrustment. The gravamen of each claim is that Caterpillar provided the Israeli Defence Force with equipment it knew would be used in the violation of international law, and thus aided and abetted those violations. The district court held that both the act of state doctrine and the political question doctrine precluded it from reaching the merits of the claims.

The Court of Appeals affirmed the lower court decision that the political question doctrine barred it from hearing the matter. In justifying its decision, the court reasoned that allowing this action to proceed would necessarily require the judiciary to question the political branch's decision to grant extensive military aid to Israel. According to the court, it is difficult to see how it could impose liability on Caterpillar without, at least implicitly, deciding the propriety of the United States' decision to pay for the bulldozers.

Furthermore, the court reasoned that it cannot intrude into the government's decision to grant military assistance to Israel, even indirectly by deciding this challenge. It observed that the plaintiffs could succeed only if a court ultimately decided that Caterpillar should not have sold its bulldozers to the Israeli Defence Force. Yet, the court noted, these sales were financed by the executive branch pursuant to a congressionally enacted program calling for executive discretion as to what lies in the foreign policy and national security interests of the United States.

The court went to a great length to discuss both classic and prudential considerations in the *Baker v. Carr* and noted that all the six factors in that case were implicated. For instance, in relation to the first factor in *Baker v. Carr*, whether there is a textually demonstrable constitutional commitment of the issue to a coordinate political department, it explained that the conduct of foreign relations is committed by the Constitution to the political departments of the federal government; and that the propriety of the exercise of that power is not open to judicial review. And that whether to grant military or other aid to a foreign nation is a political decision inherently entangled with the conduct of foreign relations,[118] and inappropriate for judicial resolution. Therefore, the Court of Appeals held that the district court did not err in dismissing the suit under the political question doctrine.

Lastly, *Schroeder v. Bush*,[119] centred around farmers who live and work within the territorial boundaries of the Tenth Circuit and who sought declaratory and injunctive relief

118 It further cited with approval the decision in *Dickson v. Ford* 521 F 2d 234 (5th Cir 1975); Dickson challenged the Emergency Security Assistance Act of 1973, which authorized $2.2 billion for military assistance and foreign military sales credit to Israel, and where the Fifth Circuit dismissed the case on political question grounds, noting that both the Congress and the President have determined that military and economic assistance to the State of Israel is necessary. Citing *Baker v. Carr*, the court held that a determination of whether foreign aid to Israel is necessary at this particular time is a question uniquely demanding single-voiced statement of the Government's views and is therefore inappropriate for judicial resolution.

119 *Schroeder v. Bush* 263 F 3d (2001), p. 1169.

against the President of the United States, the United States Secretary of Agriculture, the United States Secretary of the Treasury and the United States of America. The farmers sought an order requiring the defendants and their agents to maintain market conditions favourable to small farmers. The district court dismissed the matter for lack of subject-matter jurisdiction, noting that "the complaint seeks to have this court determine political questions which are properly addressed by the elected branches of the government."[120] The district court held that it had no jurisdiction over the discretionary acts of either defendants, and that plaintiffs' remedies are at the polling place, not the courts.[121]

On appeal, the question for the Court of Appeals was whether a constitutional action brought by farmers and ranchers for declaratory and injunctive relief against the United States, seeking an order requiring the government to maintain market conditions favourable to small farmers, was barred by the political question doctrine. The Court of Appeals agreed with the lower court that the issues presented were non-justiciable political questions, and that the plaintiffs must seek relief from the elected branches of government. The court reasoned that prudence, as well as separation of powers concerns, encourage courts to decline to hear political questions of this nature.[122] In dismissing the appeal, the court noted that the relief sought enmeshes the court in the *Baker v. Carr* threads; that no doubt this case presents textbook examples of political questions and thus was properly dismissed by the district court.

The above survey of the cases demonstrates how federal courts have grappled with and applied the test in *Baker v. Carr*. In the section that follows, I discuss the application of the political question doctrine in state courts of the United States with a view to ascertain commonalities or differences in dealing with political questions by state and federal courts.

2.7 A Survey of the Application of the Political Question Doctrine by Federal States

A fundamental principle of the US government system is that the federal government may act only if there is express or implied power in the US Constitution. On the contrary, the State governments may act unless that Constitution prohibits them from acting.[123] Two constitutional provisions succinctly capture this principle. Article I, Section 1 of the US Constitution, which creates the federal legislative authority provides that "all legislative Powers herein granted shall be vested in a Congress of the United States, which shall consist of a Senate and House of Representatives." The tenth amendment to the US Constitution,

---

120 *Id.*, at p. 1171.
121 For similar views, *see*, Justice Froneman's concurring opinion in *National Treasury*, at paras. 75-96.
122 *Schroeder v. Bush*, at p. 1173.
123 Chemerinsky, 2001, p. 91.

on the other hand, provides that "the powers not delegated to the United States by the Constitution, nor prohibited by it to the States, are reserved to the States respectively, or to the people." The tenth amendment reserves a zone of activity to the States for their exclusive control, and the federal government is prevented from intruding.[124] In a sense, as Chemerinsky has remarked, the tenth amendment provides protection to States' rights and federalism.[125] Since the US Constitution comprises delegated powers from sovereign States, the development of State constitutional traditions has been influenced by this relationship between States and the federal government.[126]

Whereas State courts are guided by their respective State constitutions, laws and traditions when adjudicating cases, commentators have observed that the political question doctrine has not escaped the attention of State courts.[127] The doctrine has been applied against the general document of limit principle that says State constitutions are documents that limit rather than grant powers.[128] Given their distinct political and constitutional traditions, one commentator has crisply noted that State courts have formulated their own political question doctrine.[129]

This section is not intended to delve into a comprehensive examination of the different approaches of the political question doctrine in State courts. Instead, a brief overview of the judicial attitudes towards the doctrine by State supreme courts will suffice, including where applicable their application or rejection of the doctrine by examining the areas where the doctrine has been considered or applied. Similarly, a general examination of whether State courts apply the political question doctrine from time to time is undertaken.

124 *Id.*, p. 114.

125 *Id. See also, Hammer v. Dagenhart* 247 US 251 (1918); *Gibbons v. Ogden* 22 US 1 (1824).

126 D. Rodriguez, 'The Political Question Doctrine in State Constitutional Law', *Rutgers Law Journal*, Vol. 43, No. 4, 2013, p. 576.

127 Rodriguez, 2013, p. 575 and N. Stern, 'The Political Question Doctrine in State Courts', *South Carolina Law Review*, Vol. 35, No. 3, 1983, p. 405. *See also, Colorado Common Cause v. Bledsoe* 810 P 2d 201 (1991) (holding that whether the speech-and-debate clause granted legislators absolute immunity from certain suits was a justiciable question); *Lobato v. State*, 218 P 3d 358 (2009) (Rice, dissenting) (holding that this court should adopt the US Supreme Court's framework in *Baker v. Carr* defining the parameters of the political question doctrine and apply it to this issue); *Connecticut Coalition for Justice in Education Funding Inc v. Rell* 990 A 2d 206 (2010); *Common Cause/Pennsylvania v. Com* 710 A 2d 108 (1998) and *State ex rel Steinke v. Lautenbaugh* 263 Neb 652, 642 NW 2d 132 (2002) (recognizing the federal political question doctrine).

128 *See*, Rodriguez, 2013, p. 576; *Gilbert v. Gladden* 87 NJ 275 (1975). *See also*, Cooley, 1868, p. 87 (arguing that the legislative department is not made a special agency for the exercise of specifically defined legislative powers, but is entrusted with the general authority to make laws at its discretion) and A. Tarr, *Understanding State Constitutions*, Princeton University Press, Princeton, 1998, p. 7 (arguing that state governments have historically been understood to possess plenary legislative powers – that is, those residual legislative powers not ceded to the national government or prohibited to them by the federal Constitution).

129 Stern, 1983, p. 407.

2.7.1 *State Court's Areas of Application*

There is no doubt that the political question doctrine exists in state constitutional law. Three areas have seen frequent application of the doctrine. These include areas involving coordinate branches of government,[130] conduct of and results of elections[131] and policy making.[132] In the discussion that follows, this section reviews the application of the doctrine in these areas.

2.7.1.1 Involving Coordinate Branches of Government

The separation of powers principle, as reflected in State constitutions, has urged State courts to encourage the coordinate branches of government to regulate themselves with minimal interference from the courts.[133] From the practice of State courts in relation to the doctrine, Stern has noted that only when a government action has the potential to violate an express constitutional prohibition is the issue detached from the scope of the political question doctrine.[134] Otherwise, claims against government conduct have been dismissed on political question grounds.

In *Fuldauer v. City of Cleveland*,[135] which involved a challenge to the city of Cleveland's municipal charter for breach of the federal constitutional guarantee of a republican form of government, the Ohio Supreme Court dismissed the challenge on the basis that the adoption of a city government plan raised "a political question, and not a judicial question, and cannot be challenged in the courts".[136]

Stern also observes that the political question doctrine has frequently been applied to cases involving a challenge to legislative decisions that are not impermissible on substantive grounds but are found wanting on procedural grounds. In other words, there is a line of cases where State courts have applied the doctrine to abstain from interfering in areas where the government is substantively permitted to act but the procedures might have not existed to regulate their conduct or been violated altogether.[137]

---

130 For state supreme court case where political question doctrine was applied to challenges to public school finance, *see, Ex parte James* 836 So 2d 813 (Ala 2002); *Marrero v. Commonwealth* 559 Pa 14, 739 A 2d 110 (1999); *Lewis v. Spagnolo* 710 NE 2d 798 (1999); *Committee for Educ Rights v. Edgar* 672 NE 2d 1178 (1996); *Coalition for Adequacy and Fairness in Sch. Funding Inc v. Chiles* 680 So 2d 400 (Fla 1996); *City of Pawtucket v. Sundlun* 662 A 2d 40 (RI1995).

131 *Meyer v. Lamm*, 846 P 2d 862 (Colo 1993), pp. 872-873 (holding that challenge by write-in candidate to voting recount procedures presented a justiciable question).

132 Rodriguez, 2013, p. 576 and Stern, 1983, pp. 408-416.

133 Stern, 1983, p. 412.

134 *Id.*, pp. 408-416.

135 *Fuldauer v. City of Cleveland* 290 NE 2d 546 (1972).

136 *Id.*, pp. 549-550. *See also, Fuldauer v. City of Cleveland* 30 Ohio App 2d 237 (1972).

137 Stern, 1983, p. 414. *See also, Gilbert v. Gladden* 87 NJ 275 (1975); *Leek v. Theis* 217 Kan 784 (1975) and *Maline v. Meekins* 650 P 2d 351 (1982).

One of the cases that demonstrates this trend is *Gilbert.*[138] The case involved an action against the constitutional provision governing the presentment of Bills to the Governor. Article V, Section 1, paragraph 14 of the New Jersey Constitution of 1947 required that "every bill which shall have passed both houses shall be presented to the Governor." If the Governor approves a Bill, the governor signs it and it becomes law. If the Governor disapproves, he or she may return it and the legislature may veto his actions by a two-thirds majority.

Within this framework, there developed an unofficial custom of long duration, known as gubernatorial courtesy, whereby Bills passed in both houses of the Legislature would not be presented to the Governor for signature or veto powers exercised over them until the Governor requests them. Accordingly, when the request for a Bill is withheld and therefore presentation not made until forty-five days before the end of the second legislative session, the Governor can prevent the Bill from becoming law merely by not signing it, and at the same time, the Legislature would have no opportunity to override that result.[139] This scheme is what formed the basis of plaintiffs' lawsuit in *Gilbert.* The plaintiff's main contention was that the practice of gubernatorial courtesy was unconstitutional. The government's response was that the questions presented to the New Jersey Supreme Court concerning the manner and the times by which Bills passed are presented to the Governor are non-justiciable political questions.

The court found that the first criterion in *Baker v. Carr* provided the basis for a conclusion that the case presented a non-justiciable political question.[140] It found that the textually demonstrable constitutional commitment of the question of presentment of Bills to the Governor can be derived from proper consideration of two constitutional provisions, namely Article IV, Section 4, paragraph 3 of the New Jersey Constitution, which gives the legislature authority "to determine the rules of its proceedings".[141] The Supreme Court also found that the Constitution of New Jersey did not limit the time frames within which presentment may be accomplished.

As a consequence, the court concluded that in the absence of constitutional standards, it is not the function of the judiciary to substitute its judgement for that of the legislature with regards to the rules it has adopted or procedures followed in giving effect to the constitutionally declared scheme.[142] The Supreme Court further reasoned that since a State constitution, unlike its federal counterpart, is not a grant but a limitation of legislative power, the legislature is vested with all powers not constitutionally forbidden.[143] It held

138 *Gilbert v. Gladden* 87 NJ 275 (1975).

139 *Gilbert v. Gladden*, at p. 279.

140 *Id.*, at p. 282.

141 *Id.*, at p. 282.

142 *Id.*, at p. 282. Contrast this with the holding in the *Impeachment case*, at para. 196 (ordering the National Assembly to discard its rules of impeachment and adopt court prescribed rules.)

143 *Gilbert v. Gladden*, at pp. 283-283, citing *State v. Muzda* 16 NJL 219 (1935).

that timing of presentment of a Bill is a non-justiciable political question that is committed to the legislature.

As demonstrated in *Gilbert*, State courts apply the criterion in *Baker v. Carr* when invoking the political question doctrine.[144] However, this is not always the case.[145] Some State courts (as opposed to federal courts) in the fifty states have rejected to incorporate the political question doctrine as formulated in *Baker v. Carr* into their jurisprudence. *Backman v. Secretary of the Commonwealth*[146] is a case in point. In this case, the Supreme Judicial Court of Massachusetts had to consider whether to restrain the Governor from putting a proposed constitutional amendment to the people for a vote because of his failure to follow the constitutionally laid out procedures. The plaintiff's basic assertion against the Governor was that the Governor acted contrary to the Massachusetts Constitution in purporting to call a joint session under Article 48 of the Amendments without first calling the General Court into session pursuant to his powers under Part II, Article 5 of the Mas-

144 *See, Nebraska Coalition for Educational Equity and Adequacy (Coalition) v. Heineman* 273 Neb 531 (2007) (holding that although we have implicitly recognized the political question doctrine, we have not previously adopted the US Supreme Court's justiciability tests under that doctrine, which we do now. We begin, however, with an overview of our separation of powers jurisprudence and an explanation of the political question doctrine).

145 For examples of cases where there is resistance in applying the doctrine, *see, Lake View Sch Dist No. 25 v. Huckabee*, 91 SW 3d 472 (2002), at p. 507 (refusing to apply the doctrine to review school funding arguing it would be a complete abrogation of our judicial responsibility); *Idaho Schools for Equal Educ. Opportunity v. Evans*, 123 Idaho 573 (1993), at p. 850 (refusing to allow other branches of government to interpret the constitution for us); *Rose v. Council for Better Educ Inc* 790 SW 2d 186 (Ky. 1989), at pp. 213-214 (held that to avoid deciding the case because of legislative discretion, legislative function, and so on, would be a denigration of our own constitutional duty.); *McDuffy v. Secretary of the Executive Office of Educ* 415 Mass 545, 615 N E 2d 516 (1993), at pp. 554-555 (citing *Marbury v. Madison* for proposition that courts have the duty to adjudicate a claim that a law and the actions undertaken pursuant to that law conflict with or fall short of the requirements of the Constitution.); *Columbia Falls Elem Sch Dist No 6 v. State*, 326 Mont 304, 109 P 3d 257 (2005), at pp. 260-261 (rejecting *Baker v. Carr*-based political question argument); *Abbott v. Burke* 693 A 2d 417 (1997), at pp. 428-429 (holding that, while deference should be given to legislative content and performance standards, it is still the courts' duty to ensure that these standards); *Campaign for Fiscal Equity, Inc. v. State*, 86 NY 2d 307, 631 NYS 2d 565, 655 NE 2d 661, 666-668 (1995); *Leandro v. State* 488 SE 2d 249 (1997), at p. 253 (rejecting political question argument and stating that when a government action is challenged as unconstitutional, the courts have a duty to determine whether that action exceeds constitutional limits); *DeRolph v. State* 78 Ohio St 3d 193, 677 NE 2d 733 (1997), p. 737 (rejecting argument that school finance challenge presents non-justiciable political question); *Abbeville County School District v. State* 335 SC 58, 515 SE 2d 535 (1999), at p. 540 (because it is the duty of this Court to interpret and declare the meaning of the Constitution, the trial court should not have used judicial restraint, separation of powers and the political question doctrine as the bases for declining to decide the meaning of the education clause); *Seattle Sch District No 1 v. State*, 90 Wash 2d 476, 585 P 2d 71, 84-87 (1978) (citing *Marbury v. Madison* and stating that a finding of non-justiciability would be 'illogical') and *Campbell County School District v. State*, 907 P 2d 1238 (Wyo. 1995), p. 1264 (rejecting separation of powers argument and stating that although this court has said the judiciary will not encroach into the legislative field of policy making, as the final authority on constitutional questions the judiciary has the constitutional duty to declare unconstitutional that which transgresses the state constitution).

146 *Backman v. Secretary of the Commonwealth* 387 Mass 549 (1982).

sachusetts Constitution. The argument advanced by government was that the issue presented to the Supreme Judicial Court was a non-justiciable political question.

In responding to this argument, the Supreme Judicial Court noted that the political question doctrine was fully developed under the US Constitution than under the Constitution of Massachusetts. Additionally, it acknowledged that despite being presented with political question doctrine-based arguments in a number of cases,[147] it has never explicitly incorporated the federal doctrine into the state jurisprudence.[148] The Supreme Judicial Court declined again to adopt the federal political question doctrine in this case. In its view, the judiciary has an obligation to adjudicate claims that particular conduct conflict with constitutional requirements.

Turning to the present matter, the Supreme Judicial Court found that there was no explicit or necessarily implicit constitutional provision directing the manner in which the Governor must call the General Court into joint session and that, in the circumstances, where the members of the General Court in joint session accepted the Governor's call and the joint session acted on various matters, it was not for the Supreme Judicial Court to disturb the procedure adopted by the Governor and accepted by the legislature.[149] It held that because the Massachusetts Constitution does not prescribe the procedures to be followed, it could not reject the means selected by the Governor to achieve a constitutionally permissible end where the legislature acquiesced in his determination.

2.7.1.2 Involving Election Processes

Another fertile ground for the possible application of the political question doctrine by state courts has been in the area of elections processes. Like in the Nigerian context discussed in detail below, State supreme courts in America routinely resist requests to intrude in election processes and determine election results. State courts consider the election process as self-monitoring and hence their reluctance to intervene.[150] The Ohio Supreme Court in *State ex rel Ford v. Board of Election of Pickaway County* justified its refusal to intervene in an election case by holding that "elections are a function of the political branch of government, are a matter of political regulation, and are not per se the subject of judicial cognizance."[151]

---

147 Citing examples of *Moe v. Secretary of Administration & Finance* 382 Mass 629 [1981], at pp. 641-642; *Colorado v. Treasurer & Receiver General* 378 Mass 550 [1979], at pp. 552-553 and *Loring v. Young*, 239 Mass 349 (1921), at pp. 360-361.

148 *Backman v. Secretary of the Commonwealth*, at p. 554.

149 *Backman v. Secretary of the Commonwealth*, at pp. 550-551.

150 Stern, 1983, p. 408.

151 *State ex rel Ford v. Board of Election of Pickaway County* 167 Ohio St 449 (1958), at p. 451. *See also, Brown v. McDaniel* 244 Ark 362 (1968) (declining to prohibit an election at the eleventh hour declaring that election is essentially the exercise of political power, and, during its progress, is not subject to judicial control. This comprehends the whole election, including every step and proceeding necessary to its completion).

Like in Nigeria where the political question doctrine has typically been applied in election cases due to the judiciary's reluctance to determine outcomes of elections, in the United States, the deference by State courts to the political branches in elections cases reaches its zenith when a challenge is raised in the aftermath of an election.[152]

The Iowa Supreme Court in *State ex rel Turner v. Scott,*[153] for example, rejected to intervene in a challenge against State Senator Scott, which sought to remove him from his seat as a State Senator. Mr Scott was elected to the Iowa Senate from the 24th district in 1976. During the campaign, the incumbent Mr Winkelman contended as a campaign issue that Mr Scott was not qualified to represent the district because he did not meet the inhabitancy requirements of the Iowa Constitution. Following the elections, the Senate credentials committee determined that Mr Scott was qualified to assume the seat to which he had been elected.

The Attorney General challenged Scott's right to hold office based on Article III, Section 5 of the Iowa Constitution, which states that the qualifications of residency and citizenship for House members also apply to Senate members. Scott resisted the action arguing, among other things, that the Attorney General had no standing to bring the claim because the legislature held the sole power to judge the qualifications of its members. His argument was predicated on Article III, Section 7 of the Iowa Constitution, which provides that:

> Each house shall choose its own officers, and judge of the qualification, election, and return of its own members. A contested election shall be determined in such manner as shall be directed by law.

Scott also argued that powers granted to the legislative branch cannot be exercised by the judicial branch of government. This argument was based on Article III, Section 1, which provides that:

> The powers of the government of Iowa shall be divided into three separate departments the Legislative, the Executive, and the Judiciary; and no person charged with the exercise of powers properly belonging to one of these departments shall exercise any function appertaining to either of the others, except in cases hereinafter expressly directed or permitted.

152 Stern, 1983, p. 408. *See generally*, Nwauche, 2010.
153 *State ex rel Turner v. Scott* 269 NW 2d 828 (Iowa 1978), at p. 831.

The trial court dismissed the case on the grounds that it lacked authority to interfere with the Senate's determination of Scott's qualifications unless a substantial violation of constitutional rights was established.[154]

In resolving the dispute, the Iowa Supreme Court found that the question of whether the judicial branch has jurisdiction to hear and determine the case is linked to the question of whether the case presented a justiciable controversy. It further noted that in order for there to be a justiciable controversy, there must exist a dispute that is capable of judicial resolution; that for a justiciable controversy to exist, a political question should not be involved.[155] After approvingly citing *Baker v. Carr*, the Supreme Court concluded that this case involved a non-justiciable political question the resolution of which is properly left to the senatorial discretion. With this conclusion, the Supreme Court affirmed the lower court decision to dismiss.

A majority of scholarly literature in the United States on the political question doctrine have focused on the federal application of the doctrine. Few scholarly commentaries have devoted to the study of the political question doctrine at the State court level. Existing literature on State court application of the doctrine shows that the doctrine forms part of a great number of State jurisprudence, and that despite the federalism imperatives that underpin the American system of government, there is room for the political question doctrine in State courts. The literature also demonstrates that the doctrine has been applied both in its classical and prudential forms. Given the distinct constitutional traditions, it is understandable that the approaches by State supreme courts towards the doctrine will differ. Some state courts, like in Massachusetts, have resisted applying the doctrine because of their unique constitutional traditions, whereas others have embraced the doctrine as formulated in *Baker v. Carr* or in its classical form.

Like at the federal court level, the impact of *Zivotofsky v. Clinton* is yet to be determined at the State level as legal commentators wrestle with the question of what is left of the doctrine. The last section in this chapter is devoted to examining the most recent political question doctrine case decided by the US Supreme Court, *Zivotofsky v. Clinton*, which has raised questions about the doctrine's future application leading some to argue that the case overruled some aspects of *Baker v. Carr*.[156]

2.8 THE POLITICAL QUESTION DOCTRINE AFTER ZIVOTOFSKY V. CLINTON

Zivotofsky v. Clinton is the most recent and significant case by the US Supreme Court addressing the political question doctrine. The case involved a dispute between Menachem

154 *State ex rel Turner v. Scott*, 1978, p. 829.
155 *Id.*, p. 831.
156 Szurkowski, 2014, pp. 358-260 (noting that certain factors in *Baker v. Carr* no longer relevant).

Zivotofsky and the Secretary of State of the United States. The facts and procedural history of the case are as important as the law that developed from the case.

To start with, Menachem Zivotofsky was born in Jerusalem in 2002. His parents were US citizens. Shortly after his birth, his mother, pursuant to Section 214(d) of the Foreign Relations Authorization Act Fiscal Year 2003[157] filed an application with the US Embassy requesting that his US passport list Jerusalem, Israel, as his place of birth. The embassy officials refused to grant the request consistent with the policy of not acknowledging any State sovereignty over Jerusalem and listed his place of birth as simply Jerusalem.[158] In 2003, Zivotofsky brought a lawsuit against the Secretary of State in the federal district court, seeking to enforce Section 214(d). That section directs the State Department to list Jerusalem-born passport applicants' birth as Israel upon request.

The district court dismissed the claim holding that Zivotofsky lacked standing and found that the case presented a non-justiciable political question. It explained that resolving Zivotofsky's claim on the merits would necessarily require the court to decide the political status of Jerusalem.[159] The Court of Appeals reversed the ruling on the grounds of standing and remanded the case for further development on the political question issue.[160] On remand, the district court dismissed the case again, this time on the ground of a non-justiciable political question,[161] and Zivotofsky appealed.

The Court of Appeals affirmed the judgement. Judge Griffith, who wrote for the panel, illuminated that "courts may not consider claims that raise issues whose resolution has been committed to the political branches by the text of the Constitution."[162] He observed that the Constitution grants the President the sole power to recognize foreign governments,[163] and given that the claim by Zivotofsky sought to negate the President's neutral

157 Section 214(d) of the Foreign Relations Authorization Act Fiscal Year 2003 provides: "For purposes of the registration of birth, certification of nationality, or issuance of a passport of a United States citizen born in the city of Jerusalem, the Secretary shall, upon the request of the citizen or the citizen's legal guardian, record the place of birth as Israel."

158 *Zivotofsky v. Clinton*, 2012, pp. 99-100.

159 *Zivotofsky v. Secretary of State* 511 F Supp 2d 97 (2007), at p. 103. *See also, Corrie v. Caterpillar* (where in justifying the application of the political question doctrine, the court reasoned that "Allowing this action to proceed would necessarily require the judicial branch of our government to question the political branches' decision to grant extensive military aid to Israel; that it is difficult to see how we could impose liability on Caterpillar without at least implicitly deciding the propriety of the United States' decision to pay for the bulldozers which allegedly killed the plaintiffs' family members.").

160 *Zivotofsky ex rel. Ari Z v. Sec'y of State* 444 F 3d 614 (DC Cir 2006), at pp. 619-620.

161 *Zivotofsky v. Secretary of State* 511 F Supp 2d, at p. 107.

162 *Zivotosfky v. Secretary of State* 571 F 3d, at p. 1230, citing *Baker v. Carr*.

163 *Zivotofsky v. Clinton*, 2012, p. 1231.

stance towards Jerusalem, it was non-justiciable.[164] In his view, Section 214(d) was of no moment to the analysis; but justiciability was a threshold matter for the court to consider.[165]

Though Judge Edwards concurred with the Griffith's opinion, he objected to the findings on the political question doctrine.[166] For Edwards, the relevant question was simply whether Section 214(d) was constitutional. He would have reached the merits and invalidate Section 214(d).[167]

The US Supreme Court vacated and remanded the case to the lower court.[168] Writing for the majority, Chief Justice Roberts elucidated that while the judiciary has the responsibility to decide cases properly before it, judicial precedent has identified a narrow exception to that requirement known as the political question doctrine.[169] He noted that the narrow exception applies where there is "a textually demonstrable constitutional commitment of the issue to a coordinate political department; or a lack of judicially discoverable and manageable standards for resolving it".[170] It is important to note that these narrow exceptions identified by Roberts are the first two factors in the test formulated in *Baker v. Carr.* I will come back to the significance of this development in Chapter 5.

Roberts concluded that Zivotofsky's case did not meet any of the narrow exceptions established in *Baker v. Carr.* He further noted that the Constitution did not commit the issue to another branch. For Roberts, the issue was not whether "to supplant a foreign policy decision of the political branches with the court's own unmoored determination of what United State policy towards Jerusalem should be".[171] Rather, the issue was whether Zivotofsky "may vindicate his statutory right ... to have Israel recorded on his passport as his place of birth".[172] That issue, in Justice Roberts view, presented the familiar judicial exercise of interpreting Section 214(d) and deciding whether it was constitutional.[173]

What is more, Justice Roberts observed that because the parties do not dispute the interpretation of Section 214(d), the only real question for determination was whether the legislation was constitutional. He noted that since *Marbury v. Madison*, it is trite that when an Act of Congress is challenged "it is emphatically the province and duty of the judiciary

164 *Id.*, pp. 1231-1232.
165 *Id.*, p. 1233.
166 *Id.*, p. 1234.
167 *Id.*, at pp. 1234-1240.
168 *Id.*, at p. 132 SCt, p. 1431.
169 *Id.*, at p. 1427, citing *Cohens v. Virginia* 6 Wheat 264 (1821), at p. 404. *See also, Third Ave Association v. Consulate Gen. of the Socialist Federal Republic of Yugoslavia* 218 F 3d 152, 164 (2d Cir 2000) (noting that political question doctrine is essentially a constitutional limitation on the courts).
170 *Zivotofsky v. Clinton*, at p. 1427, quoting *Nixon v. United States*, 506 US 224 (1993), p. 228. This language mirrors the first two factors in *Baker v. Carr. See, Baker v. Carr*, at p. 217.
171 *Zivotofsky v. Clinton*, 2012, p. 1427.
172 *Id.*, pp. 1424-1427.
173 *Id.*, p. 1427.

to say what the law is."[174] And while that duty will sometimes encompass political implications, the judiciary cannot avoid its responsibility to discharge that duty when called upon to do so.[175] Roberts remarked that in this case, the inquiry into the validity of Section 214(d) entailed deciding whether the legislation impermissibly intrudes upon Presidential powers under the US Constitution. If so, he noted, the legislation must be invalidated and the claim dismissed.

On the other hand, he reasoned that if it is found that the impugned legislation does not intrude into the President's powers, then the Secretary of State must be ordered to issue Zivotosky a passport that complies with Section 214(d). He emphasized that either way, the political question doctrine was not implicated because no policy underlying the political question doctrine suggests that Congress or the Executive can decide the constitutionality of a statute, noting that that is an issue for the judiciary to decide.[176] Justice Roberts also dismissed as invalid the lack of judicial standard argument advanced by the Secretary of State to coerce the application of the political question doctrine.

Justice Sotomayor wrote a concurring opinion in which she sought to provide a demanding inquiry on the circumstances that are appropriate for invoking the political question doctrine under *Baker v. Carr.*[177] She analyzed the six factors in *Baker v. Carr* and found that they reveal three distinct justifications for invoking the doctrine: (1) the court's lack of constitutional authority to decide the issue, (2) that cases implicating factors two and three in *Baker v. Carr* require circumstances in which a dispute calls for decision making beyond the courts' competence and (3) that factors four through six involve prudential considerations.[178] For Justice Sotomayor, although the last three factors are parts of *Baker v. Carr's* six-factor test, prudential considerations would render a case non-justiciable only in rare and exceptional cases.[179] She noted that often when prudential factors are implicated in a case presenting a political question, other factors identified in *Baker v. Carr* will likewise be apparent.[180]

Furthermore, on the future application of the doctrine, Sotomayor theorized that "it is not impossible to imagine a case involving the application or even the constitutionality of an enactment that would present a nonjusticiable issue."[181] In other words, Sotomayor

174 *Marbury v. Madison*, 1803, p. 177.
175 *Zivotofsky v. Clinton*, 2012, p. 1427.
176 *Id.*, p. 1428.
177 *Id.*, p. 1431.
178 *Id.*, pp. 1431-1432.
179 *Id.*, pp. 1431-1433.
180 *Id.*, p. 1434. *See, e.g., Nixon v. United States* 506 US 224 (1993), p. 236 (noting that in addition to the textual commitment argument, finding persuasive that opening the door of judicial review of impeachment procedures would expose the political life of the country to months, or perhaps years, of chaos) and *Baker v. Carr* 222 (explaining that the Court in *Luther v. Borden*, 7 How 1 (1849), found present features associated with each of the three rationales underlying Baker's factors).
181 *Zivotofsky v. Clinton*, 2012, p. 1435.

suggested that it is possible for a future court to find a political question in the context of statutory application.[182]

Justice Alito concurred in the judgement of Roberts. He stressed that the question presented was narrow and involved the power to regulate the contents of a passport, not whether the power to recognize foreign governments is exclusively the President's.[183] While holding that "determining the constitutionality of an Act of Congress may present a political question," Justice Alito found that the issue before the court was whether Section 214(d) infringes on the power of the President to regulate the contents of a passport.[184] In his view, this narrow question does not constitute a non-justiciable political question.

The lone dissenter in the case was Justice Breyer. He found that the case presented non-justiciable political questions on prudential grounds.[185] He concurred with Justice Sotomayor's determination that abstention from adjudication owing to prudence is appropriate only in rare cases, but Breyer, unlike Sotomayor, recognized *Zivotofsky v. Clinton* as such rare occasion.[186] Justice Breyer reached his decision by recognizing four sets of prudential considerations, taken together: firstly, he found that the case arose in the area of foreign affairs, where courts hesitate to make decisions.[187] Secondly, he found that the case required the court "to evaluate the foreign policy implications of foreign policy decisions".[188] Thirdly, the petition did not involve particularly weighty interests that courts have traditionally sought to protect or that vindicate a basic right.[189] Presumably, he meant this case was about the contents of a passport and not about a significant issue of whether Zivotofsky is entitled to a passport. Fourth, when the political branches have non-judicial methods of working out their differences, the need for judicial intervention is diminished.[190] In the light of this, Justice Breyer concluded that Zivotofsky's claim was an unusual case exemplifying several prudential considerations, which, altogether, justified abstention from judicial intervention.[191]

As one scholar, who has comprehensively studied the US Supreme Court ruling in *Zivotofsky v. Clinton* and its aftermath, has noted, it is difficult to draw any sweeping

---

182 She makes the hypothetical point that "if Congress passed a statute, for instance, purporting to award financial relief to those improperly tried of impeachment offenses. To adjudicate claims under such a statute would require a court to resolve the very same issue we found nonjusticiable in *Nixon v. United States*." Such an example is atypical, but they suffice to show that the foreclosure altogether of political question analysis in statutory cases is unwarranted. *Zivotofsky v. Clinton*, 2012, p. 1435.

183 *Zivotofsky v. Clinton*, 2012, p. 1436.

184 *Id.*

185 *Id.*, pp. 1437-1441 (Breyer J., dissenting).

186 *Zivotofsky v. Clinton*, 2012, pp. 1437-1441.

187 *Zivotofsky v. Clinton*, 2012, p. 1437.

188 *Id.*, p. 1438.

189 *Id.*, p. 1440.

190 *Id.*, p. 1441.

191 *Id.*

conclusions or declare any general trends following that judgement.[192] Shemtob has further noted that the effects of *Zivotofsky v. Clinton* in the lowers courts has been uncertain and confusing noting that lower courts have so far resisted the court's ruling.[193]

I agree with Shemtob that the implications of the judgement in *Zivotofsky v. Clinton* are yet to be seen, but it is clear that its effects will be felt beyond the borders of the United States. A few of these implications can be summarized as follows: Firstly, the judgement undermines all the prudential considerations in *Baker v. Carr* and is emphatic that only the first two factors, which represent the classical political question considerations, will be relevant in the application of the doctrine. Another commentator, Szurkowski, has correctly emphasized that *Zivotofsky v. Clinton* represents the death of the prudential strand of the political question doctrine and the reaffirmation of the classical strand.[194]

To add to this, Shemtob accurately notes that Justice Roberts adopted the classical view previously adopted by his counterparts in *Nixon v. United States.*[195] There, Chief Justice Rehnquist excluded from his analysis all four prudential factors in *Baker v. Carr* focusing solely on whether a textual demonstrable constitutional commitment of the issue to a coordinate political department was available or whether a judicially manageable standard to resolve the issue was present.[196] Roberts' position in *Zivotofsky v. Clinton* also appears to take a cue from Justice Douglas's classical approach to the doctrine. In *Massachusetts v. Laird,*[197] Justice Douglas took a classical approach to the political question when he dissented from a motion for leave to file a bill of complaint. Douglas criticized the use of prudential considerations in determining the presence of a political question.[198] In his view, the duty of the US Supreme Court was to interpret the Constitution, and it was irrelevant whether that duty offended another branch of government.[199]

Secondly, given the narrow exceptions announced by Roberts from which a political question doctrine can be determined to be present or not, the judgement in *Zivotofsky v. Clinton* suggests that the future application of the doctrine will be narrow and limited.[200]

---

192 Shemtob, 2016, pp. 1021-1025.

193 *Id.*, p. 1024, citing *Harris v. Kellogg Brown & Root Service*; *Kerr v. Hickenlooper* and *Center for Biological Diversity* 80 F Supp 3d 991 (where the court was less willing to forego *Baker v. Carr*).

194 Szurkowski, 2014. *But see*, Shemtob, 2016, p. 1010 (arguing that it is premature to argue that the test in *Baker v. Carr* has been overruled because the political question doctrine never relied solely on that test).

195 Shemtob, 2016, p. 1021.

196 *Id.*

197 *Massachusetts v. Laird* 400 US 886 (1970).

198 Shemtob, 2016, p. 1017.

199 *Massachusetts v. Laird,* 1970, pp. 894-896. *See also*, Shemtob, 2016, pp. 1017-1018. *See also*, *Roudebush v. Hartke* 405 US 15 (1972), at p. 30 (where the court had to determine whether a senate seat's recount should go forward. In his dissenting opinion, Justice Douglass advanced the classical political question arguing that all that mattered was whether there was a textually demonstrable constitutional commitment of such question to the Senate).

200 Szurkowski, 2014. *See also*, J. Barron & T. Dienes, *Constitutional Law in a Nutshell*, West, St Paul, Minnesotta, 1995.

Nonetheless, as Gil has correctly observed, the doctrine's well-established roots in American jurisprudence have been and, by all signs, shall continue to keep several politically charged issues beyond the scrutiny of the courts.[201] She notes that "more than in other fields of government conduct, foreign affairs and national security issues have been kept away from judicial review,"[202] and this trend is likely to continue under the regime of *Zivotofsky v. Clinton*.

Thirdly, there is a strong possibility that *Zivotofsky v. Clinton* may have implications in countries such as Ghana, Nigeria and Uganda and perhaps other jurisdictions where the prudential political question as formulated in *Baker v. Carr* was endorsed.[203] *Baker v. Carr* has also been criticized outside the United States. Dennison has offered a useful criticism in the context of his discussion of the issue of avoidance under the political question doctrine in Uganda.[204] His critical comments arose out of his reaction to the Constitutional Court decision in *Centre of Health Human Rights v. Attorney-General.*[205]

In *Centre of Health Human Rights v. Attorney-General,* the Court found that it was barred by the political question doctrine from determining the constitutionality of government maternal health policies. In his reaction to this decision, Dennison accepts the court's use of the political question doctrine but identified a problem with the Constitutional Court's application of the doctrine to avoid the determination of the central issue of whether there is a constitutional right to health in Uganda. For Dennison, the avoidance of the issue by the Constitutional Court is "particularly disconcerting in a Ugandan environment where courts have a tendency to exercise extreme deference to the other branches of government".[206]

Other scholars have expressed similar concerns about the inappropriate deference offered by the courts to the political branches are well documented.[207] Intensifying these concerns, Dennison observes that it is the political question doctrine as formulated in *Baker v. Carr* that legitimizes political expediency and the fear of political consequences as an appropriate legal consideration for employing the doctrine in a given case.[208] To drive his point home, Dennison emphasized the following three factors in *Baker v. Carr*:

> (1) the impossibility of a court's undertaking independent resolution without expressing lack of respect owing to coordinate branches of government, (2) an unusual need for unquestioning adherence to a political decision already made

201 Gil, 2014, p. 265.
202 *Id.*, citing *Haig v. Agee 453* US 280 (1981) 292 and *Pauling v. McNamara* 331 F 2d 796 (DC Cir 1963), p. 799.
203 *See, Onuoha v. Okafor* and *Dalhatu v. Turaki.*
204 Denisson, 2014, p. 283.
205 *Centre of Health Human Rights v. Attorney-General,* Constitutional Petition No. 16 of (2011) GCC 4.
206 Denisson, 2014, p. 283.
207 *See*, E. Bussey, 'Constitutional Dialogue in Uganda', *Journal of African Law*, Vol. 49, No. 1, 2005, p. 2.
208 Dennison, 2014, p. 283.

> or (3) the potentiality of embarrassment from multifarious pronouncements on one question.[209]

In his view, given the history of extreme deference to the political branches, the preceding three prudential factors from *Baker v. Carr* provide the legal license for Uganda's judiciary to practice issue avoidance in sensitive matters as they did in *Centre of Health Human Rights v. Attorney-General.*[210] As a result, Dennison is critical of the prudential considerations introduced in *Baker v. Carr* and questions their usefulness. His major problem, which anyone who has studied the history of judicial review in Uganda would appreciate, is that prudential factors in *Baker v. Carr* provide a fertile basis for the "executive to be more politically volatile and reactionary with respect to judicial decisions, thus increasing the legal merits for the application of the political question doctrine".[211] Professor Barkow agrees with Dennison in pointing out one of the major weaknesses of the prudential political question, which is that it gives "an even more flexible escape hatch for a court that wishes to avoid deciding a tough case".[212] It is in this context that Dennison makes an observation that sheds light into the current legal position of the law in Uganda. He observes that in his formulation of the political question doctrine in *Tinyefuza,* Justice Kanyeihamba may have deliberately left out any meaningful discussion of *Baker v. Carr* as a way of discrediting its rationale and emphasizing only the classical political question theory-based approach.[213]

It remains to be seen whether critics like Dennison would be persuaded by the views, which seek to salvage prudential considerations, expressed by Justice Sotomayor that the prudential considerations in *Baker v. Carr* rarely justify the existence of a political question doctrine;[214] that you require more than just prudential considerations to find a non-justiciable political question. These are the questions that are likely to occupy jurists and academics in those jurisdictions other than the United States when considering the political question doctrine in the aftermath of *Zivotofsky v. Clinton.*

Lastly, the elevation of the first two factors under the six factors in *Baker v. Carr* by Roberts J raises interesting questions: What is the vitality of the remaining four factors in *Baker v. Carr*? Are those factors good law after *Zivotofsky v. Clinton*? What is the future status of the prudential strand of the political question doctrine? How significant is the decision in *Zivotofsky v. Clinton* to the future application of the doctrine? Should *Zivotofsky*

---

209 *Id.*

210 American courts have confirmed that these factors in *Baker v. Carr* contain prudential considerations. *See, Wang v. Masaitis* 416 F 3d 992 (9th Cir 2005); *Corrie v. Caterpillar Goldwater v. Carter* 444 US 996 (1979).

211 Dennison, 2014, p. 283. *See also,* Bussey, 2005, pp. 12-13 (discussing some of the reactions to court decisions by President Museveni).

212 Barkow, 2002, p. 334.

213 Dennison, 2014, pp. 283-284.

214 Gill, 2014, p. 264.

v. Clinton be read as a rejection of prudential considerations all together and a return to the traditional or classical political question doctrine as others have opined? Time will tell the answers to these questions as the courts grapple with political question cases in the future.

2.9 Conclusion

As we have seen in this chapter, the political question doctrine is one of the oldest legal doctrines and remains good law in America. It has gone through transformation over the decades. Since its invention, the doctrine has been criticized by scholars and jurists over its incoherence. Based on the analysis of case law, it could be argued that the discourse around the political question doctrine among judges and academics has centred on ensuring a consistent application of the doctrine.[215] While an unpredictable application of any legal principle is not desirable, it can be expected in the development and application of a complex concept like the doctrine.[216] Courts always disagree and at times become unclear in the development and application of a significant number of legal principles, but this does not entail those principles are discredited or abandoned.[217] Due to its prominence, the political question doctrine has been considered, adopted and applied by the judiciary in Ghana.

---

215 *See*, Finkelstein, 1924, pp. 344-345 (noting that there are certain cases that are completely without the sphere of judicial interference; they are called political questions); and Redish, 1984, pp. 1031-1032 (arguing that academic debate on the political question doctrine has centred over the principled use of the doctrine; and that the doctrine is very much alive in Supreme Court decisions).

216 *See*, Finkelstein, 1924, pp. 344-345; Redish, 1984, p. 1033 and Jaffe, 2011, pp. 1043-1063 (discussing recent cases applying the political question doctrine).

217 *See*, Rautenbach, 2012, p. 28 (suggesting that the political question doctrine should not be adopted in South Africa because it is highly controversial in its land of origin). But for a discussion of disagreements among courts over the application of the doctrine of privity of contract or third-party beneficiaries, *see*, J. Perillo, *The Law of Contracts*, West Group, Minnesota, 1998, pp. 641-666; Law Reform Advisory Committee for Northern Ireland, Privity of Contract: Contracts for the Benefit of Third Parties, Report Nos. 4-6 (2006) (examining the historical origins and development of privity of contract and highlighting the practical problems that have resulted in the areas of construction, shipping, insurance, consumer law). *See also*, *Debnarayan Dutt v. Ramsadhan* AIR (1914) Cal 129 (holding that the doctrine of privity of contract is not applicable in India and that the aim of the mofussil court of justice in British India is to do complete justice according to principles of justice, equity and good conscience); *Jamna Das v. Ram Autar* (1911) 30 IA 7(where the privy council extended the doctrine to India and held that the person not party to the agreement cannot recover the amount due from one party) and *Lawrence v. Fox* 20 NY 268 (1859).

3 Separation of Powers and the Evolution of the Political Question Doctrine in Ghana*

3.1 Introduction

In most constitutional democracies, political disputes or contestations will likely end up in the courts. When this happens, judicial overreach can reasonably be perceived and judicial independence jeopardized. As one South African Judge Davis recently warned in *Mazibuko,*[1] there is a threat to judicial independence when the judiciary is drawn in to resolve political questions that are beyond its competence or jurisdiction.[2] He further said that:

> An overreach of the powers of judges, their intrusion into issues which are beyond their competence or intended jurisdiction or which have been deliberately and carefully constructed legally so as to ensure that the other arms of the state to deal with these matters, can only result in jeopardy for our constitutional democracy. In this dispute I am not prepared to create a juristocracy and thus do more than that which I am mandated to do in terms of our constitutional model.[3]

The difficulty that confronts democracies is how to jurisprudentially resolve political questions that end up in the courts, while at the same time preserve the separation of powers and rule of law. In some democracies, notably Israel, Japan, Ghana, Nigeria, Uganda and United States, the judiciaries have developed and applied the political question doctrine

---

* An earlier version of this chapter was published in 2014. *See*, M. Mhango, 'Separation of Powers in Ghana: The Evolution of the Political Question Doctrine', *Potchefstroom Electronic Law Journal*, Vol. 17, No. 6, 2014, p. 2706.

1 *Mazibuko*, 2012, p. 32. For a critical examination of *Mazibuko* 2013, *see*, F. Cachalia, 'Judicial Review of Parliamentary Rulemaking: A Provisional Case for Restraint', *New York Law School Law Review*, Vol. 60, 2015-2016, p. 379.

2 *Mazibuko*, 2012, p. 32.

3 *Mazibuko*, 2012, p. 33. *Also see*, *Mazibuko*, 2013, para. 83 (Jafta J., minority opinion) (noting that "political issues must be resolved at a political level; that our court should not be drawn into political disputes, the resolution of which falls appropriately within the domain of other fora established in terms of the Constitution.").

to resolve political questions and define their relationship with other branches of government in relation to those questions.

This chapter discusses the development and current status of the political question doctrine in Ghanaian jurisprudence. It discusses the application of the political question doctrine in Ghana with a view to draw lessons for South Africa. It argues that while there are differences of opinion on the application of the political question doctrine, the doctrine is firmly part of Ghanaian constitutional law. The chapter observes that the differences of opinion among judges in Ghana is primarily over the proper application of the doctrine rather than whether it forms part of Ghanaian constitutional law. The chapter also discusses another related issue, which is the constitutional status of Directive Principles of State Policy in Chapter 6 of the 1992 Constitution of Ghana (also referred to as the Constitution 1992) and whether these principles are justiciable.

3.2 The Application of the Political Question Doctrine

In Ghana, the political question doctrine or at least its theory can be traced to the early 1980s.[4] Even so, not only have courts and legal commentators disagreed about its wisdom and validity, they have also varied considerably over the doctrine's scope and rationale.[5] In fact, they have even diverged over whether the doctrine is applicable under Ghanaian constitutional law, given the contested case authority that adopted it.[6] However, there is agreement that the political question doctrine is a function of the separation of powers

4 *See, Tuffour v. Attorney-General* 1980 GLR 637, at pp. 651-652 (holding that "courts cannot enquire into the legality or illegality of what happened in Parliament. In so far as Parliament has acted by virtue of the powers conferred upon it by the Constitution, its actions within Parliament are a closed book.").

5 *See*, K. Asare, 'Can the Political Doctrine Question Save MP Amoateng', *GhanaWeb*, 16 November 2006, www.ghanaweb.com/GhanaHomePage/NewsArchive/artikel.php?ID=113967 (arguing against the application of the political question doctrine in Ghana); *JH Mensah v. Attorney-General* 1996-97 SCGLR 320 (holding that the political question doctrine as applied in the United States is not applicable in Ghana); *Amidu v. President Kufuor* 2001-2002 SCGLR 138, at p. 152 (Amidu) (Kpegah, dissenting opinion) (arguing that the political question doctrine is applicable to Ghana); *Ghana Bar Association v. Attorney-General* 2003-2004 SCGLR 250 (holding that the political question doctrine barred the Supreme Court from scrutinizing the decision of the President to appoint the Chief Justice) and *New Patriotic Party v. Attorney-General* 1993-94 2 GLR 35 SC; *Asare v. Attorney-General (AP)*, unreported case number 21/2006.

6 *See*, S. Bimpong-Buta, *Role of the Supreme Court in the Development of the Constitutional Law in Ghana* (LDD thesis on file at the University of South Africa, Pretoria), pp. 129-130 (suggesting that there is no proper legal authority for the application of the political question doctrine in Ghana); Redish, 1984, pp. 1033-1045 (making similar observations about the disagreements of the application of the political question doctrine in the US context) and *Asare v. Attorney-General*, 2006 (where the political question doctrine was most recently applied). *See*, L. Wishik, 'Separation of Powers and Adjudication of Human Rights Claims Under Alien Tort Claims Act – Hanoch-Tel-Oren v. Libyan Arab Republic', 726 F 2d 774 (DC Cir 1984), cert. denied, 105 SCt. 1354 (1985)', *Washington Law Review*, Vol. 60, 1985, p. 701; (discussing that scholars disagree on whether the political question doctrine exists at all, and if it does exist, on whether it is constitutionally defined or is a flexible, prudential tool to protect the court's authority).

principle enshrined in the Constitution 1992, and that its jurisprudential basis was influenced by case law from the US Supreme Court.[7] Justice Kpegah, one of the strongest advocates of the doctrine on Ghana's Supreme Court, has offered the most comprehensive and convincing articulation on the basis of the political question doctrine under the Constitution of Ghana.

In his dissenting opinion in *Amidu*,[8] Justice Kpegah explains that the Constitution of Ghana is written and underpinned by the principle of the separation of powers. In his view, being a written Constitution, it has certain attributes. Chief among them is that the form of government envisages three important pillars, namely the executive, legislature and judiciary.[9] Another attribute, maintains Justice Kpegah, is that these various pillars of government have their respective powers laid down with limits not to be infringed by any other pillar of government.[10] Kpegah reminds us that these limits expressed in the Constitution of Ghana would be meaningless and serve no purpose if freely ignored or infringed by any pillar of government.[11] Constitutional scholars agree with Justice Kpegah's pronouncements, arguing that:

> ... by simultaneously dividing power among the three branches and institutionalizing methods that allow each branch to check the other... the Constitution reduces the likelihood that one faction or interest group that has managed to obtain control of one branch will be able to implement its political agenda in contravention of the wishes of the people.[12]

Justice Kpegah goes on to explain that while the Constitution of Ghana is expressed as the supreme law of Ghana, there is an inherent indication in the text that the policy that informs

7 *See, Ghana Bar Association*, 2003-2004, pp. 272-276 (Hayfron-Benjamin J., concurring opinion) (explaining that although in *Tuffour*, the Supreme Court did not use the term non-justiciable political question, they reached conclusions that accord with justice Brennan's dictum in *Baker v. Carr*).

8 *Amidu*, 2001-2002, p. 138.

9 *Id.*, p. 153.

10 *Id.*

11 *Id.*, pp. 153-154.

12 *See*, M. Redish & E. Cisar, 'If Angels Were to Govern: The Need for Pragmatic Formalism in Separation of Powers Theory', *Duke Law Journal*, Vol. 41, No. 3, 1991-1992, p. 451. *See also*, E. Magill, 'The Real Separation in Separation of Powers Law', *Virginia Law Review*, Vol. 86, No. 6, 2000, p. 1152; S.G. Calabresi & J.L. Larsen, 'One Person, One Office: Separation of Powers or Separation of Personnel', *Cornell Law Review*, Vol. 79, No. 5, 1994, p. 1052; P.L. Strauss, 'Formal and Functional Approaches to Separation-of-Powers Questions – A Foolish Inconsistency?', *Cornell Law Review*, Vol. 72, No. 3, 1978, p. 488; L. Liberman, 'Morrison v. Olson: A Formalistic Perspective on Why the Court Was Wrong', *American University Law Review*, Vol. 38, No. 2, 1989, p. 313; H. Bruff, 'Presidential Powers and Administrative Rulemaking', *Yale Law Journal*, Vol. 88, No. 3, 1979, p. 451; S.G. Calabresi & H. Rhodes, 'The Structural Constitution: Unitary Executive, Plural Judiciary', *Harvard Law Review*, Vol. 105, No. 6, 1992, p. 1153; C. Farina, 'Statutory Interpretation and the Balance of Power in the Administrative State', *Columbia Law Review*, 1989, p. 452 and Redish, 1984, p. 1048.

or should inform any legislation and the desire to enact such legislation are matters for the political branches of government to determine.[13] On the other hand, Kpegah concedes that the interpretation and enforcement of the law passed by the legislature fall within the functions of the judiciary. In his view, the question of whether an Act of Parliament is constitutionally valid or not is not a political question and the judiciary is not barred from deciding it.[14] He teaches us that when the judiciary examines whether Parliament has breached the constitutional limits on its legislative powers, it is not engaging in determining political questions, because the judiciary has the power to make these determinations. For Kpegah, this distinction is important and must be maintained.[15] One of Kpegah's colleagues on the bench, Chief Justice Archer, agreed with the importance of maintaining this distinction when he said that:

> The Constitution gives the judiciary power to interpret and enforce the Constitution and I do not think that this independence enables the judiciary to do what it likes by undertaking incursions into territory reserved for Parliament and the executive. This court should not behave like an octopus stretching its eight tentacles here and there to grab jurisdiction not constitutionally meant for it. I hold that this court has no constitutional power to prevent the executive from proclaiming 31 December as a public holiday.[16]

Clearly, Justice Kpegah and other Justices of the Supreme Court of Ghana are of the view that the political question doctrine did not evolve in American jurisprudence due to the fact that the courts were not expressly endowed with the power of judicial review in the United States Constitution.[17] Instead, in their justifications above, they view the doctrine as a necessary function of the universal principle of separation of powers.[18] There are at

13 *Amidu*, 2001-2002, p. 154.

14 *Id.*

15 Justice Ngcobo agrees with the need to maintain this distinction and explains that "when a court decides whether parliament has complied with its express constitutional obligation, such as a provision that requires statutes to be passed by a specified majority, it does not infringe upon the principle of separation of powers or determine a political question." Ngcobo maintains that "what the court is simply doing in such a case is to decide the formal question of whether there was the required majority." *See, Doctors for Life International*, at para. 25.

16 *Amidu*, 2001-2002, p. 154, citing *New Patriotic Party v. Attorney-General*, 1993-1994, p. 49.

17 *Amidu*, 2001-2002, p. 154.

18 *Id.*, p. 155. *Also see*, S. Birkey, 'Gordon v. Texas and the Prudential Approach to Political Questions', *California Law Review*, Vol. 87, No. 5, 1999, pp. 1265-1281 (arguing that the political question doctrine is a function of the separation of powers doctrine); Y. Reich, '*United States v. AT&T*: Judicially Supervised Negotiated and Political Questions', *Columbia Law Review*, Vol. 77, No. 3, 1977, p. 466 (arguing that the judiciary's reluctance to decide political questions stems from its respect for the separation of powers between the judiciary and the elected branches of government) and D.A. Harvey, 'The *Alien Tort Statute: International Human Rights Watchdog* or *Simply Historical Trivia*', *John Marshall Law Review*, Vol. 21, No. 2, 1988, p. 356 (arguing that the political question doctrine is based on the separation of powers).

least three major Supreme Court decisions and one High Court decision that either openly applied or considered the political question doctrine in Ghana. These decisions provide a definitive statement of the law of the political question doctrine in Ghana.

3.3 A Legislative Decision to Declare a Public Holiday

The first Ghanaian case that substantively considered the political question doctrine was *New Patriotic Party v. Attorney-General.*[19] The plaintiff in this case was the New Patriotic Party, the main opposition political party at the time. It brought a law suit seeking a declaration pursuant to Section 2(1) of the Constitution 1992 that the planned public holiday and celebration of the coup d'état in Ghana on 31 December 1981 was in conflict with the Constitution 1992. In its defence, the government invoked the political question doctrine as articulated in *Baker v. Carr* to bar the Supreme Court from adjudicating the matter. It argued that the question of whether 31 December should be declared a public holiday was a non-justiciable political question.

In a five to four decision, the majority of the Supreme Court led by Justice Adade rejected the government's argument. It reasoned that since the "… Constitution, 1992 itself was essentially a political document because every matter of interpretation or enforcement which may arise from it was bound to have political dimension,"[20] this cannot be a basis to deprive the Supreme Court of its judicial powers. Further, it explained that the Supreme Court has jurisdiction to determine political questions in exercising its constitutional duty of enforcing or interpreting the Constitution under Articles 2(1)[21] and 130.[22] According to the Supreme Court, the question whether the celebration of the 31 December seizure of power from the then Government of Ghana was in conflict with the Constitution 1992 and required an interpretation of the Constitution, which the Supreme Court had jurisdiction to determine. It held that the political question doctrine was not applicable in Ghana because the Supreme Court, as the ultimate interpreter of the Constitution 1992, pursuant to Articles 2(1) and 130, may lawfully decide controversies of a political nature.

---

19 *New Patriotic Party v. Attorney-General,* 1993-1994.

20 *Id.,* pp. 38 and 65.

21 Section 2 of the Constitution of the Republic of Ghana, 1992, provides as follows: "(1) A person who alleges that – (a) an enactment or anything contained in or done under the authority of that or any other enactment; or (b) any act or omission of any person; is inconsistent with, or is in contravention of a provision of this Constitution, may bring an action in the Supreme Court for a declaration to that effect."

22 Section 130 of the Constitution provides in pertinent as follows: "The Supreme Court shall have exclusive original jurisdiction in – (a) all matters relating to the enforcement or interpretation of this Constitution; and (b) all matters arising as to whether an enactment was made in excess of the powers conferred on Parliament or any other authority or person by law or under this Constitution."

There is a general agreement among scholars that nothing prevents courts from deciding political controversies; yet, cases that are too political fall within the political question doctrine.[23]

Throwing his weight behind the majority decision, Justice Amua-Sekyi made the following observation about the reach of the Supreme Court's powers under the Constitution of Ghana:

> It was also said that the issue is a political one that the plaintiff ought to have made its complaint to Parliament… However, there is nothing to stop it from making a legal issue of it and coming to this court for redress… As the fundamental or basic law, the Constitution, 1992 controls all legislation and determines their validity. It is for the courts as the guardians of legality to ensure that all agencies of the state keep within their lawful bounds.[24]

Evidently, Justice Amua-Sekyi views Supreme Court powers as being broad enough to cover political questions.

On the other hand, the minority view was that the issue before the Supreme Court was a political question and more appropriate for the executive and legislature to determine. The minority opinion in *New Patriotic Party v. Attorney-General* converges with Justice Sotomayor's view in *Zivotofsky* that it is possible for ordinary legislation to present a non-justiciable political question. In her powerful dissenting judgement, Justice Bamford-Addo reasoned that "the fixing of a date for celebration as a public holiday is a policy decision of the government, an executive act and can be changed."[25] According to Justice Bamford-Addo, any government has the freedom to adopt a policy choice, through legislation, to scrap or insert 31 December from the list of public holidays in the legislation.[26] Since the fixing of 31 December was a policy choice, the minority opinion was that the political

23 *See*, LaTourette, 2008, p. 282 (arguing that the political question doctrine can be used to avoid deciding cases that are too complicated or politically charged); A. Fickes, 'Private Warriors and Political Questions: A Critical Analysis of the Political Question Doctrine's Application to Suits Against Private Military Contractors', *Temple Law Review*, Vol. 82, No. 2, 2009, p. 525 (arguing that the Supreme Court's willingness to determine the most politically contentious issues in recent years demonstrates that the courts will not shy away from resolving legal disputes merely because they touch upon politically controversial issues); C. Chase, 'The Political Question Doctrine: Preventing the Challenge of US Foreign Policy in 767 Third Avenue Associates v. Consulate General', *Catholic University Law Review*, Vol. 50, No. 4, 2001, p. 1045; A. Ekpu, 'Judicial Response to Coup De'tat: A Reply to Tayyab Mahmud (From a Nigerian Perspective)', *Ariz J Int'l & Comp Law*, Vol. 13, No. 1, 1996, p. 1; B. Free, 'Awaiting Does v. Exxon Mobile Corp: Advocating the Cautious Use of Executive Opinions in Alien Tort Claims Act Litigation', *Pacific Rim Law & Policy Journal*, Vol. 12, No. 2, 2003, p. 467 and S. Willig, 'Politics as Usual? The Political Question Doctrine in Holocaust Litigation', *Cardozo Law Review*, Vol. 32, No. 2, 2010, p. 723.

24 *New Patriotic Party v. Attorney-General*, 1993-1994, p. 130.

25 *Id.*, p. 153.

26 *Id.*

question doctrine barred the Supreme Court from deciding the matter as a means of demonstrating respect to the other arms of government. In his support for the minority judgement, Justice Archer defended the political question doctrine and reasoned that:

> I think if the order is granted, it would amount to judicial officiousness – poking our noses into the affairs of Parliament and intermeddling with the prerogative of the executive by directing the government not to spend moneys approved by Parliament. Such a move clearly amounts to a violation of the doctrine of separation of powers which is the core of our Constitution.[27]

It is important to point out that while siding with the majority on the question of 31 December celebrations, Justice Hayfron-Benjamin differed with the majority justices on the broad question of whether the political question doctrine was applicable in Ghana. Justice Hayfron-Benjamin confidently stated that:

> The whole principle of a non-justiciable political question is an American formulation. While it may be relevant to our situation because it is a development from a written democratic Constitution, I think there are so few parallels between the two Constitutions on this principle that its application to our Constitution, 1992 must necessarily be limited...It seems to me therefore that by the nature of our Constitution, 1992 the principle of a non-justiciable political question can only arise where the Constitution expressly commits a particular responsibility to some arm of government. A clear example may be the power of the President to appoint ambassadors under article 74(1) of the Constitution, 1992.[28]

Notwithstanding the ruling in *New Patriotic Party v. Attorney-General*, the Supreme Court in *Ghana Bar Association*[29] categorically held that the political question doctrine was applicable in Ghana.

27 *Id.*, p. 52.
28 *Id.*, pp. 178-179.
29 *Ghana Bar Association v. Attorney-General*, 2003-2004.

3.4 The Appointment of a Chief Justice

In *Ghana Bar Association*, the President, acting under Articles 91(1)[30] and 144(1)[31] of the Constitution of Ghana, nominated Justice Abban as the Chief Justice for approval by Parliament. In turn, Parliament approved the nomination and Justice Abban was duly appointed by the President on 22 February 1995. The Ghana Bar Association (GBA) objected to this appointment. It brought a lawsuit before the Supreme Court in which it sought a declaration that Justice Abban was not a person of high moral character and proven integrity and thus not appointable as Chief Justice. The GBA also sought a declaration that the appointment of Justice Abban by the President as Chief Justice, as well as the advice of the Council of State and the approval by Parliament of his nomination, was unconstitutional.

The government defended the case by challenging the jurisdiction of the Supreme Court to hear the matter. Anyone who is familiar with Barkow's work on the political question doctrine would understand that the reason the threshold question raised by the government was directed at the courts' jurisdiction is premised on the political question theory that an important "judicial task at the outset of every case is to make a threshold determination as to whether the Constitution gives some interpretive authority to the political branches on the question being raised and to specify the boundaries of what has been allocated elsewhere."[32] Barkow correctly argues that:

> just as a statute may give more or less interpretive power to agencies, the constitution also creates different degrees of interpretive power in the political branches. Similarly, just as a statute may commit a question entirely to agency discretion, so, too, does the constitution recognize that some questions rest within the absolute discretion of the political branches.[33]

In line with Barkow's thinking, the government's main argument in *Ghana Bar Association* was that by virtue of the principle of separation of powers enshrined in the Constitution 1992, the appointment of Justice Abban as Chief Justice was a non-justiciable political question specifically committed to the President, Council of State and Parliament. On the

---

30 Section 91(1) of the Constitution of the Republic of Ghana, 1992, reads as follows: "The Council of State shall consider and advise the President or any other authority in respect of any appointment which is required by this Constitution or any other law to be made in accordance with the advice of, or in consultation with, the Council of State."

31 Section 144(1) of the Constitution of the Republic of Ghana, 1992 reads as follows: "The Chief Justice shall be appointed by the President acting in consultation with the Council of State and with the approval of Parliament."

32 Barkow, 2002, p. 239.

33 *Id.*

contrary, the GBA argued that the Supreme Court, pursuant to Articles 295 and 125(3) of the Constitution, has the final judicial power to determine whether any person or authority has properly performed his, her or its functions under the Constitution or any other law. As a result, the political question doctrine was not applicable to Ghana.[34]

Justice Kpegah, who wrote for the majority, held that the political question doctrine was applicable to Ghana. He reasoned that the doctrine was implicit in the concept of the separation of powers, where certain functions are committed to a specific branch of government. In such a constitutional design, he reasoned, a political question cannot evolve into a judicial question.[35] In support of Justice Kpegah, Weinberg has argued that "the interpretation of law cannot be confided exclusively to the judiciary" but must be understood as a shared responsibility with other branches.[36] To a great extent, this view is shared by Barkow. In her view, "the political question doctrine reflects a constitutional design that does not require the judiciary to supply the substantive content of all constitutional provisions."[37]

Consistent with these views, Justice Kpegah held that Article 144 of the Constitution committed the appointment of the Chief Justice to the executive branch and legislative branch, and that any attempt by the Supreme Court to claim a power to be able to declare null and void the appointment of the Chief Justice would justly be described as a usurpation of the constitutional functions of both the executive and legislative branches.[38] Kpegah was convinced that by assuming the jurisdiction to adjudicate the matter, the Supreme Court would be engaging in policy determination for which judicially manageable standards were not available.[39] In other words, by assuming jurisdiction, the Supreme Court would

34 Defenders of the political question doctrine oppose arguments like this one raised by the GBA, which presuppose that the judiciary has the final say on the interpretation of a constitution. They argue that the judiciary shares interpretive authority with the other branches of government. *See*, Mulhern, 1988; Bickel, 1962, pp. 183-197.

35 *Ghana Bar Association*, 2003-2004, p. 294.

36 *See*, L. Weinberg, 'Political Questions and the Guarantee Clause', *University of Colorado Law Review*, Vol. 65, No. 4, 1994, p. 889.

37 Barkow, 2002, p. 239.

38 *Ghana Bar Association*, 2003-2004, p. 301.

39 In Nigeria appellate courts have taken a view similar to that of Ghanaian courts. *See*, *Onuoha v. Okafor* (holding that the lack of satisfactory criteria for a judicial determination of a political question is one of the dominant considerations in determining whether a question falls within the category of political questions); and *Balarabe Musa v. Auta Hamza* 247 (holding that the impeachment of a State governor was a political question not appropriate for judicial review. Justice Ademola reasoned that "impeachment proceedings are political and for the court to enter into the political thicket as the invitation made to it clearly implies in my view asking its gates and its walls to be painted with mud; and the throne of justice from where its judgments are delivered polished with mire."). *Also see*, M. Mhango, 'Separation of Powers and the Application of the Political Question Doctrine in Uganda', *African Journal of Legal Studies*, 2013, p. 249 (discussing the development and application of the political question doctrine in Uganda).

be supplying substantive content to the constitutional provisions concerning the appointment of a Chief Justice, which, in his view, was not constitutionally permissible.[40]

In addressing the general question of the applicability of the political question doctrine in Ghana, Justice Kpegah reasoned that there were sufficient local authorities to support its application,[41] and since the political question doctrine was a concept that emanated from the notion of the separation of powers, the Supreme Court ought to endeavour to apply it. Justice Kpegah laid down three common characteristics by which to determine whether a case raises a political question in Ghana, namely: (1) does the issue involve the resolution of questions committed by the text of the Constitution to a coordinate branch of government, (2) would a resolution of the question demand that a court move beyond areas of judicial expertise and (3) do prudential considerations counsel against judicial intervention.[42]

Justice Kpegah criticized and dismissed the proposition made by Justice Adade in the *New Patriotic Party v. Attorney-General* that the political question doctrine does not apply to the US Supreme Court, which reasoning Justice Adade had employed to deny the application of the doctrine in that case. In Kpegah's view, Justice Adade's majority opinion in the *New Patriotic Party v. Attorney-General* took a very simplistic view of a sophisticated legal concept of the political question doctrine.[43] In support of Justice Kpegah, Justice Hayfron-Benjamin commented that the political question doctrine "… is certainly one of the grounds upon which the jurisdiction of this court may be ousted."[44] He went on to observe that the judgement in *Tuffour*, which is cited as authority for the political question doctrine in Ghana, "… reached conclusions which accord with Justice Brennan's dictum in *Baker v. Carr.*"[45] Even though Justice Kpegah in *Ghana Bar Association* recognized the application of the political question doctrine in Ghana, he accepted the limits of its application and held that the mere fact that a lawsuit seeks the protection of a political right does not mean that it presents a non-justiciable political question.[46] The decision in *Ghana Bar Association* was considered in *Mensah v. Attorney-General,* in which the Supreme Court reached a different conclusion about the application of the political question doctrine in that case.

---

40 Barkow, 2002, p. 239.

41 *Tuffour* (Justice Sowah, opinion); *New Patriotic Party v. Attorney-General* (Archer, opinion; and Justice Hayfron-Benjamin, opinion).

42 *Ghana Bar Association*, 2003-2004, p. 300.

43 *Id.*, p. 294.

44 *Amidu*, 2001-2002, p. 148, citing *Ghana Bar Association.*

45 *Id.*

46 *Ghana Bar Association*, 2003-2004, p. 295.

3.5 Dismissal of a Cabinet Minister

In *Mensah v. Attorney General,* the term of office of President Rawlings had ended on 6 January 1997. The next day, President Rawlings, who had been re-elected as President in the previous month, was sworn in as President for a second term of four years. Soon after the swearing in, it was announced that the President had decided to retain in office some of his previous ministers and deputy ministers. It was also announced that since the appointment of those retained ministers had been approved by the previous Parliament, there was no need for them to be reapproved by the new Parliament. That decision was impugned by the opposition in Parliament. Subsequent to this announcement, it was also announced that one of the retained ministers, the Minister of Finance, would appear before Parliament to present the 1997 Budget Statement. Before the minister could make the presentation, the leader of the opposition political party, Mr Mensah, filed a lawsuit in the Supreme Court. Mr Mensah asked the Supreme Court to declare, among other things, that the Constitution prevented anyone from acting as a minister without the prior approval of the newly elected second Parliament. The government defended the lawsuit by arguing, *inter alia,* that the process by which Parliament exercised its powers, such as the approval of ministerial nominations, could not be examined by the judiciary under the political question doctrine.

The Supreme Court, as per Justice Acquah, held that every presidential nominee for ministerial appointment, whether retained or new, required the prior approval of Parliament. Justice Acquah reasoned that unlike the US Supreme Court, which derives its power of judicial review through jurisprudential authority, the Supreme Court of Ghana derives its power of judicial review from Articles 2 and 130 of the Constitution. Any limitation on that power, he argued, would have to find support in the language of those articles. On this point, Barkow has remarked that although judicial review is the norm, as Justice Acquah suggests, there are exceptions that are expressed in particular provisions in a constitution.[47] In the American context, Barkow asserts that a constitution carves out certain categories of issues that may be resolved as a matter of legislative or executive discretion.[48] Under this view of the political question doctrine, judicial abstinence is seen as constitutionally required and not discretionary.[49]

---

47 Barkow, 2002, pp. 247-248.

48 *Id.*

49 *Id.*; Wechsler, 1961, p. 9 (arguing that the only judgement that may lead to an abstention from decision is that the Constitution has committed the determination of the issue to another agency of government than the courts); M. Gouin, '*United States v. Alvarez-Machain*: Waltzing With the Political Question Doctrine', *Connecticut Law Review,* Vol. 26, No. 2, 1994, p. 797 (discussing the classical version of the political question doctrine and noting that the *Constitution* committed some constitutional issues to the political branches) and T. Cutaiar, '*Lane Ex Rel Lane v. Halliburton*: The Fifth Circuit's Recent Treatment of the Political Question Doctrine and What It Could Mean for *Commer v. Murphy Oil*', *Loyola Law Review,* Vol. 55, No.

However, in his analysis, Justice Acquah expressed some reservations about the political question doctrine. Specifically, he saw one potential interpretation of the doctrine that could be perceived as granting political immunity for breaches of the Constitution by the elected branches of government. In turn, he offered a preferred understanding of the doctrine, which, in his view, complied with Ghana's constitutional design and structure. I describe Acquah's preferred understanding as the compromised political question doctrine. In his characterization of this compromised version of the doctrine, Justice Acquah reasoned that:

> If by the political question doctrine, it is meant that where the Constitution allocates power or function to an authority, and that authority exercises that power or function within the parameters of that provision and the Constitution as a whole, a court has no jurisdiction to interfere with the exercise of that function, then I entirely agree that the doctrine applies in our constitutional jurisprudence. For this is what is implied in the concept of separation of powers. But if by the doctrine, it is meant that even where the authority exercises that power in violation of the constitutional provision, a court has no jurisdiction to interfere because it is the Constitution which allocated that power to that authority, then I emphatically disagree.[50]

In my own view, Justice Acquah's statement above is a perfect expression of what Cowper and Sossin identified as the main difficulty with the political question doctrine, which lies in the failure by some jurists to distinguish between:

> ...questions which the judiciary must resolve, no matter how politically sensitive, and those cases where the judiciary should decline to address the issue on the basis that it is not a proper question for adjudication by the courts.[51]

2, 2009, p. 398 (arguing that the political question doctrine is a product of constitutional interpretation rather than judicial discretion).

50 *Mensah v. Attorney-General*, 2003-2004, p. 368.

51 C.D. Geoffrey & L. Sossin, 'Does Canada Need a Political Questions Doctrine?', *The Supreme Court Law Review*, Vol. 16, No. 16, 2002, p. 343. *Also see*, Price, 2006, pp. 323-354 and J. May, '*Climate Change, Constitutional Consignment, and the Political Question', Doctrine' Denver University Law Review*, Vol. 85, No. 4, 2008, p. 953 (arguing that a political issue and a political question are two different things. The former allows judicial oversight and the latter suggests that overriding separation of powers concerns warrant judicial restraint).

It is possible that I have given Justice Acquah an unfair reading of his position; nevertheless, the failure by some jurists to appreciate the significance of the distinction highlighted by Cowper and Sossin is a common phenomenon.[52]

In explaining the distinction that must be made in cases involving political questions, Redish offered a useful suggestion that (while made in the American context during the 1980s) addresses Justice Acquah's assertion above. Redish postulates that in those cases that raise separation of powers concerns and should be dismissed, the judiciary:

> is not abdicating its power to interpret and enforce a constitutional provision; rather it is simply holding that nothing in the Constitution directs the exercise as to how to make such determinations.[53]

Redish further maintains that:

> when the Constitution's framers intended that one of the political branches has discretion to act without principles, the document effectively says so, by vesting decision making power in those branches without simultaneously indicating how that power must be exercised.[54]

In the South African case of *Doctors for Life International,* Justice Ngcobo accepts the distinction advocated by Redish. Ngcobo explains that:

> It seems to me therefore that a distinction should be drawn between constitutional provisions that impose obligations that are readily ascertainable and are unlikely to give rise to disputes, on the one hand, and those provisions which impose the primary obligation on Parliament to determine what is required of it, on the other. In the case of the former, a determination whether those obligations have been fulfilled does not call upon a court to pronounce upon a sensitive aspect of the separation of powers … It simply decides the formal question whether there was, for example, the two-thirds majority required to pass the legislation. By contrast, where the obligation requires Parliament to determine in the first place what is necessary to fulfil its obligation, a review by a court whether that obligation has been fulfilled, trenches on the autonomy

52 See my discussions in Chapter 7 and D. Moseneke, 'A Journey from the Heart of Apartheid Darkness Towards a Just Society: Salient Features of the Budding Constitutionalism and Jurisprudence of South Africa', *Georgetown* Law Journal, Vol. 101, No. 3, 2013, p. 749.

53 Redish, 1984, p. 1039. *Also see, New Patriotic Party v. Attorney-General* (Justice Adade) (arguing that "to refuse to hear a constitutional case on the ground that it is political is to abdicate our responsibilities under the Constitution and breach its provisions").

54 Redish, 1984, p. 1048.

> of Parliament to regulate its own affairs and thus the principle of separation of powers.[55]

If the political question doctrine can be understood in this way, it becomes easier to see the flaw in Justice Acquah's stance. In his pronouncement above, Justice Acquah addresses and accepts the application of the political question doctrine in circumstances where he claims the Constitution 1992 allocates power to the political branches and indicates the parameters for the exercise of such power. However, Justice Acquah fails to address the instances where the Constitution 1992 allocates power or discretion to the political branches without at the same time indicating the parameters of that discretion or substantive content of that power. By this failure, Justice Acquah creates the impression that in those other instances the judiciary will have a final say concerning those constitutional questions. Barkow disagrees with this suggestion and correctly argues that the constitution's structure and the limited powers of the judiciary require political branches to decide constitutional questions in many instances, and in such instances, they have the same authority to make decisions as the judiciary itself has in other instances.[56]

Perhaps Justice Acquah would find consolation in the classical political question theory, which views the political question doctrine as a product of constitutional interpretation rather than of judicial discretion.[57] In this regard, Professor Redish was correct in noting that it is:

> … vital to distinguish between appropriate substantive deference – in which the judiciary, while retaining power to render final decisions on the meaning of the constitutional limits, nevertheless takes into account the need for expertise or quick action – and unacceptable total procedural deference, where the court concludes simply that resort to the judiciary constitutes the wrong procedure, because the decision is exclusively that of the political branches.[58]

To some extent, Redish's arguments and comments were directed towards the views of Justice Acquah and other like-minded jurists.

55 *Doctors for Life International*, at paras. 25-26.

56 Barkow, 2002, p. 320.

57 *See*, Scharpf, 1966, p. 538 (explaining that the basic idea of the political question doctrine is that it is an outcome of constitutional interpretation); M. Kelly, 'Revisiting and Revising the Political Question: *Lane v. Halliburton* and the Need to Adopt a Case-Specific Political Question Analysis for Private Military Contractor Cases', *Miss College Law Review*, Vol. 29, 2010, p. 224 (discussing the idea that the purpose of the political question doctrine is to bar claims that threaten the separation-of-powers design of the federal government, and thus a determination as to the justiciability of a claim is a delicate exercise in constitutional interpretation, not merely plugging facts into factors.); Barkow, 2002, p. 249; *Marbury v. Madison*, 1803, pp. 167, 170-171.

58 Redish, 1984, pp. 1048-1049.

Notwithstanding Justice Acquah's omission to distinguish between justiciable and non-justiciable questions, there is something to celebrate about his perspective. There is no doubt that he endorses the political question doctrine in Ghana and accepts, like some commentators, that certain constitutional provisions require limited deference to the other branches, although Acquah has reservations about accepting that in cases involving political questions absolute deference is demanded.[59] I describe Justice Acquah's position as a compromise political question doctrine because he accepts the need to balance the judiciary's role in checking unconstitutional government action with its duty not to usurp the political power exercised by the people through the executive and legislative branches.[60] The problem, as this book attempts to demonstrate, is that Justice Acquah, at the time of his writing, had not yet fully thought out the practicalities of this balance, or may not have been convinced that the facts in *Mensah v. Attorney-General* presented an opportunity to develop that balance.

Justice Aikins agreed with Acquah's opinion in *Mensah v. Attorney-General* and wrote his own concurring opinion. Aikins dismissed the government's contention and held that the Supreme Court was entitled to decide questions of a political nature "since in Ghana it is the Constitution and not Parliament which is supreme".[61] It is important to point out what Justices Acquah and Aikins do not propose or accept, which is that the Supreme Court has authority to determine cases raising political questions. Instead, they maintained that the Supreme Court is entitled to hear and determine questions of a political nature. There is a difference between the two positions. The determination of questions of a political nature or with political implications has never been barred by the political question doctrine. Conversely, the political question doctrine is concerned with political questions, which cannot be answered by the application of the law.

Further, Aikins held that any act of Parliament, which is in conflict with the Constitution, can be declared null and void even though the Act deals with a political question.[62] While the political question doctrine was dismissed by the majority as not applicable in the case of *Mensah v. Attorney-General*, in his concurring opinion Justice Aikins conceded

59 Barkow, 2002, p. 319 (arguing that the political question doctrine is part of a spectrum of deference to the political branches' interpretation of the *Constitution*. Barkow claims that the political question doctrine requires the judiciary to determine as a threshold matter in all cases whether the question before it has been assigned by the *Constitution* to another branch of government. This initial determination of how much deference is appropriate serves a valuable function because it reminds the judiciary that not all constitutional questions require independent judicial interpretation) and Mulhern, 1988, pp. 124-127 (discussing dissenting voices against the judicial monopoly and emphasizing equal authority among the three branches on constitutional matters. Mulhern argues that there is no obvious reason why a court's assertion of judicial power should be any more authoritative than a President's assertion of executive power. Both are part of our constitutional tradition, and there is no apparent way to establish any priority between them).

60 Savitzky, 2011, p. 2043.

61 *Mensah v. Attorney-General*, 2003-2004, p. 344.

62 *Mensah v. Attorney-General*, 1996-1997, p. 344.

that the doctrine was increasingly creeping into Ghanaian legal jurisprudence.[63] To further enhance this concession and solidify the political question doctrine in Ghana, Aikins distinguished the judgement in *Tuffuor*,[64] the first case that applied the political question theory in Ghana, from *Mensah v. Attorney-General.*[65] This is an important development because as one scholar has observed, *Tuffuor,* together with the dicta from the opinions of Justices Archer and Hayfron-Benjamin in *New Patriotic Party,* has been cited as authority in support for the application of the political question doctrine in Ghana.[66] In other words, by distinguishing *Mensah v. Attorney-General* from the judgement of *Tuffuor*, Justice Aikins' pronouncement can be read as bringing clarity in the law that the political question doctrine is indeed applicable in Ghana.

3.6 A Legislative Decision to Retain a Member of Parliament

The above jurisprudence reflects the Supreme Court's efforts to formulate a consistent political question doctrine for Ghana.[67] This jurisprudence has influenced the lower court's application of the doctrine. One of the most recent lower court cases applying the political question doctrine is *Asare v. Attorney-General.*[68] In this case, a Member of Parliament Mr Eric Amoateng was arrested and detained in the United States for unlawfully importing narcotics into that country. Under the rules of Parliament, Mr Amoateng sought leave of absence from Parliament, which was granted from 17 to 24 November 2005.

In addition, Parliament's Committee on Privileges considered the reasonableness of Mr Amoateng's absence from Parliament. On the strength of the criminal law principle that everyone is presumed innocent until proven guilty by a court of law, and the need to extend compassion to Amoateng due to the slow pace of his criminal trial in the United States, the Committee on Privileges recommended that Parliament allow Amoateng the required time to defend his criminal charges.

After some debate, Parliament approved this recommendation and decided to grant Amoateng a dispensation to be absent from Parliament indefinitely. This decision was challenged by the plaintiff, Professor Stephen Asare. The plaintiff's claim was that since the Speaker permitted Amoateng to be absent from 17 to 24 November only, Amoateng's

63 *Id.*, p. 341.

64 *Tuffuor v. Attorney-General* [1980] GLR 637.

65 *Mensah v. Attorney-General*, 1996-1997, p. 348.

66 *See,* Bimpong-Buta, 2005, p. 129.

67 At least Justice Kpegah conceded that the Supreme Court has not been consistent in its application of the political question doctrine and other justiciability principles derived from the United States. He observes that the doctrine was applied in *Tuffour* without the court specifically saying so, but rejected in the *New Patriotic Party v. Attorney-General* and subsequently applied in *Ghana Bar Association*, where the *New Patriotic Party v. Attorney-General* was criticized. *See, Amidu*, 2001-2002, pp. 145-147.

68 *Asare v. Attorney-General*, 2006.

seat became vacant by operation of law and neither the Speaker nor Parliament could grant any other dispensation. Consequently, the High Court, in this case, was seized to determine whether Parliament had the authority to grant a member of Parliament a dispensation to be absent from Parliament indefinitely.[69]

In the light of the above, the High Court had to determine at least two important related questions: firstly, whether the parliamentary seat of Amoateng became vacant by operation of law, and secondly, whether Parliament's decision to grant Amoateng a dispensation to be absent indefinitely from Parliament could be called into question on legal grounds as being unreasonable and unlawful. Justice Ayebi held that the political question doctrine applied in this case. In endorsing Justice Acquah's opinion in *Mensah v. Attorney-General*, Justice Ayebi reasoned that:

> it is Parliament which as the legislative arm of government which has been mandated by the Constitution to determine the reasonableness or otherwise of [Amoateng's] explanation through the Committee on Privileges.[70]

Justice Ayebi found that this is what Parliament had done in this case. In his view "the decision of Parliament ... will stand the test of time. That apart this decision is a political question *intravires* the Constitution and therefore not subject to judicial scrutiny."[71]

To best illustrate the suitability of applying the political question doctrine in this case, Justice Ayebi employed the following hypothetical scenario and said:

> ... supposing [Amoateng] was involved in a fatal accident on this trip and he was only able to inform Mr. Speaker long after fifteen sittings of Parliament. Doctors attending to him determined that it will take some time for him to recover. Should the court declare an indefinite dispensation granted [Amoateng] in such circumstances by parliament as unreasonable? Consequent upon that, should the court declare the seat of [Amoateng] vacant? I think not.[72]

In short, Justice Ayebi's reasoning was that since Parliament found Amoateng's reasons for absence reasonable and granted indefinite dispensation in the particular circumstances of his case, that decision should not be subjected to judicial scrutiny.

Although *Asare v. Attorney-General* has been criticized, this criticism has centred on the perceived failure of Justice Ayebi to properly justify why the political question doctrine

69 As Barkow puts it, the threshold question for every court should be to determine if the questions before it have been assigned by a constitution to another branch of government. Barkow, 2002, p. 244.

70 *Asare v. Attorney-General*, 2006.

71 *Id.*

72 *Id.*

should have determined the case rather than on whether the doctrine is applicable in Ghana at all.[73] Simply put, Professor Asare, who has expressed the most critical views against the decision in *Asare v. Attorney-General*, agrees that the political question doctrine is applicable in Ghana, but that a court should offer convincing reasons for its application in any given case.[74] What seems to ignite Professor Asare's critical views on *Asare v. Attorney-General* is that Justice Ayebi's opinion does not justify or explain the rationale for allowing the political question doctrine to swallow the court's explicit powers in Article 99(1)(a) of the Constitution of Ghana.[75]

Furthermore, Asare criticizes Justice Ayebi's failure to apply the three-prong test announced in *Ghana Bar Association* to the facts in the case. Presumably, had this been done Justice Ayebi would have been forced to justify the application of the political question doctrine in the case.[76] Asare's academic criticism is reflective of the prevailing discourse around the doctrine in Ghana, namely that it forms part of Ghanaian law and *Ghana Bar Association* articulated how it ought to be applied. Therefore, it seems clear from this discourse that the critical views against the recent application of the political question doctrine are not dismissive of the doctrine but are rather directed at its proper application.

3.7 The Justiciability of Directive Principles and State Policy

What is clear from the above analysis is that the application of the political question doctrine requires an acceptance that there are certain constitutional questions or provisions that are not justiciable in Ghana. This is why the doctrine is controversial. Nonetheless, the issue of the justiciability or not of certain provisions of the Constitution of Ghana has been contested since the advent of constitutionalism in Ghana.[77] As constitutional commentators have observed, one of the areas where this issue has come to the fore is in relation to Chapter 6 of the Constitution.[78] In particular, commentators note that Article 34(1), the opening of Chapter 6, creates some ambiguity.[79] The article provides that:

> 34 (1) The Directive Principles of State Policy contained in this Chapter shall guide all citizens, Parliament, the President, the Judiciary, the Council of State,

73 Asare, 2006.

74 *Id.*

75 *Id.*

76 *Asare v. Attorney-General*, 2006.

77 K. Quashigah, 'The 1992 Constitution of Ghana', 1992, www.icla.up.ac.za/images/country_reports/ghana_country_report.pdf (last accessed 15 December 2016).

78 *Id.* and A. Atupare, 'Reconciling Socioeconomic Rights and Directive Principles with a Fundamental Law of Reason in Ghana and Nigeria', *Harvard Human Rights Journal*, Vol. 27, 2014, p. 71.

79 *Id.*, p. 86.

> the Cabinet, political parties and other bodies and persons in applying or interpreting this Constitution or any other law and in taking and implementing any policy decisions, for the establishment of a just and free society.

The observation from scholars is that the ambiguity arose from the Consultative Assembly's reliance on the *Report of the Committee of Experts on the Proposal for a Draft Constitution Ghana* to conclude that the Directive Principles in Chapter 6 should not be justiciable.[80] The rationale for the inclusion of these Directives Principles in Chapter 6 was explained by the Committee of Experts as follows:

> 94. The NCD report speaks of the need to include in the new Constitution core principles around which national political, social and economic life will revolve. This is precisely what the Directive Principles of State Policy seeks to do. Against the background of the achievements and failings of our post-independence experience, and our aspirations for the future as a people, the principles attempt to set the stage for the enunciation of political, civil, economic and social rights of our people. They may thus be regarded as spelling out in broad strokes the spirit or conscience of the constitution. The Committee used Chapter Four of the 1979 Constitution as a basis for its deliberations on this subject.
>
> 95. By tradition Directive Principles are not justiciable; even so, there are at least two good reasons for including them in a constitution. First, Directive Principles enumerate a set of fundamental objectives which a people expect all bodies and persons that make or execute public policy to strive to achieve. In the present proposals, one novelty is the explicit inclusion of political parties among the bodies expected to observe the principles. The reason for this is that political parties significantly influence government policy. A second justification for including Directive Principles in a constitution is that, taken together, they constitute, in the long run, a sort of barometer by which the people could measure the performance of their government. In effect they provide goals for legislative programmes and a guide for judicial interpretation.
>
> 96. On the basis of the foregoing considerations, the Committee proposes as follows: The Directive Principles of State Policy are for the guidance of Parlia-

80 Report of the Committee of Experts on the Proposal for a Draft Constitution Ghana (1991) (hereinafter, as Committee of Experts) 97-97; *New Patriotic Party v. Attorney-General,* 1993-1994, p. 149. In South Africa, a similar uncertainty arose over whether the death penalty was permissible under the new Constitution. The court concluded that the framers of the Constitution left it to the court to decide the issue. *See, S v. Makwanyane and Another* 1995 (3) SA 391, at paras. 5, 125 and 392.

> ment, the President, the Council of Ministers, Political Parties and other bodies and persons in making and applying public policy for the establishment of a just and free society. The Principles should not of and by themselves be legally enforceable by any Court. The Court should, however, have regard to the said Principles in interpreting any laws based on them.[81]

According to some scholars, the problem is that the final text of the Constitution 1992 omitted to expressly declare that the Directive Principles are non-justiciable, which left open the question of whether that omission points to a conclusion of non-justiciability.[82] Indeed, that omission has attracted distinct judicial pronouncements about the constitutional status of the Directive Principles in Ghana. In this section, these pronouncements and how they relate to the application of the political question doctrine in Ghana are examined.

One of the earliest judicial pronouncements on the constitutional status of the Directive Principles was made in the *New Patriotic Party v. Attorney-General.* As Atupare has observed, the judgement in the *New Patriotic Party v. Attorney-General* on the justiciability of the Directive Principles was less dynamic.[83] On the part of the majority, only Justice Adade openly tackled the issue and said that:

> I do not subscribe to the view that chapter 6 of the Constitution, 1992 is not justiciable: it is. First, the Constitution, 1992 as a whole is a justiciable document. If any part is to be non-justiciable, the Constitution, 1992 itself must say so. I have not seen anything in chapter 6 or in the Constitution generally, which tells me that chapter 6 is not justiciable. The evidence to establish the non-justiciability must be internal to the Constitution, 1992 not otherwise ... we cannot add words to the Constitution, 1992 in order to change its meaning...The very tenor of chapter 6 of the Constitution, 1992 supports the view that the chapter is justiciable... As far as the judiciary is concerned, I ask myself the question: How do the principles guide the judiciary in applying or interpreting the Constitution if not in the process of enforcing them?[84]

What is more, Justice Adade took issue with the conclusion by the Committee of Experts that Directive Principles are traditionally non-justiciable. In his view, under Chapter 4 of the Constitution 1979, Directive Principles were justiciable.[85] Adade noted that while the

81 *New Patriotic Party v. Attorney-General,* 1993-1994, p. 149.
82 Quashigah, 1992 and Atupare, 2014, p. 95.
83 Atupare, 2014, p. 95.
84 *New Patriotic Party v. Attorney-General,* 1993-1994, pp. 66-67.
85 *Id.*, p. 69.

debates in the Consultative Assembly may demonstrate some intention to make the Directive Principles non-justiciable, he concluded that "the intention was not carried into the Constitution, 1992. The debates themselves are inadmissible to contradict the language of the Constitution."[86]

On the other hand, two justices wrote minority opinions on the justiciability of the Directive Principles in the *New Patriotic Party v. Attorney-General.* Justice Abban found that the Directive Principles were not relevant to the subject-matter before the court, and that reference to them was totally misconceived.[87] Similarly, in her opinion, Justice Bamford-Addo unambiguously pronounced and reasoned as follows concerning the Directive Principles that they:

> are not justiciable and the plaintiff has no cause of action based on these articles. Those principles were included in the Constitution, for the guidance of all citizens, Parliament, the President, judiciary, the Council of State, the cabinet, political parties or other bodies and persons in applying or interpreting the Constitution,1992 or any other law and in taking and implementing any policy decisions, for the establishment of a just and free society. The judiciary is to be guided, while interpreting the Constitution, 1992 by only the specific provisions under chapter 6.[88]

Based on the above pronouncements, Atupare correctly commented that "an important tension arises from the observance of Directive Principles as legal duties of all government agencies and public officials while courts are unable to directly enforce them."[89] Atupare is critical of the fact that no clear majority or minority view on the justiciability of Directive Principles emerged in the *New Patriotic Party v. Attorney-General* because several justices addressed or omitted to conclusively address the issue. He correctly points out that:

> it is unclear whether members of the majority subscribed to the open declarations of Justice Adade that Directive Principles are justiciable or if Justice Bamford-Addo's rebuttal of that claim was supported by the other members of the minority.[90]

Beneath Atupare's criticism is the notion that the issue of the justiciability of Directive Principles remained uncertain after the *New Patriotic Party v. Attorney-General.* This is

86 *Id.*
87 *Id.*, p. 102.
88 *Id.*, p. 149.
89 Atupare, 2014, p. 96.
90 *Id.*

clear from his submission that "with Justice Adade and Justice Bamford-Addo acting alone in advancing their respective views, the case did not reach a determination of whether the Directive Principles are justiciable."[91]

Atupare's concerns were short-lived because later, in *New Patriotic Party v. Attorney-General (CIBA)*,[92] the Supreme Court revisited the issue of the justiciability of Directive Principles and clarified the law. In *New Patriotic Party v. Attorney-General (CIBA)*, the Supreme Court ruled that Directive Principles are not justiciable. Justices Ampiah and Akuffor, who wrote concurring opinions, openly found that Directive Principles are not justiciable, whereas Justice Atuguba described them as mere rules of construction.[93] Justice Bamford-Addo, who wrote for the majority, had a slightly nuanced view to the proposition that Directive Principles are not justiciable. She reasoned that:

> ... there are particular instances where some provisions of the Directive Principles form an integral part of some of the enforceable rights because either they qualify them or can be held to be rights in themselves. In those instances, they are of themselves justiciable also. Where those principles are read in conjunction with other enforceable provisions of the Constitution, by reason of the fact that the courts are mandated to apply them, they are justiciable. Further where any provision under chapter Six dealing with the Directive Principles can be interpreted to mean the creation of a legal right, ie a guaranteed fundamental human right as was done in article 37(2)(a) regarding the freedom to form associations, they become justiciable and protected by the Constitution.[94]

Despite the fact that the judgement in *New Patriotic Party v. Attorney-General (CIBA)* has been welcomed by some commentators,[95] others have criticized it arguing that the majority opinions were again indecisive about the justiciability of the Directive Principles.[96]

In other jurisdictions, the position is unambiguous that Directive Principles are not justiciable both in terms of the express terms of the relevant constitutional provisions and also in terms of judicial pronouncements. To illustrate, one of the leading cases on point is *Baitsokoli and Another v. Maseru City Council*,[97] where street vendors in the Kingdom

91 *Id.*

92 *New Patriotic Party v. Attorney-General (CIBA)*, 1997 SCGLR, p. 729.

93 *Id.*, pp. 787, 791-803; Atupare, 2014, p. 97.

94 *New Patriotic Party v. Attorney-General (CIBA)*, pp. 745-747.

95 E. Nwauche, 'The Nigerian Fundamental Rights (Enforcement) Procedure Rules 2009: A Fitting Response to Problems in the Enforcement of Human Rights in Nigeria?', *African Human Rights Law Journal*, Vol. 10, No. 2, 2010, pp. 502-514 (suggesting that courts in Nigeria adopt the approach in *New Patriotic Party v. Attorney-General (CIBA)*).

96 Atupare, 2014, p. 97.

97 [2005] LSHC 25; (2004) AHRLR 195; LAC (2005-2006), p. 85.

of Lesotho challenged a government decision to remove them from the main street in the Capital City of Maseru on the grounds that it violated their rights to life and livelihood, which form part of the principles of state policy. The High Court dismissed the case and held that the scope of the right to life being the most important and precious human right as guaranteed under Section 5 of the Constitution of Lesotho 1993 is limited to physical biological existence of people as *Homo sapiens* and should not, unless circumstances warrant, be extended to include the right to livelihood. The court also held that in Lesotho, the socio-economic and cultural rights are not justiciable. In effect, the High Court correctly interpreted the necessary intendment of Section 25 of the Constitution of Lesotho, which provides that:

> The principles contained in this Chapter shall form part of the public policy of Lesotho. These principles shall not be enforceable by any court but, subject to the limits of the economic capacity and development of Lesotho, shall guide the authorities and agencies of Lesotho, and other public authorities, in the performance of their functions with a view to achieving progressively, by legislation or otherwise, the full realisation of these principles.[98]

Unlike Atupare, I find that the judgement in *New Patriotic Party v. Attorney-General (CIBA)*, read together with the wisdom of the minority views in the *New Patriotic Party v. Attorney-General*, clarified the constitutional status of Directive Principles.

In my own view, the judgement in *New Patriotic Party v. Attorney-General (CIBA)* brought clarity to the law by holding that Directive Principles are in general not justiciable except when read with other justiciable provisions of the Constitution 1992. As Justice Bamford-Addo puts it, the effect of this judgement is that:

> having regard to the test of justiciability of any particular provision under chapter 6 of the Constitution, it is my view that each case would depend on its peculiar facts.[99]

This is because the general rule is that Directive Principles are not justiciable and a court will have to determine, in every individual case, whether the exception as pronounced in *New Patriotic Party v. Attorney-General (CIBA)* applies. Clearly, despite his criticism of that judgement, Atupare concedes that the judgement was clearer than the *New Patriotic*

98 *See, Baitsokoli and Another v. Maseru City Council and Others*, at para. 28.
99 *New Patriotic Party v. Attorney-General (CIBA)*, 1997.

Party v. Attorney-General case on the question of the constitutional status of Directive Principles.[100]

Needless to say, if the judgement in *New Patriotic Party v. Attorney-General (CIBA)* is not sufficiently clear on the issue of the justiciability of Directive Principles, as suggested by Atupare, the Supreme Court decision in *Ghana Lotto Operators Association & Others v. National Lottery Authority*[101] provides a definitive answer. In *Ghana Lotto Operators Association,* the Supreme Court considered the question of whether Chapter 6 was justiciable. Justice Date-Bah, who wrote for the majority, reasoned that the:

> starting point of analysis should be that all provisions in the Constitution are justiciable, unless there are strong indications to the contrary in the text or context of the Constitution.[102]

Justice Date-Bah further explains that:

> ... there may be particular provisions in chapter 6 which do not lend themselves to enforcement by a court. The very nature of such a particular provision would rebut the presumption of justiciability in relation to it. In the absence of a demonstration that a particular provision does not lend itself to enforcement by courts, however, the enforcement by this court of the obligations imposed in chapter 6 should be insisted upon and would be a way of deepening our democracy and the liberty under law that it entails...This court will need to be flexible and imaginative in determining how the provisions of the chapter 6 are to be enforceable.[103]

While the ambiguity concerning the justiciability of the provisions of Chapter 6 has been definitively addressed in the above paragraph, Justice Date-Bah posits that there are certain provisions that do not lend themselves to enforcement by the judiciary.[104]

Justices Date-Bah and Bamford-Addo's pronouncements in *Ghana Lotto Operators Association* and *New Patriotic Party v. Attorney-General (CIBA)*, respectively, are important ways by which Ghana's Constitution can be understood to recognize the application of the political question doctrine. It is submitted that both Justice Date-Bah and Justice Bamford-Addo probably had in mind the applicability of the political question doctrine to Ghana's constitutional circumstances when they made their pronouncements above.

100 Atupare, 2014, p. 97.
101 *Ghana Lotto Operators Association v. National Lottery Authority* 2007-2008 SCGLR, p. 1088.
102 *Id.*, p. 1099.
103 *Id.*, pp. 1106-1107.
104 Quashigah, 1992, p. 14.

To put it differently, the philosophical considerations that informed their pronouncements opens the door for the potential application of the political question doctrine. This is because both justices accept the possibility of the existence of a constitutional provision, which may not be judiciary enforceable. This is essentially what happens when a classical political question doctrine is applied.

There is another point that needs to be highlighted about the pronouncements by Justices Date-Bah and Bamford-Addo, which further demonstrates why Atupare's criticism is no longer germane. Their pronouncements have brought clarity in the law as to whether Directive Principles are justiciable. The difference between their pronouncements is that Justice Date-Bah holds that there is a presumption of justiciability of the Directive Principles, which can be rebutted, while as Justice Bamford-Addo holds that the Directive Principles are presumed not justiciable unless read with other justiciable provisions of the Constitution. In essence, the two legal positions are not in conflict with each other because both of them recognize the potential that certain provisions of the Constitution may not be justiciable. To address the potential criticism from those who might argue that these pronouncements are in conflict with each other or indecisive about the constitutional status of Directive Principles, Justice Date-Bah explains further that:

> The two positions are convergent in that, if a particular provision of chapter 6 does not lend itself for enforcement by action in court, then in our preferred approach, the presumption of justiciability would be rebutted; while, similarly, the case by case approach of Bamford-Addo JSC would result in the court finding that the provision in question does not create an enforceable right. The advantage of the presumption of justiciability is that it provides a clear starting rule that is supportive of the enforcement of fundamental human rights.

Therefore, it is clear that the question of the constitutional status of Directive Principles is no longer uncertain in Ghana, and that some categories of constitutional issues may be resolved as a matter of legislative or executive discretion. This is why the political question remains relevant and part of Ghanaian law.

3.8 CONCLUSION

From the foregoing analysis, it is clear that the holding by the Supreme Court in *Ghana Bar Association* that the political question doctrine is applicable to the Constitution of Ghana has never been overruled.[105] *Ghana Bar Association* and the wisdom in *Mensah v.*

105 For a contrary view, *see*, Bimpong-Buta, *The Role of the Supreme Court*, pp. 134-135 (arguing that the criticism in *Ghana Bar Association v. Attorney-General* on the issue of the application of the political question

Attorney-General and *New Patriotic Party v. Attorney-General* demonstrate that the political question doctrine forms part of Ghanaian constitutional law and, as in other countries where it is applied, does not apply to every political case.[106] The Supreme Court has discretion (through interpretation) to determine which matters are committed to the political branches and can be discarded on that basis. In my view, *Ghana Bar Association* is a case in point where the Supreme Court found that the questions in that case were properly committed to the political branches and decided to exercise judicial abstinence by applying the political question doctrine.

It is also apparent from the case law that courts acknowledge the importance of the political question doctrine in Ghana's constitutional democracy, which is underpinned by the principle of the separation of powers. It is evident in these cases and academic commentaries that judges disagree on philosophical grounds about which questions are most appropriate for the doctrine's application. In other words, the debate among judges in Ghana is not whether the political question doctrine forms part of Ghanaian constitutional law, rather, it is whether or when should the doctrine apply in a particular case. It is, thus, pointless to question, as others have done,[107] the validity of *Tuffour* and other local authorities that have been used to justify the political question doctrine in Ghana.

---

doctrine could be read as having overruled the decision in the *New Patriotic Party v. Attorney-General*). But for a recent case applying some aspects of a political question doctrine, *see, Professor Stephen Kwaku Asare v. Attorney-General*, [2015] GHASC 101, at pp. 64-65 (noting that "the determination of the question whether or not the President is satisfied that a commission of inquiry should be appointed once the issue to which it relates is in the public interest is a political question that we cannot inquire into.").

106 Free, 2003, p. 491; LaTourette, 2008; Fickes, 2009; Willig, 2010; Chase, 2001, p. 1055; Barkow, 2002, pp. 253, 262-263.

107 Asare, 2006 (arguing that both Justices Abeyi and Kpegah improperly rely on *Tuffour* as the authority for the political question doctrine; that this doctrine was not an issue in *Tuffour*, nor was the holding in *Tuffour* an endorsement of or even a clarification of the doctrine); and the *New Patriotic Party v. Attorney-General* (where Justice Adade found that the political question doctrine cannot have any application in Ghana). *Also see*, Bimpong-Buta, 2005, pp. 128-135 (suggesting that the political question doctrine should not apply to Ghana).

4 The Application and Evolution of the Political Question Doctrine in Uganda*

4.1 Introduction

In Uganda, courts have considered and applied the political question doctrine since the 1960s. Like in Ghana and Nigeria, the development and application of the political question doctrine in Uganda has been influenced by legal developments in the United States and from within. This chapter examines the history, case law development and trends around the application of the political question doctrine in Uganda with a view to draw lessons for South Africa. The chapter explores how courts have employed the political question doctrine to settle some of the major constitutional disputes in Uganda. Given that the political question doctrine is a contested legal concept in Uganda, the chapter deals with some of the legitimacy questions surrounding the doctrine. Notwithstanding this contestation, it is submitted that the political question doctrine is undoubtedly part of the constitutional law of Uganda, and that recent jurisprudence demonstrates that the classic political question theory is likely to dominate future applications of the doctrine.

4.2 Constitution-Making

The Uganda High Court sitting as a Constitutional Court first considered and adopted the political question doctrine in *Uganda v. Commissioner of Prisons Ex Parte Matovu.*[1] In *Ex Parte Matovu,* the plaintiff, Michael Matovu, was arrested under the Deportation Act on 22 May 1966, and then was released and detained again on 16 July, 1966, under the Emergency Powers Act and the Emergency Powers (Detention) Regulations 1966, which had come into force after his initial arrest. Before proceeding with an examination of what transpired in this case, it is important to briefly sketch the prevailing political circumstances at the time of Mr Matovu's arrest.

---

* An earlier version of this chapter was published in 2013. *See*, M. Mhango, 'Separation of Powers and the Application of the Political Question Doctrine in Uganda', *African Journal of Legal Studies*, Vol. 6, 2013, pp. 249-264.

1 *Uganda v. Commissioner of Prisons Ex Parte Matovu*, [1966] EALR 514. *See also*, D. Dennison, 'The Resurfacing Political Question Doctrine in Uganda: Self-Imposed Freedom from the Judicial Review', at p. 3. https://dullahomarinstitute.org.za/constitution-making-in-africa-conference/constitution-building-in-africa-conference-papers/brian-dennison.

Between 22 February and 15 April 1966, a series of events took place, including a declaration of a state of emergency in the region of Buganda. These events resulted in a unilateral suspension of the Constitution of 1962, which had established a federal system of government between the Kingdom of Buganda and the Republic of Uganda,[2] by the then Prime Minister Milton Obote. By this act, Prime Minister Obote had effectively taken over all powers of the government of Uganda by depriving the ceremonial President and Vice President of Uganda, contrary to the Constitution of 1962, of their offices and vested their authorities in the Prime Minister and the Cabinet through the imposition of a new Constitution of 1966.

Commentators refer to the Constitution of 1966, which was imposed on Uganda when Parliament adopted it on 15 April 1966,[3] as the pigeon hole Constitution because it is said that the members of Parliament found copies of the Constitution in their pigeonholes for them to approve.[4] The Commission of Inquiry into Violations of Human Rights described these developments of 1966 as follows:

> In February 1966, the Prime Minister suspended the 1962 Constitution. This was a unilateral action taken without consulting either Parliament or the people of Uganda. For a couple of months, Uganda was literally governed without a Constitution. The 1966 Constitution was put in the pigeonholes of the Members of Parliament and they were asked to approve it even before reading it, and they did. In other words, this Parliament suddenly, and without consulting anybody, constituted themselves into a Constituent Assembly. They enacted and promulgated a Constitution whose contents they did not even know.[5]

According to one legal commentator, the political arrangement under the Constitution of 1962 was an attempt to achieve the impossible and inevitably led to the coup of 1966.[6]

Following his arrest under the above circumstances, the plaintiff in *Ex Parte Matovu* sought an order for his release. One of the issues that had to be determined by the Court in *Ex Parte Matovu* was whether the Emergency Powers Act of 1963 and the Emergency Powers (Detention) Regulations 1966 are *ultra vires* the Constitution to the extent that

2 Eastern African Centre for Constitutional Development, 'Report of the Fact Finding Mission in Uganda on Constitutional Development', 2002, p. 15.

3 *Ex Parte Matovu*, 1966, p. 542.

4 *See*, Eastern African Centre for Constitutional Development, 2002, p. 15. *See also*, F.D. Sekindi, *A Critical Analysis of the Legal Construction of the Presidency in Post-1995 Uganda* (PhD thesis on file with the University of Pretoria, Pretoria 2015) (discussing *Ex-parte Matovu* and the political situation at the time); J. Oloka-Onyango, 'Constitutional Transition in Museveni's Uganda: New Horizons or Another False Start?', *Journal of African Law*, Vol. 39, No. 2, 1995, p. 156.

5 Eastern African Centre for Constitutional Development, 2002, p. 16, citing Report of the Commission of Inquiry into Violations of Human Rights (1994).

6 Y. Ghai, 'Matovu's Case: Another Comment', *Eastern African Law Review*, Vol. 1, 1968, p. 68.

the Act and Regulations enabled the President to take measures that may not be justifiable for purposes of dealing with the situation that existed during a state of emergency. Since there were two constitutions before the *Ex Parte Matovu* Court, namely the Constitution of 1962 and Constitution of 1966, the Court on its own accord raised the question of the validity of the Constitution of 1966. When questioned by the Court in *Ex Parte Matovu*, counsel for the plaintiff observed that he was in some doubt as to the validity in law of the Constitution of 1966.

On the other hand, the government submitted that the Court in *Ex Parte Matovu* had no jurisdiction to enquire into the validity of the Constitution of 1966 because, among other reasons, the making of a constitution is a political act and outside the scope of the functions of the Court. According to the government's argument, since there are three arms of government, it was the duty of the legislature and the executive to decide the validity of the Constitution, the issue being a political one; that the duty of the Court was to accept that decision and merely interpret the Constitution of 1966 as presented to it.

It was also the government's contention that the members of the legislature, who passed the Constitution 1966, did so as representatives of their constituencies to which they must account. Further, it pointed out that since judges were not elected but appointed and represented no specific constituencies to give account of their stewardship, the *Ex Parte Matovu* Court would usurp the functions of the legislature if it undertook to enquire into and pronounce on the validity or otherwise of the Constitution of 1966. In support of this contention, the government referred the Court to the US Supreme Court cases in *Luther v. Borden,*[7] *Marbury v. Madison*[8] and *Baker v. Carr,*[9] and the concept of the political question as discussed in those cases. In reaction to the government's contentions on the political question doctrine, the Court in *Ex Parte Matovu* observed that the government's "exposition of legal principles cannot be faulted. It is a sound doctrine."[10] To be specific, the Court approved the soundness of the political question doctrine as a legal concept for Uganda.

To fully appreciate the above observation in *Ex Parte Matovu*, it is important to briefly discuss what transpired in *Luther v. Borden*. Commentators consider *Luther v. Borden* as a classical representation of the earliest application of the political question doctrine as developed in *Marbury v. Madison.*[11] In *Luther v. Borden*, the US Supreme Court had to determine whether it had the power to legitimize the popular dissolution of an entrenched

---

7 *Luther v. Borden* (held that controversies arising under the Guaranty Clause of article four of the United States Constitution were political questions outside the purview of the court).

8 *Marbury v. Madison.*

9 *Baker v. Carr.*

10 *Ex Parte Matovu*, 1966, p. 531.

11 Redish, 1984, p. 1036; Denisson, 2014, pp. 268-269 and Savitzky, 2011, p. 2043 (arguing that *Luther* expanded considerably the notion of a political question doctrine after *Marbury*). But *see*, Henkin, 1976, p. 608 (concluding that *Luther* did not establish a pure political question doctrine).

state government. The plaintiff, Martin Luther, had been arrested after the declaration of martial law, but before the enactment of the Rhode Island Constitution of 1843. The plaintiff was arrested by martial law troops after they had entered his home and damaged his property and harassed his elderly mother.[12] The plaintiff later sued the martial law troops for trespass. The defendants, admitting an otherwise tortious breaking and entering, sought to justify their action on the ground that they were agents of the established lawful government of Rhode Island, which State was then under martial law to defend itself from active insurrection; that the plaintiff was engaged in that insurrection and that they entered his premises under orders to arrest the plaintiff.[13]

The case arose out of the political differences that agitated the people of Rhode Island between 1841 and 1842, and which had resulted in a situation wherein two groups laid competing claims for recognition as the lawful government.[14] The plaintiff's lawsuit against the troops depended on which was the lawful government of Rhode Island at the time of his arrest, namely the government under the royal charter or the one under the people's Constitution.[15] The lower court's refusals to hear argument on that issue, its charge to the jury that the earlier established or charter government was lawful and the verdict for the defendants were affirmed by the US Supreme Court.[16]

Chief Justice Taney, who wrote the majority opinion in *Luther v. Borden*, framed the issue in institutional terms and focused his analysis on the practical effects of deciding which sovereign was legitimate.[17] He observed that if the US Supreme Court could decide that the charter government was not legitimate, it could throw Rhode Island into legal chaos such as the invalidation of taxes and laws and possibly the nullification of its court decisions.[18] Taney reasoned that "when the decision of this court might lead to such results, it becomes its duty to examine very carefully its own powers before it undertakes to exercise jurisdiction."[19] He found that the power to decide which Constitution or government was legitimate belonged to state officials, the Congress and the President but not in the federal courts.[20] Additionally, he reasoned that Congress' decision under Article IV of the United

12 *Luther v. Borden*, 1849, p. 34. For a discussion of the political events during the Dorr rebellion *see*, G.M. Dennison, *The Dorr War: Republicanism on Trial 1831-1861*, University Press of Kentucky, Lexington, 1976 and G. Marvin, *The Door Rebellion: A Study in American Radicalism 1833-1849*, Random House, New York, 1973.

13 *Baker v. Carr*, 1962, p. 218.

14 *Id. See also, Luther v. Borden*, 1849, p. 34.

15 *Luther v. Borden*, 1849, p. 35.

16 *Id. See also* discussion in *Baker v. Carr*, 1962, p. 217.

17 Savitzky, 2011, p. 2039.

18 Barkow, 2002, p. 255 and Savitzky, 2011, pp. 2039-2040.

19 *Luther v. Borden*, 1849, p. 39.

20 *Id.*, pp. 39-43 (discussing the organs of government who have authority to resolve this dispute). *See also*, Savitzky, 2011, p. 2040.

States Constitution to recognize a state government or its representatives is binding on every other department of government and could not be questioned in a judicial tribunal.[21]

In her reaction to the case, Professor Barkow is correct when she argues that Chief Justice Taney expansively restated the classical theory of the doctrine by concluding that:

> This tribunal, therefore, should be the last to overstep the boundaries which limit its own jurisdiction. And while it should always be ready to meet any question confided to it by the Constitution, it is equally its duty not to pass beyond its appropriate sphere of action, and to take care not to involve itself in discussions which properly belong to other forums. No one, we believe, has ever doubted the proposition that … the sovereignty in every state resides in the people of the state, and that they may alter and change their form of government at their own pleasure.[22]

The Court in *Ex Parte Matovu* relied on *Luther v. Borden* to arrive at its decision. According to the Court, the political question doctrine as articulated in *Luther v. Borden* is a sound doctrine but was not applicable to the circumstances in *Ex Parte Matovu*.[23] It reasoned that however useful and instructive the observations of the US Supreme Court in the several matters discussed in that case may be, the government of Uganda erred in relying on it as supporting the proposition that the validity of the Constitution of 1966 was a non-justiciable political question.[24] Furthermore, the Court found that *Luther v. Borden* was irrelevant and distinguishable from the facts of *Ex Parte Matovu* on the following two grounds.

Firstly, the Court observed that *Luther v. Borden* was a contest between two rival groups as to which should control the government of Rhode Island. It argued that there was no such contest in Uganda[25] and observed that the government of Uganda is well established and has no rival. According to the Court, unlike in *Luther v. Borden*, the question that was presented to it was not the legality of the government but the validity of the Constitution of 1966.

21 *Luther v. Borden*, 1849, p. 43. *See also*, *Pacific States Telephone & Telegraph Co v. Oregon* 223 US 118 (1912) (where an Oregon tax legislation was challenged on the basis that Oregon lacked a republican form of government because the Oregon constitution improperly permitted the people to legislate by initiative and referendum. The Court discussed how all sorts of problems would emerge if it were to conclude that Oregon lacked a republican form of government. It concluded that it would open the door for every citizen to challenge taxes or other government duties).

22 *Luther v. Borden*, 1849, p. 46. *See also*, Barkow, 2002, pp. 256-257.

23 *Ex Parte Matovu*, 1966, pp. 531-533.

24 *Id.*, p. 533.

25 *Id.*, p. 533.

While it is correct that *Luther v. Borden* dealt with mainly the question of which government was legitimate, it is incorrect for the Court in *Ex Parte Matovu* to characterize *Luther v. Borden* as not examining the validity of a constitution. On the contrary, the question of the validity of a constitution was among the primary issues before the US Supreme Court in *Luther v. Borden*. In his analysis of the Dorr Rebellion, which led to the *Luther v. Borden* case, Professor Amar has observed that the charterists (one of the rival groups claiming to have established a lawful government in Rhode Island) had submitted a Constitution, which received the votes of less than one-third of the adult males or less than half of the registered vote.[26] Yet, technically this became the valid Constitution of the State of Rhode Island, and the people's Constitution, which had been submitted by the rival group, did not.[27] According to Amar, the valid Constitution received seven thousand votes, whereas the people's Constitution received nearly fourteen thousand.[28]

Chief Justice Taney considered the question of whether the people's Constitution as opposed to the charterists Constitution, which eventually became the Constitution of Rhode Island, was valid and found that the power to decide which Constitution was valid rested in state officials, the President and Congress.[29] On this point, Savitzky has argued that Taney rejected the vote that had been cast on the people's Constitution as proof of its lawful adoption and declared that:

> Certainly it is no part of the judicial functions of any court of the United States to prescribe the qualification of voters in a State ... nor has it the right to determine what political privileges the citizens of a State are entitled to, unless there is an established constitution or law to govern its decision.[30]

As argued by Savitzky, the lack of established law or Constitution authorizing popular action was at the very core of Taney's application of the political question doctrine. He observed that for Taney there was no rule by which a court could determine the qualification of the voters upon the adoption of the proposed Constitution unless there was some previous law of the State to guide it.[31] Based on the above analysis, it is my contention that *Luther v. Borden* was relevant to the resolution of *Ex Parte Matovu* to the extent that it found the validation of a constitution is a non-justiciable political question. And it was

---

26 A.R. Amar, 'The Central Meaning of Republican Government: Popular Sovereignty, Majority Rule, and the Denominator Problem', *University of Colorado Law Review*, Vol. 65, 1994, p. 775.

27 *Id.*

28 *Id.*

29 *Luther v. Borden*, 1849, pp. 39-43. *See also*, Savitzky, 2011, p. 2056 (arguing that *Luther* teaches that a court cannot competently choose a true Constitution).

30 *Luther v. Borden*, 1849, p. 41. *See also*, Savitzky, 2011, p. 2040.

31 *Id.*

incorrect for the Court in *Ex Parte Matovu* to characterize *Luther v. Borden* as being only concerned with the legality of the government of the day and not the Constitution.

Secondly, the Court in *Ex Parte Matovu* observed that *Luther v. Borden* raised all sorts of political questions, including the right to vote and the qualification for such voters. It noted that, unlike in *Ex Parte Matovu*, there were two rival governors appointed in *Luther v. Borden* and the rivalry between them produced a situation that was tantamount to a state of civil war. The Court observed that that insurrection had in fact occurred and war was levied upon the state. Further, it noted that *Luther v. Borden* also involved the question as to whether the government was republican or not, which is a political question reserved for the Congress under Article IV of the United States Constitution.[32] In the Court's view, these circumstances were not present in *Ex Parte Matovu*.

While the Court in *Ex Parte Matovu* acknowledged that *Luther v. Borden* involved political questions such as the right to vote, it failed to recognize that this political question was considered in the context of deciding the validity of the two rival constitutions in Rhode Island. Furthermore, even though the political instability in Rhode Island at the time when *Luther v. Borden* was decided may not be exactly to that which prevailed in Uganda at the time of *Ex Parte Matovu*, it is misleading for the Court in *Ex Parte Matovu* to paint a rosy picture of the political situation in Uganda at the time. The fact is that there was a considerable amount of political instability in Uganda that was predicated upon events leading up to *Ex Parte Matovu* and the surrounding political events, which eventually led to the coup d'état of 1971 that brought General Idi Amin to power.[33] Following Amin's ascendancy to power, Uganda remained relatively unstable and erupted into a civil war between 1981 and 1986. It was only in 1995 that Uganda adopted a democratic Constitution. It could be argued that the period between 1966 and 1986 can best be characterized as a period of political instability in Uganda.

It is surprising that despite finding that *Luther v. Borden* was distinguishable from *Ex Parte Matovu*, the Court reached a conclusion that is in accord with Chief Justice Taney's main considerations in *Luther v. Borden*.[34] It concluded that any decision by the judiciary as to the legality of the government could be far reaching, disastrous and wrong because the question was a political one to be resolved by the executive and legislature, which were

---

32 *See*, *Luther v. Borden*, 1849, p. 42 and Barkow, 2002, p. 256. The *Ex Parte Matovu* Court also discussed *Baker v. Carr* in ways that is not clear whether they considered it controlling in *Ex Parte Matovu*. *Ex Parte Matovu*, 1966, pp. 533-535.

33 For some discussion about the political history of Uganda, *see*, H. Ingrams, *Uganda: A Crisis of Nationhood*, HM Stationery, London, 1960; P. Mutibwa, *Uganda Since Independence: A Story of Unfulfilled Hope*, African World Press, New Jersey, 1992; and J. Okuku, *Ethnicity, State Power and the Democratisation Process in Uganda*, University Printers, Uppsala, 2002.

34 *Luther v. Borden*, 1849, pp. 38-39 (noting that "if the court could decide that the charter government was not lawful, it could throw Rhode Island into legal chaos-convictions would be reversed, compensation revoked and legislation abrogated").

accountable to their constituencies.[35] Notwithstanding this conclusion, unlike *Luther v. Borden*, the Court in *Ex Parte Matovu* held that a decision on the validity of the Constitution 1966 was within the Court's competence.[36] It found that the Constitution of 1966 was valid for a number of reasons, including the fact that it had been accepted by the people of Uganda and the international community and had been firmly established and implemented throughout the country without opposition.[37] Hence, the Court felt it could not reverse this political reality. There is probably another practical consideration that led the Court to legitimize the Constitution of 1966 and that is the fear of rendering all past acts and taxes open to legal challenges, including the legitimacy of the judges that had been appointed by the Prime Minister Obote under the impugned Constitution. Similar prudential considerations were applied in *Luther v. Borden*.

It is possible to criticize *Ex Parte Matovu* for misconstruing and misapplying *Luther v. Borden*. In spite of this, it is submitted that *Luther v. Borden* was persuasive authority in *Ex Parte Matovu* because it teaches that the act of constitutional formation is the province of the people alone as popular sovereignty, which proposition was accepted by the Court in *Ex Parte Matovu*. As Justice Woodbury observed, in his concurring opinion in *Luther v. Borden*, "our power begins after theirs end."[38] In this regards, the government of Uganda correctly relied on *Luther v. Borden* in its proposition that the judiciary had no authority over questions concerning constitutional making.

Although *Ex Parte Matovu* has been criticized by some scholars,[39] it remains good law in Uganda and has been cited with approval by judges in Uganda[40] and elsewhere.[41] Moreover, since *Ex Parte Matovu*, the political question doctrine has been the subject of consideration and application by the Uganda Court of Appeal in *Andrew Kayira v. Edward*

35 *Ex Parte Matovu*, 1966, pp. 515 and 540. *See also*, Barkow, 2002, p. 255 (observing that Chief Justice Taney was motivated by practical concerns such as the potential legal chaos that would ensure if the court had decided one way or another) and Savitzky, 2011, p. 2039 (noting that *Luther v. Borden* decided against determining which was the legitimate government because this would Rhode Island into legal chaos). Professor Weinberg has argued that the duty of courts does not evaporate because there are obstacles to enforcement or threats of crisis or chaos, and yet *Ex Parte Matovu* and *Luther v. Borden* alike seemed to have been decided on this basis. *See also*, Weinberg, 1994.

36 *Ex Parte Matovu*, 1966, pp. 515 and 540.

37 *Id.*, p. 539.

38 *Luther v. Borden*, 1849, p. 52 and Savitzky, 2011, p. 2041.

39 *See*, M. Kirya, 'The Independence and Accountability of the Judiciary in Uganda: Opportunities and Challenges', www.kituochakatiba.org/index.php?option=com_docman&task=doc_details&gid=369&Itemid=36 (criticizing *Ex Parte Matovu*); C. Kirkby, *Exorcising Matovu's Ghost: Legal Positivism, Pluralism and Ideology in Uganda's Appellate Courts, 12-21* (LLM thesis on file with the McGill University, 2007); N. Mkwentla, *The Legal Effect of a Coup D'Etat on Traditional Constitutional Concept* (LLM thesis on file with Rhodes University, 2001)(discussing *Matovu* and other cases).

40 *Attorney General v. Major General David Tinyefuza*, Constitutional Appeal No. 1 of 1997 (S.C), (unreported); *Andrew Kayira v. Edward Rugumayo & Others*, Constitutional Case No. 1 (1979); *Centre of Health Human Rights v. Attorney-General*, Constitutional Petition No. 16 (2011).

41 *See*, *Madzimbamuto v. Larder Burke* (1966) 1 AC 645; *R v. Ndhlovu* 1968 (4) SA 515.

Rugumayo & Others,[42] where the Court relying on *Ex Parte Matovu* ruled that the removal of Professor Lule from the office of President of Uganda was a political question not reviewable in the courts of law but reserved to the political organs of the state.[43] Perhaps the most cardinal application of the political question doctrine, in the context of the post-1995 Constitution of Uganda, was by the Supreme Court of Uganda in *Attorney-General v. Tinyefuza.*[44]

4.3 Military Matters

4.3.1 *Supreme Court's View*

One of the most significant cases ever decided by the Supreme Court of Uganda regarding the limits of judicial power is *Tinyefuza*. The case arose when on 29 November, 1996, General Tinyefuza gave evidence before the Parliamentary Sessional Committee (Sessional Committee) on Defence and Internal Affairs about the insurgency in Northern Uganda. In his testimony, the General made a harsh attack on the Uganda Peoples' Defence Force regarding its conduct generally and, in particular, its handling of the insurgency in Northern Uganda.[45]

Following his testimony, General Tinyefuza learned from media reports that the military authorities thought his evidence before the Sessional Committee "did not conform with the military line" and that he should resign from the army and appear before the High Command.[46] General Tinyefuza did not consider himself a member of the army at the time he addressed the Sessional Committee, but to clear the air, he resigned by a letter sent to the President.[47] He received a response from the Minister of Defence rejecting his resignation on the basis that it did not comply with the National Resistance Army (Conditions of Service) (Officers) Regulations 1993.[48] The General perceived these events as exposing him to an atmosphere of fear and felt that his rights were about to be infringed.

As a consequence, General Tinyefuza petitioned the Constitutional Court seeking a declaration that the threats to punish him for his testimony before the Sessional Committee

42 *Andrew Kayira v. Edward Rugumayo & Others,* Constitutional Case No. 1 (1979).

43 *See also,* A. Sekindi, *Critical Analysis of the Legal Construction of the Presidency in Post-1995 Uganda* (Doctoral thesis on file with Brunel University London, 2015).

44 *Attorney-General v. Tinyefuza,* Constitutional Appeal No. 1 of 1997.

45 *See, Attorney-General v. Tinyefuz* [1997] UGCC 3(Justice Manyido, opinion).

46 *Attorney-General v. Tinyefuza* (Wambuzi J., opinion), 1997, p. 2.

47 *Id.*

48 After submitting his resignation, there were media reports quoting the President saying that General Tinyefuza would have to sort out his problems with the army before he is allowed to resign. Criticisms against General Tinyefuza from other senior army officials were also reported in the media. *See, Attorney General v. Tinyefuza* [1997] UGCC 3 (Justice Manyido, opinion).

would be in conflict with Article 87 of the Constitution 1995, that the rejection of his resignation letter was unconstitutional and that the army regulations were no longer applicable to him because – at the time of his testimony – he had been appointed to a post in the public service.[49] The Constitutional Court ruled in favour of General Tinyefuza and the Attorney General appealed to the Supreme Court.[50] The Supreme Court in a five[51] to two[52] decision reversed the Constitutional Court judgement.

In his opinion in favour of the majority view, Justice Kanyeihamba remarked at the outset that in order to dispose of this appeal according to the principles of the Constitution and laws of Uganda, it was essential for him to make some preliminary observations, which he said ought to guide a court in adjudicating constitutional matters of this kind and others.[53] Justice Kanyeihamba began by examining the political question doctrine as applied in the United States and as developed by the courts in Uganda.[54] He observed that the general rule is that courts have no jurisdiction over matters that are within the constitutional and legal powers of the legislative or the executive.[55] Kanyeihamba went on to observe that even in those cases where courts feel obliged to intervene and review legislative or executive acts when challenged on the basis that the rights of an individual are infringed, they do so sparingly and with great reluctance.[56]

Further, he re-affirmed the endorsement in *Ex Parte Matovu* of the political question doctrine.[57] Constitutional observers in other jurisdictions agree with Justice Kanyeihamba's general approach to constitutional adjudication, arguing that:

> the political question doctrine requires the judiciary to decide as a threshold matter in all cases whether the question before it has been assigned by the Constitution to another co-ordinate branch of government.[58]

---

49 *Attorney General v. Tinyefuza.*

50 For a discussion of the Court of Appeal decision, *see*, C. Byamugisha, 'Administering Justice Without Undue Regard to the Technicalities', A paper presented to Green Watch Uganda. Available from http://greenwatch.or.ug/files/downloads/Administering_Justice_Without_Un_due_Regard_to_Technic.pdf. *See also, Paul Semogerere v. Attorney-General*, Constitutional Appeal No. 1 (2002) (2003); and R. Ellet, *Emerging Judicial Power in Transitional Democracies: Malawi, Tanzania and Uganda*, Northeastern University, Boston, 2008, pp. 407-498.

51 Justices Kanyeihamba, Wambuzi, Tsetooko, Karokora and Kekonyo.

52 Justices Mulenga and Oder.

53 *Attorney General v. Tinyefuza, 1997, p.* 3.

54 *Id.*, p. 11.

55 *Id.*

56 *Id.*

57 *Id.*, 1997, p. 12.

58 Barkow, 2002, pp. 243-244; Chase, 2001, pp. 1045-1046 (noting that the political question doctrine limits judicial power by curtailing the ability of courts to adjudicate issues best left to the discretion of legislative or the executive branch); M. Nixon-Graf, 'A Gathering Storm: Climate Change as Common Nuisance or Political Question?', *New York University Environmental Law Journal*, Vol. 19, No. 2, 2012, p. 353 (discussing that the political question doctrine requires courts to make a threshold determination whether a claim is

Before addressing the merits of the case, Justice Kanyeihamba highlighted some of the areas, which, in his view, would be appropriate to apply the political question doctrine in Uganda.[59] He noted that among them is whether courts should demand proof of whether a statute of the legislature was passed properly or not,[60] the conduct of foreign relations[61] and the question of when to declare and terminate wars and insurgencies.[62] Underneath this jurisprudence is a suggestion by Kanyeihamba about the areas where the judiciary will likely apply the political question doctrine in future cases. It was helpful for Justice Kanyeihamba to make these pronouncements in the development of the doctrine.

Most commentators acquiesce to Justice Kanyeihamba's suggestion of areas that are most appropriate for the application of the political question doctrine.[63] Based on his review of the common law authorities, Justice Kanyeihamba was convinced that courts should avoid adjudicating upon these kinds of questions unless in very clear cases of vio-

properly within the judicial branch of government); Gouin, 1994, p. 759 (arguing in favour of the applying the political question doctrine in foreign affairs cases); Price, 2006, p. 331 (advocating for a reformulated political question doctrine so that it is used to more carefully distinguish between those cases that raise separation of powers concerns and should therefore be dismissed, and those which do not); Breedon, 2008, p. 523 (characterizing the political question as a self-imposed restraint mechanism on the judiciary, which requires courts to dismiss a case as non-justiciable if deciding the matter in dispute would encroach upon the functions of the electoral branches of government) and A. Timothy, 'The Doctrine of Political Question: Is It's Non-Justiciability at the Brink of Erosion in the Legal Jurisprudence of Uganda?', 2014, available from http://timothyamerit.blogspot.co.za/2014/08/the-doctrine-of-political-question-is.html (critical of the political question doctrine in Uganda).

59 *Tinyefuza v. Attorney-General*, 1997, p. 12.

60 *See*, Cooley, 1868, pp. 186-187 (arguing against judicial inquiry into the legislative motives and that we must assume that legislative discretion has been properly exercised). *See also*, *People v. Draper* 15 NY 545 (1857).

61 Chief Justice Marshall described questions of foreign policy as belonging more properly to those who can place the nation in such a position with respect to foreign powers as to their own judgement shall appear wise; to whom are entrusted all its foreign relations. *See*, *United States v. Palmer* 16 US (3 Wheat) 610, 4 L Ed. 471 (1818). *See also*, Free, 2003, p. 489; Gouin, 1994, pp. 763-781; Scharpf, 1966, pp. 583-584; Nzelibe, 2004, p. 941; *Oetjen v. Central Leather Co* 246 US 297 (1918) (applying the political question doctrine to the conduct of the foreign affairs) and *United States v. Belmont* 301 US 324 (1937) (noting that the executive branch has exclusive competence in foreign affairs).

62 *Tinyefuza v. Attorney-General*, 1997, p. 12. In the United States, courts typically take the same view in cases involving military matters. *See*, *Crockett v. Reagan* 720 F 2d 1355 (DC Cir 1983), cert. denied, 467 US 1251 (1984) (finding suit regarding US military activities in El Salvador raised non-justiciable political question); *Lowry v. Reagan* 676 F Supp 333 (D DC 1987) (finding suit to compel presidential compliance with War Powers Resolution raised non-justiciable political questions); *Chicago & S Air Lines v. Waterman SS Corp* 333 US 103 (1948); *Johnson v. Eisentrager* 339 US 763 (1950), at p. 789 (holding that "certainly it is not the function of the Judiciary to entertain private litigation – even by a citizen – which challenges the legality, the wisdom, or the propriety of the Commander-in-Chief in sending our armed forces abroad or to any particular region") and *United States v. Curtiss-Wright Export Corp* 299 US 304 (1936), at p. 319 (holding that in this vast external realm, with its important, complicated, delicate and manifold problems, the President alone has the power to speak as a representative of the nation).

63 Gouin, 1994; Chase, 2001, p. 1055; Wishik, 1985, p. 697; Wechsler, 1961, pp. 11-14.

lation or threatened violation of individual liberty are shown.[64] He added that the reluctance of courts to enter into the arena reserved by the Constitution 1995 to the other arms of government reaches its zenith when it comes to the exercise and control of powers relating to the armed forces: their structure, organization, deployment and operations.[65] In his view, the accepted principle is that courts should not substitute their own views of what is in the public interest in these matters, particularly when the other coordinate arms of government are acting within the authority granted to them by the constitution.[66]

Justice Kanyeihamba's reasoning is that since military matters are within the exclusive jurisdiction of both executive and legislature, it is not for the courts to consider whether

64 *Tinyefuza v. Attorney-General*, 1997, pp. 12-13 (where Kanyeihamba stated that the "English case of Chandler v. DPP (1964) AC 763 Lord Devlin underscored this point when at p. 810 he said a court will not review the proper exercise of discretionary power but they will only intervene to correct excess or abuse. The observation by the American jurist Charles Warren in 'C. Warren, The Supreme Court in United States History, Little, Brown & Co, Boston, 1922, pp. 748-749' that courts, and especially the Supreme Court are not the only actors on the constitutional stage is equally applicable to Uganda.").

65 *Tinyefuza v. Attorney-General*, 1997, p. 12. Under US law, the greater the degree of control by the military, the more likely the courts are going to find that challenges involving the military or private military contractors present non-justiciable political questions. *See, Martin v. Mott*, 25 US (12 Wheat) 19 (1827) (holding that the President had exclusive power to determine whether the militia should be called out); *Whitaker v. Kellog Brown & Root Inc* 444 F Supp 2d 1277 (2006), p. 1281 (holding private military contractor was subject to military's orders, regulations and convoy plan, rendering suit against the private military contractor arising out of convoy accident non-justiciable); B. Davidson, 'Note, Liability on the Battlefield: Adjudicating Tort Suits Brought by Soldiers Against Military Contractors', *Public Contract Law Journal*, Vol. 37, No. 4, 2008, pp. 822-834 and J. Perez-Montes, 'Comment, Justiciability in Modern War Zones: Is the Political Question Doctrine a Viable Bar to Tort Claims Against Private Military Contractors?', *Tulane Law Review*, Vol. 83, 2008, p. 246.

66 Most judges agree with this view and have similarly held that the political branches are better placed than the judiciary to appreciate what is to the public benefit. Chief Justice Gubbay writing for a unanimous Supreme Court of Zimbabwe in the landmark case of *Nyambirai v. National Social Security Authority* 1996 1 SA 636 (ZS) 644 explained it convincingly when he upheld a legislative policy to compel employees and employers to save for their retirement and said: "I do not doubt that because of their superior knowledge and experience of society and its needs, and a familiarity with local conditions, national authorities are, in principle, better placed than the Judiciary to appreciate what is to the public benefit. In implementing social and economic policies, a government's assessment as to whether a particular service or programme it intends to establish will promote the interest of the public is to be respected by the courts. They will not intrude but will allow a wide margin of appreciation, unless convinced that the assessment is manifestly without reasonable foundation. The Minister has proclaimed that the Pensions and Other Benefits Scheme provides a service in the public interest. That is an assessment that this Court should respect." *See also, Apostolou & others v. The Republic of Cyprus* (1985) LRC (Const) 851 (rejecting the argument that the government had no authority to compel a self-employed individual to pay contributions to the social insurance fund established under the Social Insurance Law of 1980; *Sechele v. Public Officers Defined Contribution Pension Fund and Others* [2010] LSHC 94 (upholding a compulsory civil service pension fund in Lesotho); *Steward Machine Company v. Davis* 301 US 548 (1937) (upholding the provisions of the United States Social Security Act of 1935) and *Schweiker v. Wilson* 450 US 221 (1981), p. 230 (reasoning that unless a statute employs a classification that is inherently invidious or that impinges on fundamental rights, this Court properly exercises only a limited review power over Congress, the appropriate representative body through which the public makes democratic choices among alternative solutions to social and economic problems).

the discretion of the executive has been exercised properly, if at all.[67] In his view, it is Parliament that has the authority to hold the executive to account in these sorts of matters.[68]

To support Justice Kanyeihamba's view, the United States Court of Appeal in *Schneider v. Kissinger*, considered a suit against Henry Kissinger, the National Security Advisor to the President and the United States for the wrongful death of Chilean General René Schneider. In upholding the lower court decision that the political question doctrine applied in this case, it reasoned that "the lack of judicial authority to oversee the conduct of the executive branch in political matters does not leave the executive power unbounded ... the nation has recompense, and the checks and balances of the Constitution have not failed. The political branches effectively exercise such checks and balances on each other in the area of political questions."[69] It held that the allocation of political questions to the political branches must not be viewed as inconsistent with the constitutional tradition of limited government and balance of powers because it is precisely consistent, for it embodies limits and balances between the political branches without the intrusion of the judiciary into areas beyond its proper authority and expertise.[70]

Some commentators agree with these judicial sentiments. Ibrahim Imam writing with others has made a similar point that:

> we should not be overly concerned that the political question doctrine deprives the courts of enforcement power over certain constitutional provisions, because the constitution and electoral process provides an appropriate substitute.[71]

Thus, Justice Kanyeihamba cannot be faulted for pointing out that Parliament is the appropriate organ of government to check the executive on military questions, and that in the context of the political question doctrine, this is a sufficient constitutional check on executive power.[72]

Furthermore, Justice Kanyeihamba reflected on the principle of separation of powers under the Constitution of Uganda and was very clear that in Uganda, as it is in the United States, courts are not the only actors on the constitutional stage.[73] He correctly observed that the Constitution of Uganda envisages that the constitutional platform is to be shared

---

67 For a similar reasoning, *see*, *Corrie v. Caterpillar* (declining to intrude into the government decision to grant military assistance to Israel because this question was committed under the Constitution to the legislative and executive branches).

68 *Attorney-General v. Tinyefuza, 1997, p.* 12.

69 *Schneider v. Kissinger* 412 F 3d 190 (2005), at p. 200.

70 *Id.*

71 Imam et al., 2011, p. 51, citing *Obi v. INEC* (2007) 9 MJSC 1.

72 *Olson v. Morrison* 487 US 654 (1988) (Scalia J., dissenting) (arguing that another significant check is that people will replace those in the political branches who are guilty of abuse of power).

73 *Attorney-General v. Tinyefuza*, 1997, p. 13.

among the three arms of government, being the executive, judicial and legislative arms; that courts need to bear in mind the judgements of other repositories of constitutional power concerning the scope of their authority and the necessity for each to keep within its powers, including the courts themselves.[74] Professor Tribe has agreeably observed that:

> so long as the manner in which the Constitution is to be interpreted remains open to question, the meaning of the Constitution is subject to legitimate dispute, and the judiciary is not alone in its responsibility to interpret.[75]

In the light of the above views, Justice Kanyeihamba pronounced that the principle of separation of powers demands that unless there is the clearest of cases calling for intervention for purposes of determining constitutionality of action or the protection of the liberty that is presently threatened, the courts must refrain from entering arenas not assigned to them either by the Constitution or laws of Uganda.[76] Moreover, he pronounced that it is necessary in a democracy that courts refrain from entering into areas of disputes best suited for resolution by other government agents.[77]

In their discussion of the political question doctrine in Canada, Cowper and Sossin have similarly observed and argued that:

> based on the principle of separation of powers, the political questions doctrine limits judicial jurisdiction, and therefore power, in a number of circumstances where the other branches of government have a stronger claim to decide the issue raised.[78]

My argument is that Kanyeihamba's pronouncement reflects the notion that the executive and legislature have a stronger claim to decide military questions that emerged in this case. The growth of the political question doctrine in Uganda, particularly in military and foreign

74 *Id.*

75 Tribe, 1988, pp. 34-35. *See also, United States v. Butler* 297 US 1 (1936), p. 87 (Stone J., dissenting) (arguing that courts are not the only agency of government that must be assumed to have the capacity to govern); Mulhern, 1988, p. 126 (arguing that there is no obvious reason why a court's assertion of judicial power should be any more authoritative than a president's assertion of executive power. Both are part of our constitutional tradition and there is no apparent way to establish any priority between them. Courts share responsibility for interpreting the Constitution with the political branches) and Seidman, 2003, p. 442 (arguing that Constitution vests in the political branches final interpretive authority as to the meaning of some constitutional provisions; that in relation to those provisions the political branches self-monitor).

76 *Attorney-General v. Tinyefuza, 1997, p.* 13.

77 *Id.*

78 Cowper & Sossin, 2002, p. 345.

affairs matters, mirrors the growth in the same areas in other countries, such as the United States and Japan, where courts have frequently applied the doctrine.[79]

In his commentary on Justice Kanyeihamba's opinion in *Tinyefuza,* Dennison has observed that Kanyeihamba's treatment of the political question doctrine was a clear disdain of the test formulated in *Baker v. Carr.*[80] He argues that Justice Kanyeihamba was influenced by Chief Marshall's formulation of the political question doctrine in *Marbury v. Madison* as opposed to Justice Brennan's formulation in *Baker v. Carr.*[81] More simply, Dennison believes that Kanyeihamba identified with the classic political question theory as the most appropriate for Uganda, and that his lack of reliance on *Baker v. Carr* was reflective of his rejection of prudential considerations introduced in that case.[82]

Also, Dennison supports Kanyeihamba's characterization of the doctrine as a legal mechanism that allows other branches of government to conduct their constitutional business without interference.[83] He makes another important remark that given Justice Kanyeihamba's national reputation as a champion of the rule of law in Uganda, it makes his endorsement and appreciation of the political question doctrine significant and displays a strong testimony to the usefulness of the doctrine in Uganda.[84] The comments by Dennison explain why in his concluding remarks, he prays that the judiciary will continue to invoke the principled version of the doctrine as conceived by Justices Marshall and Kanyeihamba.[85] It is clear from his analysis that by principled version, Denison refers to the classical strand of the doctrine.

79 *See, Gilligan v. Morgan* 413 US 1 (1973). *See also*, E. Firmage, 'The War Powers and Political Question Doctrine', *University of Colorado Law Review*, Vol. 49, 1977-1978, p. 65; D. Cole, 'Challenging Covert War: The Politics of the Political Question Doctrine', *Harvard International Law Journal*, Vol. 26, No. 1, 1985, p. 155; *Tomabechi v. Japan*, 1955 (O) 96 *Minshu*, Vol. 14, No. 7, at p. 1206 (where the Japanese Supreme Court adopted an approach whose theory is predicated on the political question doctrine when it ruled that judicial review should be excluded from intervening in an action that is within the discretion of the political pillars of government); and *Japan v. Shigeru Sakata, Japanese Ann. International Law*, Vol. 4, 1960, pp. 105-119 (reasoning that the 1952 United States-Japan Security Treaty involved "an extremely high degree of political consideration, having bearing upon the very existence of our country as a sovereign power, and any legal determination as to whether the content of the treaty is constitutional or not is in many respects inseparably related to the high degree of political consideration or discretionary power on the part of the Cabinet which concluded the treaty and on the part of the Diet which approved it.").

80 Dennison, 2014, p. 272.

81 *Id.*, p. 284.

82 *Id.*

83 *Id.*, p. 272.

84 *Id.*, p. 272.

85 *Id.*, p. 288.

It is understandable from Justice Kanyeihamba's examination above that in Uganda, as it is Ghana,[86] Nigeria,[87] Israel,[88] Japan[89] and the United States, the political question doctrine is recognized as originating from the principle of separation of powers. Moreover, there are potential limits on the application of the doctrine; that is to say, it may not apply, as Kanyeihamba observed, in cases of clear constitutional violations or abuse of human rights.

Justice Kanyeihamba's views in this regard are similar to those of Justice Kpegah in *Amidu* where he explained that despite the Constitution of Ghana being expressed as the supreme law

> there is inherent or internal evidence in our Constitution that the policy which informs or should inform any legislation, and the desirability of enacting such a law are matters for the executive and legislature to decide.[90]

It is evident that the two justices hold similar views on the proper equilibrium of powers that should be maintained among the three arms of government by insisting on the notion that each arm of government enjoys equal constitutional powers to interpret and enforce a constitution within their respective domains.[91] *Tinyefuza* is not the most recent application of the political question doctrine in Uganda. The High Court recently adopted a different approach to political questions involving, among other things, military matters.

---

86 *Ghana Bar Association*, 2003-2004, p. 250 (held that the appointment of the chief justice was a non-justiciable political question under the Constitution of Ghana).

87 *Balarabe Musa v. Auta Hamzat*, 1983 (applying the political question doctrine in Nigeria); *Onuoha v. Okafor*, 1983 (applying the political question doctrine in Nigeria); W. Edbewole & O. Olatunji 'Justiciability Theory Versus Political Question Doctrine: Challenges of the Nigerian Judiciary in the Determination of Electoral and Other Related Case', *The Journal of Jurisprudence*, Vol. 14, 2012, p. 146 (arguing that little is now left of the political question doctrine in Nigeria) and Nwauche, 2010, pp. 31-60 (discussing the political question doctrine in Nigeria).

88 For a discussion of the political question doctrine in Israel, *see*, Cohn, 2011, p. 675; and *Jabotinsky v. Weitzmann* HCJ 65/51 (1951) (where the Israeli Supreme Court, sitting as the High Court of Justice rejected an application for an order of mandamus against the President of the State regarding his exercise of discretion in entrusting the task of forming a government to a member of the Knesset, Israel's parliament).

89 *Tomabechi v. Japan*, 1955 and *Japan v. Shigeru Sakata*, 1960.

90 *Amidu*, 2001-2002, p. 154 (Kpegah, dissenting opinion) (arguing that the political question doctrine is applicable to Ghana).

91 *See*, Mulhern, 1988; Cowper & Sossin, 2002, p. 345; Tribe, 1988; Barkow, 2002, p. 239 (arguing that the constitutional structure vests some interpretive authority with the political branches) and Seidman, 2003, p. 444 (arguing that political branches have final interpretive authority as to the meaning of the Constitution).

4.3.2 *High Court's View*

Ugandan courts are not frequented with cases raising the need to apply the political question doctrine.[92] A few reported cases have been decided by the High Court seating as the Constitutional Court or the Supreme Court. However, recently the High Court in *Ochen & Others v. Attorney-General*[93] was presented with four related matters for a decision on several preliminary points of law that were raised by the Attorney General. One of these points of law was the political question doctrine. The facts of each case were different and important to be stated separately.

The first case under consideration was *Oluka & 9 Other v. Attorney-General*[94] the plaintiffs in this case alleged that they lost property, including livestock during the war in the Teso region of Eastern Uganda. They submitted claims to the Government of Uganda for compensation. These claims have yet to be resolved. Yet, they claimed, other similarly situated claimants were compensated. They alleged this constituted discrimination.

The second case, *Okupa and 2020 Others v. Attorney-General*[95] involved a claim under Article 50 of the Constitution of Uganda. Article 50 provides that:

1. Any person who claims that a fundamental or other right or freedom guaranteed under this Constitution has been infringed or threatened is entitled to apply to a competent court for redress which may include compensation.
2. Any person or organization may bring an action against the violation of another person's or group's human rights.
3. Any person aggrieved by any decision of the court may appeal to the appropriate court.
4. Parliament shall make laws for the enforcement of the rights and freedoms under this Chapter.

The plaintiffs' claim was that the government's ineffective gun ownership policies led to Karimojong warriors to use their firearms and breach the fundamental rights of the plaintiffs. They claimed that government is liable to compensate the affected persons for loss of life, property, dependency, breach of duty and other fundamental rights and freedoms. They sought an order for the government to compensate them, including other affected persons.

---

92 *But see, Brigadier Tumukunde v. Attorney-General and Another* Supreme Court Constitutional Appeal No. 2 of 2006 (considering whether the actions of the Commander in Chief can be challenged in a court of law).

93 *Ochen & Others v. Attorney-General* Civil Suit 292/2010.

94 *Oluka & 9 Others v. Attorney-General* Civil Suit 122/2009.

95 *Okupa and 2020 Others v. Attorney-General* Civil Suit 0014/2005.

The third case, *Ochen & Others v. Attorney-General* involved a claim under Article 50 of the Constitution of 1995. The gist of the plaintiffs' claim was that between 1986 and 2006 they suffered human rights abuses, including killing, abduction, torture, rape, unlawful detention and loss of livestock. Their claim was founded upon the breach of their fundamental rights in the 1995 Constitution. They also claimed that the government of Uganda failed to protect the citizens of Teso region from the Uganda People's Army, which killed many affected citizens. Besides, they claimed that the government was in breach of the Firearms Act of 1970 that exposed the plaintiffs to brutal acts of the Karimojong cattle rustlers. The plaintiffs sought compensation from the government of Uganda.

The last case, *Edimu & 105 Others v. Attorney-General,*[96] arose from Article 50 of the Constitution. The plaintiffs claimed that they lost property at the hands of the National Resistance Army during the insurrection of 1985 and 1986 onwards. They submitted their claims to the Ministry of Defence. While these claims were admitted by the Minister of Defence, the Ministry delayed in forwarding the same to the Attorney General for payment. The Ministry of Justice later rejected the claims due to late submission. The plaintiffs claimed that the President gave direction to the government to settle certain claims, and they alleged discrimination on the part of the President and Attorney General in handling their claims. They sought a declaration from the court that their rights were infringed and must be compensated.

In response to these claims, the government raised a preliminary point of law with respect to each case. In the main, three arguments were advanced by the government relying on the political question doctrine. Firstly, citing *Baker v. Carr* and *Tinyefuza*, the government advanced the argument that issues relating to military affairs are the prerogative of the President and that courts should refrain from reviewing decisions made in that arena. For example, in relation to *Ochen & Others v. Attorney-General* where the plaintiffs claimed there was a failure to protect them against the Lord Resistance Army, the government argued that in order to determine the claim it would require the court to delve into matters of military discretion reserved for the executive branch, and that matters relating to what or how Ugandan army should have gone about to protect people of Teso region is not judicially examinable but left to the executive under the Uganda Peoples Defence Force Act 2005. To put it differently, the propriety of what may be done in the exercise of military discretion is not subject to judicial inquiry.

It is important to mention that the government's argument has successfully been used in two related American cases. In *Corrie v. Caterpillar,*[97] the United States federal Court of Appeals rejected to determine a case, which would have required it to determine the consequences of the decision by the US government to grant extensive military aid to Israel

96 *Edimu & 105 Others v. Attorney-General* Civil Suit 9/2012.

97 *Corrie v. Caterpillar* 503 F 3d 974 (9th Cir 2007).

on the ground that this was a political question.[98] The court reasoned that it was difficult to see how the court would impose liability on Caterpillar (the recipient of the military aid) without implicitly deciding the propriety of the US decision to pay for the bulldozers, which allegedly killed the plaintiff's family members.[99]

Similarly, in *Schneider v. Kissinger*, the federal Court of Appeals dismissed a claim against the United States on the basis of the political question doctrine arguing that it could not determine plaintiffs' claims without passing judgements on the decision of the executive branch to participate in the alleged covert operations against the newly elected Chilean leftist leader Dr Salvador Allende.[100]

Secondly, the Uganda government advanced a classical political question theory-based argument that there is no judicially discoverable and manageable standard to determine the actions of government vis-a-vis the Lord Resistance Army, National Resistance Movement or Karamojong castle rustlers or other rebels. In the government's view, the High Court was without competence to make these kinds of determinations, and that this role was better left to the executive, top military Council, Minister of Defence, the Court Marshall and the President as the commander-in-chief. In relation to *Oluka & 9 Other v. Attorney-General,* the government noted that a court would have to put itself in President Museveni's shoes and determine how he should have applied his discretion.[101] In the end, the government emphasized that the issues raised in all four cases should be left to the political branches to resolve.

In responding to these points of law, Judge Nahamya began by analyzing the political question doctrine as formulated in *Baker v. Carr.* She correctly noted that the doctrine essentially limits judicial review powers in limited instances.[102] And, Nahamya recognized that the doctrine had limitations noting that the mere fact that a suit seeks protection of a political right does not mean it represents a political question.[103] Nahamya made the observation that unlike in Uganda and other common law countries, she was cognizant of the fact that the United States practises a strict separation of powers among the principle organs of state. She noted that these countries prefer to have checks and balances rather than have water-tight compartmentalization. She made these observations as a prelude to a further point. In this point, she noted that the political question doctrine was neither a

98 *Id.*

99 *Id.*

100 *Schneider v. Kissinger* 412 F 3d 190 (2005).

101 A similar argument has been considered and accepted in Japan. *See, Tomabechi v. Japan,* 1955, p. 1206 (refusing to intervene in an action that is within the discretion of the political pillars of government.); and *Japan v. Shigeru Sakata,* 1960, pp. 105-107 (reasoning that the interpretation of the 1952 United States-Japan Security Treaty involved "an extremely high degree of political consideration or discretionary power on the part of the Cabinet which concluded the treaty and on the part of the Diet which approved it").

102 *Ochen & Others v. Attorney-General* Civil Suit 292/2010, p. 20. *See also, Clinton v. Zivotofsky*, 2012, p. 1427.

103 *Ochen & Others v. Attorney-General*, p. 21. *See also, Japan Whaling Ass'n v. Am Cetacean Soc'y* 478 US 221, 230, (1986) and *Kadic v. Karadzic* 70 F 3d 232, 249 (2d Cir 1995).

product of legislation nor part of the United States Constitution, but emanates from the principle of separation of powers. She remarked that while *Baker v. Carr* was cited by the government of Uganda as authority for the political question doctrine, the US Supreme Court in *Baker v. Carr* did not ultimately support the application of the political question doctrine in that case.

Nahamya's conclusive statement that the United States practises a strict version of separation of powers deserves immediate comment because it is not supported by the prevailing authorities. To the contrary, the jurisprudence of the US Supreme Court demonstrates that the principle of separation of powers contemplated under the United States Constitution was never meant to be strict or absolute.[104] In several cases, the US Supreme Court has reiterated this view. In *United States v. Nixon*,[105] a broad argument concerning the separation of powers was advanced to oppose a subpoena in connection with certain Presidential tapes and documents of value to a pending criminal investigation. The US Supreme Court rejected the argument that the United States Constitution contemplates a complete separation of powers among the three branches. The US Supreme Court held that:

> In designing the structure of our Government and dividing and allocating the sovereign power among three co-equal branches, the Framers of the Constitution sought to provide a comprehensive system, but the separate powers were not intended to operate with absolute independence.[106]

Similarly, in *Mistretta v. United States*,[107] the US Supreme Court reiterated the view that separation of powers under the United States Constitution is not meant to be rigid. The Court reasoned that:

104 *See*, Hamilton, 1999, p. 299 (where James Madison reviewing the origin of the separation-of-powers doctrine, remarked that Montesquieu, the "oracle always consulted on the subject did not mean that these departments ought to have no partial agency in, or no control over the acts of each other. His meaning, as his own words import can amount to no more than this, that where the whole power of one department is exercised by the same hands which possess the whole power of another department, the fundamental principles of a free constitution, are subverted."); M. Tully, 'The Supreme Court's Pragmatic and Flexible Approach to Federal Judicial Separation of Powers Issues: *Mistretta v. United States*', *DePaul Law Review*, Vol. 39, No. 2,1990, p. 405 (discussing flexible approach to separation of powers by Supreme Court) and Story, 1833, p. 525 (noting that "when we speak of a separation of the three great departments of government, and maintain that that separation is indispensable to public liberty, we are to understand this maxim in a limited sense. It is not meant to affirm that they must be kept wholly and entirely separate and distinct, and have no common link of connection or dependence, the one upon the other, in the slightest degree.").

105 *United States v. Nixon* 418 US 683 (1974).

106 *Id.*, p. 707. *See also*, *Nixon v. Administrator of General Services* 433 US 425 (1977) (rejecting as archaic complete division of authority among the three branches) and *Youngstown Sheet & Tube Company v. Sawyer* 343 US 579 (1952), p. 635 (Jackson J., opinion).

107 *Mistretta v. United States* 488 US 361 (1989).

> In applying the principle of separated powers in our jurisprudence, we have sought to give life to Madison's view of the appropriate relationship among the three coequal branches. Accordingly, we have recognized, as Madison admonished at the founding, that while our Constitution mandates that each of the three general departments of government must remain entirely free from the control or coercive influence, direct or indirect, of either of the others, the Framers did not require – and indeed rejected – the notion that the three Branches must be entirely separate and distinct.[108]

The US Supreme Court further explained that:

> Madison recognized that our constitutional system imposes upon the Branches a degree of overlapping responsibility, a duty of interdependence as well as independence the absence of which would preclude the establishment of a nation capable of governing itself effectively.[109]

Furthermore, Professor Story (who was later appointed Justice of the US Supreme Court), in his commentaries, argued with equal force and sagacity that:

> when we speak of a separation of the three great departments of government, and maintain that that separation is indispensable to public liberty, we are to understand this maxim in a limited sense. It is not meant to affirm, that they must be kept wholly an entirely separate and distinct, and have no common link of connexion or dependence, the one upon the other, in the slightest degree. The trust meaning is, that the whole power of one of these departments should not be exercised by the same hands.[110]

Clearly, based on these authorities, the observation and proposition by Nahamya cannot be legally sustained.

In dismissing the political question doctrine from applying in the present case, Judge Nahamya offered several reasons. Firstly, she noted that the current position in the United States is that the US Supreme Court has embraced the view that it is the only one among the three branches that has the power and competence to provide full substantive meaning of all constitutional provisions. Nahamya's views were influenced by two prominent academics Chemerinsky and Barkow. The problem with Nahamya's observations is that she

108 *Id.*, p. 380.

109 *Id.*, p. 381.

110 Story, 1833, pp. 8 and 12-13 (arguing that a rigid separation cannot be maintained).

takes an absolutist view of judicial review powers and selectively cites to Barkow's research on the subject of the political question doctrine.

In the article written by Barkow titled *More Supreme than Court? The Fall of the Political Question Doctrine and the Rise of Judicial Supremacy*,[111] which Nahamya relies on, Barkow maintains that the duty to say what the law is, which pronouncement institutionalized the power of judicial review, does not necessarily imply that a court has monopoly on constitutional interpretation.[112] Barkow argued that judicial review leaves room for deference to the constitutional interpretation of the political branches; that indeed, a constitution may contain provisions that dictate an interpretive role for the political branches. Barkow maintained that *Marbury v. Madison* itself contains the seeds for the view that the authority to answer some constitutional questions rests entirely with the political branches.[113] In essence, Barkow understood that the power of judicial review was not absolute. Nahamya did not consider these views of Barkow.

Besides, Barkow's views are not binding on Ugandan courts. Another concern is that Judge Nahamya ignores local jurisprudence on the subject. As discussed above, in his formulation of the political question doctrine for Uganda, Justice Kanyeihamba reasoned that the Constitution of Uganda provides that the constitutional platform is to be shared among the three arms of government, and that courts need to bear in mind the judgements of other repositories of constitutional power concerning the scope of their authority and the necessity for each to keep within its powers, including the courts themselves.[114] According to Kanyeihamba, other branches of government are capable of providing substantive meaning to constitutional provisions and this has to be respected. Instead of relying on the relevant local authorities, Nahamya focuses on American authorities that were not on point.

Secondly, in support of her decision to dismiss the political question doctrine argument in the case, Nahamya made another observation that the current position in the United States is that the doctrine is at odds with the US Supreme Court's view of its place in a constitutional order. She cited the case of *Bush v. Gore*[115] as an example where the US Supreme Court chose not to make mention of the doctrine in support of her view about the validity of the doctrine in the United States. Moreover, Judge Nahamya cites *Bush v. Gore* to advance the proposition that the political question doctrine was no longer favoured in the United States. She then posed the question: Why should a Ugandan court be persuaded to follow a doctrine that is almost being phased out from where it originates?

111 Barkow, 2002, p. 239.
112 *Id.*
113 *Id.*
114 *Attorney-General v. Tinyefuza*, 1997, p. 12.
115 *Bush v. Gore* 531 US 98 (2000).

I submit that Judge Nahamya's observations should be rejected on two grounds. (1) Nahamya offered no authority for her conclusion that the political question doctrine is disfavoured by the US Supreme Court or by courts in the United States in general. In fact, two years after Nahamya made her statement the US Supreme Court decided *Zivotofsky v. Clinton* in which the political question doctrine was upheld by the entire bench. The only difference among the justices was whether the doctrine should continue to incorporate prudential considerations. The US Supreme Court resolved that going forward the political question doctrine will only contain the classical considerations or the first two factors in *Baker v. Carr*. It is evident that Nahamya relied heavily and selectively on Barkow's views about the status of the doctrine at the time of her writing. She omitted to recognize that Barkow's article is probably irrelevant in the light of *Zivotofsky v. Clinton*.

Furthermore, I find the reference to *Bush v. Gore* to be misplaced. The fact that *Bush v. Gore* did not invoke the doctrine does not mean the doctrine is no longer good law.[116] Similarly, Nahamya's observation that *Baker v. Carr* did not find the questions raised in that case to be political questions does not mean that the doctrine is discredited or no longer good law. The fact is that *Baker v. Carr* laid out a principle that would be used in all future political questions cases until *Zivotofsky v. Clinton* was decided. The application of any legal principle will always dependent on facts. Evidently, the facts in *Baker v. Carr*[117] did not support the application of the doctrine, but undoubtedly the doctrine remains relevant and good law.

Before proceeding to my last point, let me draw your attention to Nahamya's dismissiveness of the political question doctrine. As mentioned above, Nahamya makes the point that the doctrine has neither legislative source nor constitutional source. This is incorrect. If one views, as most academics and US federal courts have done,[118] the political question as being divided into two versions one being classical political question and the other prudential political question, it follows that one should have the benefit of the knowledge that the classical strand views the doctrine as a command from the Constitution and focuses

116 For a discussion and criticism of *Bush v. Gore's* failure to apply the political question doctrine, *see*, S. Alton, 'From Marbury v. Madison to Bush v. Gore: 200 Years of Judicial Review in the United States', *Texas Wesleyan Law Review*, Vol. 8, 2001, p. 7; E. Chemerinsky, 'Bush v. Gore was not Justiciable', *Notre Dame Law Review*, Vol. 76, No. 4, 2001, p. 1093 and J. Raskin, 'What's Wrong With Bush v. Gore and Why We Need to Amend the Constitution to Ensure It Never Happens Again', *Maryland Law Review*, Vol. 61, 2001, p. 652.

117 As well as in *Marbury v. Madison* and recently in *Zivotofsky v. Clinton*.

118 *Corrie v. Caterpillar*; *Goldwater v. Carter* 444 US 996 (1979) (Powell J., concurring); *Nixon v. United States* 506 US 224 (1992), pp. 252-253 (Souter J., concurring) (noting that applying the political question doctrine requires case-by-case attention to prudential concerns); *Wang v. Masaitis* 416 F 3d 992, 996 (9th Cir 2005) (discussing Powell J.'s approach); *Warth v. Seldin*, 422 US 490 (1975) and 767 *Third Avenue Association v. Consulate General of the Socialist Federal Republic of Yugoslavia* 218 F 3d 152 (2d Cir 2000), p. 164 (noting that although prudential considerations may inform a court's justiciability analysis, the political question doctrine is essentially a constitutional limitation on the courts.).

on the text of the Constitution as its source,[119] while as the prudential strand focuses on the consequences of a court asserting jurisdiction on matters that are inappropriate for judicial review.[120] Nahamya's analysis seems to emphasize the prudential strand of the doctrine, which as demonstrated above has been discredited and perhaps even overruled in *Zivotofsky v. Clinton.* She ignores the Attorney General's classical political question theory-based argument in favour of the doctrine.

(2) Nahamya's view should be disdained because there is no legal authority for her proposition that the political question doctrine is almost phased out. Her views ignore the fact that federal and state courts in the United States routinely apply the doctrine in the adjudication of constitutional cases, and her hasty conclusions were based on an analysis of limited US Supreme Court authorities. Besides, the political question doctrine, as Dennison has argued, is part of Ugandan law. It no longer matters where the doctrine was borrowed from because the doctrine has taken a life of its own in Uganda. This is why two years after Nahamya's ruling, the Ugandan Supreme Court reaffirmed the doctrine in that country. Nevertheless, at the end of her analysis, Judge Nahamya found that the matters before her were not political questions but human rights questions, and, as a result dismissed the preliminary points of law.[121]

Some commentators read Nahamya's ruling as signalling the potential demise of the doctrine in Uganda.[122] Amerit Timothy has described Nahamya's ruling as "worth of celebration as it seems to nail the concept of the non-justiciability of the doctrine of political question, into the legal coffins of Uganda's jurisprudence".[123] In addition, Timothy notes that there was nothing much left of the doctrine in Uganda.[124] He argues that the political question doctrine has no space in this era of democracy, justice and constitutionalism. The views by Timothy are premature and probably redundant given that the Constitutional Court and Supreme Court upheld the doctrine in *Centre of Health Human Rights v. Attorney-General.* As early as February 2012, the Constitutional Court without mentioning the doctrine by name dismissed a case on the basis of the doctrine.

---

119 *See*, Wechsler, 1961; *Scharpf*, 1966 and Weston, 1925.

120 *Corrie v. Caterpillar*, 2007.

121 G. Skinner, 'Misunderstood, Misconstrued, and Now Clearly Dead: The Political Question Doctrine as a Justiciability Doctrine', *Journal of Law & Politics*, Vol. 29, 2013-2014, p. 479 (arguing that federal courts should not rely on the political question doctrine to avoid adjudicating individual rights claims).

122 Timothy, 2014.

123 *Id.*

124 *Id.*

4.4 Internal Affairs of Parliament

As one commentator has correctly observed, the political question doctrine led a quiet life in Uganda since *Tinyefuza* was decided.[125] The political question theory and reasoning resurfaced in *Severino.*[126] The case of *Severino* involved a constitutional challenge to the decision of Parliament to establish an *ad hoc* parliamentary committee to investigate allegations of bribery in the oil sector and to report back to Parliament. The question before the court was whether Parliament had the authority to establish the *ad hoc* committee. The Constitutional Court held that despite the political atmosphere, the setting up of the *ad hoc* committee by Parliament was constitutionally permissible under Article 90 of the Constitution of 1995,[127] and that it (the Constitutional Court) cannot interfere with Parliament's choice. The court reasoned that any intervention in this matter, as invited to do so by the plaintiff, would amount to undue meddling with the legitimate internal workings of Parliament.

Implicit in the court's holding and reasoning are theories and considerations that underpin the political question doctrine. It is inconsequential that the court did not mention the doctrine by name. Nonetheless, it is clear that the court applied the theory of the doctrine when it rejected the invitation by the plaintiff to intervene in the parliamentary process reasoning that the issue was assigned, by Article 90 of the Constitution 1995, to the legislative branch of government and that it was not appropriate for judicial review. The court recognized that to adjudicate the matter would amount to an impermissible interference in the affairs of Parliament. These are precisely the type of considerations that the political question doctrine demands of a court in theory and practice.

Dennison, who has studied the growth and development of the political question doctrine in Uganda, has similarly observed that the judgement in *Severino* was decided on political question grounds without naming the doctrine. In his analysis, Dennison comments that "this zone of non-interference with the internal workings of another branch of government is one of the most common typologies of the political question doctrine."[128]

---

125 Dennison, 2014, p. 272.

126 *Severino v. Attorney-General*, Constitutional Petition 47 of 2011 (2012).

127 Art. 90 of the Constitution provides "90. Committees of Parliament. (1) Parliament shall appoint standing committees and other committees necessary for the efficient discharge of its functions. (2) The committees of Parliament shall include sessional committees and a committee of the whole house. (3) Rules of procedure of Parliament shall prescribe the composition and functions of committees of Parliament.(4) In the exercise of their functions under this article, committees of Parliament – (a) may call any Minister or any person holding public office and private individuals to submit memoranda or appear before them to give evidence; (b) may co-opt any member of Parliament or employ qualified persons to assist them in the discharge of their functions; (c) shall have the powers of the High Court for – (i) enforcing the attendance of witnesses and examining them on oath, affirmation or otherwise; (ii) compelling the production of documents; and (iii) issuing a commission or request to examine witnesses abroad."

128 Dennison, 2014, p. 272.

He further observed that while the ruling made no mention of the doctrine, there is sufficient evidence in the reasoning of the court that the doctrine has retained its currency as an established and binding principle in Uganda.[129] A few months after *Severino* was decided, the judiciary in Uganda was presented with another task where the political question doctrine was expressly considered and applied to dismiss a case.

4.5 Maternal Health Matters

4.5.1 Constitutional Court Approach to Maternal Health Matters

As we are about to see in this section, the right to health is a contentious public policy issue in Uganda. The Constitutional Court of Uganda recently applied the judgement in *Tinyefuza* to dismiss a constitutional petition in *Centre of Health Human Rights v. Attorney-General,*[130] a case challenging government action or inaction on the basis of the political question doctrine as articulated in *Tinyefuza.*

In *Centre of Health Human Rights v. Attorney-General,* the plaintiffs petitioned the Constitutional Court, in terms of Sections 137(3) and 45 of the Constitution of 1995, in order to challenge the failure of government to provide basic maternal commodities in government health facilities. The plaintiffs sought a declaration that acts or omission of government, which have led to high maternal deaths in Uganda, were inconsistent with the constitutional right to life and health.

At the start of the proceedings, the government raised a preliminary objection to the Constitutional Court's jurisdiction to hear the matter on the basis that the political question doctrine prohibits the judiciary from adjudicating cases of this nature.[131] To some extent, the government's preliminary objection is consistent with Justice Kanyeihamba's pronouncement in *Tinyefuza* "that courts have no jurisdiction over matters which are within the constitutional and legal powers of the legislature or the executive."[132] What is more, the government can be read to be of the same mind with Professor Barkow's thinking that "the political question doctrine requires the Court to determine as a threshold matter in all cases whether the question before it has been assigned by the Constitution to another branch of government."[133]

129 *Id.*

130 *Centre of Health Human Rights v. Attorney-General,* Constitutional Petition No. 16 of (2011).

131 *Centre of Health Human Rights v. Attorney-General,* 2011, citing *Attorney-General v. Tinyefuza, Baker v. Carr;* and *R v. Cambridge Health Authority ex PB* [1995] 2 ALL ER 129.

132 *Attorney General v. Tinyefuza* (Kanyeihamba J.) 12-13.

133 Barkow, 2002, pp. 243-244.

Relying on *Tinyefuza* and other foreign authorities, the government argued that the way the petition was framed required the court to make a judicial decision involving political questions, which the court had to determine at the outset whether it had jurisdiction to determine those questions.[134] Furthermore, it argued that in adjudicating such matters, the Constitutional Court would in effect be interfering with political discretion, which by law is a preserve of the executive and legislature.[135]

Again, the government's view was that the Constitutional Court should not deal directly with questions that the Constitution of 1995 has made the sole responsibility of other branches of government; that for the Constitutional Court to determine the issues in the petition, it would be required to review all the policies of the entire health sector and make findings on them, and that the implementation of these policies was the sole preserve of the executive and legislature.[136] To further substantiate its claims, the government submitted an affidavit by the Principal Secretary of the Ministry of Health, which outlined the efforts and strategies undertaken by the government to improve maternal health services and ensure high standards in the health sector.[137] It then cited Sections 111(2)[138] and 176(2)(e)[139] of the Constitution of 1995 that it claimed preserved the right of the executive and the legislature to formulate, review and implement policies and allocate resources.

In dismissing the petition, the Constitutional Court endorsed, as good law, the political question doctrine as pronounced in *Tinyefuza.*[140] While the Court was correct in stating that that doctrine had been applied by the Supreme Court in *Tinyefuza*, it is important to point out that the Constitutional Court first adopted and applied the political question doctrine in *Ex Parte Matovu* and subsequently applied it in *Andrew Kayira v. Edward Rugumayo.*[141] In fact, in *Tinyefuza* Justice Kanyeihamba acknowledged that *Ex Parte Matovu* had adopted the political question doctrine as a sound principle to be applied in Uganda. Perhaps, one of the significance of highlighting *Tinyefuza's* application of the political question doctrine is that it was the first case that applied the doctrine after the 1995 Constitution. Prior to *Tinyefuza*, it remained uncertain whether the political question doctrine was applicable in Uganda after the adoption of the 1995 Constitution.

---

134 *Centre of Health Human Rights v. Attorney-General* 2011, at para. 14.

135 *Id.*

136 *Id.*

137 *Id.*, at paras. 14-15.

138 *Id.*, at paras. 14-15, citing Section 111(2) which provides that "the functions of the Cabinet shall be to determine, formulate and implement the policy of the Government and to perform such other functions as may be conferred by this Constitution or any other law."

139 *Centre of Health Human Rights v. Attorney-General* 2011, at paras. 14-15, citing Sections 176(2)(e) which provides that "appropriate measures shall be taken to enable local government units to plan, initiate and execute policies in respect of all matters affecting the people within their jurisdictions."

140 *Centre of Health Human Rights v. Attorney-General* 2011, at paras. 14-15, citing *Attorney-General v. Tinyefuza; Baker v. Carr*; and *Coleman v. Miller.*

141 *Andrew Kayira v. Edward Rugumayo.*

In justifying the application of the political question doctrine in *Centre of Health Human Rights v. Attorney-General*, the Court reasoned that the Constitution of 1995 clearly stipulated the different roles assigned to each of the three organs of government.[142] According to the Court, this implied that the autonomy of each organ of government must be immune from undue intrusion from the others.[143] In as much as it may be correct that the government had not allocated sufficient resources to the health sectors, the Constitutional Court reasoned that the duty to determine such matters was the preserve of the executive and no other organ of government.[144]

For this reason, the Constitutional Court pronounced that it is bound to leave certain constitutional questions of a political nature to the executive and legislature to determine.[145] The Court justified its reluctance in adjudicating the issues in the petition arguing that in doing so it would be substituting its discretion for that of the executive.[146] In other words, the Court was concerned that by adjudicating the issues in the petition, it would intrude into the domain of the executive in conflict with the principle of separation of powers.

Therefore, the Constitutional Court sustained the government's preliminary objections and held that it had no power to determine or enforce its jurisdiction on matters that required analysis of government health sector policies because the acts or omissions complained of were committed to the political branches and thus fell under the political question doctrine.[147] Professor Wechsler and other commentators characterize the judicial thinking reflected in *Centre of Health Human Rights v. Attorney-General* as the classical political question doctrine.[148] According to Trevor Cutaiar, the classical political question doctrine was recognized in the landmark case of *Marbury v. Madison*.[149] The basic premise of the classical version is that "the political question doctrine is itself a product of constitutional interpretation, rather than of judicial discretion."[150] I agree with proponents of the classical political question doctrine that the only appropriate use of the doctrine is to

142 *Centre of Health Human Rights v. Attorney-General* 2011, at para. 24.

143 *Id.*

144 *Id.*, at para. 25.

145 *Id.*, at para. 26.

146 *Id.*, at para. 25.

147 *Id.*, at paras. 25-26.

148 Wechsler, 1961, p. 9. Wechsler has been interpreted as stating that the judiciary has no basis, and or business, abstaining to hear a case where the Constitution could fairly be interpreted as requiring them to abstain. *See*, Gouin, 1994, p. 778. *See also*, Cutaiar, 2009. The other political question doctrine version is called the prudential version commonly associated from Professor Bickel. The prudential version is a judge-made overlay that courts have used at their discretion to protect their legitimacy and to avoid conflict with the other political branches. *See*, Barkow, 2002, p. 253.

149 Cutaiar, 2009, p. 398 (arguing that the political question doctrine is a product of constitutional interpretation rather than judicial discretion).

150 Scharpf, 1966, p. 538.

jurisprudentially guide the court in determining the circumstances where a constitution has committed to another branch of government the determination of a question.[151]

The Court in *Centre of Health Human Rights v. Attorney-General* has been criticized by public interest organizations as being unprogressive.[152] Most of these criticisms are either in favour or against the application of the doctrine in Uganda.[153] One of the scholarly commentaries on the judgement has come from Dennison. Dennison makes the general point that critics of the must come to grips with the established power of the political question doctrine.[154] He makes two important assertions about the source of the doctrine and how it ought to be applied in Uganda.

Firstly, he identifies two constitutional provisions that provide the basis for the doctrine in Uganda. The first provision is Article 1 of the Uganda Constitution, which provides that:

1. All power belongs to the people who shall exercise their sovereignty in accordance with this Constitution.
2. Without limiting the effect of clause (1) of this article, all authority in the State emanates from the people of Uganda, and the people shall be governed through their will and consent.
3. All power and authority of Government and its organs derive from this Constitution, which in turn derives its authority from the people who consent to be governed in accordance with this Constitution.

151 Wechsler, 1961, pp. 7-8.

152 *See*, S. Francis, 'Strict Interpretation of Political Question Doctrine a Challenge to Realizing the Right to Health-Human Rights Commission Report', 2013, available from www.cehurd.org/2013/04/strict-interpretation-of-political-question-doctrine-a-challenge-to-realizing-the-right-to-health-human-rights-commission-report-2012/ (criticizing that the Constitutional Court strictly interpreted the separation of powers thereby making it a challenge to enforce the right to health including access to quality health care and services as a Constitutional right in Uganda); Initiative For Social Economic Rights, A Political Question? Reflecting on the Constitutional Court's Ruling in the Maternal Mortality Case (*CEHURD & Others v. Attorney-General of Uganda*, 2011) (advocating against the political question doctrine in Uganda and the justiciability of social economic rights in Uganda noting that the Committee on Economic, Social and Cultural Rights has condemned the political question doctrine), at p. 2, available from www.iser-uganda.org/images/downloads/ISER_Commentary_maternal_mortality_case.pdf. *See also* General Comment No. 9, at para. 10 by the Committee on Economic, Social and Cultural Rights stating "It is sometimes suggested that matters involving the allocation of resources should be left to the political authorities rather than the courts. While the respective competences of the various branches of government must be respected, it is appropriate to acknowledge that courts are generally already involved in a considerable range of matters which have important resource implications. The adoption of a rigid classification of economic, social and cultural rights which puts them, by definition, beyond the reach of the courts would thus be arbitrary and incompatible with the principle that the two sets of human rights are indivisible and interdependent. It would also drastically curtail the capacity of the courts to protect the rights of the most vulnerable and disadvantaged groups in society."

153 Timothy, 2014.

154 Dennison, 2014, p. 279.

4. The people shall express their will and consent on who shall govern them and how they should be governed, through regular, free and fair elections of their representatives or through referenda.

Additionally, he claims that the above provisions have to be read together with Article 126(1) of the Uganda Constitution, which provides that:

(1) Judicial power is derived from the people and shall be exercised by the courts established under this Constitution in the name of the people and in conformity with law and with the values, norms and aspirations of the people.

In Dennison's view, the doctrine provides the judiciary with a legal device to give effect to Articles 1 and 126 and allows the people, through their representatives and the courts, to govern themselves.[155]

Secondly, Dennison strongly believes that there is value in the political question doctrine, and maintains that as a general rule; human rights-based claims do not bar the application of the doctrine but requires the judiciary to balance the separation of powers considerations demanded by the doctrine against any human rights interests.[156] He is critical of the way the court applied the doctrine in *Centre of Health Human Rights v. Attorney-General*. He argues that while the court had the jurisprudential license to evoke the doctrine, it was exceedingly applied.[157] In his view, the court should not have employed the doctrine to avert the determination of whether there is a constitutional right to health in Uganda.[158] He believes that before dismissing a case on political question grounds, the judiciary should know what rights exist or not.[159] Dennison claims that this was particularly true in Uganda where the existence of the right to health is uncertain. He thus disapproved the court's approach of employing the doctrine as a way of dealing with the complexity of this question and the political fallout that could have ensued from any judicial enforcement of the right to health.

Essentially, underneath Dennison's criticism is a suggestion that the judiciary in Uganda should not invoke the doctrine for fear of the political ramifications for their intervention. Instead, the focus for the application of the doctrine must be based on the principle that the issue is a political question, which is constitutionally assigned to another branch. It is difficult to disagree with Dennison's argument.

155 *Id.*, p. 281.
156 *Id.*, pp. 265, 273.
157 *Id.*, p. 281.
158 *Id.*, pp. 283-284.
159 *Id.*, p. 284.

Whereas the question of whether or not the right to health exists under Uganda's Constitution should not be avoided using the political question doctrine, Dennison is prepared to accept that if the right to health existed the next related question would be what sort of minimum threshold of health is required. According to Dennison, a court may abstain from the determination of that question on the basis of the political question doctrine since that determination is likely to intrude into the functions of the political branches. Although I agree with Dennison's observations and contentions above, it is submitted that he goes too far when he argues that the political question doctrine is a discretionary rule for courts to use or not. I disagree with this view and submit that if Dennison subscribes to the classical political question theory, he should therefore accept the fact that the doctrine is an implied command of the constitution. In this regard, the doctrine is not a discretionary rule but a constitutional necessity. Courts are required to apply the doctrine as part of their compliance with the principle of separation of powers.

Despite Dennison's critical views, Ugandan courts have consistently adhered to the classical political question doctrine and it does not appear that any future application of the doctrine will deviate from this trend. This is likely the case when one considers how the Supreme Court dealt with the maternal health matter.

4.5.2 *Supreme Court Approach to Maternal Health Matters*

The decision of the Constitutional Court in *Centre of Health Human Rights v. Attorney-General* was taken on appeal to the Supreme Court of Uganda.[160] At issue on appeal was whether the political question doctrine remained good law in Uganda. The appellant's main submission was that the Ugandan Constitution should not be interpreted or held hostage to the 19th century American jurisprudence such as *Marbury v. Madison*. The appellants sought to persuade the court to depart from its earlier landmark judgement in *Tinyefuza*, which endorsed the political question doctrine in post 1995 Uganda.[161] In addition, the appellants sought to distinguish the separation of powers principle as conceptualized in the United States from Uganda's own separation of powers.[162] In their last attempt to persuade the Supreme Court, the appellants argued that the political question doctrine was not applicable where individual rights were at issue. This legal proposition, which seeks to define the contours of the doctrine, was well articulated in *Marbury v. Madison* and suggested in *Tinyefuza* that where individual rights are at issue the doctrine would not apply.[163]

160 *Centre of Health Human Rights v. Attorney-General* Appeal No. 1 of (2013).

161 *Id.*, at para. 5.

162 *Id.*, at para. 4.

163 For a discussion about individual rights and the political question doctrine *see*, Chopper, 2005, p. 1469 and Dennison, 2014, p. 275 (arguing that there is a clear correlation between Chopper's description of the proper

Justice Kisaakye, who wrote the main judgement, found that the doctrine is both interpreted and self-imposed by the courts. Classical political question theorists like Story, Cooley, Wechsler and Fritz would disagree with the latter part of that proposition. For Wechsler, the political question doctrine is not a discretionary tool for courts, but must be understood as a command of a constitution.[164] Additionally, Justice Kisaakye held that the political question doctrine has limited application in Uganda and that it only extends to shield both the legislature and executive from judicial scrutiny where either branch is properly exercising its mandate duly vested in it by a constitution. In applying this holding to the case, the Supreme Court reasoned that while the doctrine has limited application in Uganda, the Constitutional Court erred when it dismissed the case on political question grounds without considering the merits.[165]

After considering some authorities from the United States and Uganda in his concurring opinion, Justice Katureebe summarized his findings and held that underneath the political question doctrine is the proposition that "courts will not decide on questions that are purely political and which the Constitution has reserved for determination by the other branches of government in their constitutionally mandated discretion."[166] However, he noted that the authorities recognize that the doctrine would not apply where individual rights are implicated.

Further, in his interpretation and construction of Justice Kanyeihamba's opinion in *Tinyefuza*, Katureebe found that the Supreme Court underscored that the doctrine did not rule out the judiciary from intervening where the political branches acted outside the powers granted to them by the 1995 Constitution.[167] In other words, like Justice Fatai-Williams in the Nigerian context (see discussion below),[168] Justice Katureebe views the political question doctrine as not requiring courts to abstain from adjudicating cases in those instances where a constitution specifically prescribes government procedures. He concluded by proclaiming that under Uganda's political question doctrine, courts will only decline to exercise their jurisdiction to hear and determine issues whose resolution is committed by law to a political branch and the resolution of which would involve intrusion on the executive or legislative domain given that those issues are not capable of judicial

application of the political question doctrine and Kanyeihamba's reference to the violation of individual liberties as a form of government action that is not protected from judicial review by the political question doctrine).

164 Wechsler, 1961, pp. 1-9 and Scharpf, 1966, p. 518.

165 *Centre of Health Human Rights v. Attorney-General* 2013, at para. 15.

166 *Id.*, at paras. 9-15.

167 *Id.*, at para. 10.

168 Who holds the view that the political question does not prevent courts from enforcing what the law expressly requires any political branch to do, except when the Constitution is silent about how the political branch should exercise its powers then doctrine requires courts to abstain from interfering because the political branch has discretion in this regard and its actions are only politically examinable. *AG Bendel v. AG Federation* 1982 10 SC 1, at p. 52.

resolution. Despite this declaration, Katureebe concurred with Justice Kisaakye that the political question doctrine has limited application in Uganda given the provisions of Uganda's Constitution.[169]

The decision in *Centre of Health Human Rights v. Attorney-General* is significant because it confirmed that the political question doctrine remains good law albeit under limited circumstances. While the court held that the doctrine has limited application, it did not, perhaps for good reasons, elaborate what those limited circumstances are thereby leaving this to be decided in a future case or on a case-by-case basis. However, based on the authorities, such as *Marbury v. Madison, Luther v. Borden* and *Ex Parte Matovu* cited with approval by the Supreme Court, it is reasonable to assume that by limited application, the Supreme Court was referring to the classical political question doctrine, and that the doctrine will apply only where the Constitution of 1995 expressly delegates to a specific political branch the resolution of an issue, including discretion to determine such issue. It is without doubt that the judgement by Kisaakye exhibits an endorsement of the classic political question theory in Uganda.

Another significant observation from the Supreme Court ruling in *Centre of Health Human Rights v. Attorney-General* is that it mirrors the development of the political question jurisprudence in the United States, particularly following the decision in *Zivotofsky v. Clinton.* Like *Zivotofsky v. Clinton,* the judgement in *Centre of Health Human Rights v. Attorney-General* stands for the proposition that the doctrine is a narrow exception to the institution of judicial review, and that the Supreme Court has an obligation to decide cases that come before it, unless the Constitution of 1995 has expressly delegated the power to decide the issue to a political branch.[170] Following *Centre of Health Human Rights v. Attorney-General,* it is fair to conclude that the political question doctrine will be applied only in its classical form.

4.6 Conclusion

Based on the foregoing analysis, it is plain that the political question doctrine is an integral part of Uganda's constitutional law.[171] The courts have consistently applied this doctrine to deal with some of the most significant constitutional questions in Uganda. A common feature in the application of this doctrine in Uganda is that courts place a particular emphasis on the 1995 Constitution's text and the preservation of the separation of powers.[172]

169 *Centre of Health Human Rights v. Attorney-General* 2013, at para. 20.

170 *See*, Szurkowski, 2014, p. 350 and *Zivotofsky v. Clinton,* 2012, p. 427.

171 Dennison, 2014, p. 265.

172 *See, Baker v. Carr; Ghana Bar Association; Onuoha v. Okafor* (holding that the lack of satisfactory criteria for a judicial determination of a political question is one of the dominant considerations in determining whether a question falls within the category of political questions); and *Balarabe Musa v. Auta Hamza* 1983

The discussion above demonstrates how Uganda has come to grips with the judicial response to political questions.

However, while the political question doctrine remains part of Ugandan constitutional law, I have argued that Ugandan courts are likely to tread carefully by ensuring that the doctrine has limited application by balancing the separation of powers considerations and cautiously (or attempting to) applying the doctrine. It is important to highlight that Uganda had a military regime at some point in its recent history from which the political question doctrine emerged, and that the doctrine's continued application may have different consequences under the democratic dispensation. Nevertheless, there is no doubt that the courts will develop the classical political question theory that has consistently been applied since *Ex Parte Matovu* in many ways that offer lessons for other countries like South Africa.[173]

(holding that the impeachment of a State governor was a political question not appropriate for judicial review).

173 Dennison, 2014, p. 265.

5 The Application and Evolution of the Political Question Doctrine in Nigeria

5.1 Introduction

Out of all the countries in Africa, Nigeria has had more instances where courts have considered and applied the political question doctrine since the 1960s. The political question theory was first considered in *Attorney General Eastern Nigeria v. Attorney General of the Federation*,[1] where the court held that the determination of the margin of error in census figures was a political question. While using political question theory terminology, the court did not provide any guidance about the scope or content of the doctrine.[2] Given a few changes of government and constitutions in Nigeria after it gained independence from Britain in 1960, it took almost two decades since the decision in *Attorney General Eastern Nigeria v. Attorney General of the Federation* for Nigerian courts to develop a full-fledged political question doctrine.

Some scholars argue that the development of the political question doctrine in Nigeria was largely influenced by the constitutional changes in 1979, which introduced an American presidential system of government founded on separation of powers.[3] According to this view, these changes also precipitated greater reliance on American case law and jurisprudence.[4] It is evident from existing jurisprudence and academic commentaries that Nigerian courts imported the political question doctrine as pronounced in the United States and formulated a doctrine for Nigeria. An examination of Nigerian jurisprudence further demonstrates that the doctrine has traditionally been applied in three main areas of dispute: impeachment proceedings, political parties' primary elections and internal affairs of parliament.

This chapter will examine the origins, application and status of the political question doctrine in Nigeria. It seeks to pinpoint and examine any unique aspects of the political question doctrine as applied by Nigerian courts with a view to draw lessons for South Africa. Given the constitutional changes in Nigeria since the political question doctrine was first considered, the chapter will investigate the attitudes of the courts towards the doctrine under Nigerian constitutional law post the 1999 reforms. Through an analysis of

1 *Attorney General Eastern Nigeria v. Attorney General of the Federation* (1964) ALL NLR 218 (holding that the determination of the margin of error in a census was a political question).

2 Egbewole & Olatunji, 2012, p. 125, fn. 29; and Nwauche, 2010, p. 33.

3 Egbewole & Olatunji, 2012, pp. 125-128; and Nwauche, 2010, p. 33.

4 *Id.*

the case law, the chapter will also investigate whether the political question doctrine remains good law in Nigeria. It will consider the attitude of Nigerian courts towards the usage of the classical and prudential political question theories and determine the dominant theory.

5.2 Impeachment Proceedings

The first Nigerian case to substantively consider and apply the political question doctrine is *Balarabe Musa.*[5] In this case, the Court of Appeal ruled that the impeachment of the governor of Kaduna State was a non-justiciable political question. The case arose out of impeachment proceedings initiated by the Kaduna State House of Assembly in terms of Section 170 of the Constitution of the Federal Republic of Nigeria 1979 (Constitution 1979) against the governor. The governor attacked the constitutionality of Section 170 of the Constitution 1979 on the basis of which the House of Assembly sought to carry on with the impeachment proceedings against him. Section 170 provided in pertinent part as follows:

> *Section 170*
> 1. The Governor or Deputy Governor of a State may be removed from office in accordance with the provisions of this section.
> 2. Whenever a notice of any allegation in writing signed by not less than one-third of the members of the House of Assembly:
>   a. is presented to the Speaker of the House of Assembly of State
>   b. stating that the holder of such office is guilty of gross misconduct in the performance of the functions of his office, detailed particulars of which shall be specified, the Speaker of the House of Assembly shall within 7 days of the receipt of the notice cause a copy thereof to be served on the holder of the office and on each member of the House of Assembly and shall also cause any statement made in reply to the allegations by the holder of the office to be served on each member of the House of Assembly.
> 3. Within 14 days of the presentation of the notice to the Speaker of the House of Assembly…the House of Assembly shall resolve by motion without any debate whether or not the allegation shall be investigated.
> 4. (…)
> 5. Within 7 days of the passing of a motion under the foregoing provisions the Speaker of the House of Assembly shall cause the allegation to be

5 *Balarabe Musa v. Auta Hamza*, 1983.

investigated by a Committee of 7 persons who in his opinion are of high integrity, not being members of any public service, legislative house or political party, and who shall have been nominated and, with approval of the House of Assembly, appointed by the Speaker of the House to conduct the investigation.

6. (...)
7. (...)
8. (...)
9. (...)
10. No proceedings or determination of the Committee or the House of Assembly or any matter relating thereto shall be entertained or questioned in any court.

In his constitutional attack, the governor contended that the House of Assembly had no jurisdiction to impeach him because it failed to comply with Section 170(2) and (5) of the Constitution 1979. The court construed Section 170(10) as a limitation on its powers to review any proceedings in the House of Assembly or the Committee or any determination by the House of Assembly or Committee. The court went on to rule that once the legislature commenced proceedings under Section 170(2), the jurisdiction of the court was limited by Section 170(10).[6]

In addition to the limitation in Section 170(10), the court found that judicial intervention in impeachment processes was inappropriate because the matter involved political questions. The court, as per Justice Ademola, reasoned that:

> ...the learned counsel for the appellant has called for the intervention of the judiciary in the impeachment proceedings. However, well-meaning the call might be, the law of the land... prevents such intervention. More than that, it is a political matter; self-restraint should ... be a virtue the court should cultivate. For the court to enter into the political thicket as the invitation made to it clearly implies in my view be asking its gates and its walls to be painted with mud; and the throne of justice from where its judgments are delivered polished with mire.[7]

While the court made no specific reference to the political question doctrine, part of its rationale in refusing to review the matter was that such a review is productive of insoluble

6 *Id.*, p. 257.
7 *Id.*, 1983, p. 247.

conflicts, and the court used political question theory in deciding the case.[8] Although *Balarabe Musa* was welcomed by commentators, the judgement raised more questions than answers about the future application of the doctrine. However, a few observations could be made about that judgement. What is apparent is that the judgement demonstrated an endorsement of both the classical and prudential political question theories.

In his study of the political question doctrine in Nigeria, Professor Nwauche has observed that *Balarabe Musa* is a significant case because it established two important principles.[9] Firstly, that a constitutional commitment of a function to another branch of government will be approved as grounds for applying the doctrine based on the separation of powers principle. Secondly, certain constitutional questions are more successfully resolved by the political branches of the state and are, therefore, inappropriate for judicial review.[10]

Let me elaborate that Nwauche's observation from *Balarabe Musa* represents the classical political question because the court viewed the doctrine as emanating from the Constitution itself; that the doctrine will apply if the text and Constitution commits a function or an issue, that requires to be resolved, to another branch of government and will be approved as a basis of requiring courts to abstain from supplying substantive content involving those functions or issues. More importantly, this principle is motivated by separation of powers considerations.

The second principle that emerged from *Balarabe Musa* is that it introduced the prudential political question doctrine into Nigerian law. This assertion is predicated on the fact that the court in that case established the principle that certain questions are not appropriate for judicial review. However, it was not clear from *Balarabe Musa* how future courts would determine what questions are inappropriate for judicial review. In spite of this, given the court's reference to *Baker v. Carr*, it was reasonable for every Nigerian practitioner and academic to assume that some of the prudential considerations alluded to in that case would apply in Nigeria. These two important principles in *Balarabe Musa* were affirmed by the Nigerian Supreme Court in *Onuoha v. Okafor*.

5.3 Political Party Primaries

Onuoha v. Okafor[11] is probably the case that solidified the establishment of the political question theory in Nigeria by the Supreme Court. In *Onuoha v. Okafor*, the plaintiff brought a cause of action to require the National People's Party to nominate and sponsor him for

8 *Id.*, 1983, p. 247.
9 *See*, Nwauche, 2010, p. 38.
10 *Id.*, p. 33. Egbewole & Olatunji, 2012, pp. 125-130; Imam et al., 2011.
11 *Onuoha v. Okafor* (1983) 2 NCLR 244.

a senatorial district seat and not the defendant. The two potential candidates had each contested for the senate seat and the committee set up to select a candidate, who would represent the party, chose the plaintiff. As a result, the defendant lodged a complaint, which was adjudicated by the State Working Committee of the National People's Party. The State Working Committee nullified the selection of the plaintiff and chose the defendant. The plaintiff instituted an action in the High Court, which found in his favour. The defendant appealed against this decision. His main contention on appeal was that a court of law ought not entertain an action to determine whom a political party should or should not sponsor for an elective office. The defendant was successful in his appeal and the matter ended up in the Supreme Court.

At the Supreme Court, Justice Obaseki, who delivered the leading judgement in the case, dismissed the case for lack of subject-matter jurisdiction. He framed the issue before the court as an inquiry into whether the court ought to make an order directing the National People's Party to sponsor the losing candidate. In his view, the answer to this question had to be negative because it was not appropriate for the judiciary to determine such questions. He explained that a positive response would instantly drive the court into the area of jurisdiction to run and manage political parties and politicians, and in doing so, the court would be deciding a political question which it is not fitted to do.[12]

Furthermore, Justice Obaseki reasoned that:

> implicit in the right to canvass for votes for a candidate is the right to sponsor and the right to withhold sponsorship from a candidate or not to sponsor a candidate for election.[13]

He found that the expressed intention of the Constitution 1979 and the Electoral Act of 1982 is to give a political party (such as the National People's Party) the right freely to choose the candidate it will sponsor for election to any elective office. According to Justice Obaseki, the exercise of this right is the domestic affair of the National People's Party guided by its constitution. For Justice Obaseki, the issue therefore was whether a court can justifiably interfere under any guise with the free exercise of this right by a political party. In his view, there was no legal basis for such intervention. He reasoned that since there are no judicial criteria or yardstick to determine which candidate a political party ought to choose, the judiciary is, therefore, unable to exercise any judicial power in the matter.

Besides, Justice Obaseki explained that this is a matter over which the Supreme Court had no subject-matter jurisdiction. Accordingly, the question of which candidate a political party will sponsor is more in the nature of a political question which courts are not qualified

12 *Id.*
13 *Id.*

to deliberate upon and answer. The power to decide such political questions is entrusted to the leader of a political party in terms of Section 30(4) of the Electoral Act 1982. As a result, the court refused to exercise jurisdiction on the basis that to do so would project or propel it into the area of jurisdiction to run and manage political parties.

In the end, the Supreme Court concluded that the matter in dispute was not justiciable, and that a non-justiciable dispute is presented to a court when the parties seek adjudication of only a political question.[14] Justice Obaseki further held, using American political question language, that the determination of questions of a political nature is exclusively committed to the political party, the executive and legislative branches of the government. Relying on *Baker v. Carr* and other American authorities, Justice Obaseki formulated a two-part test for the determination of the political question doctrine in Nigeria. He declared that:

> the lack of satisfactory criteria for a judicial determination of a political question is one of the dominant considerations in determining whether a question falls within the category of political questions. The other is the appropriations of attributing finality to the action of the political departments and political parties under the Nigerian Constitution and system of government.[15]

In applying the two-part test to the case, Obaseki found that there were no satisfactory judicial criteria that could be employed by the Supreme Court to adjudicate on the matter and determine the candidate to be elected for office. Lastly, Obaseki observed that the jurisdiction conferred on the Supreme Court by Section 236 of the Constitution 1979 is to hear and determine any civil proceedings in which the existence or extent of a legal right, power, duty, liability, intent, obligation or claim is in issue.[16] He found that the right to sponsorship by a political party was not vested in the plaintiff. In other words, the plaintiff was not vested with the right to be sponsored under the Constitution 1979, the Electoral Act, the common law, customary law or any other statute.[17]

The remaining justices of the Supreme Court agreed with the proposition in the main judgement by Justice Obaseki that the issue before them was not justiciable and the court

---

14 *Onuoha v. Okafor*, citing *Flast v. Cohen* 392 US 83 (1942).

15 *Onuoha v. Okafor* (Obaseki J.).

16 Section 236 of the Constitution 1979 provided: Jurisdiction: general 236. (1) Subject to the provisions of this Constitution and in addition to such other jurisdiction as may be conferred upon it by law, the High Court of a State shall have unlimited jurisdiction to hear and determine any civil proceedings in which the existence or extent of a legal right, power, duty, liability, privilege, interest, obligation or claim is in issue or to hear and determine any criminal proceedings involving or relating to any penalty, forfeiture, punishment or other liability in respect of an offence committed by any person. (2) The reference to civil or criminal proceedings in this section includes a reference to the proceedings that originate in the High Court of a State and those that are brought before the High Court to be dealt with by the court in the exercise of its appellate or supervisory jurisdiction.

17 *Onuoha v. Okafor.*

below was correct in denying jurisdiction to determine the matter. In his analysis, supportive of the leading judgement, Justice Aniagolu, who understood as being called upon to determine the proper candidate for the National People's Party, posed the following questions, which he answered in the negative and said that:

> Where the court forces a candidate on a political party, will the court proceed to campaign for votes for the candidate of its verdict? If not, in order not to render its order nugatory, will the court then proceed to make a further order that the political party must campaign for votes for the candidate of its verdict?

Justice Aniagolu observed that the negative answers to these questions demonstrate how unreasonable it is for a court to dabble itself in affairs that do not lie within its competence,[18] and that the judiciary in the prevailing constitutional order was not to determine candidates for elective office even if it was under the guise of enforcing or adjudicating political party constitutions.

Some commentators have criticized the court's refusal to adjudicate the matter on the basis of the political question doctrine by drawing an analogy between intervention by courts in disputes over political party primaries and corporate takeover disputes between contending directors and shareholders.[19] They argue that it is devoid of judicial logic for courts to abstain from adjudicating the former disputes, on the basis that it would drive courts into the jurisdiction to run and manage political parties, than to accede the adjudication of corporate takeovers bids without concern of driving themselves into the jurisdiction to run and manage corporations.[20] They assert that this state of affairs is untenable.[21]

Despite the relevance of the above analogy between political party primaries and corporate takeovers, it is submitted that the two should be distinguished in favour of sustaining the application of the political question doctrine in political party primaries. There are prudential and separations of powers considerations involved in the political party primary case that are not present in the corporate takeover cases. In the political party cases, the executive and legislature are involved at a political level, in ways that could destabilize the balance of powers contemplated by the separation of powers, than in corporate takeover cases. As one commentator has correctly observed:

> political parties are not like other private associations and cannot be treated as if they were... political parties affect the political process directly: party nomi-

18 *Id.*
19 Egbewole & Olatunji, 2012, p. 133.
20 *Id.*
21 *Id.*

> nations is the first step in the process of choosing public decision makers... the nomination is as much state action as the official election.[22]

Given these prudential and separations of power considerations, it is submitted that the Supreme Court's approach in *Onuoha v. Okafor* is logical and justified.

It is clear that the decision in *Onuoha v. Okafor* was heavily influenced by authorities from the United States on the political question doctrine. Even though the court formulated a relevant two-part test to determine whether a case presents a non-justiciable political question, the Supreme Court did not comprehensively articulate the constitutional source of the doctrine in Nigeria. Nevertheless, the *Onuoha v. Okafor* Court (and to some extent *Balarabe Musa*) has implicitly pigeonholed the doctrine as an aspect of separation of powers, but when you consider the two-part test adopted in *Onuoha v. Okafor,* it remains ambiguous whether the doctrine (at least in the Nigerian context) derived exclusively from the Constitution 1979 or from prudential considerations about the proper role of the judiciary under Nigeria's constitutional order.[23] Jurists and commentators debate and disagree on these questions.[24] The debate has centred around two theories of the doctrine.

According to the first theory, commonly referred to as the classical or textual political question theory, the doctrine must be understood as a constitutional exigency rather than discretionary.[25] It applies to cases only when the text and structure of a constitution expressly commits the resolution of a question to another branch of government.[26] According to Professor Wechsler, who is associated with the classical theory of the doctrine:

> all the doctrine can defensibly imply is that the courts are called upon to judge whether the Constitution has committed to another agency of government the autonomous determination of the issue raised, a finding that itself requires an interpretation.[27]

The proposition is that the political question doctrine is a product of constitutional interpretation rather than of judicial discretion.[28] Hence, when called upon to engage in interpretation, a court does not abdicate its duty to interpret a constitution, but rather it inter-

22 Pietzman, 1974, p. 363.

23 *See*, Nwauche, 2010, p. 57. *See also*, O. Oko, 'The Problems and Challenges of Lawyering in Developing Societies', *Rutgers Law Journal*, Vol. 35, 2004, p. 569.

24 Bickel, 1962; Wechsler, 1961; *Scharpf*, 1966; Redish, 1984; Mhango, 2014; and *Onuoha v. Okafor* (Obaseki J.).

25 Wechsler, 1961 and *Scharpf*, 1966.

26 Szurkowski, 2014, p. 347; Wechsler, 1961, pp. 6-10 and Story, 1833, pp. 345-348.

27 Wechsler, 1961, pp. 7-9 and *Scharpf*, 1966, p. 518.

28 *Scharpf*, 1966, p. 538.

prets a constitution as assigning discretion over an issue to another branch.[29] It is for these reasons that early applications of the political question doctrine were firmly grounded on constitutional text and structure.[30] As pointed out earlier in Chapter 2, commentators, in the American context, agree that following *Zivotofsky v. Clinton*, the classical political question theory of the doctrine may be all that is left of the doctrine.[31]

The second theory – prudential political question theory – was well articulated by Finklestein when he observed that:

> There are certain cases which are completely without the sphere of judicial interference. They are called, for historical reasons, political questions. What are these political questions? To what matters does the term apply? It applies to all those matters of which the court, at a given time, will be of the opinion that it is impolitic or inexpedient to take jurisdiction. Sometimes this idea of inexpediency will result from the fear of the vastness of the consequences that a decision on the merits might entail. Sometimes it will result from the feeling that the court is incompetent to deal with the particular type of question involved. Sometimes it will be induced by the feeling that the matter is too high for the courts. But always there will be a weighing of considerations in the scale of political wisdom.[32]

The prudential political question theory was later made famous by Professor Bickel's pronouncement on the passive virtue of the judiciary in which he asserts that the doctrine permits courts to decline to adjudicate cases for prudential reasons as well as textual ones.[33] Bickel was motivated by the thought that when courts frequently declare legislation or executive action to be unconstitutional, they frustrate the will of the people, which has the potential to dent the judiciary whose power arises from the perceived legitimacy in adjudicating cases rather than from passing or enforcing laws.[34] He points out that at some point,

29 Wechsler, 1961, pp. 6-10.

30 Szurkowski, 2014, p. 353. *See also, M'Culloch v. Maryland,* 17 US (4 Wheat) 316 (1819), at p. 325 (ruled that Congress, rather than the judiciary, determines the limits of the Necessary and Proper Clause); *Ware v. Hylton* 3 US (3 Dall) 199 (1796) (held that the Court would not pass on whether a treaty had been infringed); and *Martin v. Mott* 25 US (12 Wheat) 19 (1827) (holding that the President had exclusive power to determine whether the militia should be called out).

31 Szurkowski, 2014, p. 361.

32 Finkelstein, 1923-1924, p. 344; *See also*, Weston, 1925, pp. 297-298.

33 *See*, A. Kronman, 'Alexander Bickel's Philosophy of Prudence', *Yale Law Journal,* Vol. 94, 1985, p. 1567; A. Bickel, 'The Supreme Court 1960 Term Foreword: The Passive Virtues', *Harvard Law Review,* Vol. 75, No. 1, 1961, pp. 74-80; A. Nolan, 'The Doctrine of Constitutional Avoidance: A Legal Overview', *CRS Report for Congress, R43706*, 2014.

34 Bickel, 1962, pp. 16-17. For a discussion of judicial confidence, *see*, I. Mahomed, 'The Role of the Judiciary in a Constitutional State', *South African Law Journal,* Vol. 115, 1999, p. 111 (noting that "unlike Parliament or the executive, the court does not have the power of the purse or the army or the police to execute its will.

continued invalidation of the public mandate enhances the risks of losing that legitimacy. Accordingly, instead of losing legitimacy by invalidating a law or enforcing a poorly imagined policy decision by upholding it, a court may exercise the passive virtue by invoking the political question doctrine to decline to adjudicate a case.[35] Bickel maintains that when this happens, the courts facilitate a dialogue with the political branches and the public about the issues under dispute.[36]

The outlines of the prudential political question are embodied in the following famously quoted statement by Bickel where he said that:

> Such is the foundation of the political-question doctrine: the Court's sense of lack of capacity, compounded in unequal parts of (a) the strangeness of the issue and its intractability to principled resolution; (b) the sheer momentousness of it, which tends to unbalance judicial judgment; (c) the anxiety, not so much that the judicial judgment will be ignored, as that perhaps it should but will not be; (d) finally ('in a mature democracy'), the inner vulnerability, the self-doubt of an institution which is electorally irresponsible and has no earth to draw strength from.[37]

Bickel's concerns and thoughts about the proper role of courts are as much relevant in the United States as they are in other jurisdictions like Nigeria. As Szurkowski has observed, following *Marbury v. Madison* courts consistently applied the classical theory.[38] Prudential considerations only began to be intermingled with classical considerations after *Luther v. Borden* was decided, where courts dismissed cases for a combination of classical and prudential considerations.[39] For example, Szurkowski has noted that in *Luther v. Borden*, the court commenced its opinion by listing a parade of the horrible that could ensue if it had decided the case on the merits.[40] Szurkowski emphasizes that while the decision in *Luther*

The superior courts and the Constitutional Court do not have a single soldier. They would be impotent to protect the Constitution if the agencies of the state which control the mighty physical and financial resources of the state refused to command those resources to enforce the orders of the courts. The courts could be reduced to paper tigers with a ferocious capacity to roar and to snarl but no teeth to bite and no sinews to execute what may then become a piece of sterile scholarship. Its ultimate power must therefore rest on the esteem in which the judiciary is held within the psyche and soul of a nation.") and S. Ngcobo, 'Sustaining Public Confidence in the Judiciary: An Essential Condition for Realising the Judicial Role', *South African Law Journal*, Vol. 128, No. 1, 2011, p. 11 (noting that without public confidence in the judiciary, its ability to do justice is lost. Where people do not trust courts, they will resort to other means to resolve matters that properly belong to the realm of the judiciary).

35 Scharpf, 1966, pp. 537-539.

36 *Id.*

37 Bickel, 1962, p. 184.

38 Szurkowski, 2014, p. 353.

39 *Id.*, pp. 351-352.

40 *See, Luther v. Borden*, 1849, pp. 38-39.

v. Borden was grounded in the text and structure of the Constitution, it acknowledged prudential considerations to underscore the importance of accurately conducting its constitutional interpretation.[41] It was *Baker v. Carr* that formally combined classic and prudential considerations into a full-fledged doctrine.[42]

Acting under the above persuasion, Justices Obaseki and Aniagolu adopted the political question doctrine. It is not possible to clearly discern which theory of the doctrine was adopted or preferred in *Onuoha v. Okafor*. Nevertheless, when one examines the opinion by Justice Obaseki, it appears that he found favour in the classical political question theory because, in his analysis, he makes repeated references to the text of the Constitution as the basis for applying the doctrine. An additional point to make is that his two-part test resembles the first two factors in *Baker v. Carr*, which, as Szurkowski has noted, are simply reiterations of the classical political question doctrine.[43] What is more, unlike Justice Aniagolu, Justice Obaseki and the other justices emphasized a textually based commitment of a function to the political branches as the basis for the main judgement.

On the other hand, Justice Aniagolu's view seems to favour the prudential political question theory. His reasoning in favour of the application of the doctrine was not based on any constitutional text, but rather the fact or reasoning that the judiciary should be restrained from resolving issues that other branches are better suited to resolve. To say the least, Justice Aniagolu was more concerned with prudential considerations around what he perceived to be the proper role of the Nigerian judiciary in the matters at issue in that case. On the basis of the above analysis, it is fair to say that the political question doctrine in Nigeria is characterized by both the classical and prudential reflections.

In the discussion that follows, this chapter considers which theory of the doctrine is frequently applied or most preferred for purposes of identifying the contours of the doctrine in Nigeria. Commenting on the political question doctrine, Nwauche has correctly suggested that the adoption of the political question doctrine by Nigerian courts was strengthened by the fact that the Constitution 1979 was modelled out of the American presidential system.[44] He also observed that prior to *Onuoha v. Okafor, Balarabe Musa* and the Constitution 1979, Nigerian courts had applied a political question theory without categorizing it as such.[45]

41 Szurkowski, 2014, p. 354.

42 *See generally*, Tushnet, 2001.

43 Szurkowski, 2014, p. 361.

44 Nwauche, 2010, p. 33.

45 *Id.*, citing *Attorney General Eastern Nigeria v. Attorney General of the Federation* (1964) ALL NLR 218 (holding that the determination of the margin of error in a census was a political question).

5.4 The Doctrine During the Second Republic 1979-1983

5.4.1 Permissive Application

This section considers some of the cases in which the political question doctrine was applied, whether as part of the classical or prudential political question theory, to give us a sense of the areas where the doctrine was most susceptible for application, and more importantly demonstrate what the approach of the courts has been in those instances. Some commentators have observed that the application of the doctrine during the Second Republic was characterized by either the permissive or restrictive approach to the doctrine and justiciability principles.[46] Accordingly, under the permissive approach, a court often found against the application of the doctrine. Under the restrictive approach, a court often found in favour of the application of the doctrine.[47] The latter approach was prevalent during the Second Republic.[48] It is submitted that despite these characterizations, the utility of the doctrine was re-affirmed by the courts on more than one occasion during this period. Moreover, the approach taken by courts at any given point in time was influenced by the facts of the case rather than any about turn concerning the utility of the doctrine as some have suggested.

Since *Onuoha v. Okafor* and *Balarabe Musa* were decided, the courts applied the political question doctrine during the Second Republic.[49] Despite upholding *Onuoha v. Okafor*, the Supreme Court in *Alegbe v. Oloyo*[50] considered the usefulness political question doctrine and made some important pronouncements about its scope and future application.

Briefly, the plaintiff in *Alegbe v. Oloyo* was a member of the old Bendel State House of Assembly. The defendant, who was the Speaker of that House, had declared the plaintiff's seat in the House vacant on the basis that he was absent from the House's sitting for 94 times, a period more than permitted by the law. The plaintiff's main argument in the case was that it was not within the power of the Speaker to declare his seat vacant because only the judiciary exercises that power. He approached the High Court, which found in his favour. However, the Supreme Court dismissed the Speaker's appeal.

While the Supreme Court dismissed the Speaker's appeal, which effectively meant the doctrine did not apply to the case, Justice Fatai-Williams clarified the scope of the doctrine in Nigeria, particularly in areas where the doctrine has traditionally been applied. He explained that when the judiciary is presented with a task to interpret or apply any of the provisions of the Constitution 1979, this does not mean it is engaged with a political

46 Egbewole & Olatunji, 2012, p. 127.
47 *Id.*, pp. 127-136.
48 *Id.*
49 *See, Balarabe Musa v. PRP* (1981) 2 NCLR 453 and *Dalhatu v. Turaki Abaribe* (1981) 2 NCLR 763.
50 *Alegbe v. Oloyo* (1983) NSCC 315.

question despite the fact that the exercise might have political ramifications.[51] In his view, the judiciary in those instances simply performs its functions as conferred in the Constitution 1979.[52]

Justice Fatai-Williams went further to elucidate that equally when the judiciary is solicited to interpret or apply the provisions of a constitution of any organization with regards to civil rights and obligations of organization's members, the judiciary simply performs a function assigned to it by the Constitution 1979.[53] He emphasized that the judiciary is duty-bound to perform its functions regardless of whether the organization is a political party, cultural, religious or social organizations.[54]

Fatai-Williams' pronouncements are important because they clarified the distinction between political questions that courts must abstain from deciding, on the one hand, and questions that have political ramifications, and which do not necessarily require abstention by the courts, and those political questions, on the other hand, which require abstention by the courts. This is an important clarification, which courts in all countries where the doctrine has been considered and applied have had to make. As pointed out in Chapter 2, in the US case of *Baker v. Carr*, Justice Brennan made a similar point as Fatai-Williams when he emphasized the limited reach of the political question doctrine to ensure that it is employed economically in relation to discernible political questions assigned to the elected branches and not merely to cases that implicate political rights.[55]

Decades later, the US Supreme Court in *Zivotofsky v. Clinton*, where the political question doctrine was upheld, made a similar point concerning the role of courts in constitutional adjudication. Chief Justice Roberts held that when interpreting the constitutionality of a statute, the court is not engaged in a political question because the Constitution does not delegate to the political branches "the power to determine the constitutionality

51 *Alegbe v. Oloyo.*

52 Section 6(6) of the Constitution 1979 provided:

(6) The judicial powers vested in accordance with the foregoing provisions of this section –

a. (a) shall extend, notwithstanding anything to the contrary in this constitution, to all inherent powers and sanctions of a court of law;

b. (b) shall extend to all matters between persons or between government or authority and any person in Nigeria, and to all actions and proceedings relating thereto, for the determination of any question as to the civil rights and obligations of that person;

c. (c) shall not, except as otherwise provided by this Constitution, extend to any issue or question as to whether any act or omission by any authority or person or as to whether any law or any judicial decision is in conformity with the Fundamental Objectives and Directive Principles of State Policy set out in Chapter 2 of this Constitution; and

d. (d) shall not, as from the date when this section comes into force, extend to any action or proceedings relating to any existing law made on or after 15th January, 1966, for determining any issue or question as to the competence of any authority or person to make any such law.

53 *Alegbe v. Oloyo*, 1983, pp. 341-342.

54 *Id.*, p. 341.

55 *Baker v. Carr*, 1962, p. 217.

of a statute".[56] Instead, those categories of questions have always been "emphatically the province and duty of the judicial department".[57] While the exercise of that duty may have political repercussions, nonetheless, the judiciary is duty-bound to adjudicate such questions.[58] Essentially, although the court in *Zivotofsky v. Clinton* affirmed the political question doctrine, it sent a clear signal that its future application is narrow. You may recall that in the Ghanaian context, in Chapter 3 of this book, Justice Kpegah echoed similar sentiments in *Amidu*[59] that the interpretation and enforcement of the law passed by the legislature fall within the functions of the judiciary. In his view, the question of whether an Act of Parliament is constitutional is not a political question and the judiciary is not restrained from deciding it.[60] Justice Kpegah explains that when a court examines whether Parliament has breached the constitutional limits of its law-making powers, it is not engaged in the determination of political questions because courts have the authority to make these determinations.

Therefore, Justice Fatai-Williams's pronouncements should be viewed in the same light as Justices Brennan, Roberts and Kpegah that the political question doctrine is good law but its application may have a narrow application than we think. It was important for Justice Fatai-Williams to make these pronouncements in the early development of the doctrine in the same way as his counterparts in the United States and Ghana did in the preceding cases. Some commentators have suggested that the decision in *Alegbe v. Oloyo* indirectly recognized that the matter in that case involved internal proceedings of the House of Assembly and could have qualified as a political question.[61]

5.4.2 Restrictive Application

The Supreme Court took an indifferent attitude to the political question doctrine in *AG Bendel v. AG Federation*.[62] The case involved the interpretation of the Authentication Act. Section 2 of that Act had ousted the jurisdiction of the courts by providing that the Bill shall become conclusive for all purposes once passed by the two Houses of the National Assembly and upon the signature of the Clerk of the National Assembly. The effect of this wording in the Act is that the signature of the Clerk was all that was needed to determine whether a Bill had been properly passed in line with the Constitution.

56 *Clinton v. Zivotosfy*, 2012, p. 1428; 'Political Question Doctrine: Zivotofsky ex rel. Zivotofsky v. Clinton', *Harvard Law Review*, Vol. 126, No. 1, 2012, p. 307.

57 *Clinton v. Zivotosfy*, 2012, pp. 1427-1428, citing *Marbury v. Madison*.

58 *Clinton v. Zivotosfy*, 2012, p. 1428; 'Political Question Doctrine', 2012 *Harvard Law Review*, p. 307.

59 *Amidu*, 2001-2002, p. 154.

60 *Id.*

61 Egbewole & Olatunji, 2012, p. 130.

62 *AG Bendel v. AG Federation* 1982 10 SC 1.

In interpreting the impugned Act, Justice Fatai-Williams, CJN, held that the Supreme Court has the power to examine the validity of a Bill despite the signature of the Clerk. In the course of his judgement, Fatai-Williams explicated that one of the requirements of the separation of powers under Nigerian law is that courts should respect the independence of the legislature in the employment of its law-making powers.[63] This, he explicated further, required courts to abstain from pontificating on the validity of domestic affairs of the legislature, including the method of employment of its law-making powers.[64] On the contrary, Justice Fatai-Williams explained that:

> ... if the Constitution makes provision as to how the legislature should conduct its internal affairs or as to the mode of exercising its legislative powers the Court is in duty bound to exercise its jurisdiction to ensure that the legislature complies with the constitutional requirements. Sections 52, 54, 55 and 58 of our constitution clearly state how the National Assembly should conduct its internal affairs in exercise of its legislative powers. That being the case the Court is bound to exercise its jurisdiction under section 4(8) of the Constitution to ensure that the National Assembly comply with the provisions of the Constitution.[65]

Principally, in the above pronouncement, Justice Fatai-Williams clarifies that the rule of law requires courts to intervene and give effect to the law where the Constitution stipulates the procedures that the National Assembly or any other branch of government must follow in carrying out its responsibilities. In Justice Fatai-Williams's view, the political question doctrine does not prevent courts from enforcing those procedures through the process of judicial review. However, when the Constitution is silent about procedural requirements on how the legislature should conduct or manage its domestic affairs, the separation of powers and indeed the political question doctrine requires courts to abstain from interfering because the legislature has discretion (over substantive content on matters within their domain) in this regard and its actions are only politically examinable.[66] It is settled law

63 *AG Bendel v. AG Federation,* 1982.

64 *Id.*, pp. 50-52.

65 *Id.*, 1982, p. 52.

66 *See, Marbury v. Madison*; *National Treasury*, at para. 95; *Glenister v. President of the Republic of South Africa;* Weston, 1925; Finklestein, 1923-1924; Redish, 1984; Barkow, 2002 and *Economic Freedom Fighters v. Speaker of the National Assembly*, at para. 93. But allegations of individual rights violations operate as an exception to the application of the political question doctrine. *See, Malema v. Chairman of the National Council of Provinces* 2015 (4) SA 145 (WCC); *Mazibuko v. Speaker; Lekota v. Speaker* 2015 4 SA 133 (WCC); *De Lille v. Speaker* 1998 3 SA 430 (C); *Tlouamma v. Speaker* 2016 1 SA 534 (WCC); Story, 1833, pp. 346-347 (arguing that when it comes to discretionary constitutional matter conferred to the elected branches, the remedy for any disputes lies in the electoral process); and C. Okpaluba, 'Can a Court Review the Internal

and has been so pronounced very often that courts will not interfere with discretionary duties of the political branches.[67]

Therefore, it was an important clarification of the law on the part of Fatai-Williams because this goes to the heart of the political question theory as articulated in other authorities. One such authority is the case of *Doctors for Life International.* There, like Justice Fatai-Williams, Justice Ngcobo proclaimed in the South African context that:

> a distinction should be drawn between constitutional provisions that impose obligations that are readily ascertainable... on the one hand, and those provisions which impose the primary obligation ...to determine what is required of it, on the other. In the case of the former, a determination whether those obligations have been fulfilled does not call upon a court to pronounce upon a sensitive aspect of the separation of powers. An example of such a provision that comes to mind is a provision that requires statutes to be passed by a specified majority. When a court decides whether these obligations have been complied with, it does not infringe upon the principle of the separation of powers. It simply decides the formal question whether there was, for example, the two-thirds majority required to pass the legislation. By contrast, where the obligation requires Parliament to determine in the first place what is necessary to fulfil its obligation, a review by a court whether that obligation has been fulfilled, trenches on the autonomy of Parliament ...and thus the principle of separation of powers. This is precisely what the obligation comprehended in section 72(1)(a) does. While it imposes a primary obligation on Parliament to facilitate public involvement in its legislative and other processes, it does not tell Parliament how to facilitate public involvement but leaves it to Parliament to determine what is required of it in this regard.[68]

What is clear from the jurisprudence of Ngcobo and Fatai-Williams is that both have an understanding that the power of judicial review is not absolute, and that separation of powers may, in appropriate circumstances, operate as a mechanism that limits the institution of judicial review. Hence, I disagree with Professor Nwauche, who has commented that the opinion by Fatai-Williams in *AG, Bendel v. AG Federation* represents resistance by the court to apply the political question doctrine by holding that it had power to

Affairs and Processes of the Legislature?', *Comparative and International Law Journal of Southern Africa*, Vol. 48, No. 2, 2015, p. 183.

67 *Marbury v. Madison*, 1803, pp. 166-168. *See also, Luther v. Borden*; *Economic Freedom Fighters v. Speaker of the National Assembly*, at para. 93; Story, 1833; Wechsler, 1961 and Redish, 1984.

68 *Doctors for Life International*, at paras. 25-26.

determine how (procedurally) the legislature exercised its law-making powers. Nwauche did not, to my satisfaction, contextualize his comments and explain the courts' attitude to the political question in the case.

As demonstrated above, Justice Fatai-Williams is clear that courts have jurisdiction only if the Constitution provides clear parameters or procedures on how legislative powers should be employed. From a rule of law point of view, one cannot fault Fatai-Williams. Nevertheless, it is my view that Professor Nwauche is unpersuasive in his suggestion that *AG, Bendel v. AG Federation* is the authority for the proposition that judiciary has absolute power over how legislative powers are employed. This is not the preferred interpretation of *AG, Bendel v. AG Federation* and the contours of the political question doctrine. I favour alternative authorities for the proposition that the institution of judicial review is not absolute.[69]

A number of justiciability canons have been developed by courts including ripeness, mootness, avoidance and political question doctrine, which provide limits to judicial review. When courts, through any of these justiciability canons, decline jurisdiction, it is not a resistance to the value and usefulness of any particular canon, rather, it means that on the facts of a particular case, it is not appropriate to apply the relevant canon. This does not mean, as Professor Nwauche seemed to suggest, the relevant cannon is discredited or in demise. Nigerian courts displayed different attitudes to the political question doctrine during the Second Republic. Despite these distinct attitudes, the validity of the doctrine was repeatedly affirmed.[70] The next section examines the application of the doctrine in the Third Republic, particularly in light of the constitutional changes in 1999.

5.5 THE DOCTRINE DURING THE FOURTH REPUBLIC 1999 TO DATE

In 1999, Nigeria went through sweeping constitutional and democratic reforms, which led to the adoption of the Constitution of the Federal Republic of Nigeria 1999 (Constitution 1999) as the supreme law of Nigeria and ushered in the fourth Republic.[71] Additionally, the Constitution 1999 restored democratic rule to Nigeria. As a consequence of these reforms, questions arose among constitutional scholars whether the political question

69 *See, Onuoha v. Okafor; Balarabe Musa v. Autta Hamzat*; Waldron, 2006, pp. 1350, 1426; Kramer, 2004 and Tushnet, 1999.

70 *See, Abubakar Rimi v. Aminu Kano* (1982) 3 NCLR 478; *Asogwa v. Chukwu*[2004] FWLR (pt. 189) 1204; *Rimi & Musa v. PRP* (1981) 2 NCLR 734; *Ekpenkhio v. Egadon* (1993) 7 NWLR (pt. 308), p. 717 (sustained the constitutionality of the removal of a deputy speaker); *Okoli v. Mbadiwe* (1985) 6 NCLR 742; *Asogwa v. Chukwu* (2004) FWLR (pt. 189), p. 1204 (where court refused to intervene in the internal affair of the legislature concerning the removal of the speaker after it was alleged that two-thirds of members were not present in the legislature when a vote took place).

71 For a discussion of the history of constitutional reforms in Nigeria, *see*, E. Okpanachi & A. Garba, 'Federalism and Constitutional Change in Nigeria', *Federal Governance*, Vol. 7, No. 1, 2010, pp. 1-14.

doctrine would be sustained under the new dispensation.[72] In this section, I will examine a few notable cases where the political question was considered and applied in the post-1999 era with a view to determine judicial trends, if any, about the doctrine.

5.5.1 *Impeachment Question Revisited*

In post-1999 Nigeria, *Chief Enyi Abaribe*[73] was the first case to consider and apply the political question doctrine. The case involved the impeachment of the deputy governor of Abia State where the governor sought, among other things, an order to set aside the proceeding in the State House of Assembly. The High Court cited *Balarabe Musa* with approval as authority for its decision that the matter involved a political question and that it had no jurisdiction to entertain it. Supreme Court upheld the decision of the High Court that the question of the impeachment was a political question that was not appropriate for judicial review.[74] The Supreme Court, through Justice Pats-Acholonu, observed that:

> In so far as it concerns the issue of impeachment it is a political matter. However, the court at the same time may not close its eyes to serious injustice relating to the manner the impeachment procedure is being carried. That is to say it is within the province of the court to ensure strict adherent to the spirit of the Constitution for the endurance of a democratic regime. The court should not however attempt to assume for itself power it is never given by the Constitution to brazenly enter into the miasma of the political cauldron and have itself bloodied and thereby losing respect.[75]

Justice Pats-Acholonu went further to explain why the appeal was directed to a wrong forum and what ought to happen in future cases. In this respect, he ruled that:

> In this situation, as in others of like nature, appeal for relief does not belong here. Appeal must be to an informed, civically militant electorate. In a democratic society like ours, relief must come through an aroused popular conscience that sears the conscience of the people's representatives… Political question doctrine relates to those amorphous political issues which generally arise in

72 Nwauche, 2010, p. 41; Imam et al, 2011 and Egbewole & Olatunji, 2012, pp. 143-148.

73 *Chief Enyi Abaribe v. the Speaker Abia State House of Assembly & Ors* (2003) 14 NWLR (pt. 788), p. 466; *Chief Enyi Abaribe v. the Speaker, Abia State House of Assembly & Anor* (2000) LPELR-CA/PH/83M/2000.

74 *Chief Enyi Abaribe v. the Speaker Abia State House of Assembly*, 2003.

75 *Chief Enyi Abaribe v. the Speaker Abia State House of Assembly* (Pats-Acholonu J.).

> political structure of parties or in the House of Assembly and which no court should try to get involved for fear of being smeared or appear to take sides.[76]

The main issue on appeal came down to the proper interpretation of Section 188(10) of the Constitution 1999. The relevant parts of Section 188 provide that:

> *Section 188.*
> 1. The Governor or Deputy Governor of a state may be removed from office in accordance with the provisions of this section.
> 2. (...)
> 3. (...)
> 4. (...)
> 5. Within seven days of the passing of a motion under the foregoing provisions of this section, the Chief judge of the State shall at the request of the speaker of the House of Assembly, appoint a Panel of seven persons who in his opinion are of unquestionable integrity, not being members of any public service, legislative house or political party, to investigate the allegation as provided in this section.
> 6. (...)
> 7. A Panel appointed under this section shall – (a) have such powers and exercise its functions in accordance with such procedure as may be prescribed by the House of Assembly; and (b) within three months of its appointment, report its findings to the House of Assembly.
> 8. (...)
> 9. Where the report of the Panel is that the allegation against the holder of the office has been proved, then within fourteen days of the receipt of the report, the house of Assembly shall consider the report, and if by a resolution of the House of Assembly supported by not less than two-thirds majority of all its members, the report of the Panel is adopted, then the holder of the office shall stand removed from office as from the date of the adoption of the report.
> 10. *No proceedings or determination of the Panel or of the House of Assembly or any matter relating to such proceedings or determination shall be entertained or questioned in any court.* (my emphasis)

The Supreme Court reasoned that Section 188(10) denotes that impeachment is a political question, which the Constitution 1999 left to the discretion of the legislature to resolve.

76 *Id.*

The provision enables the people to remove from power those elected officials. Hence, the Supreme Court abstained from deciding the merits of the case. In the course of the judgement, Justice Ikongbeh made some important statements of law, which highlight the Supreme Court's attitude towards the political question doctrine in post-1999.

At the heart of the debate was whether Section 188(10) amounted to an ouster clause akin to those ouster clauses that prevailed during the military decrees of the 1980s. In Justice Ikongbeh's view, the interpretation of the ouster clause in the military decrees cannot provide a good guide to interpret a constitutional provision that limits judicial powers. He reasoned that:

> All governmental powers derive from the Constitution in a civilian regime. There cannot be any legitimate complaint if the Constitution withdraws a particular power from one organ of government in favour of another in the same way that one can complain about the way the military brazenly emasculated, especially the judiciary, just to pave the way for themselves to do as they pleased with the lives and property of people. This point can be better appreciated if it is realised that a Constitution is, at least in theory, the product of the planned and collective agreement of the people on how to govern themselves. When, therefore, they agree at the outset that a particular matter shall be within the competence of one organ and not of the other one cannot properly liken such situation to the situation created by ouster clauses in the military decrees.[77]

In the light of the above reasoning, Justice Ikongbeh held that the interpretation of Section 188(10) must be approached distinctly from the past. He averred that the term 'ouster clause' was not an appropriate term in the context of the new constitutional dispensation. In his view, Section 188(10) is not an ouster clause, but a separation of powers mechanism in which executive, legislative and judicial powers are allocated to the appropriate organs. He noted that each within its powers is master of its own affairs. Ikongbeh J further remarked that:

> It has been universally recognized that impeachment procedure is pre-eminently a political matter and is an affair of the legislature. The people elect officers to elective offices. The people can withdraw their mandate. They can do this either by the recall procedure or by impeachment. The latter procedure has been assigned exclusively to the legislature by the Constitution. I do not, therefore, see section 188(10) as an ouster clause. I see it as doing no more than under-

77 *Chief Enyi Abaribe v. the Speaker Abia State House of Assembly & Ors* (Ikongbeh, J.).

> scoring the recognized fact that the impeachment process is a political matter that is best left where it best belongs, i.e., with the legislature. It does not, in my view, set out to oust the jurisdiction of courts in the same way as the military decrees … did. Those decrees expressly set out to put the courts out of possession of not just the jurisdiction but, invariably, also the judicial powers vested in them by the Constitution. Those were clear cases of ouster.[78]

There are at least four reasons why the decision in *Chief Enyi Abaribe* is important and should be welcomed. Firstly, it upheld the principle in *Balarabe Musa* that impeachment is a political question that is not justiciable and therefore inappropriate for judicial review. This is a welcomed development because it creates consistency in Nigeria's political question jurisprudence.

Secondly, it upheld and clarified the application of the classical political question theory in Nigeria, particularly in relation to the impeachment of senior elected officials. In other words, the absence of any discussion of prudential considerations by Justice Ikongbeh suggests a prominent validation of the classical rather than prudential political question theory in post-1999. His application of the political question doctrine was grounded solely on the text and structure of the Constitution 1999, and the theory that where the constitutional structure and text commits an issue to another branch of government for resolution, a court should refrain from intervening. In this regard, Justice Ikongbeh is clearly in agreement with commentators, like Wechsler, Story, Cooley and Fritz, that the political question doctrine called upon him to judge whether the Constitution had committed to another branch the determination of impeachment processes. His findings based on the text and structure of the Constitution is evidently that impeachment was committed to the discretion and final say by the legislature. *Chief Enyi Abaribe,* therefore, represents a return to the classical version of the doctrine and raises questions about whether the prudential political question theory remains relevant in Nigeria.

Thirdly, the Supreme Court accepted and clarified that the political question doctrine, and by implication the separation of powers, is one of the narrow exceptions to the institution of judicial review. This is a well-settled principle of law and has been so pronounced very often.[79]

---

78 *Id.*

79 *Balarabe Musa v. Auta Hamza*; *Marbury v. Madison*; Szurkowski, 2014; *Baker v. Carr*; and *Nixon v. United States* and *Zivotofsky v. Clinton,* 2012, p. 1427 (Roberts, J.) (holding that "in general, the Judiciary has a responsibility to decide cases properly before it, even those it 'would gladly avoid…Our precedents have identified a narrow exception to that rule, known as the political question doctrine. We have explained that a controversy involves a political question where there is a textually demonstrable constitutional commitment of the issue to a coordinate political department; or a lack of judicially discoverable and manageable standards for resolving it.")

Fourthly, it explains that Section 188(10) of the Constitution 1999 is not an ouster clause, but a constitutionally permissible limitation of judicial power.

And lastly, academic commentators who argue that the political question doctrine is under threat in Nigeria are misguided because the doctrine has been endorsed in more than one occasion. I admit that the doctrine may have a limited application, but it is certainly not without utility in Nigeria. Therefore, unless Section 188(10) is amended, the proposition that impeachment is a political question remains true and sound in law.

In the light of the above analysis, it is evident that one of the debates in Nigeria around the political question doctrine has centred on the controversy over the legality of the ouster clause in Section 188 of the Constitution. *Chief Enyi Abaribe* explains that ouster clause is not an appropriate word. Rather, it is separation of powers at play; that when the Constitution 1999 divides functions among departments, it is merely a separation of powers issue at play and not an ouster clause. I agree.

5.5.2 *Political Party Primaries Revisited*

Despite the above jurisprudence, including the most recent case of *Dalhatu v. Turaki* that upheld the political question doctrine, two subsequent decisions in *Inakoju v. Adeleke*[80] and *Ugwu v. Ararume*,[81] have caused commentators to question the future relevance of the doctrine in Nigeria.[82] It is important to briefly discuss these cases in order to examine the soundness of these commentaries.

Dalhatu v. Turaki[83] involved the nomination and primary election of the gubernatorial candidate for Jigawa State. The All Nigeria Peoples Party held its primary elections on 3 January 2003. A screening of candidates was held in which Mr Turaki did not take part. Only the appellant, Mr Dalhutu attended. The latter was declared the winner. However, the All Nigeria Peoples Party held another primary election in which Mr Turaki was declared the winner and issued with a recognition certificate. The matter ended up in the

80 *Inakoju v. Adeleke* (2007) ALL FWLR (pt. 353) (which involved the former governor of Oyo State's challenge to the processes employed in the State House of Assembly's impeachment proceedings against him. The impeachment proceedings were conducted at a local hotel instead of the House of Assembly. Because of this, not all members of the House of Assembly participated in the vote that led to the removal of the governor. In reviewing the matter, the court noted that it had the power to engage in ordinary constitutional interpretation, and as such could determine this matter. According to the court, the Constitution simply requires that only the House of Assembly should try a person for the allegations that give rise to the impeachment. But this did not insulate the House from conducting the proceedings in accordance with the constitutional procedures. The court found that while the case involved political question, the issue presented to the court was justiciable because it involved the question of whether the legislature conducted itself in line with the parameters set in the Constitution 1999).

81 *Ugwu v. Ararume* (2007) 12 NWLR (pt. 1048), p. 367.

82 *See generally*, Nwauche, 2010, pp. 32, 41 and Egbewole & Olatunji, 2012, p. 126.

83 *Dalhutu v. Turaki* (2003) 15 NWLR (pt. 843), p. 310.

Supreme Court where it was dismissed on the basis of the reasoning and holding in *Onuoha v. Okafor.* To justify its decision, the Supreme Court reasoned that:

> From the decision of this court in *Onuoha's case,* it is clear that the right to sponsor a candidate by a party is not a legal right but a domestic right of the party which cannot be questioned in a court of law. The political party qua political organisation has discretion in the matter, a discretion which is unfettered; in the sense that a court of law has no jurisdiction to question its exercise one way or the other.[84]

The Supreme Court found that the issue for determination was identical to the one it decided in *Onuoha v. Okafor*, and as a consequence, Justice Edozie ruled "it seems obvious that the present case is on all fours with the *Onuoha's case* and by the doctrine of stare decisis ... is binding in the present case."[85] Justice Edozie specifically addressed the validity of *Onuoha v. Okafor* and its principles and held that "the decision of this court in *Onuoha's case* is valid today as it was in 1983."[86] A few years later, the Supreme Court upheld its holding in *Onuoha v. Okafor* and *Dalhutu v. Turaki* in *Ugwu v. Ararume.*

In *Ugwu v. Ararume*, the Supreme Court was called upon to consider the validity of its holding in *Onuoha v. Okafor* and *Dalhatu v. Turaki.* It rejected calls to overrule these judgements. Instead, it distinguished the facts in *Ugwu v. Ararume* from those in *Onuoha v. Okafor* and *Dalhatu v. Turaki* and held that the latter two judgements remained good law, and that the proposition (that the substitution of candidates for election to political office by a political party was not justiciable) enunciated in those two judgements will continue to be applied in appropriate cases in the future. The Supreme Court reasoned that:

> It is settled law that the issue of nomination or sponsorship of an election candidate is within the domestic affairs of the political parties and that the courts have no jurisdiction to determine who should be sponsored by any political party as its candidate for any election. That is the law as reflected in *Onuoha v Okafor* and *Dalhatu v Turaki*... The question for determination in the instant appeal is primarily whether that position still represents the law... Without wasting time, I will say emphatically, that *Onuoha v Okafor* and *Dalhatu v Turaki* still remain good law on the sound principles decided therein.[87]

84 *Dalhutu v. Turaki* (Tobi J.S.C.).
85 *Dalhutu v. Turaki* (Edozie J.S.C.).
86 *Dalhutu v. Turaki* (Edozie J.S.C.).
87 *Ugwu v. Ararume* as per opinion of Justice Walter Samuel Nkanu Onnoghen.

Based on the above statement, it is unambiguous that the political question doctrine remains good law in Nigeria.[88] Furthermore, recently in the case of *Alhaji Sanni Aminu Dutsima,*[89] the Abuja High Court declined to compel the People's Democratic Party to enforce its controversial zoning arrangement and struck out the action seeking to stop the incumbent President Mr Goodluck Jonathan from contesting for the same position in 2011. The High Court dismissed the case on the grounds that the provisions of the party's constitution sought to be enforced involved a political question that was non-justiciable. According to the High Court, the onus was on the party to respect the provisions of the party constitution.[90]

There is another reason that demonstrates that the political question doctrine remains a good part of the constitutional law of Nigeria and that courts will continue to apply it in appropriate cases. Before and after the Constitution 1999, Nigerian courts have consistently upheld the notion that the Nigerian Constitution is firmly based on the principle of separation of powers. Regarding the scope of this principle under the Constitution 1979, the court in *Tony Momoh*[91] eloquently stated that:

> The Nigerian Constitution separates the three arms of government- Executive, Legislative and Judicial – and each is supreme in its area of authority, but only in so far as it confines itself to, and acts within the powers conferred on it. If it exceeds such powers or acts in contravention of or in conflict with the provisions of the Constitution, it would be the duty of the judiciary to put it in check at the instance of an aggrieved party.[92]

Following the adoption of the Constitution 1999, the Supreme Court in *Attorney General Abia State*[93] reiterated the position in *Tony Momoh* and observed that the proper constitutional relationship of the executive with the courts is that the courts will respect all acts of the executive within its lawful province, and that the executive will respect all decisions of

88 Nwauche, 2010, p. 56; Imam et al., 2011, pp. 68-69. *See also, Esiaga v. University of Calabar* (2004) All FWLR (pt. 206), p. 381; *Magit v. University of Agriculture Makurdi* (2006) All FWLR (pt. 298), p. 1313 (held that it will not engage in a review of academic disputes relating to examination grades and the award of degrees); *Alhaji Atiku Abubakar v. Attorney General of the Federal* (2007) 6 MJSC 1-137; and *Abaribe v. the Speaker Abia State House of Assembly* & Ors (2003) 14 NWLR 466.

89 *Dutsima v. PDP & Another* FCT/CV/2425/2010 (2010).

90 *See*, K. Oladele, 'Political Questions and Justiciability: Two Sides of a Coin' 2012, available from Sahara Reporters, http://saharareporters.com/article/political-question-and-justiciablity-two-sides-coin. Egbewole & Olatunji, 2012, p. 147 (critically discussing the holding by Justice Lawan Hassan Gunmi in the case of *Dutsima v. PDP & Ors*).

91 *Tony Momoh v. Senate of the National Assembly* (1981) 1 NCLR 105.

92 *Tony Momoh v. Senate of the National Assembly*, 1981, p. 105.

93 *Attorney General Abia State v. Attorney General of the Federation* (2006) 9 MJSC, p. 73.

the courts as to what is within its lawful province.[94] Given that the main purpose of the political question doctrine is to preserve the separation of powers and operate as an exception to the power of judicial review, it is more likely that Nigerian courts will continue to apply the doctrine in all appropriate and future cases.

In addition, it is significant that the Supreme Court chose not to overrule *Onuoha v. Okafor* and *Dalhatu v. Turaki* when it had an opportunity to do so. This is significant in two ways: (1) it demonstrates the Supreme Court's recognition of the utility of the political question doctrine in post-1999 Nigeria and (2) it signals that there are some cases where the political question doctrine is just not appropriate for application. This explains why in *Chief Enyi Abaribe*,[95] the Supreme Court upheld the decision of the High Court that questions of impeachment involving the Deputy Governor of Abia State was a political question not appropriate for judicial review.[96]

The debate among Nigerian scholars about the political question doctrine and its current status has also centred on the key question of whether the doctrine remains good law. A number of commentators have interpreted recent jurisprudence as signifying the demise of the doctrine or at least its possible limited application.[97] Professor Nwauche has vehemently argued that signs are there to show the demise of the political question doctrine. Nwauche relies on two cases to explain his assertions. Firstly, he relies on the Supreme Court decision in *Attorney General of the Federation v. Attorney General of Abia State*,[98] where the court rejected the proposition that the determination of the seaward boundary of littoral state within the Federal Republic of Nigeria was a political question committed to the legislature.[99] Nwauche notes, with great emphasis, that only Justice Karibi-Whyte acceded to this proposition, whereas the rest of the justices did not. It is difficult to accept Professor Nwauche's argument.

The fact that one case finds no application of the political question doctrine does not mean it signals its demise. One way to look at it is that perhaps it was just not appropriate for the Supreme Court to apply the doctrine in that case. Moreover, the fact that in 2007, the Supreme Court decided *Ugwu v. Ararume*, in which it upheld the political question doctrine further weakens the argument that the political question doctrine is on the verge of demise. What may be happening is that fewer cases that are suitable for the application of the political question doctrine are reaching the courts.

---

94 *Id.*, 2006, p. 73.

95 *Chief Enyi Abaribe v. the Speaker Abia State House of Assembly & Ors*, (2003) 14 NWLR (pt. 788), p. 466; *Chief Enyi Abaribe v. the Speaker Abia State House of Assembly & Anor*, (2000) LPELR-CA/PH/83M/2000.

96 *Chief Enyi Abaribe v. the Speaker Abia State House of Assembly.*

97 Egbewole & Olatunji, 2012, pp. 143-149; Nwauche, 2010, p. 41; M. Ikhariale, 'Impeachment Proceedings and the Political Question Doctrine: The Nigerian Experience', *LASU Law Journal*, Vol. 1, 1990, p. 45 and B.O. Nwabueze, *The Presidential Constitution of Nigeria*, Enugu, Nwamife Publisher, 1982, p. 143.

98 *Attorney General of the Federation v. Attorney General of Abia State* 2001 FWLR (pt. 64), p. 202.

99 Nwauche, 2010, pp. 44-45, 59.

Lastly, Professor Nwauche relies on the dismissive views by Justice Oguntade in *Ugwu v. Ararume* to follow *Onuoha v. Okafor* as further evidence of the demise of the political question doctrine. Justice Oguntade reasoned that:

> My humble view on the decision in *Onuoha v. Okafor* ... is that it has ceased to be a guiding light in view of the present state of our political life. I have no doubt that the reasoning in the case might have been useful at the time the decision was made. It seems to me, however that in view of the contemporary occurrences in the political scene, the decision needs to be ... modified. If the political parties, in their own wisdom had written it into their Constitutions that their candidates for election would emerge from their party primaries, it becomes unacceptable that the court should run away from their duty to enforce compliance with the parties Constitution...An observer of the Nigerian political scene today easily discovers that the failure of the parties to ensure intra-party democracy and live by the provisions of their constitutions as to the emergence of candidates for elections is one of the major causes of the serious problems hindering the enthronement of a representative government in the country.[100]

For Nwauche, the above developments signify the demise of the political question doctrine. I disagree with Nwauche. Justices may differ on the need to apply a legal rule in a particular case, but this does not mean the rule is discredited or bad law. It is submitted that this is not a persuasive argument against the doctrine in Nigeria.

On the other hand, other scholars see no uncertainty or demise of the doctrine.[101] Egbewole and Olatunji have argued that there is no doubt the political question doctrine remains relevant in some instances, but have cautioned against its over application.[102] In their concluding remarks, the authors advocate for the classic political question without calling it by name. Furthermore, in their support for the application of the political question doctrine in Nigeria, Imam and others have argued that "when political institutions have no judicial remedy for a perceived constitutional violation because of the political question doctrine, they can still take to the polls and turn offending politicians out of office."[103] Additionally, they correctly urged that "we should not be overly concerned that the political question doctrine deprives the courts of enforcement power over certain constitutional

---

100 *Ugwu v. Ararume* 461.

101 *See*, Ekpu, 1996 (discussing the use of prudential considerations and recommending the adoption of the political question doctrine in relation to adjudication of cases involving coup d'etat); A. Sambo & S. Aziz, 'The Court; Insulating Itself from Politics through the Doctrine of Political Questions: A Critical Exposition', *Journal of Law, Policy and Globalization,* Vol. 4, 2012, p. 7 (suggesting improvement in the application of the political question doctrine).

102 Egbewole & Olatunji, 2012, p. 148.

103 Imam et al., 2011, pp. 51-52, citing *Obi v. INEC* (2007) 9 MJSC, p. 1.

provisions, because a constitution and the electoral process provides an appropriate substitute."[104] I agree with Imam and others to the effect that the political question doctrine is there to stay in Nigeria. From the case law analysis, the courts have had several opportunities to overrule the doctrine and in more than one occasion the doctrine has been upheld. What is evident, however, is that like the developments in Uganda and United States, courts in Nigeria are likely to be sensitive to the vital limits of the doctrine's application.

To sum up, my own view is that the doctrine remains good law in Nigeria. But its application is more likely going to be limited as in the other jurisdictions. Another observation about the future application of the doctrine is that it is likely going to hinge on whether Nigerian courts will apply the classical or prudential political question theories. If the classical theory becomes the preferred version, then its limited application is predictable. On the contrary, if courts adhere to the prudential political question theory, then its application may be wider and unpredictable. It seems clear that these are some of the future considerations concerning the political question doctrine that Nigeria's judiciary and scholars will likely debate in the coming years. These debates will provide useful guidance to South Africa.

5.6 Conclusion

From the discussions in this chapter, it seems that the application of the political question doctrine in Nigeria has occurred in three primary areas of constitutional adjudication, namely impeachment cases involving elected representatives, political party primaries and domestic affairs of the legislative processes.[105] As the doctrine developed, courts began to define its contours and clarify its foundation as being both the text and structure of the Constitution of 1979 and 1999, respectively, and prudential considerations about the proper role of the judiciary under Nigeria's constitutional order. It is significant that even after the constitutional changes in 1999, the courts have not overruled the cases that first considered and applied the doctrine, but have affirmed or distinguished the cases where the doctrine did not apply. There is an unambiguous demonstration from the jurisprudence that the political question doctrine remains relevant and firmly part of Nigerian constitutional law even though (like in Uganda) there may be different consequences, which are beyond this book, for its continued application in the democratic dispensation.[106]

104 Imam et al., 2011, pp. 51-52.

105 *See*, Nwauche, 2010, pp. 31-32.

106 *See*, Oladele, http://saharareporters.com/article/political-question-and-justiciablity-two-sides-coin (discussing the decision of the Abuja high court declining to compel the People's Democratic Party to enforce its controversial zoning arrangement and struck out a lawsuit seeking to stop the incumbent President Goodluck Jonathan from contesting for the same office on the platform of the People's Democratic Party in 2011.

The high court held that the provision of the party's constitution sought to be enforced dwelt on a political question that was non-justiciable).

6 The Development and Application of a Comprehensive Political Question Doctrine in South Africa*

6.1 Introduction

South Africa went through major constitutional changes in the early 1990s.[1] These changes, negotiated at the Convention for a Democratic South Africa (CODESA), culminated into the adoption of the Interim Constitution of Act 200 of 1993. As explained earlier, one of the most notable changes introduced by the Interim Constitution was the declaration of the supremacy of the Constitution of 1996 and that any law or act in conflict with it had no force and effect, which essentially constitutionalized judicial review.[2]

One of the political compromises reached at CODESA was that the Interim Constitution would govern South Africa for an interim period until the Constitution 1996 was adopted and certified by an independent body, namely the Constitutional Court.[3] According to Currie and De Waal, central to the implementation of the Interim Constitution was the establishment of a Constitutional Court to give effect to the supremacy of the Constitution and the bill of rights.[4]

Furthermore, Currie and De Waal observe that the idea of establishing and requiring the Constitutional Court to certify the Constitution was motivated by, among other things, "fear … amongst members of the liberation movements, that some of the old judges would use the powers to undermine the newly created democratic order".[5] Other scholars have a different take on the significance of South Africa's certification process. In his seminar piece on South Africa's transition to democracy, Professor Mutua observes that the African

---

* An earlier version of this chapter was published in 2014. *See*, M. Mhango, 'Is It Time for a Coherent Political Question Doctrine in South Africa? Lessons from the United States', *African Journal of Legal Studies*, Vol. 7, No. 4, 2014, pp. 457-493.

1 For a discussion of the transition to a democratic state, *see*, M. Bennun & M. Newitt, *Negotiating Justice: A New Constitution for South Africa*, University of Exeter Press, Exeter, 1995 (discussing the democratic transition in South Africa); H. Klug, *Constituting Democracy: Law, Globalism and South Africa's Political Reconstruction*, Cambridge University Press, New York, 2000 (discussing the constitutional changes in the 1990s) and N. Worden, *The Making of Modern South Africa: Conquest, Apartheid, Democracy*, Wiley-Blackwell, Oxford, 1994.

2 Section 4 of the Interim Constitution Act 200 of 1993.

3 Currie & De Waal, 2001, pp. 64-65.

4 *Id.*, 2001, p. 65.

5 Currie & De Waal, 2001, p. 274.

National Congress agreed to the certification process because the certifying authority – the Constitutional Court – was created by them and would likely be understanding.[6] On the other hand, he argues, the National Party agreed because the process ensured that the dominant African National Congress would not write a constitution it preferred.[7] This is because:

> the final constitution would reflect the compromise reached in 1993, effectively curbing the power of the [African National Congress] to create a completely new political and constitutional dispensation. It seems that the [National Party] got the better of the deal as it was protected against the will of the majority to substantially transform the state. What is more disturbing, however, is that CODESA, the unelected multiparty forum that produced the Interim Constitution, crafted a document that the Constitutional Assembly, the first national democratically elected body in South Africa, could not substantially alter.[8]

The above political compromise agreed at CODESA was encapsulated in Section 71 of the Interim Constitution, which provided that:

1. A new constitutional text shall:
    a. comply with the Constitutional Principles contained in Schedule 4; and
    b. be passed by the Constitutional Assembly in accordance with this Chapter.
2. The new constitutional text passed by the Constitutional Assembly, or any provision thereof, shall not be of any force and effect, unless the Constitutional Court has certified that all the provisions of such text comply with the Constitutional Principles referred to in Subsection (1) (a).
3. A decision of the Constitutional Court in terms of Subsection (2) certifying that the provisions of the new constitutional text comply with the Constitutional Principles, shall be final and binding, and no court of law shall have jurisdiction to enquire into or pronounce upon the validity of such text or any provision thereof.

Thirty-four principles were agreed upon at CODESA to inform the drafting of the Constitution. Two of these principles are most relevant for our purpose, and they provided that:

6 M. Mutua, 'Hope and Despair for a New South Africa: The Limits of Rights Discourse', *Harvard Human Rights Journal*, Vol. 10, 1997, p. 81.

7 Mutua, 1997, p. 81.

8 *Id.*

> IV. The Constitution shall be the supreme law of the land. It shall be binding on all organs of state at all levels of government.
> VI. There shall be a separation of powers between the legislature, executive and judiciary, with appropriate checks and balances to ensure accountability, responsiveness and openness.[9]

Pursuant to Section 71 of the Interim Constitution, the Constitutional Court was eventually seized with the constitutional task to certify the Constitution after it was adopted by Parliament sitting as the Constitutional Assembly.[10] As Professor Okpaluba has correctly observed, the Constitutional Court participated significantly in finalizing the democratic Constitution of 1996 through the certification process.[11]

6.2 CONSTITUTIONAL PRINCIPLES IV AND VI

The effects of constitutional principles IV and VI can be easily ascertained in the Constitution and the case law that has developed. Firstly, pursuant to constitutional principles IV, Sections 1 and 2 of the Constitution were enacted. They provide that:

> 1. The Republic of South Africa is one, sovereign, democratic state founded on the following values:
>   a. Human dignity, the achievement of equality and the advancement of human rights and freedoms.
>   b. Non-racialism and non-sexism.
>   c. *Supremacy of the constitution and the rule of law.*
>   d. Universal adult suffrage, a national common voters' roll, regular elections and a multi-party system of democratic government to ensure accountability, responsiveness and openness.

9 Analogous to the South African situation, Story has observed that "in the convention, which framed the constitution of the United States, the first resolution adopted by that body was, that a national government ought to be established, consisting of a supreme legislative, judiciary, and executive. And from this fundamental proposition sprung the subsequent organisation of the whole government of the United States." Story, 1833, p. 2.

10 Mutua, 1997, p. 81 (arguing that "the Constitutional Assembly, the body actually representing the will of all South Africans, essentially rubber-stamped prior political choices, despite projecting the perception that it was making a new constitution").

11 C. Okpaluba, 'Can a Court Review the Internal Affairs and Processes of the Legislature? Contemporary Developments in South Africa', *Comparative and International Law Journal of Southern Africa*, Vol. 48, No. 2, 2015, p. 206.

2. This Constitution is the supreme law of the Republic; law or conduct inconsistent with it is invalid, and the obligations imposed by it must be fulfilled. (my emphasis)

Since the enactment of these provisions, the judiciary has developed the concepts of the supremacy of the Constitution and the rule of law into a doctrine of law. One of the first legal challenges occasioned by South Africa's transition to democratic politics was in *Fedsure.*[12] In *Fedsure*, the plaintiffs challenged various resolutions adopted by the Greater Johannesburg Transitional Metropolitan Council (GJTMC). These resolutions provided for levies within the area of jurisdiction of the GJTMC. The plaintiffs' challenge was based on the theory that the resolutions constituted administrative action and hence it became necessary for the Constitutional Court to determine the meaning of administrative action. In resolving the dispute, the Constitutional Court developed the principle of legality, which it found emanated from the principle of rule of law and stands for the proposition that government may only act within the powers lawfully conferred on it.[13] More pointedly the Constitutional Court explained and justified the principle of legality as follows:

> It seems central to the conception of our constitutional order that the legislature and executive in every sphere are constrained by the principle that they may exercise no power and perform no function beyond that conferred upon them by law. At least in this sense, then, the principle of legality is implied within the terms of the interim Constitution. Whether the principle of the rule of law has greater content than the principle of legality is not necessary for us to decide here. We need merely hold that fundamental to the interim Constitution is a principle of legality.[14]

In essence, the Constitutional Court found that the principle of legality was implicit in the Constitution and applied to acts of government, including legislative act, executive acts and administrative action.[15] The Constitutional Court found that it was not necessary at the time to define the contours of the newly found legal doctrine, but was clear that its proposition is that all exercise of public power is only legitimate when authorized by law.[16]

12 *Fedsure Life Assurance Ltd v. Greater Johannesburg Transitional Metropolitan Council* 1998 12 BCLR 1458 (CC) (*Fedsure*).

13 *Fedsure*, at para. 56.

14 *Id.*, at para. 58.

15 *Id.*, at para. 59.

16 *Id.*, at para. 56.

In the instant case, the Court concluded that the GJTMC had acted within the powers lawfully conferred to it when it resolved to levy certain rates.[17]

Since *Fedsure*, the Constitutional Court has refined the principle of legality, which has become one of the most cited principles of law in South Africa on the basis of which the exercise of public power is reviewed.[18] Legal commentators have observed that the constitutional principle of legality has wider meaning and applies to all exercise of public power rather than the narrower meaning in administrative law noting that its detailed content continues to be worked out by the judiciary.[19] Nevertheless, based on the principle of legality, the judiciary has reviewed the exercise of public power that traditionally could

---

17 C. Hoexter, 'The Principle of Legality in South African Administrative Law', *Maquarie Law Journal*, Vol. 4, 2004, p. 165 (discussing the principle of legality in South Africa).

18 *See, National Director of Public Prosecutions and Others v. Freedom Under Law* 2014 4 SA 298 (SCA), at paras. 28-29 (the legality principle has now become well established in our law as an alternative pathway to judicial review where Promotion of Administrative Justice Act finds no application); *Pharmaceutical Manufacturers Association of South Africa: In re Ex Parte President of the Republic of South Africa* 2000 2 SA 674; *Affordable Medicines Trust v. Minister of Health* 2006 3 SA 247 (CC), at para. 49 (held that "the exercise of public power must … comply with the Constitution, which is the supreme law, and the doctrine of legality, which is part of that law. The doctrine of legality, which is an incident of the rule of law, is one of the constitutional controls through which the exercise of public power is regulated by the Constitution. It entails that public functionaries are constrained by the principle that they may exercise no power and perform no function beyond that conferred upon them by law."); *Department of Education, Free State Province v. Welkom High School* 2013 9 BCLR 989 (CC), at para. 76 (held that "state functionaries, no matter how well intentioned, may only do what the law empowers them to do. That is the essence of the principle of legality, the bedrock of our constitutional dispensation, and has long been enshrined in our law."); *MEC for Health, Eastern Cape and Another v. Kirland Investments (Pty) Ltd* 2014 3 SA 481 (CC); *Merafong City Local Municipality v. AngloGold Ashanti Limited* [2016] ZACC; *Bengwenyama Minerals (Pty) Ltd v. Genorah Resources (Pty) Ltd* 2011 4 SA 113 (CC); and *City of Cape Town v. South African National Roads Agency Ltd* 2015 6 SA 535 (WCC).

19 C. Hoexter, *Administrative Law in South Africa*, Juta, Cape Town, 2012, pp. 122, 356 (arguing that the beauty of the principle of legality is its generality that can easily encompass the full range of administrative law precepts, and that while South African has not reached that stage yet, the principle of legality has been crucial in controlling action that administrative law could not reach). Courts have held that the principle of legality acts as a safety net for checking all exercise of public power, *see, State Information Technology Agency Soc Ltd v. Gijima Holdings (Pty) Ltd* 2017 2 SA 63 (SCA), at para. 38 (held that "the proper place for the principle of legality in our law is to act as a safety-net or a measure of last resort when the law allows no other avenues to challenge the unlawful exercise of public power. It cannot be the first port of call or an alternative path to review, when [Promotion of Administrative Justice Act 2000] applies."); and *Public Servants Association of South Africa and Another v. Minister of Labour* (2016) 37 ILJ 185 (LC).

not be reviewed such as prosecutorial decisions[20] or executive appointments.[21] The principle of legality is one of the most fairly developed rules of law in South Africa today and has been the subject of numerous academic commentaries.[22]

And thirdly, pursuant to constitutional principle VI, the framers of the Constitution 1996 structured the South African state into three traditional branches and assigned each branch specific functions.[23] In *Ex parte Chairperson of the Constitutional Assembly: in re Certification of the Constitution of the Republic of South Africa 1996* (hereinafter as *First Certification Judgement*), the Constitutional Court made the following pronouncement concerning the constitutional principle VI and the separation of powers as adopted by the framers of the Constitution:

> Within the broad requirement of separation of powers and appropriate checks and balances, the [Constitutional Assembly] was afforded a large degree of latitude in shaping the independence and interdependence of government branches. The model adopted reflects the historical circumstances of our constitutional development. We find in the [Constitution] checks and balances that evidence a concern for both the over-concentration of power and the requirement of an energetic and effective, yet answerable, executive. A strict separation of powers has not always been maintained but there is nothing to suggest that the [constitutional principles] imposed upon the [Constitutional Assembly] an obligation to adopt a particular form of strict separation, such

---

20 *National Director of Public Prosecutions v. Freedom Under Law. But see, Democratic Alliance v. Acting National Director of Public Prosecutions* 2012 3 SA 486 (SCA) (where at para. 27 Navsa J.A. stated "while there appears to be some justification for the contention that the decision to discontinue a prosecution is of the same genus as a decision to institute or continue a prosecution, which is excluded from the definition of administrative action in terms of s 1(*ff*) of Promotion of Administrative Justice Act, it is not necessary to finally decide that question. Before us it was conceded on behalf of the first and third respondents that a decision to discontinue a prosecution was subject to a rule of law review. That concession in my view was rightly made.").

21 *Masetlha v. President of the Republic of South Africa and Another 2008 (1)* SA 566 (CC); *Corruption Watch NPC v. President of the Republic of South Africa* 2018 (2) SACR 442 (CC) (invalidating the appointment of the Director of Public Prosecutions); *Democratic Alliance v. President of South Africa* 2013 (1) SA 248 (CC) (invalidating the appointment of the Director of Public Prosecutions).

22 *See*, J. Mathenjwa, 'The Role of the Principle of Legality in Preserving Municipal Constitutional Integrity', *Southern African Public Law*, Vol. 29, No. 2, 2014, p. 534; R. Henrico, 'Re-Visiting the Rule of Law and Principle of Legality: Judicial Nuisance or Licence?', *TSAR*, Vol. 4, 2014, p. 742; L. Mnguni & J. Muller, 'The Principle of Legality in Constitutional Matters with Reference to Masiya v. Director of Public Prosecutions and Others 2007 5 SA 30 (CC)', *Law, Democracy and Development*, Vol. 13, No. 1, 2009, p. 112; T. Jordaan, 'Does the Principle of Legality Require Statutory Crimes to Have Specific Penalty Clauses? A Critical Analysis of the Decisions of the High Court and the Supreme Court of Appeal in DPP, Western Cape v. Prins', *South African Journal of Criminal Justice*, Vol. 25, 2012, p. 379.

23 H. Klug, 'Accountability and the Role of Independent Constitutional Institutions in South Africa's Post-Apartheid Constitutions', *New York Law School Law Review*, Vol. 60, 2015-2016, p. 153 (suggesting that the institutions established under Chapter 9 of the Constitution may be the fourth branch of government).

> as that found in the United States of America, France or the Netherlands. What [constitutional principle] VI requires is that there be a separation of powers between the legislature, executive and judiciary. It does not prescribe what form that separation should take. We have previously said that the [constitutional principles] must not be interpreted with technical rigidity. The language of [constitutional principle] VI is sufficiently wide to cover the type of separation required by the [Constitution] and the objection that [constitutional principle] VI has not been complied with must accordingly be rejected.[24]

Consequently, the Constitution establishes three great pillars of the State being the legislature, executive and judiciary.[25] The legislature's function under Chapter 4 of the Constitution is to pass legislation, to scrutinize and oversee executive action, including the implementation of legislation, and providing a national forum for public consideration of issues.[26] The allocation of these functions to the legislature is based on a constitutional theory that Parliament is a pillar that is representative of the numerous different interests of society so that what comes out of there will respect and reflect the nation's distinct interests.[27]

The Constitution vests executive authority on the President.[28] The executive's function under Chapter 5 of the Constitution is to implement the laws, develop and implement national policy and initiate legislation.[29] The allocation of these functions to a single President is based on a constitutional theory that the President can act quickly without the need to harmonize conflicting interests of society.[30] This is why in some areas like foreign relations or defence, the President is constitutionally permitted to act without the need to

24 *Certification Judgment*, at para. 132-133.

25 *See*, Chapters 4, 5 and 8 of the Constitution 1996.

26 *See*, Sections 42(3) and 55(2) of the Constitution.

27 *See*, *Democratic Alliance v. Masondo* 2003 2 SA 413 (CC) (noting that "the open and deliberative nature of the process goes further than providing a dignified and meaningful role for all participants. It is calculated to produce better outcomes through subjecting laws and governmental action to the test of critical debate, rather than basing them on unilateral decision-making. It should be underlined that the responsibility for serious and meaningful deliberation and decision-making rests not only on the majority, but on minority groups as well. In the end, the endeavours of both majority and minority parties should be directed not to exercising (or blocking the exercise) of power for its own sake, but at achieving a just society."); B. Neuborne, 'The Last Walls', a paper presented at the Great Hall at The Cooper Union on 13 December 2012 www.youtube.com/watch?v=ATK7FftBiF4. *See also*, B. Neuborne, 'Felix Frankfurter's Revenge: An Accidental Democracy Built by Judges', *New York University Review of Law and Social Change*, Vol. 35, 2011, p. 602.

28 Section 85 of the Constitution. *See*, M. Mhango, 'Constitutional Eighteenth Amendment Bill: An Unnecessary Amendment to the South Africa Constitution', *Statute Law Review*, Vol. 35, No. 1, 2014, pp. 19-34 (arguing that Section 85 means that under the South African Constitution, a single President possesses the entirety of the executive authority, which he or she exercises together with the Cabinet).

29 *See*, Section 85(1) and (2) of the Constitution.

30 Neuborne, 2012.

get prior Parliamentary approval.[31] There are several other areas where the President is constitutionally permitted to act without prior approval.[32]

The judiciary's function under Section 8 of the Constitution is to resolve disputes through the application of the law by interpreting and applying the law to a specific set of circumstances or controversies involving individuals of the state.[33] This explains why courts have consistently rejected to engage in an academic exercise by hearing a case that no longer presents an existing or live controversy that should exist if a court is to avoid giving advisory opinions on abstract propositions of law.[34] The allocation of these tasks to the judiciary is based on a constitutional theory that the judiciary is specially trained to carry out these functions and is insulated from the other branches that are politically accountable.

Apart from the text itself apportioning various powers and functions between and among the three branches of government and the constitutional principle VI, there is no constitutional text defining or codifying the principle of separation of powers.[35] In that sense, separation of powers is implied. Despite the absence of a clear textual authorization in the Constitution, the South African judiciary has constructed a constitutional doctrine defining and protecting the separation of powers.[36]

A few notable foundational cases that come to mind include the following: the case of *Western Cape Legislature v. President of South Africa,* which involved the task of the transformation of local government during the first local government elections in the mid-1990s. At issue in the case was a provision in the Local Government Transition Act 209 of 1993. Section 16A of that Act provided that the "President may amend this act and any

31 *See*, Sections 201 and 203 of the Constitution, respectively, which permit the President as head of the national executive to authorize the employment of the defence force in defence of the republic or the fulfilment of an international obligation, or to declare a state of national defence without getting prior approval from Parliament. And *see*, Section 231 of the Constitution that entrusts the national executive with the responsibility of negotiating and signing of all international agreements; Section 231(3) provides that "an international agreement of a technical, administrative or executive nature, or an agreement which does not require either ratification or accession, entered into by the national executive, binds the Republic without approval by the National Assembly and the National Council of Provinces, but must be tabled in the Assembly and the Council within a reasonable time."

32 *See*, Section 84 of the Constitution.

33 *See*, Section 165 of the Constitution.

34 *Legal Aid South Africa v. Mzoxolo Magidiwana and Others* [2015] ZACC 28; *National Coalition of Gay and Lesbian Equality v. Minister of Home Affairs* 2000 2 SA 1 (CC), at para. 21; *Radio Pretoria v. Chairman, Independent Communications Authority of SA & Another* 2005 1 SA 47 (SCA); and *Rand Water Board v. Rotek Industries (Pty) Ltd* 2003 4 SA 58 (SCA). *But see*, Okpaluba, 2015, p. 206 (noting that since the advent of the 1996 Constitution, the Constitutional Court has remained one of the few adjudicative institutions in the Commonwealth vested with the power to give advisory opinion to the executive, the President or a provincial premier, on the constitutionality of a Bill brought to the President or the premier for assent).

35 *See*, Okpaluba & Mhango, 2017; K. Hopkins, 'Some Thoughts on the Constitutionality of Independent Tribunals Established by the State', *Obiter*, Vol. 27, 2006, p. 150.

36 *See*, *South African Association of Personal Injury Lawyers v. Heath and Others* 2001 1 SA 883, at para. 20 (*Heath*) (holding that "I cannot accept that an implicit provision of the Constitution has any less force than an express provision").

schedule thereto by proclamation in the Gazette." The Constitutional Court enforced separation of powers by overturning a Proclamation by the President on the grounds that the impugned provision of the Local Government Transition Act, under which the President had acted in promulgating the Proclamation, was inconsistent with the separation of powers required by the Constitution and accordingly invalid.[37]

In *Heath*,[38] the Constitutional Court considered whether it was constitutionally appropriate for a judge of the High Court to head the Special Investigative Unit located within the executive branch and established in terms of the Special Investigating Units and Special Tribunals Act 74 of 1996. The powers of the Special Investigative Unit involved investigating and litigating on behalf of the state to recover monies lost to the state through corruption and maladministration. The court held that from a separation of powers point of view, the functions of the Special Investigative Unit were inappropriate for a judge to perform. Chaskalson P reasoned that:

> The functions that the head of the [Special Investigative Unit] is required to perform are far removed from the central mission of the judiciary. They are determined by the President who formulates and can amend the allegations to be investigated. If regard is had to all the circumstances, including the intrusive quality of the investigations that are carried out by the [Special Investigative Unit], the inextricable link between the [Special Investigative Unit] as investigator and the [Special Investigative Unit] as litigator on behalf of the State, and the indefinite nature of the appointment which precludes the head of the unit from performing his judicial functions, the first respondent's position as head of the [Special Investigative Unit] is … incompatible with his judicial office and contrary to the separation of powers required by the Constitution.[39]

Furthermore in *S v. Dodo*,[40] the Constitutional Court considered whether minimum sentencing legislation enacted by the legislature was consistent with the Constitution. Section 51 of the Criminal Law Amendment Act 105 of 1997 introduced minimum sentencing guidelines in relation to certain crimes and required the judiciary to sentence an accused person to imprisonment for life unless the judiciary was satisfied that substantial reasons exist for the imposition of a lesser sentence. The Constitutional Court held that Section 51(1) of the Criminal Law Amendment Act was not inconsistent with the principle of

37 *Executive Council, Western Cape Legislature and Others v. President of the Republic of South Africa and Others* 1995 4 SA 877 (CC).
38 *Heath*, 2001, para. 29.
39 *Id.*, para. 45.
40 *S v. Dodo*, 2001, 5 BCLR 423 (CC). *See also, Bernstein v. Bester* 1996 4 BCLR 449, at para. 105 (where the Constitutional Court suggested that an Act of Parliament that sought to bring the judiciary under the control of the political branches could be struck down under the principle of separation of powers).

separation of powers because both Parliament and the Judiciary have obligations in relation to sentencing of convicted offenders. Justice Ackerman, who wrote for the majority, reasoned that:

> There is under our Constitution no absolute separation of powers between the judicial function, on the one hand, and the legislative and executive on the other. When the nature and process of punishment is considered in its totality, it is apparent that all three branches of the state play a functional role and must necessarily do so. No judicial punishment can take place unless the person to be punished has been convicted of an offence which either under the common law or statute carries with it a punishment. It is pre-eminently the function of the legislature to determine what conduct should be criminalised and punished … Both the legislature and executive share an interest in the punishment to be imposed by courts, both in regard to its nature and its severity. They have a general interest in sentencing policy, penology and the extent to which correctional institutions are used to further the various objectives of punishment. The availability and cost of prisons, as well as the views of these arms of government on custodial sentences, legitimately inform policy on alternative forms of non-custodial sentences and the legislative implementation thereof.[41]

Lastly, in *Magidiwana,*[42] where the applicants sought an order to compel the state and Minister of Justice to pay the legal bills arising from their participation in the Marikana Commission of Inquiry, the Constitutional Court refused to grant the interim relief sought based on the principle of separation of powers. The Constitutional Court rejected to hear the case based on the understanding that the issues were not justiciable.[43] In the light of this brief discussion, it is clear-cut that through the institution of judicial review, the judiciary has engaged in the development of the law of separation of powers.[44] But has this development been refined to encompass a clear political question doctrine?

41 *S v. Dodo*, at paras. 22-23.

42 *Magidiwana and Others v. President of the Republic of South Africa* 2013 11 BCLR 1251 (CC).

43 For a discussion of *Magidiwana and Others v. President of the Republic of South Africa, see,* discussions generally, Okpaluba & Mhango, 2017.

44 *See*, Mojapelo, 2013, p. 37; K. O'Regan, 'Checks and Balances Reflections on the Development of the Doctrine of Separation of Powers Under the South African Constitution', *Potchefstroom Electronic Law Journal,* Vol. 8, No. 1, 2005, p. 120 (noting how far South Africa has progressed in this task of developing a distinctively South African model of the separation of powers).

6.3 Emergence of the Political Question Theory

During the reign of the Interim Constitution, the Constitutional Court in *Ferreira v. Levin*[45] had to determine the constitutionality of Section 417(2)(b) of the Companies Act 61 of 1973.[46] It was provided in that subsection that any person summoned for an examination into the affairs of a company may be required to answer questions, and notwithstanding that the answer to such questions might incriminate him, any response could be used in evidence against him. The Constitutional Court ruled that Section 417(2)(b) was in conflict with the right to freedom and security of the person, which included the right not to be detained without trial in Section 11(1) of the Interim Constitution.

In his concurring opinion, Chaskalson P used this case to explain what he thought is the constitutionally envisaged relationship between the judiciary and the political branches of government in connection to the determination of political questions under the new democratic order. He pronounced that:

> Implicit in the social welfare state is the acceptance of regulation and redistribution in the public interest … Whether or not there should be regulation and redistribution is essentially a *political question* which falls within the domain of the legislature and not the court. It is not for the courts to approve or disapprove of such policies. What the courts must ensure is that the implementation of any political decision to undertake such policies conforms with the Constitution. It should not, however, require the legislature to show that they are necessary if the Constitution does not specifically require that this be done.[47] (my emphasis)

President Chaskalson made the above remark in support of his view against a broad interpretation of Section 11(1) of the Interim Constitution. He cautioned South Africa against falling into the pitfall of *Lochner v. New York* era,[48] which gave rise to serious questions about judicial review and the relationship between the judiciary and the elected branches of government in the United States. In his view, Section 11 should not be construed

45 *Ferreira v. Levin*, 1996.
46 The Companies Act 1973 has since been repealed by the Companies Act 71 of 2008.
47 *Ferreira v. Levin*, 1996, at para. 180. (emphasis added).
48 *Lochner v. New York* 198 US 45 (1905) (invalidating maximum working hours for bakers). It is estimated that almost 200 state laws were declared unconstitutional as violating the due process clause of the fourteenth amendment. For a discussion of what has been termed as the *Lochner* era, *see*, B. Wright, '*The Growth of American Constitutional Law*', Greenwood Press, Westport, 1942, p. 154; and D. Bernstein, 'Lochner's Legacy's Legacy', *Texas Law Review*, Vol. 92, 2003, p. 1 (arguing that *Lochner's* legacy provides a particularly telling example of the danger of applying an ideological construct to constitutional history for present purposes, while ignoring or neglecting contrary evidence).

so broadly that "we overshoot the mark and trespass upon the terrain that is not rightly ours."[49] He explained that in a democratic society the role of the legislature, as a body reflecting the dominant opinion, should be acknowledged. He emphasized the need to bear in mind that there are functions that are properly the concern of the political branches, and that while these functions may overlap, the terrains are separate and should be kept separate.[50]

Regarding the determination of political questions, the above pronouncement by President Chaskalson's should be understood in light of what Justice Kpegah said in *Amidu.*[51] There, Kpegah remarked that "there is inherent or internal evidence in our Constitution that the policy which informs or should inform any legislation... are matters for the executive and legislature."[52] Like Kpegah, Chaskalson considers those policy choices to be of no concern to the judiciary and notes that it is not for the judiciary to approve or disapprove such choices.[53] Likewise, in his pronouncement, Chaskalson's suggestion is that the Constitution bars the judiciary from requiring the political branches of government to demonstrate the necessity under the Constitution for the policy choices that inform legislative measures because the political branches have discretion in this regard.[54] In other words, the suggestion by Chaskalson, as Redish has agreeably argued elsewhere, is that when the Constitution is silent concerning the need for legislation in a particular area, the Constitution should be understood as granting the political branches discretion to formulate new policies in those areas without judicial interference.[55]

Evidently, Chaskalson would agree that the determination of whether regulation 28 of the Pension Funds Act 24 of 1956, which regulates the investment of private pension funds in South Africa, should exist or is necessary under the Constitution is a political question and the judiciary may not approve or disapprove the choices taken by the political branches responding to that question. The discretion can be sourced from Section 85(2) of the Constitution, which gives the executive power to initiate and develop policy, and Section 44(1)(a)(ii) of the Constitution, which grants the power to the National Assembly to pass legislation. Although these provisions grant powers to the political branches, the same do not require that these powers be exercised. There are only a few provisions in the Consti-

49 *Ferreira v. Levin,* 1996, at para. 106.

50 *Id.*, at para. 106.

51 *Amidu,* 2001-2002.

52 *Id.*, p. 154.

53 *Ferreira v. Levin,* 1996, at para. 105.

54 *See,* Sections 84(2), 85(2), 55 and 44(1) of the Constitution 1996.

55 Redish, 1984, *Northwestern LR* 5-10 and 24-25. Justice Ngcobo makes a similar suggestion in *Doctors for Life International,* at para. 26, and says when a constitutional obligation requires a political branch of government to determine in the first place what it necessary to fulfil its obligation by leaving to the political branch to determine what is required of it in this regard, a review by a court on whether the obligation has been fulfilled intrudes the separation of powers principle. Ngcobo suggest that political branches have discretion to determine how to fulfil the obligation in such circumstances.

tution where the political branches are required to initiate and enact legislation.[56] In all other areas, the decision of whether to develop policy or initiate legislation and eventually pass such legislation remains the discretion of the political branches.[57] The views by Chaskalson in *Ferreira v. Levin*, which recognize the limits of judicial power in determining political questions, were confirmed by the Constitutional Court during the certification of the Constitution.

The certification process was the first time the Constitutional Court had the occasion to interpret the Constitution before it became enforceable. In the *First Certification Judgement*, the Constitutional Court described its functions and powers in the certification process (which are not different from its ordinary powers and functions) as follows:

> First and foremost it must be emphasised that the Court has a judicial and not a political mandate. Its function is clearly spelt out in Interim Constitution 71(2): to certify whether all the provisions of the [new text] comply with the [constitutional principles]. That is a judicial function, a legal exercise. Admittedly a constitution, by its very nature, deals with the extent, limitations and exercise of political power as also with the relationship between political entities and with the relationship between the state and persons. But this Court has no power, no mandate and no right to express any view on the political choices made by the [constitutional assembly] in drafting the [new text], save to the extent that such choices may be relevant either to compliance or non-compliance with the [constitutional principles]. Subject to that qualification, the wisdom or otherwise of any provision of the [new text] is not this Court's business.[58]

56 *See*, Section 33 of the Constitution (requiring national legislation to give effect to the right to administrative action, which was complied with by passing the Promotion of Administrative Justice Act, 2000); Section 9(4) of the Constitution (requiring national legislation to give effect to the right to equality, which was complied with by passing the Promotion of Equality and Prevention of Unfair Discrimination Act, 2000; Section 32(2) of the Constitution (requiring national legislation to give effect to the right to access to information, which was complied with by the passage of the Promotion of Access to Information Act, 2000).

57 For authorities on the proposition that where Constitution delegates a power or function to a political branch of government without imposing how the power or function delegated should be exercised, the political branch of government has discretion on how to execute that power, *see*, *Economic Freedom Fighters v. Speaker of the National Assembly*, at para. 93; Mhango, 2014, p. 471; *Glenister*, at para. 146; Redish, 1984, p. 1048; Ngcobo, 2016, pp. 21-23; Barkow, 2002, p. 239; and *Ferreira v. Levin*, 1996, at para. 105. *But see*, *Minister of Justice and Constitutional Development and Others v. Prince* [2018] ZACC 30; 2018 (10) BCLR 1220 (CC); 2018 (6) SA 393 (CC) (ordering parliament to pass legislation to permit and regulate the private use of marijuana); and *My Vote Counts NPC v. Minister of Justice and Correctional Services and Another* [2018] ZACC 17; 2018 (8) BCLR 893 (CC); 2018 (5) SA 380 (CC) (ordering parliament to pass legislation governing campaign finance).

58 *In re: Certification of the Constitution of the Republic of South Africa*, 1996, at para. 27.

Despite not mentioning the doctrine by name, for the following two reasons I argue that the above statements of law in *Ferreira v. Levin* and the *First Certification Judgement* are judicial authorities for the political question theory in South Africa.

Firstly, in both cases, the Constitutional Court recognized the limits of the power of judicial review in dealing with political questions. It recognized, without saying more, that these questions are reserved for the political branches, and that courts must not intrude in them; that political questions present a narrow limitation over the court's power of judicial review.

Secondly, the Constitutional Court recognized that this limitation is predicated upon respect for separation of powers. As intimated in Chapter 1 of this book, the South African judiciary before and after the new constitutional dispensation has always recognized that the institution of judicial review is not absolute but has certain narrow limitations to it.[59] To this extent, these statements of the law (from *Ferreira v. Levin* and the *First Certification Judgement*) can be equated with the famous authoritative words from *Marbury v. Madison*,[60] *Tuffuor*,[61] *Onuoha v. Okafor*[62] and *Ex Parte Matovu*[63] as legal authorities for the political question doctrine in the United States, Ghana, Nigeria and Uganda, respectively.

59 *See, Brown v. Leyds NO* (where the Supreme Court of South African acceded to the concept of judicial review in *Marbury v. Madison* but like *Marbury v. Madison* it also recognized the limits of judicial review); *Cassim and Solomon v. the State* (1862) 9 *Cape Law Journal* 58 (applying judicial review of legislation); *National Coalition for Gay and Lesbian Equality v. Minister of Home Affairs* 2000 1 BCLR 54 (incorporating the doctrine of ripeness as applied in the United States into South African law); *Wiese v. Government Employees Pension Fund,* 2012, 6 BCLR 599 (CC), at paras. 21-24 (holding that the issues between the parties had moot due to recent legislative interventions); Currie & de Waal, *The Bill of Rights,* pp. 79-96 (discussing the justiciability doctrines of mootness, ripeness and other noting that these now forms part of South African law).

60 *Marbury v. Madison,* 1803, p. 170 (holding that the province of the court is, solely, to decide on the rights of individuals, not to enquire how the executive, or executive officers, perform duties in which they have a discretion. Questions, in their nature political, or which are, by the constitution and laws, submitted to the executive, can never be made in this court).

61 *Tuffuor,* 1980, pp. 651-652 holding that there is a longline of authorities which establishes two important principles governing the relationship that subsists or should exist between Parliament and the courts: (a) that the courts can call in question a decision of Parliament; but the courts cannot seek to extend their writs into what happens in Parliament; and (b) that the law and custom of Parliament is a distinct body of law and, as constitutional experts do put it, unknown to the courts. And therefore the courts take judicial notice of what has happened in Parliament. The courts do not, and cannot, inquire into how Parliament went about its business. The courts cannot therefore inquire into the legality or illegality of what happened in Parliament. In so far as Parliament has acted by virtue of the powers conferred upon it by the provisions of article 9(1), its actions within Parliament are a closed book. *See also, Ghana Bar Association*; *Ex Parte Matovu,* 1966; *Attorney General v. Tinyefuza*; Cooley, 1868, pp. 186-187 (arguing against judicial inquiry into the legislative motives) and *Collins v. Minister of the Interior and Another* 1957 (1) SA 552 (A) 565.

62 *Ouoha v. Okafor,* 1983, p. 507 (holding that the lack of satisfactory criteria for a judicial determination of a political question is one of the dominant considerations in determining whether a question falls within the category of political questions. The other is the appropriations of attributing finality to the action of the political departments and political parties under the Nigerian Constitution and system of government).

63 *Ex Parte Matovu,* 1966, p. 531 (holding that the government' exposition of political question doctrine as elaborated in *Luther v. Borden* cannot be faulted).

Clearly, even before the *First Certification Judgement*, Chaskalson, motivated by separation of powers concerns, was apprehensive about the judiciary not to overreach and determine political questions that were the preserve of the political branches in the new South Africa.[64] It is apparent from Chaskalson's pronouncements that certain political questions are not appropriate for determination by the courts. The problem with Chaskalson's pronouncement is that he did not give details on how his pronouncement would be given effect to. That is, he did not elaborate how the judiciary would identify those political questions that are the preserve of the political branches and which courts may not interfere with.

It is my submission that the pronouncements by the Constitutional Court in *Ferreira v. Levin* and the *First Certification Judgement* can only be explained in the context of the political question theory because they advance the objectives of the doctrine. In fact, Chaskalson's views in *Ferreira v. Levin* are indistinguishable from the compromised political question doctrine articulated by Justice Acquah in *Mensah v. Attorney-General.* Seedorf and Sibanda have made a similar observation that:

> Like courts in other jurisdictions, the Constitutional Court of South Africa has on frequent occasions employed the idea of judicial restraint, a conscious decision based on separation of powers concerns not to interfere with decisions by the other branches of government, provided that they are in line with the Constitution.[65]

In subsequent cases decided after the Interim Constitution, the Constitutional Court consistently expressed similar views concerning the role of the judiciary in adjudicating certain political questions and the need not to intrude into the domain of the other branches.

6.4 Political Question Doctrine or Mere Deference: Jurisprudence from the Constitutional Court

Some of the jurisprudence emerging from the Constitutional Court has pointed to the reluctance of the Court to adjudicate on political questions or willingness to exercise

---

64 H. Corder, 'Lessons from (North) America (Beware the Legalization of Politics and the Political Seduction of the Law)', *South African Law Journal*, Vol. 109, 1992, p. 211 (arguing that the new South Africa must take note of lessons on constitutional adjudication from the United States and Canada and resolve what he described as the Madisonian dilemma: the conflict between the principle of self-government by the majority and that of protection of the minority against the tyranny of the majority. According to Corder, the lesson for South Africa was the need to ensure that courts are active to protect human rights while being proportionately conscientious to respect the rights of majorities or the popular mandate to govern the country).

65 Seedorf & Sibanda, 2008, pp. 12-55-12-56.

judicial restraint.[66] It is not certain from this jurisprudence whether the Constitutional Court is merely exercising deference to the other branches of government or applying a political question doctrine. And the courts themselves have frequently failed to clarify whether they are truly abstaining or merely giving deference to another branch in the resolution of a political question. What explains this confusion? What would prompt a court to be less clear about the nature of its rulings when it relies on a political question theory? In all these cases, the Constitutional Court has not developed a rule for future application or guide lower courts.

One of the early cases that illustrates this irony is *United Democratic Movement.*[67] In *United Democratic Movement,* the Constitutional Court upheld three Acts of Parliament – the Constitution of the Republic of South Africa Amendment Act 18 of 2002, the Constitution of the Republic of South Africa Second Amendment Act 21 of 2002 and the Local Government: Municipal Structures Amendment Act 20 of 2002 – that allowed members of Parliament to cross the floor in Parliament without losing their seats. It struck down the Loss or Retention of Membership of National and Provincial Legislatures Act 22 of 2002, which had been tabled together with the other three Acts.

The context which led to the case is that the four pieces of legislation were enacted to take political profit of the demise of the New National Party from the Democratic Alliance in 2001. In terms of the legal framework applicable at the time, candidates elected to represent a particular political party could not switch to another party without losing their seats in the legislature.[68] When the New National Party broke away from the Democratic Alliance to join the African National Congress in 2001, the New National Party councillors who had won seats in the 2000 elections faced the possibility of losing their seats to the Democratic Alliance.

In a swift move to prevent the loss of political power in the legislature, the African National Congress tabled four bills mentioned above. The common feature in these Bills is that they all sought to grant a fifteen-day window period on two occasions every four years during which floor-crossing could happen without a member losing their seat. The Bills also granted an immediate window period for those wishing to switch political parties.

---

66 *See,* Okpaluba, 2003-2004, p. 184 (arguing that it is also common knowledge that this judicial restraint stems not only from the courts' deference to the other arms of government on considerations of the separation of powers; it also derives from the doctrine of justiciability underlying judicial avoidance of those issues not properly suited for adjudication and which rightly belong to the domain of the executive, the legislature, or the political sphere). *See also,* C. Okpaluba, 'Constraints on Judicial Review of Executive Conduct: The Juridical Link Between the Marikana Mineworkers' Imbroglio and the Gauteng E-Tolling Saga', *TSAR,* No. 2, 2015, pp. 286-287 (arguing that courts decline to entertain any action the subject-matter of which properly resides in the political arena) and C. Okpaluba, 'Justiciability and Constitutional Adjudication in the Commonwealth: The Problem of Definition (1) and (2)', *Journal for Contemporary Roman-Dutch Law,* Vol. 66, No. 4, 2003, pp. 424, 610.

67 *United Democratic Movement v. President of the Republic of South Africa* 2003 (1) SA 495.

68 *See,* Section 27 of the Local Government: Municipal Structures Act 117 of 1998.

Two of the Bills required a constitutional amendment in terms of Section 74(3) of the Constitution, which stipulates the procedure for amendments to any part of the Constitution.

The United Democratic Movement, a political party represented in Parliament, challenged the process by which the Bills were passed. In describing the issue before it, the Constitutional Court explained that:

> This case is not about the merits or demerits of the provisions of the disputed legislation. That is a political question and is of no concern to this Court. What has to be decided is not whether the disputed provisions are appropriate or inappropriate, but whether they are constitutional or unconstitutional. It ought not to have been necessary to say this for that is true of all cases that come before this Court. We do so only because of some of the submissions made to us in argument, and the tenor of the public debate concerning the case which has taken place both before and since the hearing of the matter.[69]

While the current position in South Africa is that legislators cannot cross the floor in the legislature without losing their seats, the outcome in the *United Democratic Movement* signalled the need for the Constitutional Court to give absolute deference to the elected branches of government in cases involving interpretation of constitutional provisions that assign certain questions to the political branches.[70] It is important to point out that even though *United Democratic Movement* was widely criticized by commentators,[71] none of the criticisms is developed around the Constitutional Court's acknowledgement and expression of the political question theory sentiments above. What is evident from *United Democratic Movement* is that the Constitutional Court is silent on what kind of political questions it will not entertain and how those questions will be identified and what legal tools will be used to justify abstention.

Another significant case that demonstrates the reluctance of the Constitutional Court to determine political questions is *Kaunda*.[72] This case involved the question of whether the plaintiffs, who were South African citizens, were entitled to diplomatic protection under the Constitution and international law, when they were arrested on criminal charges in Zimbabwe. The Constitutional Court ruled they were not, and explained that while it had jurisdiction to decide matters involving diplomatic protection, courts could not command the executive how to make diplomatic interventions for the protection of its

69 *United Democratic Movement v. President of the Republic of South Africa*, at para. 11.

70 *See*, Constitution Fourteenth Amendment Act of 2008, General Notice 31791.

71 *See*, G. Devenish, 'Political Musical Chairs – the Saga of Floor-Crossing and the Constitution', *Stellenbosch Law Review*, Vol. 15, 2004, p. 64.

72 *Kaunda v. President of the Republic of South Africa* 2004 1 BCLR 1009 (CC).

nationals.[73] Why? Is it because the executive has discretion in this area? In his concurring opinion to the majority judgement, Justice Ngcobo addresses these questions by expressing the separation of powers imperatives in this way:

> The conduct of foreign relations is a matter which is within the domain of the executive. The exercise of diplomatic protection has an impact on foreign relations. Comity compels states to respect the sovereignty of one another; no state wants to interfere in the domestic affairs of another. The exercise of diplomatic protection is therefore a sensitive area where both the timing and the manner in which the intervention is made are crucial. The state must be left to assess foreign policy considerations and it is a better judge of whether, when and how to intervene. It is therefore generally accepted that this is a province of the executive, the state should generally be afforded a wide discretion in deciding whether and in what manner to grant protection in each case and the judiciary must generally keep away from this area.[74]

In her dissenting opinion, Justice O'Regan offered the following rationale, which was in accord with Justice Ngcobo's views above:

> It is clear ...that under our Constitution the conduct of foreign affairs is primarily the responsibility of the executive, for the executive is the arm of government best placed to conduct foreign affairs... It is clear from the existing jurisprudence of this Court that all exercise of public power *is to some extent justiciable under our Constitution, but the precise scope of the justiciability will depend on a range of factors including the nature of the power being exercised.* Given that the duty to provide diplomatic protection can only be fulfilled by government in the conduct of foreign relations, the executive must be afforded considerable latitude to determine how best the duty should be carried out... [In] any proceedings in which the exercise of the power is challenged, a court will bear in mind that foreign relations is a sphere of government reserved by our Constitution for the executive and it will accordingly be careful not to attribute to itself superior wisdom in relation to it.[75] (my emphasis)

73 *Id.*, p. 1029.

74 *Id.*, at para. 172.

75 *Id.*, at paras. 243-245. *See*, T. Roux, 'The Constitutional Framework and Deepening Democracy in South Africa', *Policy: Issues and Actors,* 2006, p. 16 www.sarpn.org/documents/d0002299/PIA_18-6_Roux_Oct2005.pdf (arguing that O'Regan's opinion in *Kaunda v. President of the Republic of South Africa* is the most preferred).

Short of articulating an intelligible political question theory in *Kaunda*, the majority of the Constitutional Court concluded that decisions made by the government in foreign affairs are subject to constitutional control.[76] It held that whereas courts are required to deal with such matters, they will, however, give particular weight to the government's special responsibility for and particular expertise in foreign affairs and the wide discretion that it must have in determining how best to deal with such matters.[77] It is problematic that the Constitutional Court did not recognize or consider the possibility of granting absolute deference to elected branches on those foreign affairs questions even though it recognizes the inability for courts to determine these matters for lack of expertise.

By failing to grant absolute deference, the Constitutional Court misses the point that the political question doctrine requires more than mere deference in determining matters that are committed to the political branches to resolve. Clearly, the Constitutional Court is mindful of the limits of its own power and the separation of powers concerns in determining foreign affairs. But, the Court fails to adequately define the boundaries of discretion afforded to the executive or the jurisprudential justification for such discretion.

Despite the fact *Kaunda* was clear that executive action was subject to constitutional control, presumably as part of the demands of the rule of law and checks and balances, it is silent concerning the contours of the limits on judicial powers. In other words, the Constitutional Court did not specifically consider or apply the political question doctrine, which operates as a limitation on judicial powers even though it decided the case based on sentiments with the doctrine.[78] What the Constitutional Court did was to provide some foundation for a potential development or application of the doctrine in future cases. The closest it got to articulate a political question theory is when Justice O'Regan in the above quotation spoke of the extent to which the exercise of public power is justiciable, but failed to take this discussion to its logical conclusion by developing a lucent political question doctrine.

It is this double speak that you encounter from the justices in cases such as *United Democratic Movement, Kaunda* and others that makes the case for the Constitutional

76 *Kaunda v. President of the Republic of South Africa* 1045, at para. 172.

77 *Id.*, at paras. 144, 172. *See also*, Tushnet, 2002, p. 1232 (advocating that the judiciary should be restrained from resolving issues that other branches are better suited to resolve such as foreign affairs); Free, 2003, p. 490 (arguing that the political question doctrine enjoys special potency in foreign affairs); Scharpf, 1966, pp. 567, 583-584 (agreeing with the Supreme Court's approach of treating foreign affairs questions as political questions).

78 *See, e.g.*, Chase, 2001, p. 1045 (arguing that the political question doctrine limits judicial power); Endicott, 2010, p. 538 (arguing that the political question doctrine represents the judicial effort to ensure that courts do not hamper the functioning of the political branches of government); Gouin, 1994 (advocating for the political question in foreign affairs); *US Dep't of Commerce v. Montana* 503 US 442, 458 (1992) (noting that the political question doctrine recognizes that a constitutional provision may not be judicially enforceable; that a political question doctrine is a restraint mechanism on the judiciary) and *Baker v. Carr*, 1962, pp. 217-218 (stating that particular issues are non-justiciable because they fall outside of the province of the judiciary).

Court to develop a clear-witted political question doctrine that would bring certainty in the law. In this regard, I welcome the proposition by Professor Asare in the Ghanaian context that courts must provide justification when they invoke the political question doctrine sentiments because it forces them to clarify the doctrine and its application. South African courts have not done this in those cases where they have made statements that can only be read as expressions of the political question theory.[79]

Perhaps, the most recent expression of the political question theory can be found in *International Trade Administration Commission.*[80] This case arose out of South Africa's World Trade Organisation obligations on tariffs and trade. These obligations are given effect to in terms of a number of domestic legislation that governs anti-dumping duties, imports and other trade remedies, including the primary legislation known as the International Trade Administration Act 2002.[81]

The International Trade Administration Act established the International Trade Administration Commission (the International Trade Commission) with the authority to, among other things, make recommendations to the Minister of Trade and Industry (Minister of Trade), who may then request the Minister of Finance to lift or impose anti-dumping duties on goods introduced into South Africa.

In 2002, the Board on Tariffs and Trade, the predecessor to the International Trade Commission, conducted an investigation into alleged dumping of stranded wire, rope and cables of iron streel from several countries including the United Kingdom. Following this investigation and the recommendation by the Board on Tariffs and Trade to the Minister of Trade, the Minister of Finance imposed five-year anti-dumping duties on certain steel products. A few months before these anti-dumping duties were to expire, Scaw South Africa (Pty) Ltd (Scaw), South Africa's largest manufacturer of steel products, requested the International Trade Commission to conduct a sunset review. The purpose of this

79 *See, Mazibuko*, 2012 (where based on separation of powers concerns judge Davis refused to intervene in a matter involving political questions pertaining to a motion of no confidence); *United Democratic Movement v. Speaker of the National Assembly* [2017] ZACC 21, at para. 92-93, p. 69 (where the Constitutional Court was asked to order the Speaker of Parliament to make all the necessary arrangements to ensure that the motion of no confidence is decided by secret ballot. The Court found that no legal basis exists for that radical and separation of powers-insensitive move and that to order a secret ballot would trench separation of powers. The Court reasoned that our decision that the power to prescribe the voting procedure in a motion of no confidence reposes in the Speaker, accords with the dictates of separation of powers. It affirms the functional independence of Parliament to freely exercise its powers); and *Democratic Alliance v. President of the Republic of South Africa* [2017] ZAWCHC 34 (where the court dismissed a political party's action to review the president's decision to reshuffle cabinet on the basis that the decision to reshuffle involves a political discretion that is not susceptible to judicial review).

80 *International Trade Administration Commission v. Scaw South Africa (Pty) Ltd*, 2012, (4) SA 618 (CC) (International Trade Administration).

81 *See, Government Gazette*, GG 25684, GN 3197, 14 November 2003; Customs and Excise Act, 1964; and Board of Tariffs and Trade Act, 1986.

request was to persuade the International Trade Commission to extend the life of the existing anti-dumping duties.[82]

Following the sunset review, the International Trade Commission concluded that the lifting of existing anti-dumping duties would not result in further dumping of steel products from the United Kingdom.[83] Hence, in October 2008, the International Trade Commission decided to recommend to the Minister of Trade that the existing anti-dumping duty on imports from the United Kingdom should be terminated. This decision led Scaw to lodge an urgent application to restrain the International Trade Commission, Minister of Trade and Minister of Finance from terminating the existing anti-dumping duties.

The High Court granted a temporary relief to Scaw, pending a review to set aside the International Trade Commission's decision, and later refused the International Trade Commission's leave to appeal the court decision. The International Trade Commission then approached the Supreme Court of Appeal, which also rejected its application for leave to appeal.[84] As a last resort, the International Trade Commission appealed to the Constitutional Court.

In considering the merits of the appeal in the majority opinion, Justice Moseneke began his analysis with a discussion of the emergence of separation of powers jurisprudence in South Africa, including his thoughts on what should guide the development of this jurisprudence. He reasoned that:

> It is now clear from a steady trickle of judgments that the doctrine of separation of powers is part of our constitutional architecture. Courts are carving out a distinctively South African design of separation of powers. It must be a design which in the first instance *is authorised by our* Constitution itself. In other words it must sit comfortably with the *democratic system of government* we have chosen. It must find the careful equilibrium that is imposed on our constitutional arrangements by our *peculiar history*. For instance, it must ensure *effective executive government* to minister to the endemic deprivation of the poor and marginalised and yet all public power must be under constitutional control. Our system of separation of powers must give due *recognition to the popular will* as expressed legislatively provided that the laws and policies in issue are consistent with constitutional dictates.[85] (my emphasis)

82 *See*, Regulation 53.2 provides: "If a sunset review has been initiated prior to the lapse of an anti-dumping duty, such anti-dumping duty shall remain in force until the sunset review has been finalised."

83 *International Trade Administration Commission*, at para. 22.

84 *Id.*, at para. 24.

85 *Id.*, at para. 91.

In the above statement of law, Justice Moseneke, despite not being his objective, offers useful suggestions on how South Africa can develop a sound political question doctrine. In my view, Moseneke provided five key requirements that are suitable elements for the development and application of a political question doctrine in South Africa, which are:

1. it must be authorised by our Constitution itself.
2. It must sit comfortably with the democratic system of government we have chosen.
3. It must find the careful equilibrium that is imposed on constitutional arrangements by our peculiar history.
4. It must ensure effective government.
5. It must give due recognition to the popular will.[86]

These requirements are a good standing point for the judiciary to finally construct a transparent political question doctrine for South Africa. Moreover, there is no doubt that these requirements favour the classical political question doctrine because of their emphasis on authorization by the Constitution itself. In other words, there has to be a constitutional basis for the doctrine, which is a point of emphasis for the classical political question theorists. I will come back to this point later in this chapter.

Further, in explaining the effects of the separation of powers principle, Justice Moseneke correctly observed that each branch of state is required to act within the domain set for it, but explains that in the end, the judiciary must determine whether a breach of separation of powers has occurred.[87] In this respect, Moseneke noted that the courts are likely to question whether to venture into the territory of other branches, but even in these circumstances, the Deputy Chief Justice accepts that courts must observe the limits of their own power.[88] While Moseneke's pronouncements are persuasive, they are short of elaborating on how the courts should observe these limits. However, his analysis did not end there. He pronounced further that:

> Where the Constitution or valid legislation has entrusted specific powers and functions to a particular branch of government, courts may not usurp that power or function by making a decision of their preference. That would frustrate the balance of power implied in the principle of separation of powers. The primary responsibility of a court is not to make decisions reserved for... other branches of government... This would especially be so where the decision in issue is policy-laden as well as polycentric.[89]

86 *Id.*, at para. 91.
87 *Id.*, at para. 92.
88 *Id.*, at para. 93.
89 *Id.*, at para. 95.

The pronouncements above came in response to two related arguments advanced by the Minister of Trade and the International Trade Commission, respectively, in opposition to the restraining order. The Minister of Trade contended that the restraining order would hinder the proper administration of economic policy, a matter which the Constitution bestows on the national executive.[90]

In his additional response to this argument, Moseneke observed that the Minister of Trade had wide discretion to accept or reject the recommendations made by the International Trade Commission or remit them. To put it differently, a recommendation from the International Trade Commission was not the sole predictor of what the Minister of Trade is likely to decide. Instead, the Minister of Trade has discretion to weigh a number of considerations, including the country's balance of payments, diplomatic relationships, the regional and global trading conditions, goods needed to foster economic growth and other factors. Thus, it was a concern for Justice Moseneke that the High Court was silent on these separation of powers considerations, especially in relation to the role of the executive in policy formulation on matters of national and international trade, when it restrained the executive from acting in their terrain.

Secondly, the International Trade Commission advanced another argument that the High Court breached separation of powers because a court may not interfere with the discretionary and polycentric discretion bestowed on the International Trade Commission and the two responsible ministers. Moseneke acceded to this argument. He reasoned that:

> when a court is invited to intrude into the terrain of the executive, especially when the executive decision-making process is still uncompleted, it must do so only … when irreparable harm is likely to ensue.[91]

For Justice Moseneke, a court in that situation must accord due weight to findings of fact and policy decisions made by those with experience in the field.

In any event, Justice Moseneke noted that the formulation and implementation of international trade policy lies at the heartland of national executive. In the end, he pronounced that courts may not trench upon the policy domain of international trade and its associated foreign relations and diplomatic considerations reserved by the Constitution for the national executive.[92] He concluded that the High Court breached the separation of

90 *Id.*, at para. 97.

91 *Id.*, at para. 101. *See also, Glenister v. President of the Republic of South Africa and Others*, 2009, 2 BCLR 136 (CC).

92 In the above proclamation, Justice Moseneke offers useful suggestions on how South Africa can develop a sound political question doctrine. In the above suggestion, Moseneke provided key requirements for a political question doctrine: "It must be authorised by our Constitution itself. It must sit comfortably with the democratic system of government we have chosen. It must find the careful equilibrium that is imposed on constitutional arrangements by our peculiar history. It must ensure effective government. Finally, it

powers. Moseneke's reasoning in *International Trade Administration Commission* was adopted in *National Treasury.*[93]

In *National Treasury*, the Constitutional Court was seized to determine whether the High Court was correct in granting the temporary restraining order against several government departments to prevent them from implementing the controversial Gauteng Freeway Improvement Project (GFIP).[94] A major component of this implementation was a policy decision taken by the national executive branch at the Cabinet level that the expenditure related to the GFIP would be funded by tolling some roads in the province on a user-pay principle.[95]

The Constitutional Court ruled that the High Court did not take sufficient consideration of separation of powers concerns when it granted the restraining order. It reasoned that the duty of determining how public resources are to be used is delegated to the executive and legislative arms of government, and that courts must refrain from entering the exclusive terrain of the other arms of government.[96]

Justice Moseneke, who wrote for the majority in *National Treasury*, applied his reasoning in *International Trade Administration Commission* and found that the formulation, implementation and funding of the GFIP was a matter entrusted to the political branches of the state and that the courts may not overthrow that power lest they frustrate the separation of powers. It is my contention that Justice Moseneke's finding in *National Treasury* was an acknowledgement of the political question theory that when the Constitution reserves decision-making powers or functions to a specific arm of government, the other arms may not overthrow that power or function.[97]

It is important to mention that the Constitutional Court, through *National Treasury*, endorsed the proposition that the Constitution allocates certain matters to specific branches, and that other branches of government must abstain from interfering in those matters. In this regard, Justice O'Regan in *Kaunda*, once remarked that a variety of constitutional

must give due recognition to the popular will." *International Trade Administration Commission*, at para. 104.

93 Commenting on the Constitutional Court decision in *National Treasury*, one commentator has argued that "this is unquestionably the most important judgment because it shows that the South African judiciary is acutely conscious of not interfering in core areas of legislative and executive competence." Sergeant at the Bar 'E-tolling case an opportunity for Concourt to define its ambit', *Mail & Guardian*, 9 September 2012.

94 One of South African Roads Agency Limited's largest projects to date. It comprises different phases to upgrade and implement new freeway networks in the Gauteng province. The ultimate freeway network will be 560 km. *See*, www.roadsandtransport.gpg.gov.za/media/Category%20Media/GFIP%20fact%20sheet.pdf.

95 The Cabinet took a decision in 2007 that approved an extensive upgrade of roads in the economic hub of the Gauteng province as part of the GFIP. *National Treasury v. Opposition to Urban Tolling Alliance*, at para. 1.

96 *National Treasury*, at paras. 44, 67.

97 *See*, *Kaunda v. President of the Republic of South Africa* (Justice O'Regan's opinion).

provisions,[98] suggests that the Constitution commits the conduct of a great deal of foreign affairs matters to the executive branch, which according to Justice O'Regan 'is hardly surprising'[99] presumably because of the expertise possessed by the executive in these matters.

Similarly, recently in *United Democratic Movement v. Speaker of the National Assembly and Others,* the Constitutional Court had to determine whether the Speaker of the National Assembly had constitutional discretion to determine the voting procedure in a motion of no confidence in the President. The Court held that "how best and in terms of which voting procedure to hold the President accountable in a particular instance is a responsibility constitutional allocated to the National Assembly."[100] The Court also found that the National Assembly delegated this discretion to the Speaker in terms of Rule 104 of the National Assembly.[101]

In articulating a similar view, former Chief Justice Ngcobo recently commented that "it is important, as the decisions of the Constitutional Court indicate, to understand that there are matters that, for good reasons, are reserved for political branches of government."[102] The question that arises is when should the judiciary intervene and when should it not? What sort of justifications should be provided where a court decides not to interfere to preserve the balance of power implied in the principle of separation of powers?

6.5 JUSTICIABILITY OF FOREIGN AFFAIRS

In 2001, the High Court decided the case of *Kolbatschenko v. King.*[103] The case considered what Okpaluba calls the American version of the political question doctrine to resolve a dispute involving foreign affairs.[104] I will point out later in this chapter that there is no such thing as the American version of the political question doctrine because the doctrine can potentially emerge from any constitutional system underpinned by the principle of separation of powers. In *Kolbatschenko v. King,* the second respondent, the Director of Public Prosecutions (DPPs) was granted permission by means of a court order to request assistance from a foreign state in obtaining information for use in an investigation into

98 *Kaunda* and Others *v. President of the Republic of South Africa,* at para. 243.

99 *Kaunda v. President of the Republic of South Africa,* at para. 243. *See also, Harksen v. President of the Republic of South Africa* 2000 5 BCLR 478 (CC) (confirming that matters of foreign affairs are committed to the legislative and executive branches); *National Treasury,* at para. 84 (Justice Froneman held that the formulation and implementation of policy is a matter committed to the heartland of national executive function).

100 *United Democratic Movement v. Speaker of the National Assembly,* 2017, at para. 64.

101 *Id.,* 2017, at paras. 64-66.

102 Ngcobo, 2016, p. 24.

103 *Kolbatchenko v. King NO* [2001] 4 All SA 107 (C).

104 *See,* Okpaluba, 2003-2004, p. 331 (discussing that *Kolbatchenko v. King NO and Another* standards for the proposition that there are issues of foreign affairs, which are non-justiciable since courts have no judicial standards by which to judge them).

an alleged offence. This permission was granted pursuant to Section 2 of the International Cooperation in Criminal Matters Act 75 of 1996. Also at issue was a letter of request to the government of Liechtenstein for assistance in obtaining certain information relating to three entities with which the applicant had nefarious links.[105] The letter of request was acted upon by the Liechtenstein government, which led Mr Robert von Palace Kolbatschenko to apply to rescind the order granted by the court.

The DPP defended the application on two grounds. The first ground was that the application involved political questions, which were non-justiciable, and that certain disputes are non-justiciable in that the nature and subject matter are not susceptible to the judicial process.[106] This argument was enhanced by reliance on the wording of Section 34 of the Constitution, which provides that:

> everyone has the right to have any dispute that can be resolved by the application of law decided in a fair public hearing before a court or, where appropriate, another independent and impartial tribunal or forum.

Based on the above provision, the DPP submitted that a dispute may be regarded as non-justiciable if it cannot be resolved by the application of the law or other legal norms,[107] and that many acts in the realm of foreign affairs are not governed by legal norms but involve the consideration of polycentric social, economic and political interests. As such, courts should exercise restraint because of the lack of judicially manageable standards by which to judge such issues.[108] It is important to note that the DPP's argument was developed

105 *Kolbatchenko v. King*, 2001, p. 111.

106 *Kolbatchenko v. King*, 2001, p. 120, citing *Council of Civil Service Union and Others v. Minister for the Civil Service* [1984] 3 All ER 935 (HL).

107 *Kolbatchenko v. King*, p. 120, citing with approval *Mankatshu v. Old Apostolic Church of Africa and Others*, 1994, 2 SA 458; *Amod v. Multilateral Motor Vehicle Accidents Fund (Commission for Gender Equality Intervening)* 1999 4 SA 1319 (SCA) (where the courts were reluctant to intervene in cases involving religious doctrine or dogma).

108 Many academic commentaries agree with this view. *See*, Free, 2003, p. 490 (arguing that the political question doctrine enjoys special potency in foreign affairs); Scharpf, 1966, p. 6 (agreeing with the Supreme Court's approach of treating foreign affairs questions as political questions). *See also*, *Chicago & Southern Air Lines v. Waterman SS Corp* 333 US 103, 111 (1948) (reasoning that foreign affairs should be undertaken only by those directly responsible to the people whose welfare they advance or imperil. They are decisions of a kind for which the Judiciary has neither aptitude, facilities nor responsibility and have long been held to belong in the domain of political power not subject to judicial intrusion or inquiry); M. Schiraldi, 'Rising Temperatures, Political Questions, and Public Nuisances: The Second Circuit Weighs in on the Climate Change Debate in Connecticut v. American Electricity Power Co', *Villanova Environment Law Journal*, Vol. 22, No. 2, 2011, pp. 330-333 (observing that the political question doctrine is raised more often in the foreign affairs context than in any other area where cases that directly implicate foreign affairs issues are sometimes deemed non-justiciable because their resolution frequently turns on standards that defy judicial application, or involve the exercise of a discretion demonstratively committed to the executive or legislature); *Atlee v. Laird* 347 F Supp 689 (DC Pa 1972) (where the court found that cases touching on foreign policy suffer from several procedural concerns that may give rise to political questions); R. Watson & D. Becker, 'Recent

from the six factors articulated by Justice Brennan in *Baker v. Carr.*[109] The High Court dismissed the argument, a point that I will return to later in this chapter.

An argument similar to the one in *Kolbatschenko v. King* was advanced in *National Treasury*. However, unlike in *Kolbatschenko v. King*, the argument was raised in *National Treasury* to achieve the opposite result, namely to prevent the application of the political question theory in the case. The respondents in *National Treasury* argued that the policy decision of government to implement the GFIP was not so political, economic or policy-laden to warrant judicial deference (or in the language of this book to warrant the application of the political question doctrine), and that the impugned decision is not of the executive and polycentric character as was the case in *United Democratic Movement* and other cases.[110] At the heart of this argument is an acknowledgement by the respondents that had the case involved certain types of political or policy-laden questions,[111] the Constitutional Court would be expected to abstain from adjudicating the matter on separation of powers or political question theory grounds. The Court rejected the respondent's argument because it found that the impugned decision was political or policy-laden in nature, and hence was outside the scrutiny of the courts because of separation of powers concerns.[112]

The second ground of defence by the DPP in *Kolbatschenko v. King* was that the request for international assistance was a political act in the realm of foreign affairs and thus non-justiciable. What is the basis for this argument? Matters involving foreign affairs are routinely considered to be within the competence of the political branches and constitutionally reserved for those branches.[113] Even at the time of *Marbury v. Madison* where Chief Justice

---

Decisions of the United States Court of Appeals for the District of Columbia Circuit', *George Washington Law Review*, Vol. 73, No. 4, 2006, p. 706 (concluding that foreign affairs issues will often render a case non-justiciable under the political question doctrine); G. O'Donoghue, 'Precatory Executive Statements and Permissible Judicial Responses in the Context of Holocaust-Claims Litigation', *Columbia Law Review*, Vol. 106, No. 5, 2006, p. 1148 (noting that some foreign affairs cases may present non-justiciable political questions); G. Noyes, 'Cutting the President Off from Tin Cup Diplomacy', *University California Davis Law Review*, Vol. 23, No. 4, 1991, p. 864 (observing that some courts avoid adjudication by finding that foreign affairs cases present non-justiciable political questions) and *Coleman v. Miller* 307 US 433 (1939), at p. 454.

109 *Baker v. Carr*, 1962, p. 217.

110 *National Treasury*, 2012, at para. 39, citing *Glenister v. President of the Republic of South Africa and Others* 2009 2 BCLR 136 (CC) and *International Trade Administration Commission*, 2012.

111 This is just another word to describe political questions or non-justiciable questions.

112 *National Treasury*, 2012, at para. 39.

113 *See*, *International Trade Administration Commission*, 2012; *Kaunda v. President of the Republic of South Africa*; *Glenister v. President of the Republic of South Africa*, at paras. 89-90 (where Justice Ngcobo made a profound statement about emphasizing this point. In explaining the place of international law in South Africa's legal framework, Ngcobo reasoned the constitutional scheme of Section 231 [of the Constitution] is deeply rooted in the separation of powers, in particular the checks and balances between the executive and the legislature. It contemplates three legal steps that may be taken in relation to an international agreement, with each step producing different legal consequences. First, it assigns to the national executive the authority to negotiate and sign international agreements. But an international agreement signed by the executive does not automatically bind the Republic, unless it is an agreement of a technical, administrative or executive nature. To produce that result, it requires, second, the approval by resolution of Parliament.

Marshall conceptualized the political question doctrine, the little detail that he was able to provide was that the doctrine would apply in matters involving foreign affairs and the president's power to nominate persons to the Senate.[114]

Thus, it is not surprising that the respondent in *Kolbatschenko v. King* advanced this argument to try and prevent the High Court from adjudicating the merits of the case that were purely political. To support its argument, the DPP relied on some South African authorities where courts had refused to evaluate decisions in the realm of foreign affairs involving issues of high executive nature.[115]

The approval of an agreement by Parliament does not, however, make it law in the Republic unless it is a self-executing agreement that has been approved by Parliament, which becomes law in the Republic upon such. Otherwise, and third, an international agreement becomes law in the Republic when it is enacted into law by national legislation). *See also*, C. Bradley, 'Chevron Deference and Foreign Affairs', *Virginia Law Review*, Vol. 86, No. 4, 2000, pp. 661-662; J. Goldsmith, 'The New Formalism in United States Foreign Relations Law', *University of Colorado Law Review*, Vol. 70, 1999, pp. 1401-1402; A. Ketchel, 'Deriving Lessons for the Alien Tort Claims Act from the Foreign Sovereign Immunities Act', *Yale Journal of International Law*, Vol. 32, No. 1, 2007, p. 201 (noting that while past administrations have invoked the political question doctrine in cases that implicate treaties signed by the United States, the Bush Administration has invoked the political question doctrine in ATCA cases where treaties are not implicated and only a general foreign policy interest exists); *Chaser Shipping Corp v. United States* 649 F Supp 736 (SDNY 1986) (dismissing damages action in connection with mining of Nicaraguan harbours as political question); *Khulumani v. Barclay Nat'l Bank Ltd* 504 F 3d 254, 263 (2d Cir 2007) (per curiam) (reiterating that in evaluating executive statements, courts are guided by our application of the political question doctrine); *First Nat'l City Bank v. Banco Nacional de Cuba*, 406 US 759, 767 (1972) (ruling that this court has recognized the primacy of the Executive in the conduct of foreign relations); T. Sutcliffe, 'The Nile Reconstituted: Executive Statements, International Human Rights Litigation and the Political Question Doctrine', *Boston University Law Review*, Vol. 89, 2009, p. 295 (encouraging courts to reconceptualize the political question doctrine, at least with respect of foreign affairs, by incorporating a multi-factored balancing test into the political question framework. Such a balancing test could draw from the balancing tests already contained in the act of state and international comity doctrines.); and M. Glennon, 'Foreign Affairs and the Political Question Doctrine', *American Journal of International Law*, Vol. 83, 1989, p. 814.

114 *Marbury v. Madison*, pp. 166-167. *See also*, *Ware v. Hylton*.

115 *Kolbatschenko*, 2001, pp. 123-124, citing *Inter-Science Research and Development Services (Pty) Ltd v. Republica Popular de Mocambique* 1980 2 SA 111 (T). *See also*, *Swissbourgh Diamond Mines (Pty) Ltd and Others v. Government of the Republic of South Africa and Others* 1999 2 SA 279 (T); 1998 JOL 4144 (T), at pp. 108-109 (where the court held that "the basis of the application of the act of State doctrine or that of judicial restraint is just as applicable to South Africa as it is to the USA and England... The judicial branch of government ought to be astute in not venturing into areas where it would be in a judicial no-man's land. It would appear that in an appropriate case, as an exercise of the court's inherent jurisdiction to regulate its own procedure, the court could determine to exercise judicial restraint and refuse to entertain a matter, notwithstanding it having jurisdiction to do so, in view of the involvement of foreign States therein. In the present matter, it is apparent that decisions have to be made in regard to the alleged unlawful conduct of [government of Lesotho] in Lesotho and the control of [government of Lesotho] and its relationship with [South Africa]. As far as the latter is concerned there can be little doubt that this is not an area for the judicial branch of government. It belongs to international law.... The Court would be in judicial no-man's land. It would have no judicial or manageable standards by which to judge the issue. It clearly is a matter in respect of which this Court should exercise judicial restraint."). *See also*, *Van Zyl v. Government of the Republic of South Africa* 2008 (3) SA 294 (SCA) [5] (discussing the judgement in *Swissbourgh Diamond Mines (Pty) Ltd v. Government of the Republic of South Africa* with approval).

In dismissing the argument, the High Court observed that the decision to request international assistance did not involve the evaluation of social and economic policy among competing claims. Rather, it implicated legal questions such as the interpretation of the International Cooperation in Criminal Matters Act and the requirements for judicial review of administrative decision making encapsulated in the Constitution and case law.[116] Furthermore, the High Court rejected the view that the case involved matters of high executive nature directly impacting upon the relationship between South Africa and a foreign state as was the case in *Swissbourgh Diamond Mines (Pty) Ltd v. Government of the Republic of South Africa*.[117]

Instead, it found that the case involved the relationship between South Africa and an individual, the applicant, as a person who is suspected of having committed various offences in South Africa. In addition, the High Court dismissed the argument developed from *Baker v. Carr* that in assessing the legality of the requests, it (the High Court) would lack a judicially manageable standard by which to judge the issues involved.[118] It found that the subject matter of the case was justiciable.

Despite the outcome in *Kolbatschenko v. King*, it seems evident from the arguments, reasoning and holding in the case, including the authorities cited in it, that the High Court accepted the plausibility of the political question doctrine as being applicable to constitutional adjudication in South Africa but found it inapplicable to the facts of the case. In other words, while rejecting the application of the political question doctrine, the High Court in *Kolbatschenko v. King* can be credited with finding the basis for a potential application of the doctrine in a future case. Nevertheless, there are problems with the case law developments involving the political question in South Africa, which is the subject of the following discussion.

116 *Kolbatchenko v. King*, 2001, p. 124.

117 Chase, 2001, p. 1046 (arguing that the recognition of a foreign state or nation is a political question committed to the political branches of government). *But see, Japan v. Shigeru Sakata*, 1960, pp. 105-119 (where the Supreme Court of Japan ruled that the determination of the constitutionality of the 1952 Security Treaty between Japan and the United States involved a high degree of discretionary powers on the part of the cabinet and Diet such that courts were not competent to adjudicate the issues, and that an act of a government of high political nature, having direct relationship to the sovereign act of state, is beyond the province of judicial review. Accordingly, the determination of disputes of that nature should be delegated to the political department like the government or Diet, which owes political responsibility to the people within whom rest the sovereign power of the state, and ultimately to the political decision of the people themselves. It further reasoned that the sovereign act of the government as a limitation imposed upon the judicial authority is predicated upon the separation of powers and it must be interpreted that such is the design inherent in the Constitution of Japan) and P. Chen & J. Wada, 'Can the Japanese Supreme Court Overcome the Political Question Doctrine Hurdle?', *Washington International Law Journal*, Vol. 26, No. 2, 2017, p. 362 (arguing that scholars have approved the *Japan v. Shigeru Sakata* judgement popularly known as the *Sunagawa case* on three main rationales: prudential view, separation of powers and judicial competence).

118 This argument was accepted as a basis for declining to hear the merits of a case. *See, Swissbourgh Diamond Mines (Pty) Ltd and Others v. Government of the Republic of South Africa*, at para. 334.

6.6 Challenges with Implementation of the Doctrine

There are three main challenges with the current implementation of the political question theory in South Africa. Firstly, the case law developments demonstrate that an incomprehensive political question theory exists in South Africa. In the same way that Cowper and Sossin have observed in the Canadian context, in South Africa the political question doctrine has been advanced and considered, but in a gradual manner without being recognized as an element of a lucid doctrine.[119] There are a number of cases in which South African courts have acknowledged the necessity of abstaining from deciding certain political questions.[120]

The Constitutional Court has frequently held that "courts must be conscious of the vital limits on judicial authority and the Constitution's design to leave certain matters to other branches of government," yet, no rule has been developed to give effect to this profound statement of law. What is missing is a clearly stated and acceptable rule of law to guide courts when similar questions arise in the future. Seedorf and Sibanda appear to agree with this assessment in their study of separation of powers and the political question doctrine in South Africa.[121]

In their reflection on the opinion of Justice Chaskalson in *Ferreira v. Levin*, they remarked that the Constitutional Court has followed the US model in so far as it has accepted its power to decide a case may be limited by a lack of judicially discoverable and manageable standards.[122] Moreover, they argue that the South African case law also validates the view that there are some questions that courts cannot decide, such as political or moral questions, but the Constitutional Court has not abstained from deciding these questions as would be the case in other jurisdictions.[123] Seedorf and Sibanda observe that while the:

---

119 Cowper & Sossin, 2002, p. 347.

120 *Kaunda v. President of the Republic of South Africa*; *Ferreira v. Levin*; *Mazibuko*, 2012; *Mazibuko v. Sisulu*, 2013 (Jafta J., minority opinion); *United Democratic Movement v. President of the Republic of South Africa*; *Economic Freedom of Fighters v. Speaker of the National Assembly and Others*, 2016; *National Treasury*, 2012 *MEC: Social Development, Western Cape v. the Justice Alliance of South Africa* [2016] ZASCA 88, at para. 19 (holding that "in view of the above, orders (iii) – (v) clearly trench on the decision-making powers of the executive. The decisions as to the establishment, appropriate spread and conduct of child and youth care centres in terms of the Children's Act are ones (to borrow a phrase from D.C.J. Moseneke, in *International Trade Administration Commission*, at para. 44 that reside in the heartland of the exercise of national and provincial executive authority. The separation of powers doctrine requires a court to refrain from intervening in decisions of this nature, particularly as they are polycentric and policy-laden in nature. The appellants correctly submitted that the granting of orders (iii) – (v) clearly impinge on the function of the executive by effectively determining where and how public funds and resources should be deployed.").

121 Seedorf & Sibanda, 2008, p. 12-52.

122 *Id.*, p. 12-53. *See also, Swissbourgh Diamond Mines (Pty) Ltd and Others v. Government of the Republic of South Africa*; *Kolbatchenko v. King*; *and Mazibuko v. Sisulu* (Jafta J., dissenting).

123 Seedorf & Sibanda, 2008, pp. 12-52-12-53, citing the example of *Minister of Home Affairs & Another v. Fourie & Others; Lesbian & Gay Equality Project v. Minister of Home Affairs & Others* 2006 3 BCLR 355 (CC), p. 390 (involving same sex marriage in South Africa).

> the Constitutional Court of South Africa has on frequent occasions employed the idea of judicial restraint, a conscious decision based on separation of powers concerns not to interfere with decisions by the other branches of government, provided that they are in line with the Constitution … it is necessary that the courts themselves formulate, articulate and apply principles for guiding the limits of their own powers and preventing their abuse. The formulation and application of these principles is important for the actual self-constraint which the courts exhibit.[124]

In the main, Seedorf and Sibanda accept that despite the existence of elements of the political question theory in South African jurisprudence, there is a need for the development of clear principles for guiding the limits of judicial authority.[125] I share the views of Seedorf and Sibanda that the problem lies with the judiciary, which has failed to articulate and apply a coherent political question doctrine and its purpose.[126] It is not clear from the case law whether or when the judiciary will hear or dismiss a matter involving political questions and what jurisprudential justifications will be offered. The uncertainty in South Africa is exacerbated by the fact that the Constitution expressly granted the courts the power of judicial review as opposed to courts organically developing it over time like in other jurisdictions. The effect of this is that the judiciary has been disinclined to organically develop the institution of judicial review, including its inherent limitations, like in other jurisdictions. In other words, judicial review is a product of deliberate constitutional design and not of historical development like in other jurisdictions.

While the judiciary has recognized the limits of the power of judicial review in the context of separation of powers cases such as the landmark case of *Doctors for Life International* and *Economic Freedom Fighters v. Speaker of the National Assembly*,[127] it has not devised a rule of law to be applied in future cases to give effect to this recognition. Professor Okpaluba also believes in the benefits of developing a limpid political question doctrine for South Africa. In one of the first studies about the political question doctrine in South Africa, Okpaluba suggested that for a matter raising a purely political question to emerge, it must be clear that judicial intervention lacks constitutional foundation,[128] and that "that is a political question over which a court cannot assume jurisdiction, entertain its cause of complaint or grant any relief in any exercise of judicial authority."[129] He concluded by suggesting that:

124 Seedorf & Sibanda, 2008, pp. 12-54-12-55.
125 *Id.*, pp. 12-54-12-55.
126 *Id.*, 2008, p. 12-55.
127 *Economic Freedom Fighters v. Speaker of the National Assembly* 2016 5 BCLR 618 (CC).
128 Okpaluba, 2003-2004, p. 331.
129 *Id.*, p. 331.

> such a matter, whether it is expressed in the language of the political question doctrine of American vintage, or simply dismissed for being unamenable to the judicial process as the common law courts would put it, is non-justiciable in a South African court as it is in the courts of the United States, Australia, Canada, England and Nigeria.[130]

Secondly, and more recently, former Chief Justice Ngcobo has remarked that the challenge facing South African courts arises from the need to develop a coherent theory of judicial review, which is rooted in the principle of separation of powers, and that will guide the courts on whether to accept or reject disputes that often appear to have heavy political lifting brought before them.[131] Ngcobo is emphatic in his suggestion that in the development of such a theory, the following propositions of law should be accepted:

> First, our Constitution contemplates three co-equal branches of government; an all too powerful judiciary is a threat to our constitutional democracy in which government is based on the will of the people just as an all too powerful executive or legislature is a threat to our democracy;
> Second, the very principle of separation of powers which forms part of our Constitution, presupposes that there are limitations on the exercise of the power of judicial review and requires the judiciary to observe the vital limits on the exercise of this power;
> Third, limitations must be sought in, and be derived from the Constitution; and
> Fourth, while concepts such as the principle of deference or margin of appreciation or political question doctrine provide a useful starting point in considering limits on the power of judicial review, it is important to bear in mind that the principle to be developed must be informed by our Constitution and be anchored in our constitutional democracy which gives courts the central role in upholding and protecting the Constitution.
> Fifth, as the Constitutional Court has recently emphasized, it must be informed by the need to allow space to the political branches of government to discharge their constitutional obligations unimpeded by the judiciary save where the Constitution permits it.[132]

130 *Id.*, p. 131.
131 Ngcobo, 2016, p. 22.
132 Id., pp. 22-23.

Thirdly, more than a decade ago, Professor Motala and Ramaphosa[133] advocated for the application of the political question doctrine in a number of areas.[134] They identified the following areas as being suitable for the application of the political question doctrine: (a) the removal of a president or cabinet through a motion of no confidence because it is not appropriate for a court to render a decision on the conditions for the validity of such an action;[135] (b) the finding by the Judicial Service Commission to remove a judge from office supported by a two-thirds majority vote of the National Assembly; (c) the internal arrangements, proceedings and procedures of Parliament. Given their view, Motala and Ramaphosa would probably subscribe to the dissenting opinions in the *Impeachment case* and (d) cases involving matters of foreign affairs because a country needs to speak with one voice and the other branches of government are better fortified to make decisions in this area.[136]

Lastly, while the courts, particularly the Constitutional Court, have recognized in a number of cases, the limits of judicial power in general and in relation to the adjudication of political questions, they have been unsuccessful to explain this in the context of the political question doctrine, which is predicated upon the principle of separation of powers, the text and structure of the Constitution. Although the political question doctrine was not the substance of the case, Justice Ngcobo in *Doctors for Life International*[137] identified an important characteristic of the political question doctrine that is missing in South African case law, which can be used to develop the doctrine in South Africa when he said that:

> Courts must be conscious of the vital limits on judicial authority and the Constitution's design to leave certain matters to other branches of government. They too must observe the constitutional limits of their authority. This means that the judiciary should not interfere in the processes of other branches of government unless to do so is mandated by the Constitution.[138]

From the above statement, I read in a duty on the judiciary to develop a rule of law to give effect to the obligations created in that statement. The Constitutional Court has not successfully given effect to the obligations in the above pronouncement. In order to give effect to this pronouncement, the Constitutional Court would need to link separation of powers concerns, similar to the ones identified by Ngcobo above, with the limits on judicial powers,

133 At the time of this writing, Mr Ramaphosa was serving as the President of South Africa.
134 *Motala & Ramaphosa, 2002, p.* 123.
135 *Id.*
136 *Id., p.* 124.
137 *Doctors for Life International,* at para. 37.
138 *Id.*

particularly in relation to political questions constitutionally allocated to other branches of government. Consequently, this has led to the failure of the Constitutional Court to develop a clear political question doctrine that would be used to dispose of such questions in the future.[139] To put it differently, there is a disjuncture between the Constitutional Court's rationale and recognition of its limits in the adjudication of certain political questions in the cases discussed above with the principle of separation of powers.

In its proper application, the effect of the political question doctrine requires courts to abstain from hearing a matter due to separation of powers concerns, and based on the Constitution's text and structure, it requires that the issues be deferred to the relevant political branch.[140] However, what the case law in South Africa demonstrates is that courts acknowledge political questions in cases brought before them and the limits of the courts' power to deal with those questions, but at the same time take a flexible approach, as Seedorf and Sibanda observed, and proceed to adjudicate those cases instead of abstaining and allowing them to be resolved through democratic contestation.[141] This is a major challenge to the development and implementation of the political question doctrine in South Africa.

6.7 The Limits of the Doctrine

It is important to emphasize at the outset that the application of the political question doctrine does not entail that every political question is immune from judicial review.[142] As indicated earlier, courts that have applied this doctrine expressly recognize the limits of its reach and apply it only in those cases that raise purely political questions and where

139 The failure to develop a political question doctrine has on occasion prevented government from taking timely measures to transform society. *See*, *SARIPA v. Minister of Justice and Constitutional Development* 2015 2 SA 430 (WCC) (overturning affirmative action measure involving insolvency practitioners); *Opposition to Urban Tolling Alliance v. South African National Roads Agency Ltd* [2012] ZAGPPHC 323 (where an interdict was issued against the implementation of the e-tolling in the province of Gauteng); *National Treasury v. Opposition to Urban Tolling Alliance* 2012 6 SA 223 (CC) (overturning the interdict of the High Court); O'Regan, 2012, p. 129 (arguing that the role of the Constitutional Court is not to thwart or frustrate the democratic arms of government, but is rather to hold them accountable for the manner in which they exercise public power) and *Glenister v. President of the Republic of South Africa* 2011 3 SA 347 (CC) (where the court invalidated an Act of Parliament that frustrated the crime-fighting efforts of government).

140 *See*, *US Department of Commerce v. Montana* 458 (noting that the political question doctrine restrains judicial authority); Chase, 2001, p. 1045 (noting that political question doctrine limits judicial authority).

141 *See*, Endicott, 2010, p. 538 (emphasizing that as a procedural mechanism, the political question doctrine mandates dismissal of a claim if adjudication revolves around policy choices constitutionally committed for resolution to the political branches). *See also*, Seedorf & Sibanda, 2008, p. 12-52.

142 *See*, *Immigration and Naturalization Serv v. Chadha* 462 US 919, 1982 (stating that the presence of constitutional issues with significant political overtones does not automatically invoke the political question doctrine); 2006 *Harvard LR 2292* (observing that the US Supreme Court has not closed its doors to cases touching on foreign affairs; after all, separation of powers dictates that courts avoid political questions, not political cases) and Chase, 2001, p. 1055.

the Constitution has committed the determination of the question to another branch of government or when no judicial standard exists to determine the question.[143] Writing in the American context, Jared Cole once remarked that as an initial matter, it is significant to distinguish the political question doctrine from cases that involve political issues.[144] He noted that courts repeatedly determine cases with political consequences or implications.[145] On the other hand, the doctrine applies to issues that the Constitution determines are dedicated to the political branches or cannot be resolved through the application of the law.[146]

In *Baker v. Carr,* the case that has influenced the application of the doctrine in many countries, Justice Brennan makes it evident that the doctrine should be applied cautiously to political questions committed to the elected branches and not simply cases that have political consequences.[147] His Ghanaian counterpart, Justice Kpegah in *Ghana Bar Association* subscribes to this view and recognizes the limited reach of the doctrine when observing that:

> it is… legitimate to say that the mere fact that a suit seeks the protection of a political right does not mean that it presents a political question and therefore non-justiciable.[148]

Furthermore, Ugandan Supreme Court Justice Kanyeihamba in *Tinyefuza* expresses a similar view and argues that courts should avoid adjudicating upon political questions unless in very clear cases of violation or threatened violations of individual liberty.[149] In the South African context, these limitations will have to be recognized in the development and application of a clear doctrine for South Africa. This is important in the light of what the Constitutional Court has said about the political consequences of its functions.[150]

143 *See*, Wechsler, *Principles* 7-8.

144 Cole, 2014, p. 2.

145 *Id.*, citing *Terry v. Adams*, 345 US 461 (1953).

146 Cole, 2014, p. 2.

147 *Baker v. Carr*, 1962, p. 217. *See also*, *Zivotofsky v. Clinton*, 2012 (noting that courts cannot avoid their responsibility merely because the issue have political implications) (Roberts J., opinion); and Justice Sotomayor (noting that a court may not refuse to adjudicate a dispute merely because a decision may have significant political overtones) and Gil, 2014, p. 253 (noting that where there is no legal question, there should be no judicial review.).

148 *Ghana Bar Association*, 2003-2004, p. 295.

149 *Attorney General v. Major General David Tinyefuza*, 1997, p. 12.

150 *See*, *President of the Republic of South Africa and Others v. South African Rugby Football Union* 1999 7 BCLR 725, pp. 762-763 (CC) (explaining that "one of the functions of the Constitutional Court is to exercise exclusive jurisdiction in a number of crucial political areas in respect of issues which would inevitably have important political consequences"). Similarly, the Supreme Court of Appeal has ruled that the invalidation of an Act of Parliament for breach of the constitutional duty to facilitate public involvement in its processes would be pre-eminently a crucial political question, which the Constitution reserved for the Constitutional Court to decide. *See*, *King and Others v. Attorneys Fidelity Fund Board of Control and Another*, 2006 4 BCLR

In *Doctors for Life International,* Justice Ngcobo made an important observation that it was envisaged that this [Constitutional Court] would be called upon to adjudicate finally in respect of issues that could inevitably have important political consequences. Consistent with this role, he noted, Section 167(4) confers exclusive jurisdiction on the Constitutional Court in a number of crucial political areas.[151] He explained that the purpose of giving the Court exclusive jurisdiction to decide issues that have important political consequences is to preserve the comity between the judicial branch of government and the other branches of government by ensuring that only the highest court may intrude into the domain of other branches of government.[152] Recognizing the political consequences of a broad construction of Section 167(4), Justice Ngcobo held that the section should be given a narrow meaning.[153] Ngcobo's explanation is very key. It recognizes the distinction between political questions cases and cases with political consequences. The latter does not attract the need to invoke the political question doctrine, while the former does.

Thus, if anything is to be learned from the analysis of the countries discussed in this book, it is that the political question doctrine is not absolute in its application because it only applies where the Constitution itself commits a question to other branches of government or when there is no judicial standard to decide a case.[154] Courts will inevitably adjudicate cases that have political implications and may even be required to give some deference

462 (SCA). *See also, Premier of the Province of Mpumalanga v. Executive Committee of the Association of Governing Bodies of State-Aided Schools, Eastern Transvaal,* 1999 2 BCLR 151 (CC), at p. 171 (Justice O'Regan holding that just because a decision has political implications does not necessarily mean it is not an administrative decision with the context of Section 33 of the Constitution). Another case that I believe involved a political question but which would not fall within the political question doctrine is *Khosa and Others v. Min of Social Development and Others; Mahlaule and Another v. Min of Social Development and Others,* 2004 6 BCLR 569 (CC) (dealing with the question of whether permanent residents should have access to social welfare grants).

151 Section 167(4) provides:
(4) Only the Constitutional Court may:
a. decide disputes between organs of state in the national or provincial sphere concerning the constitutional status, powers or functions of any of those organs of state;
b. decide on the constitutionality of any parliamentary or provincial Bill, but may do so only in the circumstances anticipated in Section 79 or 121;
c. decide applications envisaged in Section 80 or 122;
d. decide on the constitutionality of any amendment to the Constitution;
e. decide that Parliament or the President has failed to fulfil a constitutional obligation; or
f. certify a provincial constitution in terms of Section 144.

152 In terms of the Constitution Seventeenth Amendment Act of 2012, the Constitutional Court is no longer the highest court on constitutional matters. It is the apex court.

153 *Doctors for Life International,* 2006, p. 1403 and *Economic Freedom Fighters v. Speaker of the National Assembly,* 2016.

154 *See,* V. Pappalardo, 'Isolationism or Deference? The Alien Tort Claims Act and the Separation of Powers', *Michigan Journal of International Law,* Vol. 10, 1989, p. 902 (arguing that while the political question doctrine may stand as a hurdle to adjudication of issues touching on foreign policy, it clearly does not represent an absolute bar to their judicial resolution) and Kelly, 2010, p. 224 (suggesting that not every political question invokes the political question doctrine).

to the political branches, but these cases must be distinguished from those cases involving political questions in which absolute deference is required.[155]

6.8 JUSTIFYING THE DOCTRINE

In a constitutional democracy with a supreme constitution like South Africa, every principle, rule or doctrine of law has to have an express or implied constitutional basis. The judiciary has consistently applied this notion. In *Fedsure*, the Constitutional Court found that the principle of legality is implied from Section 1 of the Constitution. Similarly, in *Glenister*, the Constitutional Court found that Section 7 of the Constitution implicitly requires the state to establish an independent corruption fighting body, and in *Heath* the Constitutional Court found that separation of powers is implied in the Constitution.

Similarly, for the political question doctrine to be constitutionally sustained, there is a need to identify a constitutional basis for it. In the South African context, there are at least three constitutional provisions that form the basis for the political question doctrine. These are:

> PREAMBLE
> We, the people of South Africa …through our freely elected representatives, adopt this Constitution as the supreme law of the Republic so as to… *Lay the foundations for a democratic and open society in which government is based on the will of the people and every citizen is equally protected by law*; (my emphasis)
> 34 Access to Courts
> Everyone has the right to have any dispute that can be resolved by the application of law decided in a fair public hearing before a court or, where appropriate, another independent and impartial tribunal or forum.
> 167 Constitutional Court
> (3) The Constitutional Court:
> a. is the highest court of the Republic; and
> b. may decide:
>   i. constitutional matters; and
>   ii. any other matter, if the Constitutional Court grants leave to appeal on the grounds that the matter raises an arguable point of law of general public importance which ought to be considered by that Court, and

155 Barkow, 2002, pp. 243-244 (arguing that absolute deference is expected in cases involving political questions). *See also*, *Doctors for Life International*, 2006, p. 1414 (noting that the Constitution envisaged the Constitutional Court would decide cases with important political consequences); and *King and Others v. Attorneys Fidelity Fund Board of Control and Another* 2006 (1) SA 474 (SCA), at para. 23.

c. makes the final decision whether a matter is within its jurisdiction.

The political question doctrine provides the judiciary with a legal mechanism to give effect to the above constitutional imperatives. My reasons for this conclusion are: firstly, the preamble to the Constitution entrenches the notion that the government that is envisioned in South Africa is based on the will of the people. When the political question doctrine is invoked, it allows the people, who are represented by members of the political branches, to govern themselves by determining and resolving the issues at play thereby reinforcing the notion that government is based on the will of the people. Hence, it was significant for Justice Moseneke to have pronounced in *International Trade Administration Commission* the five requirements that are highlighted in this chapter. His second and fifth requirements are motivated by the imperative to reinforce the values in the preamble to the Constitution 1996.

My argument is that the second and fifth requirements are useful elements in the development of the political question doctrine in South Africa. I apply them to advance the objectives of the doctrine by ensuring that the doctrine "must sit comfortably with the democratic system of government we have chosen" and "must give due recognition to the popular will". While Moseneke developed these requirements as part of his contribution to the development of the separation of powers principle and did not envisage that these requirements would be construed in the manner that I propose, it is not difficult to imagine the relevance and usefulness of the application on account of the intimate relationship between separation of powers and the political question doctrine. Similarly, Zuma's pronouncements cited in Chapter 1 of this book were predicated upon his desire to reinforce the language and values in the preamble.

In addition, as Professor Bickel once pointed out, when the judiciary invalidate acts of the politically accountable branches of government they frustrate the will of the people.[156] This has never been disputed. Instead, in the South African context it is justified on the basis that that frustration is mandated by the Constitution.[157] Ngcobo has explained this

156 Bickel, 1962, pp. 16-17. For a discussion of judicial confidence, *see*, Mahomed, 1999, p. 111 (noting that unlike Parliament or the executive, the court does not have the power of the purse or the army or the police to execute its will. The superior courts and the Constitutional Court do not have a single soldier. They would be impotent to protect the Constitution if the agencies of the state that control the mighty physical and financial resources of the state refused to command those resources to enforce the orders of the courts. The courts could be reduced to paper tigers with a ferocious capacity to roar and to snarl but no teeth to bite and no sinews to execute what may then become a piece of sterile scholarship. Its ultimate power must therefore rest on the esteem in which the judiciary is held within the psyche and soul of a nation) and Ngcobo, 2011, p. 11 (noting that without public confidence in the judiciary, its ability to do justice is lost. Where people do not trust courts, they will resort to other means to resolve matters that properly belong to the realm of the judiciary).

157 *Economic Freedom Fighters v. Speaker of the National Assembly*, 2016, at para. 92; *Doctors for Life International*, 2006, at para. 37.

justification by noting that, similarly, "when the president declines to assent to a Bill passed by Parliament… this interferes with Parliament's law-making powers."[158] He notes that in the same way the President interferes with the judicial powers when he pardons convicted offenders or when Parliament passes legislation to prescribe minimum sentencing guidelines thereby interfering with the court's power to impose a sentence.[159] Ngcobo claims that all these interferences are mandated by the constitutional principle of separation of powers.[160] However, when the political question doctrine is applied, it allows the judiciary to reinforce the notion that government is based on the will of the people who get to decide how the issues should be resolved.

Secondly, Section 34 of the Constitution provides us with another basis for the political question doctrine. The section enjoins the judiciary to entertain disputes that can be resolved through the application of the law. Implicit in this provision is the notion that if a dispute brought before the judiciary is not capable of being resolved through the application of the law, the judiciary would not have subject-matter jurisdiction to hear the dispute.[161] For example, consider the recent decision by the South African government to withdraw from the Rome Statute of the International Criminal Court 1998, which established the International Criminal Court. Recently, the High Court ruled that it was procedurally defective for the government to give notice of its intention to withdraw from the Rome Statute of the International Criminal Court.[162]

Assume for a moment that there are no procedural problems arising from the Constitution against South Africa's decision to withdraw. If the matter were to be heard by the Constitutional Court, would it be able to resolve the dispute through the application of the law? Is there a legal standard that governs what should inform a sovereign state's decision to enter or withdraw from a treaty on the basis on which a court can assess the merits or demerits of the decision? Would the judiciary have a judicially manageable norm to determine the dispute? If the judiciary were to decide to hear the dispute, would it not impermissibly interfere with the functioning of the executive and legislature who are constitutionally entrusted with the powers concerning treaty making? Would not allowing this action to proceed necessarily require the judicial branch of government to question the propriety of South Africa's decision to withdraw from the Rome Statute which is a

158 Ngcobo, 2011, p. 20.

159 *Id.*

160 *Id.*

161 *See, Mazibuko*, 2012, p. 33 (declining subject-matter jurisdiction to hear political question cases that have been deliberately and carefully been constructed legally to ensure they fall within the court's jurisdiction).

162 *Democratic Alliance v. Minister of International Relations and Cooperation,* 2017, ZAGPPHC 53. For an argument that substantively nothing stops South African from withdrawing from the Rome Statute, *see,* N. Dyani-Mhango, 'South Africa's (unconstitutional) withdrawal from the Rome Statute: A Note on Democratic Alliance v. Minister of International Relations an Cooperation', *South African Journal on Human Rights,* Vol. 34, No. 2, 2018, p. 268.

political question allocated to the political branches? In the main, is the substantive decision to withdraw from the Rome Statute justiciable under Section 34? This book submits that it is not.

Section 34 implicitly recognizes that disputes incapable of resolution through the application of the law are not justiciable. A dispute is non-justiciable if there is no judicial standard to determine the dispute, if it has been constitutionally committed for resolution to the elected branches or if it cannot be resolved through the application of the law.[163] In other words, the converse of the jurisdictional facts for invoking Section 34 is what provides the basis for the doctrine.

In *Kolbatschenko v. King* and *Swissbourgh Diamond Mines (Pty) Ltd v. Government of the Republic of South Africa* the High Court accepted the proposition that if there is no judicially discoverable method to resolve a dispute, a court should exercise restraint and not determine the merits of a dispute because it is not capable of judicial resolution as contemplated in Section 34. The question remains: in a system governed by the rule of law, how does the judiciary exercise such restraint without developing a rule of law that governs how to identify those non-justiciable questions? Therefore, implicit in Section 34 is an obligation on the judiciary to develop a legal mechanism or rule to assist it in identifying those non-justiciable political questions because the provision imposes limits on judicial powers. The political question doctrine is that legal mechanism.

Lastly, Section 167 of the Constitution as amended provides a further basis for the political question doctrine. Section 167(b) widely defines the jurisdiction of the Constitutional Court. By prefacing its sentence with the word 'may', Section 167(b) gives the Constitutional Court wide discretion to decide constitutional matters and any other matter of public importance. Additionally, Section 167(c) provides discretion on the Constitutional Court by giving it final say on whether a matter falls within its defined jurisdiction. When one reads the two provisions together, it is clear that within this newly formulated jurisdiction, the Constitutional Court can formulate a political question doctrine that it could use to abstain from deciding cases either because the issues presented are not constitutional matters, but purely political questions, or lack public importance. It may be difficult to dismiss a political question for lacking public importance because by definition political questions have public importance and the reason for requiring abstention is to allow the political process, which involves the public dialogue, to resolve them. This highlights the need for a rational doctrine. Unlike the other constitutional basis for the political question

163 *Kolbatschenko v. King*, 2001 and *Swissbourgh Diamond Mines (Pty) Ltd and Others v. Government of the Republic of South Africa. See also, State of Rajasthan v. Union of India* 1977 3 SCC 590, at para. 149 (holding that if a question brought before the court is purely a political question not involving determination of any legal or constitutional right or obligation, the court would not entertain it, since the court is concerned only with adjudication of legal rights and liabilities).

doctrine, Section 167 is significant because of the discretion it provides the Constitutional Court in formulating the doctrine.[164]

The above provisions – preamble, Sections 34 and 176 – are deeply rooted in separation of powers and function as the constitutional basis for developing a political question doctrine. Their content is closely associated with the political question doctrine. What is more, these provisions are reinforced by case law discussed earlier and other constitutional provisions where political accountability is envisioned.

6.9 Reinforcement of the Doctrine: Political Accountability Provisions

In addition to the analysis concerning the constitutional basis for the political question doctrine, there are a number of provisions in the text of the Constitution that contemplate political (and not judicial) accountability thereby emphasizing the need for a coherent doctrine in South Africa. The text of the Constitution envisages that there should be political accountability in relation to certain constitutional questions as a mechanism to preserve separation of powers and promote the will of the people through participatory democracy.[165] In other words, these provisions give discretion to the political branches in relation to some political or policy questions, which are not judiciary examinable.[166] The

164 For cases where the Constitutional Court widely interpreted what constitutes a constitutional matter, *see, S v. Boesack* 2000 1 SA 912 (CC); *National Education Health & Allied Workers Union (NEHAWU) v. University of Cape Town and Others* 2003 3 SA 1 (CC); *Ingledew v. Financial Services Board* 2003 4 SA 584 (CC); *Bato Star Fishing (Pty) Ltd v. Minister of Environmental Affairs and Tourism and Others* 2004 4 SA 490 (CC).

165 *See*, D. Moseneke, 'Shades of the Rule of Law and Social Justice', *Annual Helen Suzman Memorial Lecture*, 2016, p. 12, https://hsf.org.za/publications/lectures/helen-suzman-memorial-lecture-2016-1 (where after cautioning against using courts to resolve political disputes observes that the highest form of public accountability is not in the courts, or in the work of the Public Protector or of the Auditor General, but it is electoral accountability which would be useful only when communities understand and embrace what is truly in their interest.).

166 *See*, *Impeachment Case*, 2017, at para. 73 (noting that "section 53(1)(c) of the Constitution is to the effect that all questions before the Assembly are decided by a majority of the votes cast…A litigant cannot, therefore, ask a court to make a decision that should be the outcome of votes cast in the National Assembly when he or she fears that the majority in the National Assembly might not support the decision he or she wants."); *Merafong Demarcation Forum and Others v. President of the Republic of South Africa and Others* 2008 (5) SA 171 (CC), at para. 308 (holding that "if voters perceive that their democratically elected politicians have disrespected them or believe that the politicians have failed to fulfil promises made by the same politicians without adequate explanation, then the politicians should be held accountable by the voters. Courts deal with bad law; voters must deal with bad politics. The doctrine of separation of powers, to which our constitutional democracy subscribes, does not allow this Court, or any other court, to interfere in the lawful exercise of powers by the legislature. A democracy such as ours provides a powerful method for voters to hold politicians accountable when they engage in bad or dishonest politics: regular, free and fair elections."); *Fedsure*, 1999, SA 374, at para. 41 (held that the municipal "council is a deliberative legislative body whose members are elected. The legislative decisions taken by them are influenced by political consid-

purpose is to promote (and not curtail) democratic dialogue. Justice Froneman endorses the latter proposition. In his concurring opinion in *National Treasury,* Froneman J. found that it is a breach of separation of powers for a court to intrude by granting an interdict against the implementation of government policy to fund infrastructure projects by means of tolling the roads on a user-pay principle[167] because that matter resides in the heartland of national executive.[168] Furthermore, Froneman declared that "the playing field for the contestation of executive government policy is the political process, not the judicial one" because in his view the

> courts of this country do not determine what kind of funding should be used for infrastructural funding of roads and who should bear the brunt for that cost. The remedy in that regard lies in the political process.[169]

erations for which they are politically accountable to the electorate"; *Certification Judgment,* 1996, at para. 186 (where in upholding the proportional representation system the court held that "under a list system of proportional representation, it is parties that the electorate votes for, and parties which must be accountable to the electorate"); and *Oosthuizen v. Lur, Plaaslike Regering en Behuising, en 'n Ander,* 2004 1 SA 492 (O) (held that it was not open to a member of any of the legislative chambers to compel a cabinet minister to account in court for the performance of his or her duties where a legislator has failed to secure such accountability in the legislature. The high court rejected to issue orders that would compel the executive to provide answer to a question posed by the legislator under the standing orders of the provincial legislature. It was held that Sections 57 and 116 of the Constitution authorises the National Assembly and the provincial legislatures to be masters of their internal arrangements and proceedings, and that this prevents the courts from enquiring into due compliance with the rules of the legislature. Given that what had occurred in the legislature in this case had taken place during the course of its internal proceedings, issuing the order sought would clearly amount to inappropriate interference in such proceedings. The question posed in the legislature and the failure to answer it appropriately would fall within the accountability clause of Section 133(2) of the Constitution. The court was consequently not empowered to interfere.).

167 The Cabinet took a decision in 2007 that approved an extensive upgrade of roads in the economic hub of the Gauteng province as part of the GFIP. *National Treasury,* 2012, at para. 1.

168 *National Treasury,* 2012, at para. 84. There are other matters in the Constitution that are committed to the elected branches of government. *See, President of the Republic of South Africa and Another v. Hugo* 1997 6 BCLR 708 (CC) (recognizing that the exercise of pardon powers is committed to the executive branch). In addition, Sections 206(1) and 207(2) of the Constitution commit policing matters to the executive branch such that it is free to structure the South African Police without substantive judicial scrutiny. *See, Glenister,* 2017, at paras. 65, 120, 162 (holding that the elected branches of government are free to decide where to locate a specialized corruption-fighting unit. In this case, the elected branches had decided to locate such unit within and not without the South African Police Service as previously was the case.).

169 *National Treasury,* 2012, at paras. 93-95. *See also,* Sections 59; 85(2)(d); 118; 195(1)(e); 72 of the Constitution, 1996. *And see, Doctors for Life International*; 2006. *See also, Chief Enyi Abaribe v. the Speaker Abia State House of Assembly & Ors,* 2003, 14 NWLR (pt. 788), p. 466; (Nigeria) (explaining that "in cases involving political questions appeal for relief does not belong here. Appeal must be to an informed, civically militant electorate. In a democratic society like ours, relief must come through an aroused popular conscience that sears the conscience of the people's representatives"); *Schneider v. Kissinger* 412 F 3d 190, 2005, (in addressing concern about the effects of leaving political questions to the political process, the court reasoned that the lack of judicial authority to oversee the conduct of the executive branch in political matters did not leave executive power unchecked because political branches effectively exercise checks and balances on each other in the area of political questions) and J. Story, *Commentaries on the Constitution,* William S.

Justice Froneman's opinion is a confirmation that the text or structure of the Constitution envisages political rather than judicial accountability when it comes to certain political or policy questions and is another reminder of the need for the judiciary to develop a coherent political question theory to implement its constitutional obligation to ensure courts are conscious of their vital limits.[170]

More than three hundred years ago, Chief Justice Marshall (while formulating the political question doctrine in the United States) explained that when "the executive possesses a constitutional or legal discretion, nothing can be more perfectly clear than that their acts are only politically examinable".[171] Former Chief Justice Ngcobo of South Africa agrees with this view. He recently remarked that:

> It is important also to understand that having regard to their proper role on judicial review, courts cannot provide solutions to all political, economic and social problems that afflict societies in modern times...the appropriate solution to most political, economic or social problems can only be found through the political process. These problems are usually complex and they involve many conflicting interests and may involve the use and allocation of limited resources... It is to the political process that the citizen must look for an appropriate resolution of these problems. The responsibility for the proper and effective functioning of the political process in the interests of the community rests of course with the executive and the legislature. Judicial review ensures that the political branches of government perform their constitutional obligations and do so in accordance with and within the limits of their constitutional authority and obligations.[172]

To enhance Justice Ngcobo and Justice Froneman's above observations, the following constitutional provisions give authority to the proposition that the Constitution contemplates political accountability by committing issues arising from them to the discretion of the relevant political branch:

> 57. (1) The National Assembly may:
> a. determine and control its internal arrangements, proceedings and procedures; and

---

Hein & Company, New York, 1905, p. 525 (arguing that in cases involving questions exclusively of political character, the supreme authority as to these questions belongs to the political branches of government and that the remedy in such cases is solely by an appeal to people at the elections).

170 *See also*, Okpaluba, 2015, p. 195, discussing *Oosthuizen v. Lur, Plaaslike Regering en Behuising, en 'n Ander*, 2004.

171 *Marbury v. Madison*, 1803, p. 166.

172 Ngcobo, 2016, p. 24.

b. make rules and orders concerning its business, with due regard to representative and participatory democracy, accountability, transparency and public involvement.[173]

84 Powers and functions of President

1. The President has the powers entrusted by the Constitution and legislation, including those necessary to perform the functions of Head of State and head of the national executive.
2. The President is responsible for:

   (...)

i appointing ambassadors, plenipotentiaries, and diplomatic and consular representatives;

j pardoning or reprieving offenders and remitting any fines, penalties or forfeitures; and

k conferring honours.[174]

85 Executive authority of the Republic

1. The executive authority of the Republic is vested in the President.
2. The President exercises the executive authority, together with the other members of the Cabinet, by:
   a. (...)
   b. developing and implementing national policy[175];
   c. (...)
   d. preparing and initiating legislation[176];
   e. (e) (...)

91 Cabinet

1. The Cabinet consists of the President, as head of the Cabinet, a Deputy President and Ministers.

173 *See, United Democratic Movement v. Speaker of the National Assembly and Others* 2017 (5) SA 300 (CC), at para. 64 (where interpreting Section 57 of the Constitution held that "it bears emphasis that the absence of a prior determination of the voting procedure by our Constitution for a motion of no confidence means that it neither prohibits nor prescribes an open ballot or a secret ballot. The effect of this is to leave it open to the National Assembly, when the time comes to vote on that motion, to decide on the appropriate voting procedure. This can only reinforce the conclusion that the Assembly has the power to make that determination. It is for it to decide on the voting procedure necessary for the efficiency and effectiveness of the institution in holding the Executive accountable. In sum, how best and in terms of which voting procedure to hold the President accountable in the particular instance is the responsibility constitutionally-allocated to the National Assembly."). *See also, Maloy v. Marietta*, 11 Ohio, NS 639 (holding that the judiciary cannot interfere with legislative discretion).

174 *See, Kaunda v. President of the Republic of South Africa*, 2004, at para. 243; *President of the Republic of South Africa and Another v. Hugo*, 1997; *Mansingh v. General Council of the Bar and Others*, 2014 (2) SA 26 (CC).

175 *Electronic Media Network Limited and Others v. e.tv (Pty) Limited and Others*, 2017.

176 *Glenister v. President of the Republic of South Africa and Others* (*Glenister I*) 2009 (1) SA 287 (CC).

2. The President appoints the Deputy President and Ministers, assigns their powers and functions and may dismiss them[177];

231 International Agreements[178]

1. The negotiating and signing of all international agreements is the responsibility of the national executive.
2. An international agreement binds the Republic only after it has been approved by resolution in both the National Assembly and the National Council of Provinces, unless it is an agreement referred to in Subsection (3).
3. An international agreement of a technical, administrative or executive nature, or an agreement which does not require either ratification or accession, entered into by the national executive, binds the Republic without approval by the National Assembly and the National Council of Provinces, but must be tabled in the Assembly and the Council within a reasonable time.[179]

The above provisions are a strong basis for the political question doctrine because the content of these provisions envisage political accountability, which can only be achieved through a court invoking the doctrine when presented with certain substantive disputes or questions arising from them. The provisions confer authority and obligations on the political branches of government and place no substantive parameters in the text or define the strictures within which the National Assembly and the President, respectively, is to operate in their efforts to fulfil their respective functions and obligations in them. The mechanics of how best to go about fulfilling these constitutional functions and obligations is a discretionary matter left to the National Assembly and the President in a given situation.[180] The latter proposition of the law is an integral part of the political question doctrine

177 *See, Democratic Alliance v. President of the Republic of South Africa and Another*, 2017, ZAWCHC 34, at para. 7 (reasoned that "it is difficult to imagine a power closer to the heartland of the President's personal preferences than the power to appoint and dismiss ministers and deputy ministers; it is by its nature highly discretionary … In general, though, I think it can be said that the primary consequence of decisions to appoint and fire cabinet ministers which the public or sectors of it regard as bad decisions, is political rather than legal.").

178 *See, Glenister* 2011, at para. 98 (held that "the constitutional scheme of section 231 is deeply rooted in the separation of powers, in particular the checks and balances between the executive and the legislature").

179 For a discussion of these provisions, *see Glenister*, 2011; *Democratic Alliance v. Minister of International Relations and Cooperation*, 2017 and Dyani-Mhango, 2018.

180 *Economic Freedom Fighters v. Speaker of the National Assembly*, 2016, at para. 93 (holding that the National Assembly has discretion on how to hold the executive to account); *Democratic Alliance v. President of the Republic of South Africa and Another*, 2017, ZAWCHC 34 (held that "the power to appoint and dismiss ministers and deputy ministers; it is by its nature highly discretionary"); *United Democratic Movement v. Speaker of the National Assembly and Others* 2017 (5) SA 300 (CC), at para. 64 (held that "it how best and in terms of which voting procedure to hold the President accountable in the particular instance is the

to the extent that it recognizes constitutional discretion on the part of the political branches, which is not susceptible to judicial review.

The proposition was first articulated by Justice Ngcobo in *Doctors for Life International* in the context of Parliament's obligations to facilitate public involvement where he held that:

> where the obligation requires Parliament to determine in the first place what is necessary to fulfil its obligation, a review by a court whether that obligation has been fulfilled, trenches on the autonomy of Parliament ...and thus the principle of separation of powers. This is precisely what the obligation comprehended in section 72(1)(a) does. While it imposes a primary obligation on Parliament to facilitate public involvement in its legislative and other processes, it does not tell Parliament how to facilitate public involvement but leaves it to Parliament to determine what is required of it in this regard.[181]

Ngcobo revisited this proposition in his minority judgement in *Glenister*,[182] where the Constitutional Court had to consider the constitutionality of the decision to establish the Directorate for Priority Crime Investigation (DPCI) and locating it within the South African Police Service (SAPS) as opposed to the National Prosecuting Authority as was the case previously. Both the minority and majority held that:

> section 179 of the Constitution does not oblige Parliament to locate a specialised corruption-fighting unit within the National Prosecuting Authority (NPA) and nowhere else. The creation of a separate corruption-fighting unit within the SAPS was not in itself unconstitutional and thus the DPCI legislation cannot be invalidated on that ground alone. Similarly, the legislative choice to abolish the Directorate of Special Operations (DSO) and to create the DPCI did not in itself offend the Constitution.[183]

---

responsibility constitutionally-allocated to the National Assembly"); *Glenister*, 2011, at para. 67 (holding that when making laws, Parliament will exercise its judgement as to the appropriate policy to address the situation. This judgement is political and may not always coincide with views of social scientists or other experts. It is not for the court to disturb political judgements); *General Council of the Bar and Another v. Mansingh and Others*, 2014, at para. 28 (holding that the wording of Section 84(2) is both permissive and broad, affording a wide discretion to the President); *Glenister v. President of the Republic of South Africa and Others*, 2009 (rejecting an application to intervene in the initiation of legislation); and *Amidu*, 2001-2002, p. 154 (holding that the intrinsic proposition in the Constitution is that the policy that should inform any legislation are matters for the political branches to decide).

181 *Doctors for Life International*, 2006, at paras. 25-26.

182 *Glenister*, 2011.

183 *Id.*, at para. 162; *See also, Helen Suzman Foundation v. President of the Republic of South Africa*, 2015, 1 BCLR 1 (CC).

In a minority judgement delivered by Justice Ngcobo, he reasoned that:

> The decision to disband the DSO and establish the DPCI and locate it within the SAPS must be understood in the context of the Constitution. Section 179 of the Constitution makes provision for a single national prosecuting authority... On the other hand, section 205 makes provision for the national police service... It is therefore within the power of Parliament to establish an anti-corruption unit and to locate it within the SAPS. The Constitution does not prescribe to Parliament where to locate the anti-corruption unit. It leaves it up to the executive, which initiates legislation under section 85(2)(d), and ultimately to Parliament to make a policy choice.[184]

Ngcobo dismissed the argument that the impugned legislation in the case was unconstitutional because it sought to implement a political resolution adopted by the governing political party, the African National Congress at its 52nd national conference in Polokwane in December 2007. The resolution called for a single police service and the dissolution of the DSO. In dismissing the argument, Ngcobo reasoned that:

> Assume, for the moment, that the impugned laws were in fact motivated by the Polokwane Resolution. This does not render the scheme unconstitutional... Indeed, it may well be the central role of a political party to formulate policy recommendations with the intention that they be implemented, and there is nothing untoward in the Cabinet taking up such recommendations... these recommendations become law only if the executive embodies them into legislation which it initiates, Parliament passes the legislation, and the President signs the legislation.[185]

Ngcobo found that it was a policy decision by the government to transfer this investigative component of the NPA to the SAPS, and the suggestion is that such policy choices are within the political branches' discretion to make. He reasoned further that:

> Under our constitutional scheme it is the responsibility of the executive to develop and implement policy. It is also the responsibility of the executive to initiate legislation in order to implement policy. And it is the responsibility of Parliament to make laws. When making laws Parliament will exercise its judgment as to the appropriate policy to address the situation. This judgment

184 *Glenister*, 2011, at paras. 64-65.
185 *Id.*, at para. 62.

> is political and may not always coincide with views of social scientists or other experts.[186]

Ultimately, Justice Ngcobo held that:

> What must be stressed here is that it is not the judicial role to dictate to other branches what is the most appropriate way to secure the independence of an anti-corruption agency. The judicial role is limited to determining whether the agency under consideration complies with the Constitution. Indeed the legislature here had to exercise a political judgment. That there is more than one permissible way of securing the structural and operational autonomy of the DPCI does not make the choice of one rather than the other unconstitutional.[187]

The principle that emerged from Justice Ngcobo's jurisprudence in *Glenister* and *Doctors for Life International* is this where the text of the Constitution grants a power to a political branch without prescribing the parameters on how such power should be exercised, the political branch is deemed to have discretion in exercising that power and courts may not interfere in that process.[188]

The Constitutional Court in *Economic Freedom Fighters v. Speaker of the National Assembly*[189] endorsed, without overruling the majority in *Glenister*, the above proposition of law in relation to its determination of whether the National Assembly breached its constitutional obligation to hold the President to account in relation to his conduct involving upgrades at his private residence. In addressing this question, a unanimous court observed that the Constitution neither gives details on how the National Assembly is to discharge the duty to hold the executive to account nor are the mechanisms for doing so outlined in the Constitution.[190] As a consequence, the court reasoned, the National Assembly must be construed as having "been given the leeway to determine how best to carry out its constitutional mandate".[191] The Constitutional Court reasoned that:

> It falls outside the parameters of judicial authority to prescribe to the National Assembly how to scrutinise executive action, what mechanisms to establish and which mandate to give them, for the purpose of holding the Executive accountable and fulfilling its oversight role of the executive or organs of State

186 *Id.*, at para. 67.
187 *Id.*, at para. 146.
188 *See*, Ngcobo, 2016, pp. 22-23 (discussing this principle of law).
189 *Economic Freedom Fighters v. Speaker of the National Assembly*, 2016.
190 *Id.*, at para. 43.
191 *Id.*, at para. 87.

> in general. The mechanics of how to go about fulfilling these constitutional obligations is a discretionary matter best left to the National Assembly. Ours is a much broader and less intrusive role ... these are some of the vital limits on judicial authority and the Constitution's design to leave certain matters to other branches of government.[192]

It is my submission that the Constitution carves out, as seen in the above cases, certain categories of constitutional questions that may only be resolved as a matter of legislative or executive discretion, and that in this context, judicial abstinence is constitutionally required.

In the light of the uncertainties in the constitutional law of South Africa identified in this book, scholars agree that what needs to transform is for the courts, particularly the Constitutional Court, to develop the political question doctrine and clarify its purpose, when it applies and how.[193] The starting point in this development should be in line with Justice Moseneke's suggestions in *International Trade Administration Commission* where he advocated for the adoption of distinctively South African separation of powers and suggested five critical requirements, which would assist the development of a lucid political question doctrine. Also relevant are Ngcobo's suggestions that he made above around the development of what he calls a coherent theory of judicial review.

In addition to the South African constitutional basis for the doctrine, the body of case law from Ghana, Nigeria, Uganda and United States are valuable as examples of how other judiciaries have come to constrain judicial reactions to political questions. This body of law demonstrates the notion that old and recent constitutional democracies have jurisprudentially defined and developed, within their constitutional histories and designs, some constitutional mechanism for dealing with political questions that threaten or implicate the equilibrium of power among the three arms of government while at the same time giving effect to constitutional provisions that assign certain questions for resolution to the political branches. South Africa is lagging behind in this regard and, as I have argued in this chapter, the Constitutional Court should resolve this legal uncertainty. Any blanket rejection of the political question doctrine, as Justice Kpegah warned over a decade ago in the context of Ghana, will create judicial legitimacy, jurisdictional and separation of powers problems for South Africa in the future,[194] due to, at least, three reasons.

Firstly, I subscribe to Justice Moseneke's recent cautionary statement on one of the local radio stations Power FM's Breakfast Show on 18 October 2016 concerning the current

192 *Id.*, at para. 93.

193 *See*, Seedorf & Sibanda, 2008, pp. 12-54-12-55 and Okpaluba, 2003-2004.

194 *Amidu*, 2001-2002, p. 159.

state of affairs where courts are routinely drawn in to resolve political disputes.[195] In his statement, Moseneke explained that this practice is straining the judicial system enormously. He noted that presently all disputes, including political ones, end up in court. He cited examples of student protests, battles within the cabinet, battles among members of Parliament, battles involving agencies constitutionally entrusted with policing in South Africa. He correctly observed that in a normal constitutional system, these disputes should ideally be resolved at the sites where they emerge before they reach the judiciary. In the case of Parliament, for example, he noted that Parliament should have an efficient dispute resolution system to resolve any differences in ways that are acceptable to all members, who will not rush to court. He was emphatic that currently there is a huge burden that South Africa is placing on judges arguing that if a conflict has underlying political questions, courts are obliged under Section 34 of the Constitution to hear the dispute so long as the claim is couched in such a way that law is applicable.[196]

It is worth noting that Justice Moseneke did not address (as he should have) the question of how the judiciary should determine political disputes that are not capable of being resolved through the application of the law. He, however, cautioned that:

> we need to rethink if our democracy is working properly because one day the wall containing the volume of water that is ever increasing may just burst and we may get flooded.[197]

Justice Moseneke subsequently reiterated his views at the Annual Helen Suzman Lecture where he stated that:

> Plainly, courts have become sites of resolving disputes on political power and rivalry absent other credible sites for mediating political strive. A properly functioning democracy should eschew lumbering its courts with so much that properly belong at other democratic sites or the streets. We will over time over-politicise the courts and thereby tarnish their standing and effectiveness. That is true also of manifold and costly commissions of enquiry headed by judges only to give respite to dithering political or state functionaries.[198]

---

195 D. Moseneke Power FM Radio Interview 2016. Moseneke is not the only retired judge who has responded to the concerns about the proper role of the judiciary in a democracy. Justice Ngcobo recently remarked that some are concerned that issues that should be resolved through the ballot box are increasingly being resolved in Bloemfontein and in Braamfontein. *See*, Ngcobo, 2016, p. 18. *See also*, Editorial, *BusinessDay*, 7 July 2016 (arguing that parliament is notionally the institution that should be holding the executive to account ... because courts are strictly speaking not designed to solve these kinds of [political] problems).

196 Moseneke, 2016.

197 *Id.*

198 *Id.*, p. 10. https://hsf.org.za/publications/lectures/helen-suzman-memorial-lecture-2016-1.

It is significant to note that Justice Moseneke did not suggest a political question doctrine as the solution to this well-articulated problem. While he prefers to see courts get less involved in dealing with cases that are openly political or economic in nature, his suggested solution is to encourage disputants to try and resolve these types of cases before they go to court. This is not enough. South Africa requires a rule of law-based response to this problem.

Similarly, in addressing the Cape Town Press Club on 25 October 2017, Chief Justice Mogoeng correctly warned that:

> those of us who are inclined to litigate as we should… make sure that we are careful about the responsibilities that we impose on our courts to deal with … because if we push our courts to the point where they literally become raw political players we are exposing them to criticism that could have been avoided… We are putting them in a space that could easily cause people to delegitimize the crucial role that we play in our constitutional democracy. We owe it to prosperity to challenge every wrong doing but let us be very careful in our choices … sometimes almost refusing to deal as we should with challenges of a political nature than be quick to have courts deal with them. This applies to different political parties. Shouldn't you as a political family go out of your way to resolve your internal problems … before you go to court and only go to court if you are left with no choice… this extends to every dispute that different political parties might have … but it also extends to disputes different political parties might have in parliament or any other setting… let us treasure the role of our courts that we do not inadvertently place courts in an unenviable position where it has to deal with matters of a nature that it ought not ordinarily have to deal with.[199]

Mogoeng's warning should be welcomed. Like Moseneke, the problem with Mogoeng's caution is that he neglects to recognize that the judiciary is capable of solving the problem than relying solely on litigants to avoid bringing disputes of a political nature to court. By way of explanation, it is submitted that the judiciary has the responsibility to devise a remedy to the problem identified by both Moseneke and Moegoeng and others instead of surrendering that responsibility to litigants.

---

199 M. Mogoeng, 'Judicial Overreach', a speech presented at the Cape Town Press Club on 25 October 2017 www.youtube.com/watch?v=xGAe_zHg9dw, at 14:18-17:08. Mogoeng made this speech two months before he would pen a strong dissenting opinion against what he termed as 'textbook case of judicial overreach' in referring to the majority judgement. In his dissent, he would repeat these cautionary statements and criticize the majority's failure to apply the principle adopted in two previous cases. *See, Impeachment Case*, 2018, at paras. 235, 252-255.

Secondly, I subscribe to another cautionary statement made by Judge Davis in *Mazibuko* about the threat to judicial independence when the judiciary is drawn in to resolve political questions that are beyond its competence or jurisdiction. Judge Davis had this to say:

> It is necessary to say something ... about this particular application. Courts do not run the country, nor were they intended to govern the country. Courts exists to police the constitutional boundaries, as I have sketched them. Where the constitutional boundaries are breached or transgressed, courts have a clear and express role. And must then act without fear or favour. There is a danger in South Africa however of the politicisation of the judiciary, drawing the judiciary into every and all political disputes, as if there is no other forum to deal with a political impasse relating to policy, or disputes which clearly carry polycentric consequences beyond the scope of adjudication. In the context of this dispute, judges cannot be expected to dictate to Parliament when and how they should arrange its precise order of business, matters.... I regret the need to emphasise this point, but it appears to me to be vital to the future integrity of the judicial institution. An overreach of the powers of judges, their intrusion into issues which are beyond their competence or intended jurisdiction or which have been deliberately and carefully constructed legally so as to ensure that the other arms of the state to deal with these matters, can only result in jeopardy for our constitutional democracy.[200]

The above observation is yet another acknowledgement by a sitting judge that a political question doctrine is indispensable to preserve South African constitutional democracy. On appeal to the Constitutional Court, Justice Jafta, in the opening paragraph of his dissenting opinion, echoed Judge Davis's concerns and said that:

> Political issues must be resolved at a political level. Our courts should not be drawn into political disputes, the resolution of which falls appropriately within the domain of other fora established in terms of the Constitution. A timely warning was issued in this case by Davis J in a judgment delivered by the High Court.

Thirdly, there is a tendency by detractors to reject (without proper justification) the political question doctrine as an American concept. I hereby argue that this rejection is

200 *Mazibuko*, 2012, pp. 32-33.

unfounded and simplistic at best.[201] The political question doctrine, as Justice Kpegah puts it, is not developed from any specific provision of the United States Constitution.[202] Instead, he correctly says it is a necessary derivative of the concept of separation of powers, which concept underpins the South African Constitution.[203] Justice Kpegah teaches us the

> fact that it was developed and so named within the American jurisprudence should not give us goose pimples and make us averse to its application to our constitutional adjudication. After all, what is in a name? A rose will always smell sweet even if it is called ammonia.[204]

Justice Kpegah's observations are applicable to South Africa. It should not matter that the political question doctrine is associated with or has gained prominence in the United States' jurisprudence. The focus of any examination of this doctrine should be on the text of each constitution, its usefulness and what it is designed to achieve, which is to preserve the separation of powers and advance the will of the people. What is more, the Constitution of 1996 is underpinned by the concept of separation of powers, which suggests that South Africa is not immune from experiencing similar separation of powers concerns and challenges as the other countries discussed above that have already developed a political question doctrine as a legal mechanism to solve those problems and define the contours of judicial authority.[205]

Even though the Constitutional Court has correctly said "no separation of powers is absolute",[206] it has emphasized that:

> pursuant to constitutional principle VI the Constitution provides for a system of separation of powers among the three co-equal branches of government, in which checks and balances result in the imposition of restraints by one branch of government upon another.[207]

---

201 *See*, Rautenbach, 2012; Asare, 2006; *Ghana Bar Association*, 2003-2004, pp. 294-295 and T. Roux, 'Baker v. Carr in South Africa, or How Political Questions Become Legal Questions', Address at the Conference on Law, Language and Politics in South Africa: The Impact of the Constitution, 2006.

202 *Amidu*, 2001-2002, p. 159.

203 *Id.*

204 *Id.*

205 *See*, *Heath*, 2000, at para. 22 (holding that there can be no doubt that our Constitution provides for such a separation, and that laws inconsistent with what the Constitution requires in that regard are invalid); *Certification Judgement*, 1996, pp. 1298-1300; *Executive Council, Western Cape Legislature v. President of the Republic of South Africa and Others* 1995 10 BCLR 1289 (CC); *De Lange v. Smuts* 1998 7 BCLR 779 (CC); *Pharmaceutical Manufacturers Association of SA: In re Ex parte President of the Republic of South Africa and Others* 2000 3 BCLR 241,260 (CC) and *Bernstein and Others v. Bester* 1996 4 BCLR 449, 499 (CC).

206 *Certification Judgement*, pp. 1298-1300. *See also*, *De Lange v. Smuts* 804.

207 *Certification Judgement*, 1996, p. 1299. *See also*, *Heath*, 2000 (confirming the separation of powers concept in the South African Constitution).

The Court has also imposed an obligation on itself to respect the vital limits of its judicial power.[208]

Also, the Constitutional Court has invalidated acts of the State on the basis of their conflict with the separation of powers imperatives in the Constitution,[209] and as a result, it can be argued that the Constitution does not contemplate the taking by one branch of government functions which in essence belong or are constitutionally assigned to another branch. Hence, South Africa's constitutional order is not uniquely designed from those countries like Ghana, Uganda, Nigeria and the United States that have developed and applied the political question doctrine.

6.10 Response to Opponents of the Doctrine

There is existing literature in which arguments have been made against the adoption of the political question doctrine in South Africa.[210] It is submitted that the arguments advanced in this body of literature are misplaced because the theory of the doctrine already exists, but requires clarity and comprehensiveness. For the reasons already articulated, this book argues that it is a misplaced view to suggest that the doctrine is an American concept.

In his critical discussion of the application of the political question doctrine in South Africa, Rautenbach describes it as an American concept.[211] In his attempt to convince the readers to disfavour the doctrine, he observes that "in its land of origin it is highly controversial and has after more than two hundred years not produced clear guidelines on how it must be applied."[212] The fact that that doctrine is controversial in the United States is not a rational basis for South African courts not to consider it and adapt it to the South African context. There are many legal doctrines that South African courts have borrowed from abroad.[213]

208 *See, Doctors for Life International*, 2006; *Economic Freedom Fighters v. Speaker of the National Assembly*, 2016.

209 *See, Executive Council, Western Cape Legislature v. President of the Republic of South Africa* (invalidating the Local Government Transition Act 209 of 1993 on separation of powers grounds).

210 Rautenbach, 2012, p. 28.

211 *Id.*

212 *Id.*

213 For a discussion of some of the justiciability doctrines that have been borrowed from abroad, *see, National Coalition for Gay and Lesbian Equality and Others v. Minister of Home Affairs* (incorporating the doctrine of ripeness as applied in the United States into South African law); *Ferreira v. Levin*, at paras. 164-165 (discussing other justiciability doctrines like standing requirement from the US perspective noting that it is important for courts not to be required to deal with abstract or hypothetical issues); Currie & De Waal, 2005, pp. 79-96 (discussing the justiciability doctrines of mootness, ripeness and other noting that these now forms part of South African law); *R v. Garnsworthy and Others*, 1923 WLD 17 (importing the English doctrine of common purpose into South African criminal law); *See also, S v. Mgedezi*, 1989 1 SA 687 (A)

In justifying the concept of legal borrowing, Wiktor has noted that since there are no sufficient legal doctrines, legal borrowing has become an acceptable practice worldwide. Certainly, there is no other doctrine that seeks to address the problems associated with courts adjudicating political questions than the political question doctrine. Furthermore, the fact that courts in the United States have not produced clear guidelines on how it ought to be applied is also not a good reason to discard any consideration of US authorities on the subject. In fact, this state of affairs presents an opportunity for South African courts to learn from the experiences in the United States and other countries that have applied it.[214]

As revealed above, it is submitted that the theory of the doctrine or some elements of it already form part of South African law, and thus examining the experiences in other countries allows South African courts to develop it further as contemplated by Justice Ackerman in *De Lange v. Smuts.* Ackerman said that:

> I have no doubt that over time our courts will develop a distinctively South African model of separation of powers, one that fits the particular system of government provided for in the Constitution and that reflects a delicate balancing, informed both by South Africa's history and its new dispensation, between the need, on the one hand, to control government by separating powers and enforcing checks and balances and, on the other, to avoid diffusing power so completely that the government is unable to take timely measures in the public interest.[215]

If courts were to adhere to Rautenbach's suggestion, they would miss the opportunity to develop a clear political question doctrine from the principle of separation of powers as suggested by Justice Ackerman. Such development should require a straightforward and

(applying the doctrine of common purpose); *Thebus and Another v. S*, 2003 10 BCLR 1100 (CC) (the constitutional court upholding the validity of the doctrine of common purpose under the Constitution); and *see*, *Swissbourgh Diamond Mines (Pty) Ltd and Others v. Government of the Republic of South Africa and Others*, 1998, JOL 4144 (T) (holding that the act of state doctrine is applicable to South Africa as it is to the United States, and that the judicial branch of government ought to be astute in not venturing into areas where it would be in a judicial no-man's land. It would appear that in an appropriate case, as an exercise of the court's inherent jurisdiction to regulate its own procedure, the court could determine to exercise judicial restraint and refuse to entertain a matter, notwithstanding it having jurisdiction to do so, in view of the involvement of foreign states therein). *See also*, Wishik, 1985, p. 698 (discussing that Judge Bork has used the political question and act of state doctrines as evidence of underlying separation of powers issues that in his view justify judicial abstention on a broad range of foreign relations issues).

214 For a discussion of the political question doctrine in Israel, *see*, Cohn, 2011, p. 675 and *Jabotinsky v. Weitzmann*, HCJ 65/51 (1951) (where the Israeli Supreme Court, sitting as the High Court of Justice rejected an application for an order of mandamus against the President of the State regarding his exercise of discretion in entrusting the task of forming a government to a member of the Knesset, Israel's parliament).

215 *De Lange v. Smuts NO* 1998 7 BCLR 779 (CC), at para. 60.

acceptable principle to guide courts to determine whether to hear cases involving political questions.

Additionally, it is submitted that an examination of the constitutional experiences in the United States, Ghana, Nigeria, and Uganda offers South Africa an opportunity to confront once and for all the political question doctrine as developed and applied by courts in those countries and determine how relevant it might be to the South African circumstance instead of the current selective application of American and other doctrines.[216] As seen in this book, this approach has worked well in Uganda, Israel, Japan, Nigeria and Ghana where the courts have adopted and modified the political question doctrine to fit the system of government contemplated in their respective supreme constitutions.

Another of Rautenbach's main objections to the doctrine is that its application in South Africa would conflict with the supremacy of the Constitution, as contemplated by Section 2 of the Constitution.[217] He argues that the supremacy clause does not permit the exclusion of any action from judicial review.[218] This argument is misplaced based on at least two grounds.

Firstly, the problem with Rautenbach's argument is that it is premised on an incorrect assumption that the power of judicial review is absolute. This is further from the truth. The Constitutional Court has conceded to the fact that the power of judicial review is not absolute. In *Doctors for Life International*,[219] it held that "courts must be conscious of the vital limits on judicial authority and the constitution's design to leave certain matters to other branches of government."[220] Lately, in *Economic Freedom Fighters v. Speaker of the National Assembly*, the Constitutional Court reiterated this view holding that the judiciary "does not have unlimited powers and must always be sensitive to the need to refrain from undue interference with the functional independence of other branches of government".[221]

In addition, even *Marbury v. Madison*, which is revered for institutionalizing the power of judicial review recognized that that power has limitations. Similarly, earlier cases in South Africa such as *Brown v. Leyds NO* and *Cassim and Solomon v. the State* also recognized the inherent limitation of the power of judicial review. However, even if Rautenbach was correct in his assertion, how should we explain the Constitutional Court's endorsement of other justiciability doctrines such as mootness, ripeness and standing, all of which seek

216 *See, e.g., Swissbourgh Diamond Mines (Pty) Ltd*, 1998, p. 108 (adopting the act of state doctrine from the US Supreme Court). There are other justiciability doctrines such as ripeness, advisory opinion mootness that have been discussed and applied in South Africa. Free, 2003; Yoshino, 2009 and Currie & De Waal, 2005, pp. 79-96.

217 Section 2 of the South African Constitution provides that "this Constitution is the supreme law of the Republic; law or conduct inconsistent with it is invalid, and the obligations imposed by it must be fulfilled."

218 Rautenbach, 2012, p. 28.

219 *Doctors for Life International*, 2006.

220 *Id.*, at para. 37.

221 *Economic Freedom Fighters, 2016*, at para. 92.

to limit the power of judicial review?[222] Are those doctrines in conflict with Section 2 of the Constitution as well to the extent that they limit the power of judicial review? These justiciability doctrines have been applied by the Constitutional Court since the Constitution was adopted. There is, therefore, no conflict between the political question doctrine and Section 2 of the Constitution 1996. More simply, as noted in Chapter 1 in my discussion of the study by Margit Cohn, the political question doctrine is a member of the justiciability canons.[223] It would be irrational to embrace all justiciability canons, except the doctrine.

Secondly, if Section 2 read with Section 167(3) of the Constitution is seen as implying that the Constitutional Court has a special guardianship role in constitutional interpretation and enforcement, then it could equally be said that it (the Constitutional Court) alone must have the final say in all constitutional questions in South Africa. This is hardly a true reflection of the South African constitutional scheme. I make this submission with a clear benefit in mind of Section 167(3) of the Constitution, which assigns the Constitutional Court as the highest court on all matters and the power to finally decide whether a matter is within its jurisdiction. This is not the entire picture of the envisaged constitutional scheme.

Based on the doctrine of coordinate construction, Fisher and Devins have convincingly argued that the elected branches have both the authority and the competence to engage in constitutional interpretation.[224] According to this view,

> the elected branches participate before the courts decide and they participate afterwards as well … the process is circular, turning back on itself again and again until society is satisfied with the outcome.[225]

---

222 *See*, *National Coalition for Gay and Lesbian Equality v. Minister of Home Affairs* (discussing the doctrine of ripeness in South Africa); *Ferreira v. Levin*; 1996; *Albutt v. Centre for the Study of Violence and Reconciliation* 2010 3 SA 293 (CC); *Port Elizabeth Municipality v. Prut NO* 1996 4 SA 318 (E); *New Party of South Africa v. Government of the Republic of South Africa* 1999 3 SA 191 (CC); *Kruger v. President of the Republic of South Africa* 2009 1 SA 417 (CC); *Bio Energy Afrika Free State v. Freedom Front Plus* 2012 2 SA 88 (FB); *JT Publishing v. Minister of Safety and Security*; *National Coalition of Gay and Lesbian Equality v. Minister of Home Affairs* 2000 2 SA 1 (CC) [21]; *S v. Dlamini* 1999 4 SA 623 (CC); *Janse van Rensburg NO v. Minister of Trade and Industry* 2001 1 SA 29 (CC); *President of the Ordinary Court Martial v. Freedom of Expression Institute* 1999 4 SA 682 (CC); *Chairman, State Tender Board v. Digital Voice Processing (Pty) Ltd* 2012 2 SA 16 (SCA); *Ritcher v. Minister of Home Affairs* 2009 3 SA 615 (CC); *S v. Friedland* 1996 8 BCLR 1049 (W); *Transvaal Agricultural Union v. Minister of Land Affairs* 1997 2 SA 621 (CC); *Minister of Education v. Harris* 2001 4 SA 1297 (CC) and *Legal Aid South Africa v. Magidiwana (2)* 2014 4 All SA 570 (SCA).

223 Cohn, 2011, p. 677 and Yoshino, 2009, p. 559 (noting that the political question doctrine is a doctrine of justiciability. Other such doctrines include standing, ripeness, mootness and the bar on advisory opinions).

224 Fisher & Devins, 1992, p. 10. For further discussion about the doctrine of coordinate construction, *see*, G. Neuman, 'Variations for Mixed Voices', *University of Pennsylvania Law Review*, Vol. 137, 1989, 1851.

225 Fisher & Devins, 1992, p. 10.

Justice Kanyeihamba of the Uganda Supreme Court shared this view when he declared in the landmark case of *Tinyefuza* that the constitutional platform is to be shared among the three arms of government, and that courts need to bear in mind the judgements of other repositories of constitutional power concerning the scope of their authority and the necessity for each to keep within its powers, including the courts themselves.[226]

South African academics such as Currie and de Waal agree with Fisher and Devins and Justice Kanyeihamba. They observe that "while the courts have the final word they are by no means solely responsible for interpreting the Constitution."[227] Similarly, former Chief Justice Ngcobo agrees that the South African constitutional design contemplates interaction among the three branches of government when he spoke of the notion of 'constitutional dialogue' and dismissed the perceived notion that when courts "strike down unconstitutional action or legislation … it is perceived as the end of the matter".[228] To the contrary, he argued that a "dialogic theory appreciates that a judicial finding of constitutional invalidity is more often than not merely the beginning"[229] of a dialogue among the three branches of government. Justice Ngcobo advocates that "this dialogue must be rooted in the shared obligation among all branches of government to uphold the Constitution."[230]

What is more, I submit that Ngcobo's concept of a constitutional dialogue was influenced by Professor Bickel's notion of the passive virtue.[231] As noted in Chapter 5, Bickel advocated for courts to abstain from determining cases that raise political questions to prevent them from losing their legitimacy. He advocated that instead of losing this legitimacy by invalidating acts of the political branches, courts should exercise the passive virtue by invoking the political question doctrine to decline to adjudicate a case.[232] In Bickel's view, which ties in with Justice Ngcobo's, invoking the political question doctrine in these

226 *Attorney General v. Tinyefuza*, 1997, p. 3. *See also*, M. Mhango, Transformation and the Judiciary, in Hoexter & Olivier (Eds.), *The Judiciary in South Africa*, Juta, Cape Town, 2014, pp. 95-96.

227 *See*, Currie & de Waal, 2005, p. 394 fn. 184 (commenting on the comments by Justice Chalskalson in *Executive Council, Western Cape Legislature v. President of the Republic of South Africa*.)

228 S. Ngcobo, 'South Africa's Transformative Constitution: Towards an Appropriate Doctrine of Separation of Powers', *Stellenbosch Law Review*, Vol. 22, No. 1, 2011, pp. 37-48 (arguing that the constitutional dialogue is the underpinning and defining feature of South African separation of powers).

229 *Id.*, pp. 38-48.

230 *Id. See also*, Story, 1833, p. 346 (arguing that "it may arise in the course of the discharge of the functions of any one, or of all, of the great departments of government, the executive, the legislative, and the judicial. The officers of each of these departments are equally bound by their oaths of office to support the constitution of the United States, and are therefore conscientiously bound to abstain from all acts, which are inconsistent with it. Whenever, therefore, they are required to act in a case, not hitherto settled by any proper authority, these functionaries must, in the first instance, decide, each for himself, whether, consistently with the constitution, the act can be done. If, for instance, the president is required to do any act, he is not only authorized, but required, to decide for himself, whether, consistently with his constitutional duties, he can do the act.")

231 *See*, Ngcobo, 2016, p. 19 (noting that Bickel's argued against judicial review because "it thwarts the will of the representatives of the actual people").

232 Scharpf, 1966, pp. 537-539 (expressing agreement with Bickel's basic theory but critical of the political question doctrine as a means to achieving the end of legitimacy).

circumstances enables a constitutional dialogue between the people and the political branches, and society at large about the issues under dispute.

While Justice Ngcobo does not mention the term 'political question doctrine' in his articulation of the notion of a constitutional dialogue, his objectives for advocating for such dialogue are similar to Bickel's, which is to ensure that political questions are resolved in the political process without court interference. Justice Ngcobo recently crystalized his views. In his examination of the arguments for and against judicial review, he argues that "at the core of these arguments and counter-arguments is the doctrine of separation of powers and the limits of the power of judicial review."[233] Other scholars like Professor Devenish observe that the "Constitutional Court is not the ultimate protector of democracy."[234] Clearly, for these academics and jurist, the South African judiciary share responsibility for interpreting the Constitution with the elected branches of government.

Therefore, contrary to Rautenbach, it is submitted that the preferred interpretation of Section 2 read with Section 167 of the Constitution is that the Constitutional Court has authority to adjudicate constitutional issues only when they are properly within its jurisdiction and that it shares the responsibility for interpreting the Constitution with other branches of government.[235] It is proposed that Section 2 does not bar courts from applying the political question doctrine just like it does not under the supremacy clauses in the constitutions of Uganda,[236] Ghana,[237] Nigeria and the United States.[238]

The common feature in these constitutional provisions is that they all declare their constitutions supreme law, and yet the highest courts in those countries have ruled that the political question doctrine is applicable. What is more, these constitutions (unlike the United States) are fairly new having been adopted in the 1990s like the Constitution 1996. Thus, it is difficult to understand the uniqueness, which seems to be suggested by Rauten-

233 Ngcobo, 2016, p. 19.

234 Devenish, 2004, p. 64.

235 Moreover, the jurisdiction of court in Section 34 of the Constitution is implicitly limited to those disputes that can be resolved by the application of legal principles. *See, Kolbatschenko v. King*, 2001, p. 1399 (discussing the threshold question of whether the Constitutional Court has jurisdiction to interfere during the legislative but before process a legislative bill is signed into law, thereby confirming the proposition that the Constitutional Court has authority to adjudicator constitutional issues that are properly within its jurisdiction).

236 Section 2 of the Uganda Constitution provides: 2. (1) This Constitution is the supreme law of Uganda and shall have binding force all authorities and persons throughout Uganda. (2) If any other law or any custom is inconsistent with any of the provisions of this Constitution, the Constitution shall prevail, and that other law or custom shall, to the extent of the inconsistency, be void.

237 Art. 1(2) of the Constitution of Ghana provides that: (2) This Constitution shall be the supreme law of Ghana and any other law found to be inconsistent with any provision of this Constitution shall, to the extent of the inconsistency, be void.

238 Art. VI(2) of the United States Constitution provides that: This Constitution, and the Laws of the United States which shall be made in Pursuance thereof; and all Treaties made, or which shall be made, under the Authority of the United States, shall be the supreme Law of the Land; and the Judges in every State shall be bound thereby, anything in the Constitution or Laws of any State to the Contrary notwithstanding.

bach about the supremacy of the South African Constitution that would prevent the application of the political question doctrine.

It is clear from the discussions of the case law from Ghana, Nigeria, Uganda and the United States that courts frequently apply the doctrine without compromising the supremacy clause in their constitutions. To reject the doctrine as being contrary to Section 2 of the Constitution 1996 is tantamount to suggesting that Section 2 conflicts with the principle of separation of powers, which is the genesis of the doctrine. This is legally unsound because the two principles co-exist, and there is no reason why the doctrine, as articulated in the countries discussed, cannot be applied in harmony with the supremacy clause in South Africa.

Notwithstanding the supremacy clause, the book concurs with Justice Kpegah that there is an inherent suggestion in modern constitutions, and I would add the South African Constitution that the policy that should inform any legislation and desire to enact such legislation are discretionary matters for the elected branches to decide.[239] This book submits that those policy decisions should not concern the judiciary because the elected branches have discretion for which they must be held politically accountable and the "province of the [judiciary]... is not to inquire how the executive or [legislative] officers perform duties in which they have discretion."[240]

Finally, Rautenbach maintains that it would make no sense to adopt the political question doctrine in South Africa because of the critical remarks of Professor Henkin in an article published in 1976.[241] In this article, Henkin contends that the political question doctrine does not exist.[242] He reasoned that the doctrine is an unnecessary packaging of several established doctrines, but is no more than the sum of its parts and courts should do away with them.[243]

The problem with Rautenbach's reliance on Henkin is that he fails to acknowledge that many other prominent legal scholars support the application of the doctrine and have discredited Henkin's views.[244] Clearly, it would be irrational to abandon an important legal

239 *See, Amidu*, 2001-2002, p. 154.
240 *Marbury v. Madison*, 1803, p. 170.
241 Henkin, 1976, p. 597.
242 *Id.*, pp. 598-599.
243 *Id.*, p. 622.
244 *See*, Redish, 1984 (generally arguing that the political question doctrine does exist and is critical of Henkin's views but suggests that the doctrine should not exist); Tushnet, 2002, pp. 1203-1208; H. Wechsler, 'Toward Neutral Principles of Constitutional Law', *Harvard Law Review*, Vol. 73, No. 1, 1959, pp. 9, 6-9; O. Field, 'The Doctrine of Political Questions in the Federal Courts', *Minnesota Law Review*, Vol. 8, 1924, p. 512 (recognizing the formulation of the political question doctrine); Mulhern, 1988, pp. 104-124, and Seidman, 2003, *John Marshall LR* 449 (arguing that the political question doctrine is an important tool to modern constitutional adjudication, and that it manifests itself in three strands); Barkow, 2002, pp. 242-244, 301-336 (arguing that the political question doctrine forces the Court to confront the institutional strengths of the political branches – and the Court's weaknesses – in resolving some constitutional questions) and C. Carter, 'Halliburton Hears a Who? Political Question Doctrine Developments in the Global War on Terror

principle like the political question doctrine solely on the basis that one prominent academic is critical of it. Moreover, Rautenbach fails to recognize that even after Henkin's article was published, a plurality of the US Supreme Court in *Goldwater v. Carter*[245] expressly invoked the doctrine to avoid adjudicating a constitutional challenge by several members of Congress to the President's unilateral notice of termination of a mutual defence treaty with the Republic of China.[246]

Another critic of the political question doctrine is former Deputy Chief Justice Moseneke. In a public lecture at the Georgetown Law Center in 2013,[247] Justice Moseneke discussed his views about the political question doctrine as applied in the United States, and noted that the judiciary in South Africa has not adopted such a doctrine. He explained that in the South African context, if a dispute is properly raised as a constitutional question, the Constitutional Court is not free to take refuge in the political question doctrine despite the political implications arising from the dispute.[248] In explaining why the political question doctrine is not suitable in South Africa, Justice Moseneke maintains that it is because the Constitutional Court has a duty to resolve disputes despite the potential political implications; that the Constitution has installed the Constitutional Court as the final arbiter that will give full voice to our constitutional norms.

It is difficult to agree with Moseneke to the extent he seems to suggest that the political question doctrine applies to disputes that have political implications hence the doctrine gains no favour in South Africa because Constitutional Court is permitted to decide these types of cases.[249] In fact, in many jurisdictions where some version of the doctrine is applied, courts have made clear that the doctrine does not apply to any question that has political implications.

In *Baker v. Carr*, Justice Brennan considered the scope of the political question doctrine and pronounced that it has limited reach so that it applies to political questions "not simply to cases that involve political issues".[250] This view was recently endorsed by the US Supreme

---

and Their Impact on Government Contingency Contracting', *Military Law Review*, Vol. 201, 2009, p. 86 (discussing the importance of the political question doctrine in modern contingency environment).

245 444 US 996 (1979).

246 Redish, 1984, p. 1032.

247 Moseneke, 2013, p. 749.

248 There is nothing that stops South African courts from applying the political question doctrine in some limited areas. *See*, Motala & Ramaphosa, 2002, pp. 123-124 (where in arguing in favour of the application of the political question doctrine, they observed that "even though the German Constitution, like the South African Constitution, requires the Constitutional Court to adjudicate cases rightly brought before it, the German Constitutional Court in *Pershing 2 and Cruise Missile 1 case* (1983) 66 BVerfGe 39 held that foreign affairs is an area where it lacks manageable judicial standards and should be treated as a political question better left to be decided by the other branches of government.").

249 *President of the Republic of South Africa and Others v. South African Rugby Football Union* 1999 4 SA 147 (CC), at para. 72 (holding that it was envisaged that this Constitutional Court would be called upon to adjudicate finally in respect of issues that would inevitably have important political consequences).

250 *Baker v. Carr*, 1962, p. 217.

Court in *Zitovsky v. Clinton* where the court upheld the doctrine but found that "the political question doctrine does not apply to the interpretation of a federal statute passed by Congress and signed by the President."[251] Similarly, in Ghana, Justice Kpegah in *Ghana Bar Association*[252] held that the mere fact that a lawsuit seeks the protection of a political right does not mean that it presents a non-justiciable political question.[253]

Therefore, it is submitted that Justice Moseneke's understanding of the political question doctrine is not consistent with the application of the doctrine in the countries where it is applied. I believe it is wrong to consider, as Justice Moseneke does, the political question doctrine as a legal concept that requires courts to abstain from deciding a question because of the political implications. Instead, the doctrine applies to those political questions that are either constitutionally delegated to the discretion of the political branches for resolution or those where there is no judicial norm or standard to resolve them.[254] In short, a distinction has to be drawn, which Justice Moseneke omits to do, between questions that have political implications, which courts may resolve and questions themselves political that courts should abstain from deciding.[255]

By his own admission, Moseneke accepts that the Constitutional Court has stepped aside in matters that affect the political branches when the Constitution requires it. He cited cases such as *Ferreira v. Levin,*[256] *United Democratic Movement,*[257] and I would add other recent cases like *International Trade Administration Commission* and *National Treasury* to the list of cases. While it is accurate that the Court has stepped aside, the problem is that the Constitutional Court has not provided a coherent principle or theory that explains how and when it will step aside in any given case.

Therefore, while this book accepts Justice Moseneke's basic proposition that the Constitutional Court "has attempted to explain the separation of powers, abide by its precepts and defer to the other branches of government when appropriate",[258] the problem, which I suspect has caused the judiciary to be repeatedly accused of judicial overreach, is that a coherent theory of separation of powers that incorporates a political question doctrine has not been developed in South Africa.[259] The judiciary has not created a sufficient principle

251 *Zivotofsky v. Clinton,* 2012, p. 1425; C. Michel, 'There's No Such Thing as a Political Question of Statutory Interpretation: The Implications of *Zivotofsky v. Clinton*', *Yale Law Journal,* Vol. 123, No. 1, 2013, p. 253 and Shemtob, 2016, p. 1001.

252 *Ghana Bar Association,* 2003-2004, p. 250.

253 *Id.*, p. 295.

254 *Zivotofsky v. Clinton*. And *see,* the reasoning in *Betsy v. Bank Mauritius,* 1993.

255 Mhango, 2014, p. 464.

256 *Ferreira v. Levin,* 1996.

257 *United Democratic Movement v. President of South Africa,* 2004.

258 D. Moseneke, 'Separation of Powers: Have the Courts Crossed the Line?', p. 10, 2015. www.groundup.org.za/article/separation-powers-have-courts-crossed-line_3152.

259 Recently in the *Impeachment Case,* Chief Justice Mogoeng characterized the majority judgement as a text book example of judicial overreach. *See, Impeachment Case,* at para. 223.

on how separation of powers will be adhered to when faced with political questions that are textually allocated to the heartland of the national executive or legislature. Instead, the courts have opted to deal with these questions on an *ad hoc* manner. If the courts developed a coherent separation of powers, which I submit should incorporate a political question doctrine for South Africa, that, as Justice Moseneke has suggested, should be distinctly South African in design; authorized by the Constitution and sit comfortably with our democratic system, less attacks from other branches, judges or interests will be had because courts will be required to give the political process a chance and the circumstances under which the courts may intervene will become clear.

Other opponents of the political question have dismissed the application of the doctrine in South Africa on the basis that the Constitution does not assign any issue of constitutional interpretation to a coordinate branch of government for final decision.[260] This argument is not valid. The fact that the Constitution is underpinned by the concept of separation of powers means that the Constitution assigns particular matters to the discretion of specific branches of government, which inevitably requires interpretation.

Recently, in the *United Democratic Movement v. Speaker of the National Assembly,* Chief Justice Mogoeng reiterated this principle when he held that the determination of the best "voting procedure to hold the President accountable … is the responsibility constitutionally-allocated to the National Assembly."[261] Furthermore, in *Kaunda,* Justice O'Regan agrees that the Constitution committed the conduct of foreign affairs to the executive branch. O'Regan held "it is clear, though perhaps not explicit, that under our Constitution the conduct of foreign affairs is primarily the responsibility of the executive."[262] She observed that:

> a variety of constitutional provisions including those that state that the President is responsible for receiving and recognising foreign diplomatic and consular representatives,[263] appointing ambassadors, plenipotentiaries and diplomatic and consular representatives,[264]

suggests that the Constitution commits the conduct of foreign affairs to the executive branch.[265] Justice O'Regan correctly asserts that:

260 Roux, 2006.

261 *United Democratic Movement v. Speaker of the National Assembly* 2017 (8) BCLR 1061 (CC), at para. 64.

262 *Kaunda v. President of the Republic of South Africa,* at para. 243.

263 *See,* Section 84(2)(h) of the Constitution.

264 *See,* Section 84(2)(i) of the Constitution.

265 *Kaunda v. President of the Republic of South Africa,* at para. 243.

> this is hardly surprising [because] under most, if not all constitutional democracies, the power to conduct foreign affairs is one that is appropriately and ordinarily conferred upon the executive, for the executive is the arm of government best placed to conduct foreign affairs.[266]

Justice Moseneke in *National Treasury* agreed with O'Regan and said the following:

> Where the Constitution or valid legislation has *entrusted* specific powers and functions to a particular branch of government, courts may not usurp that power or function by making a decision of their preference. That would frustrate the balance of power implied in the principle of separation of powers. The primary responsibility of a court is not to make decisions reserved for or within the domain of other branches of government, but rather to ensure that the concerned branches of government exercise their authority within the bounds of the Constitution. This would especially be so where the decision in issue is policy-laden as well as polycentric.[267]

Justices Mogoeng, O'Regan and Moseneke's pronouncements above are an acknowledgement that the Constitution commits certain provisions, and the questions arising from those provisions, to the other arms of government.[268] In my view, this commitment involves constitutional interpretation by the relevant branch.

---

266 *Id. See also, Harksen v. President of the Republic of South Africa and Others* 2000 5 BCLR 478 (CC) (confirming that matters of foreign affairs are committed to the legislative and executive branches).

267 *National Treasury,* 2012, at para. 63.

268 *See, National Treasury,* 2012, at para. 84 (Froneman J., concurring holding that "it is a breach of separation of powers for a court to intrude, by granting an interdict against government, upon the formulation and implementation of policy, a matter that resides in the heartland of national executive function"); *President of the Republic of South Africa and Another v. Hugo,* 1997 (recognizing that the exercise of pardon powers is committed to the executive branch). In addition, Sections 206(1) and 207(2) of the Constitution commit policing matters to the executive branch such that it is free to structure the South African Police without judicial scrutiny. *See, Glenister v. President of the Republic of South Africa,* 2011, at para. 162 (holding that the elected branches of government are at liberty to decide where to locate a specialized corruption-fighting unit. In this case, the elected branches had decided to locate such unit within and not without the South African Police Service as previously was the case. The court also noted that international law matters are committed to the political branches of the state); *South African Reserve Bank v. Public Protector and Others,* 2017, ZAGPPHC 443, at paras. 43-44 (held that the power to amend the Constitution is constitutionally assigned to Parliament) and *United Democratic Movement v. Speaker of the National Assembly and Others* 2017 (5) SA 300 (CC), at para. 64 (confirming that the determination "of which voting procedure to hold the President accountable in the particular instance is the responsibility constitutionally-allocated to the National Assembly").

6.11 Conclusion

Since its emergence in *Marbury v. Madison*, the political question doctrine has been applied by courts in the United States. Due to its prominence, the doctrine has been adopted and applied in various forms in African countries such as Nigeria, Uganda and Ghana. In South Africa, its consideration or application has been problematic. The problem is that the courts have failed to articulate and develop a comprehensive doctrine to adjudicate political questions. It has been submitted throughout this book that just as the Constitutional Court in *Fedsure*[269] created and articulated the doctrine of legality as a function of the rule of law contained in Section 1 of the Constitution, the same must happen in relation to the political question doctrine as an incident of the principle of separation of powers.

In the same way that the doctrine of legality has been clarified over the years since it was first articulated, the Constitutional Court must develop and clarify the political question doctrine, which as this book maintains, its theory is already part of South African constitutional law. The Constitutional Court must do this to prevent jurisdictional problems affecting the three arms of government that are bound to emerge in the future. More importantly, the Constitutional Court must do this because the framers of the Constitution did not intend to ordain the judiciary with unlimited powers.

269 *Fedsure*, 1998, p. 1482 (CC). *See also*, *Pharmaceutical Manufacturers Association of SA; In Re: Ex Parte Application of President of the Republic of South Africa*, 2000, 3 BCLR 241 (CC).

7 The Future of the Political Question Doctrine in South Africa

7.1 The Main Arguments

The arguments advanced during the course of this book are the following: firstly, it has been argued that the existence of the political question theory in South Africa can be discerned from prevailing jurisprudence that has emerged over the years. In other words, through constitutional adjudication, the judiciary has developed an incomprehensive political question doctrine jurisprudence, which remains to be fully developed into a lucid doctrine. In developing this argument, this book has considered notable cases by the judiciary such as *Ferreira v. Levin, Doctors for Life International* and *Economic Freedom Fighters v. Speaker of the National Assembly, National Treasury, Kolbatschenko v. King* and *Swissbourgh Diamond Mines (Pty) Ltd v. Government of the Republic of South Africa* and others where the judiciary decided the issues using political question doctrine theories without referring to the doctrine by name.

It has been contended throughout this book that *Ferreira v. Levin* and *First Certification Judgement* provides the legal basis for developing a political question theory in South Africa. In these cases, the Constitutional Court emphatically accepted the proposition that political questions fall within the domain of the political branches and outside the judicial boundaries, and that the democratic role of the political branches as reflecting the dominant opinion of the people of South Africa should be acknowledged and respected. The submission in this book is enhanced by the views of Moseneke expressed in *International Trade Administration Commission* that in developing separation of powers for South Africa, which in my own view incorporates a political question doctrine, we must adopt "a design which in the first instance is authorised by our Constitution itself… [and] must give due recognition to the popular will."[1] In this proposition, Justice Moseneke should be seen as giving credence to the classical political question doctrine.

Secondly, this book has argued that the judiciary has a constitutional obligation to develop a rule of law that will give effect to its most cited pronouncement on separation of powers that "courts must be conscious of the vital limits on judicial authority and the Constitution's design to leave certain matters to other branches of government."[2] It has been argued that the judiciary has not given effect to this rule of law, and that in order to

1 *International Trade Administration Commission*, 2010, at para. 91.
2 *Doctors for Life International*, 2006, at para. 37.

do so, the judiciary is obliged to develop a comprehensive political question doctrine. In this regard, the political question doctrine in South Africa must be seen as a constitutional requirement. The point I have tried to make is that *Doctors for Life International* requires the judiciary to develop a rule, and according to this book, the political question doctrine is that rule, which will permit the judiciary to observe the constitutional limits of their authority vis-à-vis the political branches in relation to political questions constitutionally assigned to these branches.

Thirdly, this book has argued that there are at least three constitutional provisions that provide the basis for the political question doctrine:

1. the preamble to the Constitution 1996 provides that one of the values upon which South Africa was founded is that government is based on the will of the people. This value provides the constitutional basis for the political question doctrine. This book has pointed out that when the political question doctrine is properly invoked, it reinforces the commitment to self-government by ensuring that important public issues are left to be decided by the people through their elected representatives and participatory democracy.
2. Section 34 of the Constitution provides another basis for the political question doctrine. The argument is that whereas Section 34 gives everyone the right to have their dispute that can be resolved by the application of the law decided by the judiciary, the converse is true. A dispute that cannot be resolved through the application of the law is necessarily non-justiciable, and the judiciary has no subject-matter jurisdiction over such dispute. An example would be a dispute that raises a political question (not a question that has political implications). Therefore, it is my view that the section enjoins the judiciary to develop a mechanism to determine or identify those non-justiciable disputes that fall outside its provisions, namely those that cannot be resolved through the application of the law. It is submitted that political questions fall within these non-justiciable disputes because by their very nature they are not capable of resolution through the application of the law. Political questions can only be resolved through democratic dialogue and compromise.
3. Section 167 of the Constitution gives the Constitutional Court discretion to decide constitutional or any other matters of public importance. This discretion could be employed as an additional basis for developing a political question doctrine.

Fourthly, it has been argued that based on existing case law as well as the plain reading of relevant constitutional provisions, the Constitution envisages that there should be political accountability (and not judicial accountability) in relation to certain constitutional questions. One of the ways in which political accountability is envisaged and manifested is when the Constitution delegates a function to a political branch of government without imposing principles or restrictions in the text on how the function should be exercised. In those instances, the political branch of government is deemed to have discretion on how to execute that power.[3] For example, the Constitutional Court has ruled that how the National Assembly should hold the executive to account is a discretionary power constitutionally assigned to the National Assembly and thus political and not judicial accountability is envisaged.[4] More simply, the judiciary cannot provide substantive content on how the National Assembly should hold the executive to account.

Likewise, the question of what kind of funding models should be employed for national infrastructure projects and who should pay for that cost has been found to be a political question whose resolution lies in the political process.[5] A number of constitutional provisions, including Sections 85, 84 and 55, support this proposition. The fact that the Constitution contemplates political accountability in relation to certain questions bolsters the argument that there is a need for a political question doctrine to apply in certain disputes arising from those constitutional provisions.

Lastly, the book argues that case law developments in Ghana, Nigeria, the United States and Uganda are useful to South Africa's own process of developing a comprehensive political question doctrine. It is also suggested that Justice Acquah's views in *Mensah v. Attorney-General* on the doctrine might particularly be useful as it resembles the reasoning that was shared by the then President of the Constitutional Court in *Ferreira v. Levin.*

7.2 WHAT DOCTRINE TO IMPLEMENT

Based on the above arguments, the following three suggestions, which if implemented, could address the problems identified in this book. Firstly, in recognition of South Africa's constitutional history and current dispensation, it is submitted that a political question

3 *See, Economic Freedom Fighters v. Speaker of the National Assembly*, 2016, at para. 93; Mhango, 2014; *Glenister v. President of the Republic of South Africa*, 2011, at para. 146; *South African Reserve Bank v. Public Protector and Others* [2017], at paras. 43-44 (finding that the Public Protector does not have the power to prescribe to Parliament how to exercise its discretionary legislative power, and that an order directed at Parliament to amend the Constitution offends the separation of powers by seeking too fetter in advance the legislative discretion vested in Parliament and the independent judgment vested in members of Parliament); Redish, 1984; Ngcobo, 2016 and Barkow, 2002.

4 *See, Economic Freedom Fighters v. Speaker of the National Assembly*, 2016.

5 *National Treasury*, 2012, at para. 95; *Merafong*, 2008, at para. 60 (held that "politicians, who are perceived to disrespect their voters or fail to fulfil promises without explanation, should be held accountable. A democratic system provides possibilities for this, one of which is regular elections."); *Certification Judgment*, at para. 186 (where in upholding the proportional representation system the court held that "under a list system of proportional representation, it is parties that the electorate votes for, and parties that must be accountable to the electorate") and S. Woolman, 'Understanding South Africa's Aspirational Constitution As Scaffolding,' *New York Law School Law Review*, Vol. 60, 2015-2016, p. 286 (arguing that "if a constitutional democracy wishes to last more than a few decades, several pre-conditions must obtain." One of those conditions is to "ensure political accountability [namely] the ability of to kick the bums now and again" in exchange for better policies or outcomes).

doctrine should be developed based on a classical political question theory. Part of what should be considered in this development are the suggestions by Justice Moseneke in *International Trade Administration Commission*[6] and Justice Ngcobo.[7] Chief Justice Ngcobo identified the lack of a coherent theory of judicial review as a major problem in South Africa and advocated its development by taking into account a number of factors discussed in the preceding chapter.[8]

The suggestions by these jurists are relevant and support the development of the classical political question theory. They both emphasize the need to identify a constitutional basis for a rule that develops either the separation of powers or judicial review. The two suggestions are linked. In a greater scheme of things, Ngcobo's suggestions are in fact linked to the development of a political question doctrine, although he does not use that term.

In any event, the practical effects of what is being advocated in this book is that when presented with an issue a court must ask, as a threshold question, whether the issue has been constitutionally assigned to the discretion of a political branch. In the event that an issue is constitutionally assigned for resolution to a political branch, the court should abstain from determining the issue and allow its merits to be resolved through democratic dialogue and compromise.

Secondly, a court presented with an issue should, as threshold question, inquire whether there is a judicially ascertainable standard by which the issue can be resolved, that is to say, whether the issue can be resolved through the application of the law. If a court is called upon to serve as a forum for re-examining the wisdom of discretionary decisions made by the political branches, then the political question doctrine should apply and the courts should abstain from proceeding in such an exercise.

For example, the doctrine should apply to the substantive issue over the policy decision of South Africa to withdraw from the Rome Statute because that question is constitutionally assigned to the discretion of the political branches. Moreover, there is no judicially ascertainable standard for a court to substantively evaluate the decision to withdraw from the Rome Statute without delving into political and international relations matters that are outside the domain of the judiciary.[9] In *Democratic Alliance v. Minister of International Relations and Cooperation,*[10] the High Court held that the delivery of the notice of withdraw from the Rome Statute to the Secretary General of the United Nations was procedurally flawed and invalid. However, when requested to determine the substantive aspects of the

---

6 *See, International Trade Administration Commission v. Scaw South Africa (Pty) Ltd* [91] and *see* discussion in Chapter 6.

7 Ngcobo, 2016, pp. 22-23.

8 *See,* discussions in Chapter 6.

9 *See, Glenister*, 2011, at paras. 89-90 (Ngcobo discussing that international law matters are assigned to the political branches as part of separation of powers principle).

10 *Democratic Alliance v. Minister of International Relations and Cooperation*, 2017, at para. 71.

decision to withdraw from the Rome Statute, the High Court correctly abstained from expressing any view on the substantive question. It offered two reasons for this abstention: (1) that the:

> decision to withdraw from the Rome Statute is policy-laden and one residing in the heartland of the national executive in the exercise of foreign policy, international relations and treaty making.[11]

In my own view, this is just another way of saying the decision involves non-justiciable questions or political questions that are not appropriate for judicial determination or resolution through the application of the law; (2) the court found that

> there is nothing patently unconstitutional … about the national executive's policy decision to withdraw from the Rome Statute, because it is within its powers and competence to make such a decision.[12]

Underneath the High Court decision in *Democratic Alliance v. Minister of International Relations and Cooperation* is an acknowledgement that the judiciary may intervene in the procedural aspects relating to the policy decision to withdraw from the Rome Statute (given the elaborate procedures in the Constitution concerning how these decisions may be carried out), but it may not intervene substantively in the matter for obvious separation of powers considerations.[13] Professor Dyani-Mhango, who has recently published a convincing commentary on the High Court judgement in *Democratic Alliance v. Minister of International Relations and Cooperation*, correctly summarizes her take on the case by arguing that the High Court's ruling was predicated on the notion that South Africa's

> decision to withdraw from the Rome Statute involves political choices that are not suitable for judicial determination through the application of the law [and] this militated against the High Court's consideration of the substantive matters.[14]

It is submitted that the reasoning of the High Court applies to the decision of South Africa to join the BRICS. If this decision were to be challenged in court as well as a dispute as to

11 *Id.*, at para. 77.

12 *Id.*, at para. 81.

13 In his commentaries on the United States Constitution, Story made a convincing argument, which is applicable to the South African context when he said "So the power to make treaties being confided to the president and senate, when a treaty is properly ratified, it becomes the law of the land, and no other tribunal can gainsay its stipulations." Story, 1833, p. 346. *See also*, Dyani-Mhango, 2017. *But see, SADC Tribunal Case,* 2018 (suggesting that courts may intervene on substantive aspects of treaty making).

14 Dyani-Mhango, 2017, p. 14.

whether the National Assembly breached its constitutional obligations when it failed to remove, through a vote of no confidence, the President following accusations of mismanaging the country's affairs. These would be political questions because whether to enter into a treaty with other sovereign states or how to hold the executive to account are matters within the discretion of the political branches and thus the judiciary should be constitutionally restrained from supplying substantive context to them.[15]

Lastly, in the light of the above, it is further submitted that South Africa's political question doctrine should be developed and applied to the following areas: policy formulation, development and implementation; foreign affairs matters; internal political party rivalries;[16] internal affairs of Parliament, except where individual rights are involved,[17] and perhaps other areas such as those involving some head of state powers.[18]

---

15 *Economic Freedom Fighters v. Speaker of the National Assembly*, 2016.

16 *See, Ramakatsa and Others v. Magashule and Others* 2013 (2) BCLR 202 (CC) and *Dube and Others v. Zikalala and Others* [2017] ZAKZPHC 36 [159] (held that "as in *Ramakatsa* this court should be disinclined to determine how the [African National Congress] should regulate its internal processes, given the powers in Rules 11.3 and 12.2.4 of the [African National Congress] constitution providing for continuity. Consequences will follow from the declaration of invalidity which, going forward, are best dealt with by the ANC itself in regulating its internal processes."). *See also, O'Brien v. Brown 409 US 1 (1972)* (where the US Supreme invoked the political question doctrine to find that federal courts had no authority over national political conventions as long as the convention itself could resolve the disputes. The large public interest was best served by allowing the political process to function instead of judicial supervision) and Pietzman, 1974.

17 *See*, Mazibuko, 2012; *Lekota v. Speaker* 2015 4 SA 133 (WCC); *De Lille v. Speaker* 1998 3 SA 430 (C); and Okpaluba 2015 CILSA, pp. 287-290; Cachalia, 2015-2016, p. 405 (advocating for a limited and contextual non-justiciability doctrine in South Africa in areas involving internal matters of Parliament arguing that judicial intervention should be limited to cases of a clear breach of the bill of rights or express constitutional provision). For cases dealing with individuals rights violations in Parliament, *see*, Chairperson of the *Nation Council of Provinces v. Malema* 2016 5 SA 335 (SCA) (where Supreme Court of Appeal found that a member of parliament was protected when he said the following in Parliament: "The ANC government massacred the people in Marikana."); *Primedia Broadcasting (a division of Primedia (Pty) Ltd) and Others v. Speaker of the National Assembly and Others* 2017 1 SA 572 (SCA) (where the Supreme Court of Appeal ruled that the manner in which the State of the Nation proceedings in February 2015 was broadcast was unconstitutional and unlawful, and that the use of a telecommunication signal jamming device in Parliament, without the permission of the Speaker of the National of Assembly and the Chairperson of the National Council of Provinces, was contrary to Section 4(1) of the Powers, Privileges and Immunities of Parliament and Provincial Legislatures Act 4 of 2004 and is unlawful.); *Democratic Alliance v. Speaker of the National Assembly and Others* 2016 3 SA 487 (CC) (where the Constitutional Court upheld the constitutional validity of a provision of a law that permits the arrest of members of parliament for causing disturbance in Parliament); *Democratic Alliance v. Speaker of the National Assembly and Others* 2015 4 SA 351 (WCC). For a case dealing with internal affairs of Parliament, *see, United Democratic Movement v. Speaker of the National Assembly and Others* [2017] ZACC 21 (where the court held that it has no authority to order the Speaker to determine the voting procedure on a motion of no confidence, and that the speaker has the authority to determine such voting procedure).

18 *President of the Republic of South Africa v. South African Rugby Football Union* 1999 2 BCLR 175 (CC) [146] (held that Section 84(2) [of the Constitution] powers are discretionary powers conferred upon the President that are not constrained in any express manner by the provisions of the Constitution. Their scope is narrow: the conferral of honours; the appointment of ambassadors; the reception and recognition of foreign diplomatic representatives; the calling of referenda; the appointment of commissions of inquiry and the pardoning of offenders. They are closely related to policy; none of them is concerned with the implementation of leg-

More than a decade ago, Motala and Ramaphosa made a similar suggestion concerning the application of the political question doctrine in South Africa.[19] They suggested that the doctrine should be applied in relation to cases arising out of a motion of no confidence in the President or the cabinet because there are no judicial standards for establishing what is appropriate for purposes of determining the lack of confidence.[20] In addition, for prudential reasons, Motala and Ramaphosa advocated that the political question doctrine should apply to cases involving the removal of a judge by the Judicial Service Commission supported by a two-thirds majority vote by the National Assembly; internal arrangements, proceedings and procedures of Parliament that are entrusted to Parliament and foreign affairs because it is an area where the country needs to speak with one voice and the other branches of government are better placed to make decisions in this area.[21] This book agrees with their suggestions and urges courts to consider them in developing the doctrine.

The rationale behind the suggestions about the future implementation of the doctrine in this chapter is that the Constitution grants discretion to the political actors in the above areas and that it envisages these actors should be held politically accountable in the performance of these discretionary functions in the respective areas. The Court has put it plain that if South Africans feel that their members of Parliament have disrespected them or failed to fulfil their promises made, then the politicians should be politically accountable to voters. It observed that "courts deal with bad law, voters must deal with bad politics."[22] Moreover, there are no judicial standards for determining answers to these questions.

In relation to political party rivalries, the fact that the Constitution does not regulate political parties means that discretion is afforded to political party functionaries where the electorate holds the power of accountability.[23] To put it differently, the principle articulated

islation. Several of them are decisions that result in little or no further action by the government: the conferral of honours, the appointment of ambassadors or the reception of foreign diplomats, for example. In the case of the appointment of commissions of inquiry, it is well-established that the functions of a commission of inquiry are to determine facts and to advise the President through the making of recommendations. The President is bound neither to accept the commission's factual findings nor is he or she bound to follow its recommendations).

19 Motala & Ramaphosa, 2002, pp. 122-126.

20 *Id.*, p. 123.

21 *Id.*, pp. 123-124 (noting that even though the German Constitution, like the South African Constitution, requires the Constitutional Court to adjudicate cases rightly brought before it, the German Constitutional Court in *Pershing 2 and Cruise Missile 1 case* (1983) 66 BVerfGe 39 held that foreign affairs is an area where it lacks manageable judicial standards and should be treated as a political question better left to be decided by the other branches of government).

22 *Merafong*, 2008, at paras. 308-309.

23 Recent jurisprudence confirms that the framers of the Constitution deliberately chose not to regulate political parties in favour of a system where parties will govern their own internal affairs. In this regard, the courts have extended discretion to political parties. *See, Ramakatsa and Others v. Magashule and Others* 2013 (2) BCLR 202 (CC) [125] (where after invalidating a provincial election of the African National Congress (ANC), the court held that "we are disinclined to determine how the political party concerned should regulate its internal process in the light of the declaration made by this Court. We are satisfied that

in *Glenister v. President of the Republic of South Africa, Economic Freedom Fighters v. Speaker of the National Assembly* and *Doctors for Life International* that where the Constitution grants power to a functionary without prescribing or imposing limitations on how such power should be exercised, such functionary is deemed to have discretion in exercising that power, applies forcefully to political parties in South Africa and hence the political question doctrine should be extended to political party rivalries. The Nigerian judiciary also applies the doctrine to political party rivalries focusing more on prudential considerations.

Unlike in Nigeria, the argument in this book is that South Africa's political question doctrine should be predicated upon the classical political question theory. While prudential considerations should not be precluded from being considered in the political question doctrine analysis, South Africa's doctrine should, in the first instance, be expressly authorized by the Constitution. Similarly, regardless of the merits of any prudential considerations, without a classical political question theory-based argument, no case should be dismissed on political question grounds. Finally, given South Africa's constitutional history and jurisprudence that has emphasized constitutional control of all exercise of public power, the political question doctrine should be narrowly applied in the same way that the exclusive jurisdiction of the Constitutional Court over crucial questions involving the political branches is applied.[24]

It needs to be emphasized that there are certain assumptions that have to be made concerning the propositions in this book. Given that the political question doctrine advocates leaving certain questions to be resolved through democratic decision making, there is an assumption that the political system is functioning properly. It is also assumed that political leaders will take their constitutional obligations seriously and believe in the constitutional values for which they have taken an oath to defend and uphold. If these assumptions are not manifested on the ground, it may be difficult for a court to justify invoking the political question doctrine and ensure effective government based on the will of the people.

---

the ANC's constitution confers on the [National Executive Committee] or the National Conference adequate authority to regulate its affairs in the light of the decision of this Court"); and *Dube and Others v. Zikalala and Others* [2017] ZAKZPHC 3 [159] (where after invalidating a recent provincial election of a political party, the court ruled that "as in *Ramakatsa* this court should be disinclined to determine how the ANC should regulate its internal processes, given the powers in Rules 11.3 and 12.2.4 of the ANC constitution providing for continuity. Consequences will follow from the declaration of invalidity which, going forward, are best dealt with by the ANC itself in regulating its internal processes.").

24 *See, Doctors for Life International*, 2006, at paras. 19-20 (held that the phrase fulfils a constitutional obligation in Section 167(4)(e) of the Constitution should be given a narrow meaning); *President of the Republic of South Africa and Others v. South African Rugby Football Union*, 1999) (held that in the context of the conduct of the President, expressed the view that the words fulfil a constitutional obligation in Section 167(4)(e) should be given a narrow meaning). *See also, Kaunda v. President of the Republic of South Africa*, at para. 78 (hold that the exercise of all public power is subject to constitutional control).

7.3 CONSEQUENCES OF FAILURE TO IMPLEMENT

What happens if the courts do nothing about the issues identified in this book? It is submitted that the failure to develop a separation of powers principle that is underpinned by a political question doctrine is problematic and may lead to, *inter alia*, the following problems: firstly, the potential for producing court orders that are ineffective or unenforceable. To put this into context, one should be reminded of what the Constitutional Court said in *S v. Mamabolo* concerning the role of the judiciary and its enforcement powers in our constitutional order. It said that:

> Under the doctrine of separation of powers it stands on an equal footing with the executive and the legislative pillars of state; but in terms of political, financial or military power it cannot hope to compete. It is in these terms by far the weakest of the three pillars; yet its manifest independence and authority are essential. Having no constituency, no purse and no sword, the judiciary must rely on moral authority. Without such authority it cannot perform its vital function as the interpreter of the Constitution, the arbiter in disputes between organs of state and, ultimately, as the watchdog over the Constitution and its Bill of Rights – even against the state.[25]

Flowing directly from the latter quoted part, one eminent jurist has argued that:

> .. the judiciary is naturally, and almost necessarily ... the weakest department. Its powers can never be wielded for itself. It has no command over the purse or the sword of the nation. It can neither lay taxes, nor appropriate money, nor command armies, appoint to offices. It is never brought into contact with the people by the constant appeals and solicitations, and private intercourse, which belong to all the other departments.[26]

Given these weaknesses of the judiciary, particularly the fact that the judiciary has no military to enforce its orders and rely on the executive to enforce them, if South Africa's separation of powers is continuously developed without a coherent political question doctrine, the political branches, especially the executive, could ignore court orders that are deemed to deal with purely political questions.

---

25 *S v. Mamabolo* 2001 3 SA 409 (CC) [16].

26 Story, 1833, pp. 17, 23. (remarking further the following as other weaknesses thatcharacterize the judiciary "cannot punish without law. It cannot create controversies to act upon. It can decide only upon rights and cases, as they are brought by others before it. It can do nothing for itself. It must do everything for others. It must obey the laws; and if it corruptly administers them, it is subjected to the power of impeachment.").

A recent example is the case of *Southern Africa Litigation Centre v. Minister of Justice and Constitutional Development.*[27] This case involved the invitation by the South African government of President of the Republic of Sudan Omar Al Bashir to attend the African Union Summit in South Africa. It is common knowledge that President Al Bashir has an outstanding warrant of arrest against him issued by the International Criminal Court for, among other things, crimes against humanity. Upon his arrival in South Africa, the Southern Africa Litigation Centre sought to enforce this warrant in terms of the Implementation of the Rome Statute of the International Criminal Court Act, 27 of 2002. The Southern Africa Litigation Centre obtained a court order against the government of South Africa ordering it to take steps and arrest President Al Bashir while in South Africa. The order could not be enforced because President Al Bashir managed to surreptitiously depart from South Africa.[28]

The point I wish to make is that aside from the law that formed the basis of the High Court order to arrest President Al Bashir, the High Court should have known that it was unlikely that the government was going to enforce the order particularly after it had invited President Al Bashir arguably with full knowledge of the legal consequences of his visit and without doubt made certain assurances to him regarding his visit. Courts must be mindful of their limits and context when crafting court orders so as not to make a mockery of the judicial system. If this (the disregard of court orders) were to become a trend, the public trust in the judiciary could be severely compromised.

The Constitutional Court has pronounced itself concerning what considerations to make when determining an appropriate remedy. It has noted that in terms of Section 172(1)(b) of the Constitution, the judiciary is granted authority and may "make any order that is just and equitable" as part of a relief.[29] But in *Masetlha v. President of the Republic of South Africa and Another,*[30] Justice Ngcobo held that "the requirement of just and equitable means that the remedy must be fair and just in the circumstances of the particular case."[31] He noted that "what is required is a careful balancing of … various interests."[32] Justice Ngcobo further cited with approval the Constitutional Court decision in *Hoffman v. South African Airways*[33] where it elaborated on the type of considerations to be under-

27 *Southern Africa Litigation Centre v. Minister of Justice and Constitutional Development* 2015 5 SA 1 (GP).

28 For a discussion of the implications and dilemma of South Africa's decision not to arrest President Al-Bashir, *see,* D. Dyani-Mhango, 'South Africa's Dilemma: Immunity Laws, International Obligations and the Visit by Sudan's President Omar Al Bashir', *Washington International Law Journal,* Vol. 26, No. 3, 2017, p. 535.

29 *Masetlha v. President of the Republic of South Africa and Another* 2008 1 SA 566 (CC); and *Hoffmann v. South African Airways* 2001 1 SA 1 (CC).

30 *Masetlha v. President of the Republic of South Africa and Another,* 2008, at para. 212.

31 *Id. See also Hoffmann v. South African Airways* 2001 1 SA 1 (CC) [42].

32 *Id.,* at para. 45.

33 *Hoffmann v. South African Airways,* 2001, at para. 42.

taken when determining a fair and equitable remedy. In *Hoffman v. South African Airways*, the Court pronounced that:

> The determination of appropriate relief … calls for the balancing of the various interests that might be affected by the remedy. The balancing process must at least be guided by the objective, first, to address the wrong occasioned by the infringement of the constitutional right; second, to deter future violations; third, *to make an order that can be complied with; and fourth, of fairness to all those who might be affected by the relief.* Invariably, the nature of the right infringed and the nature of the infringement will provide guidance as to the appropriate relief in the particular case. Therefore, in determining appropriate relief, we must carefully analyse the nature of the constitutional infringement, and strike effectively at its source.[34] (my emphasis)

Similarly, in the Ghanaian case of *New Patriotic Party v. Attorney-General* (discussed earlier in this book),[35] Chief Justice Archer made a related observation concerning the order sought by the plaintiff in that case. He reasoned that:

> I have always held the view that this court like equity must not act in vain. In other words, it should not make orders that could be lawfully and legitimately circumvented so as to make the court a laughing stock. Under the Constitution, 1992 the President is the commander-in-chief of the Ghana Armed Forces. Suppose he accepts the declaration sought and confers with his commanders and service chiefs not to hold any route marches on 31 December 1993, yet the non-commissioned officers who were instrumental in staging the 31 December 1981 coup d'etat choose to parade through the streets of Accra, who can stop them? Is this court going to send judges, magistrates, registrars, court bailiffs and ushers to erect barricades in the paths of the marchers? Again suppose notwithstanding the orders of this court, the members of the governing party, and their allies choose to celebrate 31 December with picnics, processions and dances, who can stop them? I must confess that the more I ponder over the reliefs sought, the more I become convinced of the futility of the orders being sought. I think this is a case which requires realism, pragmatism and foresight on the part of this court.[36]

---

34 *Id.*, at para. 45.

35 *New Patriotic Party v. Attorney-General,* 1993-1994. For a discussion of the case and subsequent developments, *see,* M. Mhango, 'Separation of Powers in Ghana: The Evolution of the Political Question Doctrine', *Potchefstroom Electronic Law Journal,* Vol. 17, No. 6, 2014, pp. 2706-2746.

36 *New Patriotic Party v. Attorney-General,* 1993-1994, pp. 50-51.

This book agrees with Chief Justice Archer's reasoning. While the justices in the *New Patriotic Party v. Attorney-General* disagreed over whether the political question doctrine applied, it is submitted that any constitutional system without a political question doctrine, coupled with perceived breaches of separation of powers, is likely to witness an increase in the frequency of ineffective or unenforceable court orders. In the South African context, the development of a coherent political question doctrine could assist in preventing this risk from materializing.

Secondly, the absence of an intelligible political question doctrine enhances the likelihood that jurisdictional problems will emerge and impede the achievements of popular transformation objectives in South Africa. There are a number of cases that illustrate this point, including the case involving Gauteng Freeway Improvement Project, street name change cases across the country, and affirmative action measures involving insolvency practitioners, cabinet appointments and others.[37]

Thirdly, as was said in *S v. Mamabolo*, the judiciary's legitimacy and powerful tool is its public trust. The absence of a rational political question doctrine increases the risk of court orders, which are deemed to be breaches of the separation of powers, from being implemented against the political branches. The frequency of this occurring will more likely dent the legitimacy of and public trust in the judiciary, and as Chief Justice Archer warned, turn the judiciary into a laughing stock.

37 *See, e.g., SARIPA v. Minister of Justice and Constitutional Development* 2015 2 SA 430 (WCC) (overturning affirmative action measures involving insolvency practitioners); *Opposition to Urban Tolling Alliance v. South African National Roads Agency Ltd* (where an interdict was issued against the implementation of the e-tolling in the province of Gauteng); O'Regan, 2012, p. 129 (arguing that the role of the Constitutional Court is not to thwart or frustrate the democratic arms of government, but is rather to hold them accountable for the manner in which they exercise public power); *Glenister v. President of the Republic of South Africa*, 2017 (where the court invalidated an Act of Parliament that frustrated the crime-fighting efforts of government) and *Minister of Constitutional Development and Another v. South African Restructuring and Insolvency Practitioners Association and Others* 2018 (5) SA 349 (CC) (invalidating affirmative action measures).

Bibliography

Books and Book Chapters

Barron, J. & Dienes, T. (1995). Constitutional Law in a Nutshell. Minnesotta: West.

Bennun, M. & Newitt, M. (1995). Negotiating Justice: A New Constitution for South Africa. Exeter: University of Exeter Press.

Bickel, A. (1962). The Least Dangerous Branch. New Haven, CT: Yale University Press.

Bickel, A. & Schmidt, B. (1984). History of the Supreme Court of the United States: The Judiciary and Responsible Government, 1910-21. Cambridge: Cambridge University Press.

Cappelletti, M. (1971). Judicial Review in the Contemporary World. Indiana: Bobbs-Merril.

Chemerinsky, E. (2001). Constitutional Law. New York: Aspen Law & Business.

Cooley, T.M. (1868). A Treatise on the Constitutional Limitations Which Rest Upon the Legislative Power of the States of the American Union. Boston: Little, Brown & Co.

Currie, I. & De Waal, J. (2001). The New Constitutional and Administrative Law. Cape Town: Juta.

Currie, I. & de Waal, J. (2005). The Bill of Rights Handbook. Cape Town: Juta.

Currie, I. & de Waal, J. (2013). The Bill of Rights Handbook. Cape Town: Juta.

Dugard, J. (1978). Human Rights and the South African Legal Order. Princeton: Princeton University Press.

Ellet, R. (2008). Emerging Judicial Power in Transitional Democracies: Malawi, Tanzania and Uganda. Boston: Northeastern University.

Fisher, L. & Devins, N. (1992). Political Dynamics of Constitutional Law. St. Paul, Minnesota: West Publishing.

Hamilton, A. (1999). The Judiciary. In C. Rossiter (Ed.), The Federalist Paper No. 78. New York: Signet Classic.

Hand, L. (1958). The *Bil! of Rights.* Cambridge: Harvard University Press.

Hasen, R. (2007). Leaving the Empty Vessel of "Republicanism" Unfilled: An Argument for the Continued Non-Justiciability of Guarantee Clause Cases. In B. Cain & N. Mourtada-Sabbah (Eds.), The Political Question Doctrine and the Supreme Court of the United States. Lanham: Lexington Books.

Hoexter, C. (2012). Administrative Law in South Africa. Cape Town: Juta.

Ingrams, H. (1960). Uganda: A Crisis of Nationhood. London: HM Stationery.

Klug, H. (2000). Constituting Democracy: Law, Globalism and South Africa's Political Reconstruction. New York: Cambridge University Press.

Kramer, L. (2004). *The People Themselves: Popular Constitutionalism and Judicial Review. New York:* Oxford University Press.

Locke, J. (1996). Second Treatise of Government. In M. Cohen & N. Fermon (Eds.), Princeton Readings in Political Thought Essential Texts Since Plato. Princeton: Princeton University Press.

Madison, J., Hamilton, A. & Jay, J. (1961). The Federalist Papers. In C. Kesler & C. Rossiter (Eds.). New York: Signet Classic.

Montesquieu, B. (1989). The Spirit of the Laws 163 (A. Cohler, Trans.) New York: Cambridge University Press. (Original work published 1748).

Mutibwa, P. (1992). Uganda Since Independence: A Story of Unfulfilled Hope. New Jersey: African World Press.

Nwabueze, B.O. (1982). The Presidential Constitution of Nigeria. Enugu: Nwamife Publisher.

Nwauche, E. (2010). Is the End Near for the Political Question Doctrine in Nigeria? In C. Fombad & C. Murray (Eds.), Fostering Constitutionalism in Africa. Pretoria: Pretoria University Law Press.

Okuku, J. (2002). Ethnicity, State Power and the Democratisation Process in Uganda. Uppsala: University Printers.

Perillo, J. (1998). The Law of Contracts. Minnesota: West Group.

Seedorf, S. & Sibanda, S. (2008). Separation of Powers. In S. Woolman *et al.* (Eds.), Constitutional Law of South Africa. Juta: Cape Town.

Story, J. (1833). Commentaries on the Constitution 525. New York: William S. Hein & Company.

Story, J. (1833). Commentaries on the Constitution of the United States with a Preliminary Review of the Constitutional History of the Colonies and States, Before the Adoption of the Constitution. Cambridge: Hilliard Gray & Co.

Tribe, L. (1988). American Constitutional Law. New York: Foundation Press.

Tushnet, M. (1999). Taking the Constitution Away from the Courts. Princeton, NJ: Princeton University Press.

Wechsler, H. (1961). Principles, Politics, and Fundamental Law. Cambridge Massachusetts: Harvard University Press.

Wiecek, W. (1972). The Guarantee Clause of the United States Constitution. Ithaca: Cornell University Press.

Worden, N. (1994). The Making of Modern South Africa: Conquest, Apartheid, Democracy. Oxford: Wiley-Blackwell.

Case Law

Abaribe v. The Speaker Abia State House of Assembly & Ors, 14 NWLR 466 (2003).

Abbeville County School District State, 335 S.C. 58, 515 SE 2d 535 (1999).

Abbott v. Burke, 693 A 2d 417(1997).

Abubakar Rimi v. Aminu Kano (1982) 3 NCLR 478 (1982).

African Personnel Services v. Government of Namibia and Others, [2008] NAHC 148.

Albutt v. Centre for the Study of Violence and Reconciliation, 2010 (3) SA 293 (CC).

Alegbe v. Oloyo, (1983) NSCC 315.

Alhaji Atiku Abubakar v. Attorney General of the Federal, (2007) 6 MJSC 1.

Amidu v. President Kufuor, 2001-2002 SCGLR 138.

Anderson v. Jordan, 343 US 912 (1952).

Andrew Kayira v. Edward Rugumayo & Others, Constitutional Case no. 1 (1979).

Antolok v. United States 873 F 2d 369 (DC Cir 1989).

Apostolou & Others v. The Republic of Cyprus, (1985) LRC (Const) 851.

Arakaki v. Lingle, 305 F Supp 2d 1161 (2004).

Asare v. Attorney-General (AP), unreported case number 21/2006.

Asogwa v. Chukwu, (2004) FWLR (pt. 189) 1204.

Attorney General v. Tinyefuza Const. Appeal No.1 of 1997 (S.C).

Attorney General Abia State v. Attorney General of the Federation, (2006) 9 MJSC 1.

Attorney General Eastern Nigeria v. Attorney General of the Federation, (1964) ALL NLR 218.

Avery v. Midland Country 390 US 474 (1968).

Backman v. Secretary of the Commonwealth, 387 Mass. 549 (1982).

Baker v. Carr, 369 US 186 (1962).

Balarabe Musa v. Auta Hamza, (1983) 3 NCLR 229.

Bato Star Fishing (Pty) Ltd v. Minister of Environmental Affairs, 2004 (4) SA 490 (CC).

Bernstein v. Bester No and Others, 1996 (2) SA 751 (CC).

Betsy v. Bank of Mauritius, 1993 3 LRC 75.

Bio Energy Afrika Free State v. Freedom Front Plus, 2012 (2) SA 88(FB).

Black Sash Trust v. Minister of Social Development and Others, [2017] ZACC 8; 2017 (5) BCLR 543 (CC); 2017 (3) SA 335 (CC).

Brigadier Tumukunde v. Attorney General, Constitutional Appeal No. 2 of (2006).

Brown v. Leyds NO, 4 Off Rep 17 (1897).

Brown v. McDaniel, 244 Ark 362 (1968).

Campaign for Fiscal Equity, Inc. v. State, 86 NY 2d 307, 55 NE 2d 661 (1995).

Campbell County School District v. State, 907 P 2d 1238 (Wyo1995).

Centre of Health Human Rights v. Attorney-General, Constitutional Pet No 16, (2011) UGCC 4.

Centre for Health Human Rights & Development v. Attorney General, [2012] UGCC 4.

Certification of the Constitution of the Republic of South Africa, 1996, 1996 (4) SA 744 (CC).

Certification of the KwaZulu-Natal Constitution, 1996 (11) BCLR 1419.

Chairman, State Tender Board v. Digital Voice Processing (Pty) Ltd, 2012 (2) SA 16 (SCA).

Chairperson of the Nation Council of Provinces v. Malema, [2016] 3 All SA 1 (SCA); 2016 (5) SA 335 (SCA).

Chicago & S Air Lines v. Waterman SS Corp, 333 US 103 (1948).

Chief Enyi Abaribe v. The Speaker, Abia State House of Assembly & Anor, (2000) LPELR-CA/PH/83M/2000.

Chief Enyi Abaribe v. The Speaker Abia State House of Assembly & Ors., (2003) 14 NWLR (pt. 788).

City of Pawtucket v. Sundlun, 662 A 2d 40 (R.I.1995).

Coalition for Adequacy & Fairness Sch Funding v. Chiles, 680 So 2d 400 (Fl 1996).

Cohens v. Virginia, 19 US 264 (1821).

Colegrave v. Green, 328 US 549 (1946).

Colegrove v. Barrett, 330 US 804 (1947).

Collins v. Minister of the Interior and Another, 1957 (1) SA 552 (A) 565.

Colorado v. Treasurer & Receiver General, 378 Mass 550 [1979].

Colorado Common Cause v. Bledsoe, 810 P 2d 201 (1991).

Columbia Falls Elem Sch Dist No 6 v. State, 109 P 3d 257 (2005).

Committee for Educ. Rights v. Edgar, 672 NE 2d 1178 (1996).

Common Cause/Pennsylvania v. Com, 710 A 2d 108 (1998).

Connecticut Coalition for Justice in Education Funding, Inc. v. Rell 990 A 2d 206 (2010).

Cooper v. Aaron 358 US 1 (1958).

Corrie v. Caterpillar 403 F Supp 2d 1019 (2005).

Corrie v. Caterpillar 503 F 3d 974, 980 (9th Cir 2007).

Cowigan (Pty) Ltd & Others v. Thwala NO, [2012] SZSC 25.

Crockett v. Reagan, 720 F 2d 1355 (DC Cir 1983).

Dada NO and Others v. Unlawful Occupiers of Portion 41, [2008] ZAGPHC 48.

Dalhatu v. Turaki, (2003) 15 NWLR (pt. 843) 310.

Davoyan v. Republic of Turkey, 116 F Supp 3d 1084 (2013).

De Lange v. Presiding Bishop of the Methodist Church of Southern Africa, 2016 (2) SA 1 (CC).

Debnarayan Dutt v. Ramsadhan, AIR (1914) Cal 129.

Democratic Alliance v. Acting National Director of Public Prosecutions, 2012 (3) SA 486 (SCA).

Democratic Alliance v. Minister of International Relations and Cooperation, [2017] AGPPHC 53.

Democratic Alliance v. President of the Republic of South Africa, [2017] ZAWCHC 34.

Democratic Alliance v. President of the Republic of SA; In re: Democratic Alliance v. President of the Republic of S A and Others, 2017 (4) SA 253 (GP).

Democratic Alliance v. Speaker of the National Assembly and Others, 2015 (4) SA 351 (WCC); [2015] 3 All SA 72 (WCC).

Democratic Alliance v. Speaker of the National Assembly and Others, 2016 (5) BCLR 577 (CC); 2016 (3) SA 487 (CC).

DeRolph v. State, 78 Ohio St 3d 193, 677 NE 2d 733 (1997).

Dickson v. Ford, 521 F 2d 234 (5th Cir.1975).

District of Columbia v. United States Dep't of Commerce, 789 F Supp 1179, 1184 (D DC 1992).

Doctors for Life International v. Speaker of the National Assembly, 2006 (12) BCLR 1399 (CC).

Doe v. Bush, 322 F 3d 109 (1st Cir 2003).

Dr. James Rwanyarare and Another v. Attorney General, [2000] UGCC 2.

Dube and Others v. Zikalala and Others, [2017] ZAKZPHC 3.

Dutsima v. PDP & Another, FCT/CV/2425/2010 (2010).

Economic Freedom Fighters v. Speaker of the National Assembly, [2016] ZACC 11.

Economic Freedom Fighters and Others v. Speaker of the National Assembly and Another, 2018 (2) SA 571 (CC)

E.E.O. C. v. Peabody W. Coal Co., 400 F 3d 774, 785 (9th Cir 2005).

Ekpenkhio v. Egadon, (1993) 7 NWLR (pt. 308) 717.

El-Shifa Pharmaceutical Industries Co v. US, 607 F 3d 836 (2010).

Esiaga v. University of Calabar, (2004) All FWLR (pt. 206) 381.

Ex parte James, 836 So 2d 813 (Ala. 2002).

Fedsure Life Assurance Ltd v. Greater Johannesburg Transitional Metropolitan Council, 1998 (12) BCLR 1458 (CC).

Ferreira v. Levin, 1996 (1) BCLR 1 (CC).

Flast v. Cohen, 392 US 83 (1942).

Fuldauer v. City of Cleveland, 119 NE 2d 546 (1972).

Ghana Bar Association v. Attorney-General, 2003-2004 SCGLR 250.

Ghana Lotto Operators Association v. National Lottery Authority, 2007-2008 SCGLR 1088.

Gibbons v. Ogden, 22 US 1 (1824).

Gilbert v. Gladden, 87 NJ 275 (1975).

Gilligan v. Morgan, 413 US 1 (1973).

Glenister v. President of the Republic of South Africa, 2011 (3) SA 347 (CC).

Goldwater v. Carter, 444 US 996 (1979).

Gonzales-Vera v. Kissinger, 449 F 3d 1260 (2006).

Gray v. Sanders, 372 US 368 (1963).

Haig v. Agee, 453 US 280, 292 (1981).

Hammer v. Dagenhart, 247 US 251 (1918).

Harris v. Kellogg Brown & Root Service, 80 F Supp 3d 991 (3d Cir 2013).

Highland Farms Dairy v. Agnew, 300 US 608 (1937).

Idaho Schools for Equal Educ Opportunity v. Evans, 123 Idaho 573 (1993).

In re South African Apartheid Litigation, 617 F Supp 2d 228 (2009).

Inakoju v. Adeleke, (2007) ALL FWLR (pt. 353).

International Trade Administration Commission v. SCAW South Africa (Pty) Ltd, 2012 (4) SA 618 (CC).

Jamna Das v. Ram Autar, (1911) 30 IA 7.

Janse van Rensburg v. Minister of Trade and Industry, 2001 (1) SA 29 (CC).

Japan v. Shigeru Sakata, 4 *Japanese Ann. International Law*, (1960) 103.

Japan Whaling Assoc v. American Cetacean Society, 478 US 221 (1986).

Johnson v. Eisentrager, 339 US 763 (1950).

JT Publishing v. Minister of Safety and Security, 1997 (3) SA 514 (CC).

Kadic v. Karadzic, 70 F 3d 232 (2d Cir 1995).

Kahawaiolaa v. Norton, 386 F 3d 1271 (9th Cir 2004), cert denied by the US Supreme Court 545 US 1114 (2005).

Kidd v. McCanless, 352 US 920 (1956).

Kiernan v. City of Portland, 223 US 151 (1912).

Koohi v. United States, 976 F 2d 1328 (9th Cir 1992).

Kruger v. President of the Republic of South Africa, 2009 (1) SA 417 (CC).

Lake View Sch Dist No. 25 v. Huckabee, 91 SW 3d 472 (2002).

Lane v. Halliburton, 529 F 3d 548 (2008).

Law Society of South Africa and Others v. President of the Republic of South Africa and Others, [2018] ZACC 5.

Lawrence v. Fox, 20 NY 268 (1859).

Leandro v. State, 488 SE 2d 249 (1997).

Leek v. Theis, 217 Kan 784 (1975).

Legal Aid South Africa v. Magidiwana (2), 2014 (4) All SA 570 (SCA).

Lekotholi v. Attorney-General, [1994] LSCA 153.

Lewis v. Spagnolo, 710 NE 2d 798 (1999).

Lobato v. State, 218 P 3d 358 (2009).

Lochner v. New York, 198 US 45 (1905).

Loring v. Young, 239 Mass 349 (1921).

Lowry v. Reagan, 676 F Supp 333 (D.D.C. 1987).

Luftig v. McNamara, 373 F 2d 664 (DC Cir 1967).

Luther v. Borden, 48 US 1 (1849).

M'Culloch v. Maryland, 17 US (4 Wheat.) 316 (1819).

MacDougall v. Green, 335 US 281 (1948).

Madzimbamuto v. Larder Burke, (1966) 1 AC 645.

Magidiwana v. President of the Republic of South Africa, 2013 (11) BCLR 1251 (CC).

Magit v. University of Agriculture Makurdi, (2006) All FWLR (pt. 298) 1313.

Maline v. Meekins, 650 P 2d 351 (1982).

Maloy v. Marietta, 11 Ohio, NS 639.

Marbury v. Madison, 5 US (1 Cranch) 137 (1803).

Marrero v. Commonwealth, 559 Pa 14, 739 A 2d 110 (1999).

Marshall v. Dye, 231 US 250 (1913).

Martin v. Mott, 12 Wheat 29, 25 US 19 (1872).

Masetlha v. President of the Republic of South Africa, 2008 (1) SA 566 (CC).

Mashavha v. President of the Republic of South Africa, 2005 (2) SA 476 (CC).

Massachusetts v. Laird, 400 US 886 (1970).

Matthews v. Handley, 361 US 127 (1959).

Mazibuko v. Sisulu, 2013 (6) SA 249 (CC).

Mazibuko, Leader of the Opposition in the National Assembly v. Sisulu MP Speaker of the National Assembly, [2012] ZAWCHC 189.

McDuffy v. Secretary of the Executive Office of Educ., 415 Mass 545 (1993).

MCulloch v. Maryland, 17 US (4 Wheat) 316 (1819).

Meyer v. Lamm, 846 P 2d 862, 872-873 (Colo 1993).

Minister of Constitutional Development and Another v. South African Restructuring and Insolvency Practitioners Association and Others, 2018 (5) SA 349 (CC).

Minister of Education v. Harris, 2001 (4) SA 1297 (CC).

Minister of Justice and Constitutional Development and Others v. Prince, [2018] ZACC 30; 2018 (10) BCLR 1220 (CC); 2018 (6) SA 393 (CC).

Mistretta v. United States, 488 US 361 (1989).

Moe v. Secretary of Administration & Finance, 382 Mass. 629 [1981].

Mountain Timber Company v. Washington, 243 US 219 (1916).

My Vote Counts NPC v. Minister of Justice and Correctional Services and Another, [2018] ZACC 17; 2018 (8) BCLR 893 (CC); 2018 (5) SA 380 (CC).

National Coalition of Gay & Les Equality v. Min of Home Affairs, 2000 (2) SA 1 (CC).

National Director of Public Prosecutions v. Freedom Under Law, 2014 (4) SA 298 (SCA).

National Treasury v. Opposition to Urban Tolling Alliance, 2012 (6) SA 223 (CC).

Native Village of Kivalina v. ExxonMobil Corp, 663 F Supp 2d 863 (2009).

Nebraska Coalition for Educational Equity and Adequacy v. Heineman, 273 Neb 531 (2007).

New Party of South Africa v. Government of the Republic of South Africa, 1999 (3) SA 191 (CC).

New Patriotic Party v. Attorney-General, 1993-94 2 GLR 35 SC.

New Patriotic Party v. Attorney General (CIBA), 1997 SCGLR 729.

New York v. United States, 505 US 144 (1992).

Nixon v. Administrator of General Services, 433 US 425 (1977).

Nixon v. United States, 506 US 224 (1993).

Nyambirai v. National Social Security Authority, 1996 (1) SA 636 (ZS).

Obi v. INEC, (2007) 9 MJSC 1.

O'Brien v. Brown, 409 U.S. 1 (1972).

Ochen & Others v. Attorney General, Civil Suit 292/2010.

Oetjen v. Central Leather Co, 246 US 297 (1918).

Ohio ex rel Bryant v. Akron Metro Park Dist, 281 US 74 (1930).

Ohio ex rel Davis v. Hildebrant, 241 US 565 (1916).

Okoli v. Mbadiwe, (1985) 6 NCLR 742.

Okupa and 2020 Others v. Attorney General, Civil Suit 0014/2005.

Olson v. Morrison, 487 US 654 (1988).

Oluka & 9 Others v. Attorney General, Civil Suit 122/2009.

O'Neill v. Leamer, 239 US 244 (1915).

Onuoha v. Okafor, (1983) NSCC 494.

Oregon v. Mitchel, 400 US 112 (1970).

Pacific States Telephone & Telegraph Co v. Oregon, 223 US 118 (1912).

Paul Semogerere v. Attorney-General, Constitutional Appeal No 1 (2002).

Pauling v. McNamara, 331 F 2d 796 (DC Cir 1963).

Pharmaceutical Manufacturers Association of South Africa: In re Ex Parte President of the Republic of South Africa, 2000 (2) SA 674 (CC).

People v. Draper, 15 NY 545 (1857).

Port Elizabeth Municipality v. Prut NO, 1996 (4) SA 318 (E).

Powell v. McCormack, 395 US 486 (1969).

Premier of the Eastern Cape v. Ntamo, 2015 (6) SA 400 (ECB).

President of the Ordinary Court Martial v. Freedom of Expression Institute, 1999 (4) SA 682 (CC).

President of the Republic of South Africa v. Hugo, 1997 (6) BCLR 708 (CC).

President of the Republic of South Africa v. Quagliani, President of the Republic of South Africa and Others v. Van Rooyen; Goodwin v. Director-General, Department of Justice and Constitutional Development, 2009 (4) BCLR 345 (CC).

Primedia Broadcasting v. Speaker of the National Assembly and Others, [2016] 4 All SA 793 (SCA); 2017 (1) SA 572 (SCA).

R v. Cambridge Health Authority ex PB, [1995] 2 ALL ER 129.

R v. Ndhlovu, 1968 (4) SA 515.

Radford v. Gary, 352 US 991 (1957).

Radio Pretoria v. Chairman, Independent Communications Authority of SA, 2005 (1) SA 47 (SCA).

Ramakatsa and Others v. Magashule and Others, 2013 (2) BCLR 202 (CC).

Rand Water Board v. Rotek Industries (Pty) Ltd, 2003 (4) SA 58 (SCA).

Remmey v. Smith, 342 US 916 (1952).

Reynolds v. Sims, 377 US 533 (1964).

Rhode Island v. Massachusetts, 37 US (12 Pet.) 657 (1838).

Rimi & Musa v. PRP, (1981) 2 NCLR 734.

Ritcher v. Minister of Home Affairs, 2009 (3) SA 615 (CC).

Rose v. Council for Better Educ Inc, 790 SW 2d 186 (Ky. 1989).

Roudebush v. Hartke, 405 US 15 (1972).

S v. Cloete, [2008] NAHC 116.

S v. Dlamini, 1999 (4) SA 623 (CC).

S v. Friedland, 1996 (8) BCLR 1049 (W).

Saldana v. Occidental Petroleum Corporation, 774 F 3d 544 (2014).

Schneider v. Kissinger, 412 F 3d 190 (2005).

Schroeder v. Bush, 263 F 3d 1169 (2001).

Schweiker v. Wilson, 450 US 221 (1981).

Seattle Sch. District No 1 v. State, 90 Wash.2d 476, 585 P 2d 71 (1978).

Sechele v. Public Officers Defined Contribution Pension Fund, [2010] LSHC 94.

Severino v. Attorney General, Constitutional Petition 47 of 2011 (2012).

South African Reserve Bank v. Public Protector and Others, [2017] ZAGPPHC 443.

State v. Muzda, 16 NJL 219 (1935).

State ex rel Ford v. Board of Election, 167 Ohio St 449 (1958).

State ex rel Steinke v. Lautenbaugh, 263 Neb 652, 642 NW 2d 132 (2002).

State ex rel Turner v. Scott, 269 NW 2d 828 (Iowa 1978).

State of Georgia v. Stanton, 73 US 50 (1867).

State of Idaho v. Freeman, 529 F Supp 1107 (1981).

State of Rajasthan v. Union of India, 1977 3 SCC 590.

States v. Belmont, 301 US 324 (1937).

Steward Machine Company v. Davis, 301 US 548 (1937).

Sunagawa Case, 1959 (A) 710.

Taylor & Marshall v. Beckham, 178 US 548 (1900).

Tedesco v. Board of Supervisors, 339 US 940 (1950).

Tel-Oren v. Libyan Arab Republic, 726 F 2d 774 (DC Cir 1984).

Third Ave Association v. Consulate Gen of the Socialist Federal Republic of Yugoslavia, 218 F 3d 152 (2d Cir 2000).

Tomabechi v. Japan, 1955 (O) 96 Minshu Vol. 14, No. 7.

Tony Momoh v. Senate of the National Assembly, (1981) 1 NCLR 105.

Transvaal Agricultural Union v. Minister of Land Affairs, 1997 (2) SA 621 (CC).

Tuffour v. Attorney-General, 1980 GLR 637.

Turman v. Duckworth, 329 US 675 (1946).

Uganda v. Commissioner of Prisons Ex Parte Matovu, [1966] EALR 514.

Ugwu v. Ararume, (2007) 12 NWLR (pt. 1048) 367.

United Democratic Movement v. President of the Republic of South Africa, (1) 2002 (11) BCLR 1179 (CC).

United Democratic Movement v. Speaker of the National Assembly, [2017] ZACC 21.

United States v. Belmont, 301 US 324 (1937).

United States v. Butler, 297 US 1 (1936).

United States v. Curtiss-Wright Export Corp., 299 US304 (1936).

United States v. Nixon, 418 US 683 (1974).

United States v. Palmer, 16 US (3 Wheat) 610, 4 L Ed 471 (1818).

US ex rel Joseph v. Cannon, 642 F 2d 1373 (1981).

Van Huysteen NO Minister, 1996 (1) SA 283 (C).

Van Huysteen NO v. Minister of Environmental Affairs and Tourism, 1996 (1) SA 283 (C).

Vieth v. Jubelirer, 541 US 267 (2004).

Warth v. Seldin, 422 US 499 (1975).

Wells v. Rockefeller, 394 US 542 (1969).

Wesberry v. Sanders, 376 US 1 (1964).

Whitaker v. Kellog Brown & Root Inc, 444 F Supp 2d 1277 (2006).

Youngstown Sheet & Tube Company v. Sawyer, 343 US 579 (1952).

Zivotofsky ex rel Ari Z v. Sec'y of State, 444 F 3d 614 (DC Cir 2006).

Zivotofsky v. Secretary of State, 511 F Supp 2d 97, 103 (2007).

Zivotofsky v. Clinton, 132 S Ct 1421 (2012).

Constitutions

Constitution of Ghana, 1992

Constitution of the Federal Republic of Nigeria, 1979

Constitution of the Federal Republic of Nigeria, 1999

Constitution of the Republic of South Africa Act 200 of 1993

Constitution of the Republic of South Africa, 1996

Constitution of Uganda, 1962

Constitution of Uganda, 1966

Constitution of Uganda, 1995

United States Constitution, 1787

International Treaties

Contingent Reserve Arrangement Treaty of the BRICS (2014)

Rome Statute of the International Criminal Court, 1998

Internet Sources

Asare, K. Can the Political Doctrine Question Save MP Amoateng. Available from www.ghanaweb.com/GhanaHomePage/NewsArchive/artikel.php?ID=113967.

Cole, J. The Political Question Doctrine: Justiciability and the Separation of Powers, 2014. Available from www.fas.org/sgp/crs/misc/R43834.pdf.

Dennison, D. The Resurfacing Political Question Doctrine in Uganda: Self-Imposed Freedom from the Judicial Review, 3. Available from www.dullahomarinstitute.org.za.

Francis, S. Strict Interpretation of Political Question Doctrine a Challenge to Realizing the Right to Health – Human Rights Commission Report 2012, 2013. Available from www.cehurd.org/2013/04/strict-interpretation-of-political-question-doctrine-a-challenge-to-realizing-the-right-to-health-human-rights-commission-report-2012/.

Kirya, M. The Independence and Accountability of the Judiciary in Uganda: Opportunities and Challenges. Available from www.kituochakatiba.org/index.php?option=com_docman&task=doc_details&gid=369&Itemid=36

Mogoeng, M. Judicial Overreach, a speech presented at the Cape Town Press Club on 25 October 2017. Available from www.youtube.com/watch?v=xGAe_zHg9dw at 14:18-17:08.

Oladele, K. Political Questions and Justiciability: Two Sides of a Coin, 2012. Available from http://saharareporters.com/article/political-question-and-justiciablity-two-sides-coin.

Quashigah, K. The 1992 Constitution of Ghana. Available from www.icla.up.ac.za/images/country_reports/ghana_country_report.pdf.

Timothy, A. The Doctrine of Political Question: Is It's Non Justiciability At The Brink of Erosion in the Legal Jurisprudence of Uganda? 2014, http://timothyamerit.blogspot.co.za/2014/08/the-doctrine-of-political-question-is.html.

Journal Articles

A.R. Amar, 'The Central Meaning of Republican Government: Popular Sovereignty, Majority Rule, and The Denominator Problem', *University of Colorado Law Review*, Vol. 65, 1994, p. 775.

A. Atupare, 'Reconciling Socioeconomic Rights and Directive Principles with a Fundamental Law of Reason in Ghana and Nigeria', *Harvard Human Rights Journal*, Vol. 27, 2014, p. 71.

S. Banner & J. May, 'American Electric Power Company Inc et al., Petitioners v State of Connecticut, et al., Respondents', *Valparaiso University Law Review*, Vol. 46, 2012, p. 459.

R. Barkow, 'More Supreme than Court? The Fall of the Political Question Doctrine and the Rise of Judicial Supremacy', *Columbia Law Review*, Vol. 102, 2002, p. 237.

G.N. Barrie, 'Impeachment on the Highveld: The Dismissal of Chief Justice Kotze by President Kruger on 16 February 1898', *Tydskrif vir die Suid-Afrikaanse Reg*, Vol. 4, 2014, p. 817.

A. Bickel, 'The Supreme Court 1960 Term Foreword: The Passive Virtues', *Harvard Law Review*, Vol. 75, 1961, p. 40.

J. Blum, 'How Much Process Is Due: The Senate Impeachment Trial Process after Nixon v. United States', *Catholic University Law Review*, Vol. 44, 1994-1995, p. 243.

A. Bonfield, 'The Guarantee Clause of Article IV, Section 4: A Study in Constitutional Desuetude', *Minnesotta Law Review*, Vol. 46, 1962, p. 513.

K. Breedon, 'Remedial Problems at the Intersection of the Political Question Doctrine, the Standing Doctrine and the Doctrine of Equitable Discretion', *Ohio Northern University Law Review*, Vol. 34, 2008, p. 523.

E. Bussey, 'Constitutional Dialogue in Uganda', *Journal of African Law*, Vol. 49, 2005, p. 2.

C. Byamugisha, 'Administering Justice Without Undue Regard to the Technicalities', *Greenwatch*, 2003.

F. Cachalia, 'Judicial Review of Parliamentary Rulemaking: A Provisional Case for Restraint', *New York Law School Law Review*, Vol. 60, 2015-2016, p. 379.

C. Chase, 'The Political Question Doctrine: Preventing the Challenge of US Foreign Policy in 767 Third Avenue Associates v Consulate General', *Catholic University Law Review*, Vol. 50, 2001, p. 1045.

E. Chemerinsky, 'Cases Under the Guarantee Clause Should Be Justiciable', *University of Colorado Law Review*, Vol. 65, 1994, p. 849.

P. Chen & J. Wada, 'Can the Japanese Supreme Court Overcome the Political Question Doctrine Hurdle?', *Washington International Law Journal*, Vol. 26, No. 2, 2017, p. 362.

J.H. Choper, 'The Political Question Doctrine: Suggested Criteria', *Duke Law Journal*, Vol. 54, 2005, p. 1457.

D. Cole, 'Challenging Covert War: The Politics of the Political Question Doctrine', *Harvard International Law Journal*, Vol. 26, 1985, p. 155.

M. Corbett, 'Judicial Review and the Problems of Southern Africa', *Loyola University Chicago Law Journal*, Vol. 12, 1981, p. 175.

H. Corder, 'Lessons from (North) America (Beware the Legalization of Politics and the Political Seduction of the Law)', *South African Law Journal*, Vol. 109, 1992, p. 204.

G. Cowper & L. Sossin, 'Does Canada Need a Political Questions Doctrine?', *Supreme Court Law Review*, Vol. 16, 2002, p. 343.

T. Cutaiar, '*Lane Ex Rel Lane v. Halliburton*: The Fifth Circuit's Recent Treatment of the Political Question Doctrine and What it Could Mean for *Commer v. Murphy Oil*', *Loyola Law Review*, Vol. 55, 2009, p. 393.

B. Davidson, 'Note, Liability on the Battlefield: Adjudicating Tort Suits Brought by Soldiers Against Military Contractors', *Public Contract Law Journal*, Vol. 37, 2008, p. 822.

B. Dennison, 'The Political Question Doctrine in Uganda: A Reassessment in the Wake of *CEHURD*', *Law, Democracy and Development*, Vol. 18, 2014, p. 264.

N. Dyani-Mhango, 'South Africa's (Unconstitutional) Withdrawal from the Rome Statute: A Note on *Democratic Alliance v. Minister of International Relations an Cooperation*', *South African Journal on Human Rights*, Vol. 34, 2018, p. 268.

Eastern African Centre for Constitutional Development. 'Report of the Fact Finding Mission in Uganda on Constitutional Development', 2002, p. 15.

W. Egbewole & O. Olatunji, 'Justiciability Theory Versus Political Question Doctrine: Challenges of the Nigerian Judiciary in the Determination of Electoral and Other Related Cases', *Journal Jurisprudence*, Vol. 14, 2012, p. 1.

A. Ekpu, 'Judicial Response to Coup D'etat: A Reply to Tayyab Mahmud (From A Nigerian Perspective)', *Arizona Journal of International and Comparative Law*, Vol. 13, 1996, p. 1.

D. Ellis, '*Powell v. McCormack* and the Power to Expel: Some Unanswered Questions Regarding the Framers' Intent', *Georgia Law Review*, Vol. 5, 1971, p. 203.

A. Endicott, 'The Judicial Answer? Treatment of the Political Question Doctrine in Alien Tort Claims', *Berkeley Journal of International Law*, Vol. 28, 2010, p. 537.

C. Engberg, 'Note, Taking the Initiative: May Congress Reform State Initiative Lawmaking to Guarantee a Republican Form of Government?', *Stanford Law Review*, Vol. 54, 2001, p. 569.

R. Fallon, 'Marbury and the Constitutional Mind: A Bicentennial Essay on the Wages of Doctrinal Tension', *California Law Review*, Vol. 91, 2003, p. 5.

M. Finkelstein, 'Judicial Self-Limitation', *Harvard Law Review*, Vol. 37, 1923-1924, p. 338.

E. Firmage, 'The War Powers and Political Question Doctrine', *University of Colorado Law Review*, Vol. 49, 1977-1978, p. 65.

Y. Ghai, 'Matovu's Case: Another Comment', *Eastern African Law Review*, Vol. 1, 1968, p. 68.

E. Gil, 'Judicial Answer to Political Question: The Political Question in the United States and Israel', *Boston University Public Interest Law Journal*, Vol. 23, 2014, p. 245.

M. Gouin, 'United States v. Alvarez-Machain: Waltzing with the Political Question Doctrine', *Connecticut Law Review*, Vol. 26, 1994, p. 759.

T.L. Grove, 'The Lost History of the Political Question Doctrine', *New York University Law Review*, Vol. 90, 2015, p. 1908.

D.A. Harvey, '*The Alien Tort Statute: International Human Rights Watchdog or Simply Historical Trivia*', *John Marshall Law Review*, Vol. 21, 1988, p. 341.

L. Henkin, 'Is There a Political Question Doctrine?', *Yale Law Journal*, Vol. 85, 1976, p. 597.

C. Hoesly, 'Reforming Direct Democracy: Lessons from Oregon', *California Law Review*, Vol. 93, 2005, p. 1191.

C. Hoexter, 'The Future of Judicial Review in South African Administrative Law', *South African Law Journal*, Vol. 117, 2000, p. 484.

C. Hoexter, 'The Principle of Legality in South African Administrative Law', *Maquarie Law Journal*, Vol. 4, 2004, p. 165.

A.C. Hutchinson, 'A Hard-Core Case Against Judicial Review', *Harvard Law Review*, Vol. 25, 2008, p. 121.

M. Ikhariale, 'Impeachment Proceedings and the Political Question Doctrine: The Nigerian Experience', *LASU Law Journal*, Vol. 1, 1990, p. 45.

I. Imam, *et al.* 'Judicial Activism and Intervention in the Doctrine of Political Questions in Nigeria: An Analytical Exposition', *African Journal of Law and Criminology*, Vol. 1, 2011, p. 50.

J. Jaffe, 'The Political Question Doctrine: An Update in Response to Recent Case Law', *Ecology Law Quarterly*, Vol. 38, 2011, p. 1037.

M. Kelly, 'Revisiting and Revising the Political Question: *Lane v. Halliburton* and the Need to Adopt a Case-Specific Political Question Analysis for Private Military Contractor Cases', *Miss College Law Review*, Vol. 29, 2010, p. 219.

L.D. Kramer, 'Popular Constitutionalism', *California Law Review*, Vol. 92, 2004, p. 959.

A. Kronman, 'Alexander Bickel's Philosophy of Prudence', *Yale Law Journal*, Vol. 94, No. 7, 1985, p. 1567.

S. LaTourette, 'Global Climate: A Political Question?', *Rutgers Law Journal*, Vol. 40, 2008, p. 219.

R. Layman, 'Aftermath of *Baker v. Carr*', *William & Mary Law Review*, Vol. 4, 1963, p. 93.

H. Linde, 'Who is Responsible for Republic Government', *University of Colorado Law Review*, Vol. 64, 1994, p. 709.

I. Mahomed, 'The Role of the Judiciary in a Constitutional State', *South African Law Journal*, Vol. 115, 1999, p. 111.

J. May, '*Climate Change, Constitutional Consignment, and the Political Question Doctrine*', *Denver University Law Review*, Vol. 85, 2008, p. 919.

T. McAffee & C. Johnson, 'Note, A Dialogue on the Political Question Doctrine', *Utah Law Review*, Vol. 1978, 1978, p. 523.

M. Mhango, 'Separation of Powers and the Application of the Political Question Doctrine in Uganda', *African Journal of Legal Studies*, Vol. 6, 2013, p. 249.

M. Mhango, 'Is it Time for a Coherent Political Question Doctrine in South Africa? Lessons from the United States', *African Journal of Legal Studies*, Vol. 7, 2014, p. 471.

P. Mojapelo, 'The Doctrine of Separation of Powers (a South African Perspective)', *Advocate*, Vol 26, 2013, p. 37.

H. Monaghan, 'Marbury and the Administrative State', *Columbia Law Review*, Vol. 83, 1983, p. 7.

D. Moseneke, 'A Journey from the Heart of Apartheid Darkness Towards a Just Society: Salient Features of the Budding Constitutionalism and Jurisprudence of South Africa', *Georgetown Law Journal*, Vol. 101, No. 3, 2013, p. 749.

U. Mubig, 'At the Roots of European Legal Culture: Crossborder Influences of Locke and Montesquieu', *Fundamina: A Journal of Legal History*, Vol. 15, No. 2, 2009, p. 112.

P. Mulhern, 'In Defense of the Political Question Doctrine', *University of Pennsylvania Law Review*, Vol. 137, 1988, p. 97.

M. Mutua, 'Hope and Despair for a New South Africa: The Limits of Rights Discourse', *Harvard Human Rights Journal*, Vol. 10, 1997, p. 63.

P. Neal, 'Baker v. Carr: Politics in Search of Law', *Supreme Court Review*, Vol. 1962, 1962, p. 252.

B. Nelson, 'Originalism and Interpretive Conventions', *University of Chicago Law Review*, Vol. 70, 2003, p. 519.

S. Ngcobo, 'Sustaining Public Confidence in the Judiciary: An Essential Condition for Realising the Judicial Role', *South African Law Journal*, Vol. 128, No. 1, 2011, p. 11.

S. Ngcobo, 'Why Does the Constitution Matter?', Public Lecture delivered at the Gallagher Estate, 2016.

M. Nixon-Graf, 'A Gathering Storm: Climate Change as Common Nuisance or Political Question?', *New York University Environmental Law Journal*, Vol. 19, 2012, p. 353.

A. Nolan, 'The Doctrine of Constitutional Avoidance: A Legal Overview', *CRS Report for Congress*, 2014, R43706.

E. Nwauche, 'The Nigerian Fundamental Rights (Enforcement) Procedure Rules 009: A Fitting Response to Problems in the Enforcement of Human Rights in Nigeria?', *African Human Rights Law Journal,* Vol 10, 2010, p. 502.

J. Nzelibe, 'The Uniqueness of Foreign Affairs', *Iowa Law Review,* Vol. 89, 2004, p. 941.

C. Okpaluba, 'Justiciability and Constitutional Adjudication in the Commonwealth: The Problem of Definition (1) and (2)', *THRHR,* Vol. 66, 2003, p. 424.

C. Okpaluba, 'Justiciability and Standing to Challenge Legislation in the Commonwealth: A Tale of the Traditionalist and Judicial Activists Approaches', *Comparative and International Law Journal of Southern Africa,* Vol. 36, No. 1, 2003, p. 25.

C. Okpaluba, 'Justiciability, Constitutional Adjudication and the Political Question in a Nascent Democracy: South Africa', *South African Public Law,* Vol. 18, 2003-2004, p. 331 (Part 1) and *South African Public Law* Vol. 19, 2003-2004, p. 131 (Part 2).

C. Okpaluba, 'Can a Court Review the Internal Affairs and Processes of the Legislature?', *Comparative and International Law Journal of Southern Africa,* Vol. 48, 2015, p. 183.

C. Okpaluba, 'Constraints on Judicial Review of Executive Conduct: The Juridical Link Between the Marikana Mineworkers' Imbroglio and the GAUTENG E-Tolling Saga', *Tydskrif vir die Suid Afrikaanse Reg,* Vol. 2, 2015, p. 286.

C. Okpaluba & M. Mhango, 'Between Separation of Powers and Justiciability: Rationalising the Constitutional Court's Judgement in the Gauteng E-tolling Litigation in South Africa', *Law, Democracy and Development,* Vol. 21, 2017.

E. Okpanachi & A. Garba, 'Federalism and Constitutional Change in Nigeria', *Federal Governance,* Vol. 7, 2010, p. 1.

J. Oloka-Onyango, 'Constitutional Transition in Museveni's Uganda: New Horizons or Another False Start?', *Journal of African Law,* Vol. 39, 1995, p. 156.

K. O'Regan, 'A Forum for Reason: Reflections on the Role and Work of the Constitutional Court', *South African Journal on Human Rights,* Vol. 28, 2012, p. 132.

W. Osiatynski, 'Paradoxes of Constitutional Borrowing', *International Journal of Constitutional Law,* Vol. 1, 2003, p. 244.

M. Paulsen, 'Judging Judicial Review: Marbury in the Modern Era', *Michigan Law Review*, Vol. 101, 2003, p. 2706.

L. Peitzman, 'The Supreme Court and the Credentials Challenge Cases: Ask a Political Question, You Get a Political Answer', *California Law Review*, Vol. 62, No. 4, 1974, p. 1344.

J. Perez-Montes, 'Comment, Justiciability in Modern War Zones: Is the Political Question Doctrine a Viable Bar to Tort Claims Against Private Military Contractors?', *Tulane Law Review*, Vol. 83, 2008, p. 246.

J. Pettinato, 'Executing the Political Question Doctrine', *Northern Kentucky Law Review*, Vol. 33, 2006, p. 61.

R. Post & R. Siegel, '*Popular Constitutionalism, Departmentalism and Judicial Supremacy*', *California Law Review, Vol. 92, 2004, p. 1027.*

L. Price, 'Banishing the Specter of Judicial Foreign Policymaking: A Competence-Based Approach to the Political Question Doctrine', *New York University Journal of International Law & Politics*, Vol. 38, 2006, p. 323.

R. Pushaw, 'Justiciability and Separation of Powers: A Neo-Federalist Approach', *Cornell Law Review*, Vol. 81, 1996, p. 393.

R. Pushaw, 'Bush v. Gore: Looking at Baker v. Carr in a Conservative Mirror', *Constitutional Commentary*, Vol. 18, 2001, p. 359.

R. Pushaw, 'The Presidential Election Dispute, the Political Question Doctrine, and the Fourteenth Amendment: A Reply to Professors Krent and Shane', *Florida State University Law Review*, Vol. 29, 2001, p. 603.

R. Pushaw, 'Judicial Review and the Political Question Doctrine: Reviving the Federalist Rebuttable Presumption Analysis', *North Carolina Law Review*, Vol. 80, 2002, p. 1192.

I.M. Rautenbach, 'Policy and Judicial Review – Political Questions, Margins of Appreciation and the South African Constitution', *Tydskrif vir die Suid Afrikaanse Reg*, Vol. 1, 2012, p. 28.

M.H. Redish, 'Judicial Review and the Political Question', *Northwestern Law Review*, Vol. 79, 1984, p. 1031.

D. Rodriguez, 'The Political Question Doctrine in State Constitutional Law', *Rutgers Law Journal*, Vol. 43, 2013, p. 573.

A. Sambo & S. Aziz, 'The Court; Insulating Itself from Politics through the Doctrine of Political Questions: A Critical Exposition', *Journal of Law, Policy and Globalization*, Vol. 4, 2012, p. 7.

T. Sandalow, 'Comment on Powell v. McCormack', *UCLA Law Review*, Vol. 17, 1969, p. 164.

G. Sant, 'So Banks Are Terrorists Now? The Misuse of the Civil Suit Provision of the Anti-Terrorism Act', *Arizona State Law Journal*, Vol. 45, 2013, p. 533.

A. Savitzky, 'The Law of Democracy and the Two *Luther v. Borden's*: A Counter History', *New York University Law Review*, Vol. 86, 2011, p. 2030.

F. Scharpf, 'Judicial Review and the Political Question: A Functional Analysis', *Yale Law Journal*, Vol. 75, 1966, p. 517.

D. Schuman, 'The Origin of State Constitutional Direct Democracy: William Simon U'Ren and the Oregon System', *Temple Law Review*, Vol. 67, 1994, p. 947.

L. Seidman, 'Secret Life of the Political Question Doctrine', *John Marshall Law Review*, Vol. 37, 2003, p. 442.

Z. Shemtob, 'The Political Question Doctrines: *Zivotofsky v. Clinton* and Getting Beyond the Textual-Prudential Paradigm', *The Georgetown Law Journal*, Vol. 104, 2016, p. 1001.

S. Shrewsbury, 'Marbury v. Madison: The Origins and Legacy of Judicial Review', *Military Law Review*, Vol. 173, 2002, p. 160.

G. Skinner, 'Misunderstood, Misconstrued, and Now Clearly Dead: The Political Question Doctrine as a Justiciability Doctrine', *Journal of Law & Politics*, Vol. 29, 2013-2014, p. 427.

T. Smith, 'The Rule of Law and the States: A New Interpretation of the Guaranty Clause', *Yale Law Journal*, Vol.93, 1984, p. 561.

O. Stephens, 'John Marshall and the Confluence of Law and Politics', *Tennesse Law Review*, Vol. 71, 2004, p. 241.

N. Stern, 'The Political Question Doctrine in State Courts', *South Carolina Law Review*, Vol. 35, 1983, p. 405.

C. Szurkowski, 'The Return of Classical Political Question Doctrine in Zivotofsky Ex Rel. Zivotofsky v. Clinton', *Harvard Journal of Law & Public Policy, Vol. 37, No. 1, 2014, p. 347.*

N. Tebe & R. Tsai, 'Constitutional Borrowing', *Michigan Law Review*, Vol. 108, 2009, p. 456.

M. Tully, 'The Supreme Court's Pragmatic and Flexible Approach to Federal Judicial Separation of Powers Issues: Mistretta v. United States', *DePaul Law Review*, Vol. 39, 1990, p. 405.

M. Tushnet, 'Law and Prudence in the Law of Justiciability: The Transformation and Disappearance of the Political Question Doctrine', *North Carolina Law Review*, Vol. 80, 2002, p. 1203.

J. Van Detta, 'Some Legal Considerations for EU Based MNES Contemplating High-Risk Foreign Direct Investments in the Energy Sector After Kiobel v. Royal Dutch Petroleum and Chevron Corporation v. Naranjo', *South Carolina Journal of International Law & Business*, Vol. 9, 2013, p. 161.

J. Waldron, 'The Core Case Against Judicial Review', *Yale Law Journal*, Vol. 115, 2006, p. 1346.

L. Weinberg, 'Political Questions and the Guarantee Clause', *University of Colorado Law Review*, Vol. 65, 1994, p. 849.

M.F. Weston, 'Political Questions', *Harvard Law Review*, Vol. 38, 1925, p. 296.

N. Williams, 'Direct Democracy, the Guaranty Clause, and the Politics of the "Political Question" Doctrine: Revisiting *Pacific Telephone*', *Oregon Law Review*, Vol. 87, 2008, p. 979.

L. Wishik, 'Separation of Powers and Adjudication of Human Rights Claims Under Alien Tort Claims Act-Hanoch-Tel-Oren v. Libyan Arab Republic 726 F2D 774 (D.C.CIR.1984), Cert. Denied 105 S.CT. 1354', *Washington Law Review*, Vol. 60, 1985, p. 697.

S. Woolman, 'Understanding South Africa's Aspirational Constitution as Scaffolding', *New York Law School Law Review*, Vol. 60, 2015-2016, p. 286.

K. Yoshino, 'Restrained Ambition in Constitutional Interpretation', *Willamette Law Review*, Vol. 45, 2009, p. 557.

Reports

Law Reform Advisory Committee for Northern Ireland, *Privity of Contract: Contracts for the Benefit of Third Parties*, Report Nos. 4-6 (2006).

Thesis and Dissertation

Bimpong-Buta, S. *Role of the Supreme Court in the Development of the Constitutional Law in Ghana, 129-130* (LLD Thesis, University of South African 2005).

Kirkby, C. *Exorcising Matovu's Ghost: Legal Positivism, Pluralism and Ideology in Uganda's Appellate Courts* (LLM Theses, McGill University 2007).

Mkwentla N *The Legal Effect of a Coup D'Etat on Traditional Constitutional Concept* (LLM Theses, Rhodes University 2001).

Sekindi, F.D. *A Critical Analysis of the Legal Construction of the Presidency in Post-1995 Uganda* (PhD Theses, University of Pretoria 2015).

Index

Democracy and the Rule of Law (Series editor: Miodrag A. Jovanović)

Volume 1: Miodrag A. Jovanović and Đorđe Pavićević (eds.), Crisis and Quality of Democracy in Eastern Europe, ISBN 978-94-9094-767-5
Volume 2: Miodrag A. Jovanović and Dragica Vujadinović (eds.), Identity, Political and Human Rights Culture as Prerequisites of Constitutional Democracy, ISBN 978-94-6236-077-8
Volume 3: Miodrag A. Jovanović and Kenneth Einar Himma (eds.), Courts, Interpretation, the Rule of Law, ISBN 978-94-6236-096-9
Volume 4: Lidija R. Basta Fleiner and Tanasije Marinković (eds.), Key Developments in Constitutionalism and Constitutional Law, ISBN 978-94-6236-396-0
Volume 5: Miodrag A. Jovanović (ed.), Constitutional Review and Democracy, ISBN 978-94-6236-512-4
Volume 6: Kenneth Einar Himma and Bojan Spaić (eds.), Fundamental Rights: Justification and Interpretation, ISBN 978-94-6236-656-5
Volume 7: Hauke Brunkhorst, Dragica Vujadinović, and Tanasije Marinković (eds.), European Democracy in Crisis: Polities under Challenge and Social Movements, ISBN 978-94-6236-799-9
Volume 8: Violeta Beširević (ed.), New Politics of Decisionism, ISBN 978-94-6236-897-2
Volume 9: Mtendeweka Owen Mhango, Justiciability of Political Questions in South Africa: A Comparative Analysis, ISBN 978-94-6236-918-4

Printed by Libri Plureos GmbH in Hamburg, Germany

9 789462 369184